OXFORD TEXTBOOKS IN LING

Pragmatics

Second edition

OXFORD TEXTBOOKS IN LINGUISTICS

Pragmatics

Second edition

Yan Huang

OXFORD
UNIVERSITY PRESS

OXFORD

UNIVERSITY PRESS

Great Clarendon Street, Oxford, OX2 6DP,
United Kingdom

Oxford University Press is a department of the University of Oxford.
It furthers the University's objective of excellence in research, scholarship,
and education by publishing worldwide. Oxford is a registered trade mark of
Oxford University Press in the UK and in certain other countries

Published in the United States of America by Oxford University Press
198 Madison Avenue, New York, NY 10016, United States of America

British Library Cataloguing in Publication Data
Data available

ISBN 978-0-19-957776-7

Dedication

In loving memory of and with profound gratitude to my mother,
Hexia Feng (1921–2010), and my father,
Yongzeng Huang (1922–2013)

Contents

Preface to the second edition

The continuing demand for my *Pragmatics* necessitates a new edition. In this second edition, while the aim, readership, and overall structure of the first edition are retained, the material in the entire book has been thoroughly revised, refreshed, and updated to reflect the continuing, rapid development of pragmatics since the publication of the first edition, thus rendering the whole text more forward-looking. In terms of coverage, the most notable change is that a new chapter on reference has been added to Part I. Reference is an important topic in both linguistics and the philosophy of language. Since at least Strawson (1950), it has been considered to be largely pragmatic in nature, given that it is essentially a context-dependent aspect of utterance meaning. Whereas there is an extensive body of literature on reference in both linguistics and the philosophy of language, much of the work (especially in the tradition of the philosophy of language) has been written at such an intimidating level of technicality that it is not easily accessible to the student. Furthermore, most of the existing textbooks on pragmatics do not provide an (adequate) account of this important topic in both linguistics and the philosophy of language. I believe that with the addition of reference, the range of classic topics of pragmatics that should be dealt with in this book is complete. Other significant changes include a new section on upward and downward entailment in Chapter 1, on current debates about conversational implicature and on embedded (conversational) implicature in Chapter 2, on impoliteness in Chapter 4, on emotional deixis in Chapter 5, on contextualism versus semantic minimalism in the philosophy of language in Chapter 8, and on elimination of binding conditions in Chapter 9. Where appropriate, works in experimental pragmatics and in lexical pragmatics have also been added to various chapters throughout the entire book. In compensation for these additions, some of the less important content contained in the first edition has been condensed or even removed. This edition contains an even richer collection of cross-linguistic data drawn from a wider range of the world's languages than the first edition. Finally, the key concepts, exercises, and essay questions, and further readings sections at the end of each chapter, and the glossary, references, and suggested solutions to exercises sections at the end form important parts of this book, and consequently they too have been revised, updated, and slightly expanded.

Auckland, New Haven, Cambridge MA, and Beijing   Y. H. 黄衍
July 2013

Acknowledgements to the second edition

A number of people have contributed to the preparation of this second edition. I am particularly grateful to Barbara Abbott and Fred Kroon for reading through the chapter on reference, and to Bart Geurts for reading through the section on embedded (conversational) implicature while they were in draft. Thanks to their very insightful comments, the chapter and the section have been improved significantly. I owe a debt of gratitude to Abdullah al-Saqqaf, Guohua Chen, David Cram, Michael Haugh, Larry Horn, Richard Larson, Steve Levinson, and Yi'an Wu for helping me in one way or another. My thanks also go to Sara Amani, Beidi Li, and Danyang Zheng for their assistance with the references section.

I would like to take this opportunity of expressing my appreciation to Hae-Yun Lee for translating the first edition into Korean, Puteri Roslina Abdul Wahid for translating it into Malay, and to Ziran He and Yaxin Wu for writing an introduction to the Chinese reprint of that edition. I would also like to thank Keith Allan, Alessandro Capone, Cedric Ginestet, Gregory Glasgow, the late Robert Harnish, Stacia Levy, Dunlai Lin, Yunqing Lin, Chaoqun Xie, and Ren Zhang for reviewing the first edition in various journals of linguistics, philosophy, and psychology, the *International Cognitive Linguistics Association Book Reviews*, and the Linguist List.

Since the publication of the first edition, portions of the material, especially the new material, contained in this edition have been presented to various audiences at the Uniwersytetu im. Adama Mickiewicza, Aalborg Universitet, Anhui University, Universiteit Antwerpen, University of Auckland, Universität Augsburg, University of the Basque Country, Beijing University of Aeronautics and Astronautics, Beijing Foreign Studies University, Beijing Language and Culture University, Beijing Normal University, University of Cambridge, Chinese University of Hong Kong, Communication and Media University of China, National Dong Hwa University, East China Normal University, Finnish National Graduate School in Language Studies (Langnet), Freie Universität Berlin, Fujian Medical University, Fujian Normal University, Fuyang Teachers' College, Fuzhou University, Université de Genève, Guangdong University of Foreign Studies, Harvard University, Hefei University of Technology, University of Helsinki, Henan University, University of Hong Kong,

Hongkong Polytechnic University, Hsuan Chuang University, Hunan University, Institute of Linguistics at Academia Sinica, Institute of Linguistics at the Chinese Academy of Social Sciences, Jiangxi Normal University, Université de Kairouan, Kansai University, Kyoto Prefectural University, Katholieke Universiteit Leuven, Uniwersytet Łodzki, University of London, Lunghwa University of Science and Technology, Universidade de Macau, Universität Mainz, Nankai University, University of Nanking/Nanjing, Nanjing Normal University, Nanjing University of Science and Technology, University of New South Wales, Ninbo University, University of North Carolina, Université d'Orléans, University of Oxford, Peking University, Universität Regensburg, Rice University, San Francisco State University, Seoul National University, Shandong University, Shanghai International Studies University, Shanghai Jiao Tong University, Shih-Hsin University, Soochow University, Tsinghua University (Beijing), National Tsing Hua University (Hsinchu), Tohoku University, University of Tokyo, University of Waikato, Victorian University of Wellington, Xi'an International Studies University, Yale University, Zhejiang University, and Zhengzhou University. I have benefited from the comments received on all these occasions. I wish to extend my gratitude to all the people who have invited me. In addition, I am indebted to the undergraduate and graduate students at the universities of Reading, Oxford, and Auckland, and the PhD students at Beijing Foreign Studies University who attended my (advanced) courses on semantics and pragmatics in which some of the new material was tested.

The preparation of the final version of this edition was partially made while I spent my sabbatical/research leave at the Department of Linguistics, Yale University; the Department of Linguistics, Harvard University; and the National Research Centre for Foreign Language Education, Beijing Foreign Studies University. I am grateful to Larry Horn, Maria Polinsky, Gennaro Chierchia, and Qiufang Wen for inviting me, and to the three departments for providing me with the opportunity to work in a stimulating and congenial environment.

In connection with the preparation of this edition for publication, I would like to thank John Davey, Julia Steer, Victoria Hart, and Kate Gilks at Oxford University Press for their professionalism. My gratitude also goes to Lucy Hollingworth and Lesley Rhodes for an excellent job of copy-editing and proofreading, respectively. Since 2000, I have published three books (this edition not included) with Oxford University Press. In particular, I am grateful to John Davey (who has now retired from

Oxford University Press) for the interest he has shown in my research and the encouragement he has given me over these years.

On a more personal note, I wish to thank my wife and daughter for being a continual source of love, encouragement, and support. My parents passed away while I was working on this edition. I wish to express my indebtedness to them, especially my mother, for all they did for me. During the dark days of Mao's 'Cultural Revolution' in China, it was they who tried their best to bring me up, educate me, and teach me how to be a decent person. This edition is therefore dedicated to their memory.

Preface to the first edition

The aim of this book is to provide an authoritative, up-to-date, and yet accessible introduction to contemporary linguistic pragmatics.

In contemporary pragmatics, two main schools of thought can be identified: Anglo-American and European Continental. Within the former conception of linguistics and the philosophy of language, pragmatics is defined as the systematic study of meaning by virtue of, or dependent on, language use. The central topics of inquiry include implicature, presupposition, speech acts, and deixis. This is known as the component view of pragmatics, namely, the view that pragmatics should be treated as a core component of a theory of language, on a par with phonetics, phonology, morphology, syntax, and semantics. By contrast, other areas such as anthropological linguistics, applied linguistics, and psycholinguistics would lie outside this set of core components. Within the Continental tradition, pragmatics is defined in a far broader way, encompassing much that goes under the rubric of, say, sociolinguistics, psycholinguistics, and discourse analysis. The Continental approach represents the perspective view of pragmatics, namely, the view that pragmatics should be taken as presenting a functional perspective on every aspect of linguistic behaviour. Given the degree of overlap among the phenomena dealt with in other relatively well-established interdisciplinary fields of linguistics such as sociolinguistics, psycholinguistics, and neurolinguistics, it is rather difficult to see how a coherent research agenda for pragmatics can be made within the wider Continental tradition. By contrast, the narrower Anglo-American, component view of pragmatics, which focuses on topics emerging from the traditional concerns of analytical philosophy, delimits the scope of the discipline in a relatively coherent, systematic, and principled way. In this book, therefore, my discussion of pragmatics will largely be from the Anglo-American, component point of view.

This book is primarily written for second- or third-year undergraduate and postgraduate students specializing in linguistics with little or no prior knowledge of pragmatics. It should also be suitable for students taking a linguistics option as part of a language, humanities, or social science degree. Moreover, it should be of interest to researchers in anthropology, artificial intelligence, cognitive science, literature, philosophy, and psychology, as well as linguistics.

The plan of the book is as follows. Chapter 1 is an introductory chapter. The remainder of the book is then divided into two parts. Part I covers those topics that are standardly included in a pragmatics textbook. Within this part, Chapter 2 is concerned with classical and neo-Gricean pragmatic theories of implicature. The focus of Chapter 3 is on presupposition. Chapter 4 is devoted to speech act theory, concentrating on the classic work by Austin and Searle. Chapter 5 provides an in-depth descriptive analysis of various types of deixis. Of these chapters, Chapters 2, 4, and 5 are relatively self-contained, and can be used independently. But Chapter 3 should ideally be read after Chapter 2, and certain sections of Chapter 1 such as Section 1.2 should be revisited after Chapters 2 and 8 have been read. Part II deals with topics which represent new ground in pragmatics, but which are under-represented in any of the existing pragmatics text-books. In particular, it focuses on various interfaces between pragmatics and other (core) areas of inquiry. Chapter 6 discusses the pragmatics–cognition interface, concentrating on relevance theory. The interface between pragmatics and semantics is the topic of Chapter 7. Finally, Chapter 8 examines the interaction and the division of labour between pragmatics and syntax, focusing on anaphora and binding. The material in this part is more advanced than that in Part I. Of the three chapters in Part II, Chapter 6 should be read after Chapter 2, and Chapter 7 after Chapters 2 and 6. Chapters 6, 7, and 8 are also linked to the student's parallel courses in cognitive science, semantics, and syntax. Each chapter of the book contains an extensive set of exercises and essay questions, and suggested solutions to the exercises can be found after the references. A glossary is provided before the references.

The survey and analysis made in this book are based on a rich collection of cross-linguistic data. While English is the main exemplar language, data (where relevant and possible) is also drawn from a wide range of the world's languages. This is especially the case for Chapters 4, 5, and 8.

Oxford and Reading   Y. H. 黃衍
September 2005

Acknowledgements to the first edition

My greatest intellectual debt is to Steve Levinson, my mentor in pragmatics. At Cambridge, I was extremely fortunate to be personally taught also by John Lyons, Peter Matthews, and Nigel Vincent. The influence on me of these four great scholars and inspiring teachers has been profound. I am very grateful to them and to Anna Morpurgo Davies for the guidance, encouragement, and support they have given me over the years. I owe a special debt of gratitude to David Cram and Sophia Marmaridou, who read through a complete draft of this book and made many invaluable comments on both substance and form. I wish particularly to thank Jay Atlas for reading the chapter on presupposition; Deirdre Wilson and Robyn Carston for reading the chapter on relevance theory; and Kent Bach and François Recanati for reading the chapter on the pragmatics–semantics interface. Their comments have improved these chapters significantly. I would also like to extend a special note of thanks to Eva Clark, Jonathan Cohen, Gerald Gazdar, Larry Horn, Jim Miller, Carita Paradis, Dingfang Shu, Ken Turner, Junju Wang, and several anonymous Oxford University Press referees for helping me in one way or another. I am grateful to Peter Strawson for the anecdotes he told me about Paul Grice, and I was honoured to co-present the John Searle–Yan Huang Symposium (Shanghai, 2002) with John Searle.

Parts of the material contained in this book, especially that used in Chapters 2, 7, and 8 were presented to various audiences at the Universiteit Antwerpen, the Universitat de Barcelona, Beijing Normal University, the University of Cambridge, Charles University in Prague, the National Chengchi University, the National Chungcheng University, Cornell University, the École des Hautes Études en Sciences Sociales Paris, the University of Essex, the University of Exeter, Fudan University, Georgetown University, the Rijks Universiteit Groningen, Harvard University, Heinrich Heine Universität Düsseldorf, the University of Hong Kong, the Humboldt-Universität zu Berlin, Johns Hopkins University, the Universität zu Köln, the University of Lancaster, the Rijks Universiteit Leiden, the Linguistics Institute of the Academia Sinica, the Linguistics Institute of the Chinese Academy of Social Sciences, the Max-Planck-Institut für

Evolutionäre Anthropologie Leipzig, the University of Lisbon, University College London, Lund University, Lunghwa University of Science and Technology, the Universität Mainz, the University of Manchester, the University of Maryland, MIT, the University of Massachusetts at Amherst, Middlesex University, the University of Nanking, the Nanking University of Aeronautics and Astronautics, the Nanking University of Science and Technology, the University of Newcastle upon Tyne, the Occean University of China, the University of Oxford, the Université de Paris 6, the Université de Paris 8, the Université Pierre et Marie Curie, Providence University, the University of Reading, the Universität des Saarlandes, the Shanghai International Studies University, the Universidad de Sevilla, Shandong University, the Southeast University, SOAS, the University of Surrey, the National Taiwan Normal University, the Universiteit Utrecht, the University of Wales at Bangor, the University of York, the University of Wolverhampton, the Zentrum für Allgemeine Sprachwissenschaft Typologie und Universalienforschung Berlin, and Zhejiang University. I have benefited from the comments received on all these occasions.

The bulk of this book has grown out of a series of pragmatics lectures I have delivered for linguistics undergraduate and postgraduate students at the University of Cambridge, the University of Oxford, and the University of Reading since 1989. I owe a debt of gratitude to generations of my students, whose great enthusiasm, positive responses, and helpful comments and criticisms have helped shape this book. More recently, Sophia Marmaridou and Carita Paradis have used parts of the draft of this book as course book with their students in the University of Athens and Lund University, respectively. I am also grateful to them and their students.

I would like to thank John Davey of Oxford University Press for his advice and patience. I am particularly grateful to Alison Kelly, who did an outstanding job of copy-editing. The research reported on in this book was in part supported by a Research Leave Award from the Arts and Humanities Research Board, which provided the time much needed to complete the writing. In addition, I am indebted to the Research Board of the University of Reading for awarding me a number of grants from its Grant and Travel Fund. Once more, I dedicate this book to my daughter, my wife, and my parents: without their love, I would not have completed it. I am grateful to Blackwell Publishing Ltd., Cambridge University Press, Elsevier Science Publishers B.V., and Oxford University Press for permission to reprint material from my published work.

Symbols and abbreviations

Symbols

~	negation
+>	conversationally implicates
~ +>	does not conversationally implicate
+>>	conventionally implicates
~ +>>	does not conventionally implicate
>>	presupposes
~ >>	does not presuppose
‖-	entails
~ ‖-	does not entail
< >	Q- or Horn-scale
[ ]	I-scale
{ }	M-scale
K	speaker knows that
*	example sentence that follows is syntactically ill-formed or semantically anomalous
?	the example utterance that follows is pragmatically anomalous

Abbreviations

ACC	accusative case
ADDR	addressee pronoun
AFF	affirmative
AGR	agreement
ART	article
ASP	aspect
AUX	auxiliary
CAUS	causative
CL	classifier

CLI	clitic
CMP	comparative
CNJ	conjunctive
COMP	complementizer
CTR	contrastive
DAT	dative
DECL	declarative
DEF	definite
DEM	demonstrative
DIR	directional
DUL	dual
DUR	durative
EMPH	emphatic
ERG	ergative
EVD	evidential
F	feminine gender
FOC	focus
FUT	future
GEN	genitive
GER	generic
HON	honorific
IMPF	imperfective
IMPV	imperative
INDEF	indefinite
INDIC	indicative
INF	infinitive
INS	instrumental
IRR	irrealis
LF	Logical Form
LOC	locative
LOG	logophor/logophoric
M	masculine gender
MOD	modality
N	neuter gender
NEG	negative
NOM	nominative/nominalizer
NP	noun phrase
OBJ	object

OBV	obviative
PASS	passive
PAST	past tense
PERF	perfective
PF	Phonological Form
PL	plural
POSS	possessive
PREP	preposition
PRES	present tense
PROG	progressive
PRON	pronoun
PROX	proximate
PRT	particle
PURP	purposive
Q	question marker
REAL	realis
REFL	reflexive
REL	relative marker
SBJV	subjunctive
SBOR	subordinator
SEQ	sequential
SG	singular
SIM	simultaneous
SUBJ	subject
TNS	tense
TOP	topic
1	first person
2	second person
3	third person

The abbreviations used in the glosses of the original sources are retained, except for those that have been altered for the sake of uniformity. For abbreviations that are non-conventional and/or language-specific, consult the original examples.

1

Introduction

1.1. What is pragmatics?

1.1.1. A definition

Pragmatics is one of the most vibrant and rapidly growing fields in contemporary linguistics and the philosophy of language. In recent years, it has also become increasingly a central topic in cognitive science, artificial intelligence, informatics, neuroscience, language pathology, anthropology, and sociology.

But what is pragmatics? Pragmatics can be broadly defined as the study of language in use. However, such a definition may be too general and too vague to be of much use. This is because pragmatics is a particularly complex subject with all kinds of disciplinary influence, and few, if any, clear boundaries (see e.g. Levinson 1983: 5–35 and Ariel 2010 for a discussion of how to define pragmatics).[1] Here, I shall not repeat Levinson's and

---

[1] In Huang (2013a), the representative research areas in contemporary pragmatics are surveyed and an authoritative, up-to-date, and comprehensive description of the contemporary landscape of pragmatics is presented.

Ariel's discussions, but simply propose a working definition of pragmatics (see also Levinson 2000).

(1.1)   A definition of pragmatics
        Pragmatics is the systematic study of meaning by virtue of, or dependent on, the use of language. The central topics of inquiry of pragmatics include implicature, presupposition, speech act, deixis, and reference.

I shall return to the issue of how to define pragmatics in Chapter 8, where the interface and division of labour between pragmatics and semantics is to be discussed.

1.1.2. A brief history of pragmatics

Pragmatics as a modern branch of linguistic inquiry has its origin in the philosophy of language. Its philosophical roots can be traced back to the work of the philosophers Charles Morris, Rudolf Carnap, and Charles Peirce in the 1930s. Influenced by Peirce, Morris (1938: 6–7), for example, presented a threefold division into **syntax**, **semantics**, and pragmatics within **semiotics**—a general science of signs.[2] According to this typology, syntax is the study of the formal relation of one sign with another, semantics deals with the relation of signs to what they denote, and pragmatics addresses the relation of signs to their users and interpreters[3] (Levinson 1983: 1; Horn and Ward 2004). This trichotomy was taken up by Carnap (1942), who, following Morris's insight that syntax, semantics, and pragmatics are ranked hierarchically, posited a similar order of degree of abstractness for the three branches of inquiry: syntax is the most and pragmatics the least abstract, with semantics lying somewhere in between. Consequently, syntax provides input to semantics, which in turn provides input to pragmatics.

When it came to the 1950s, two loosely structured, opposing schools of thought or movements emerged within the analytic philosophy of language: the school of **ideal language philosophy** and the school of **ordinary** or **natural**

---

[2] Morris was also credited with having coined the term 'pragmatics' in English, borrowed from *pragmatisch* in German, as used by the German philosopher Immanuel Kant in his *Kritik der reinen Vernunft* (Critique of pure reason).

[3] Cf. Stalnaker's (1972) definitions: 'Syntax studies sentences. Semantics studies propositions. Pragmatics is the study of linguistic acts and the contexts in which they are performed'.

language philosophy. The central ideas underlying the former originated with the philosophers Gottlob Frege, Alfred Tarski, Bertrand Russell, and the early Ludwig Wittgenstein. The philosophers involved in ideal language philosophy were primarily interested in the study of the logical system of artificial language. However, the partially successful application of its theory and methodology to natural language in the 1950s and 1960s by followers of the movement such as Richard Montague, David Donaldson, and David Lewis led to the development of today's formal semantics. By contrast, within the tradition of ordinary language philosophy, particular attention was paid to natural language, especially natural language use rather than the formal language studied by logicians. Everyday linguistic usages as a means of resolving problems created when they are adopted as philosophical terms were analysed. Under the leadership of the British philosopher J. L. Austin, the school of ordinary language philosophy flourished principally at Oxford University in the 1950s and 1960s. Other leading thinkers of the movement included the philosophers Gilbert Ryle, H. P. Grice, Peter Strawson, John Searle, and the later Ludwig Wittgenstein (Huang 2003a; Recanati 2004a, 2004b).[4] It was within the tradition of ordinary language philosophy that Austin developed his theory of speech acts, and Grice, his theory of conversational implicature. Both theories have since become landmarks on the path towards the development of a systematic, philosophically inspired pragmatic theory of language use.

On the linguistics front, in the late 1960s and early 1970s a campaign was launched by some of Noam Chomsky's disaffected pupils in **generative semantics** (as it was then called), notably George Lakoff, Paul Postal, and J. R. Ross, to challenge their teacher's treatment of language as an abstract, mental device divorced from the uses and functions of language. In their search for the means to undermine Chomsky's position, the **generative semanticists**, who were attracted to the philosophical work by Austin, Grice, Strawson, and Searle, helped to empty what the Israeli philosopher Yehoshua Bar-Hillel called the 'pragmatic wastebasket' (see Harris 1993 for a discussion of the 'linguistics wars' they waged). As a result, a great deal of important research was done in the 1970s by linguists such as Laurence Horn, Gerald Gazdar, and Charles Fillmore to 'bring some order into the content of [the pragmatic] wastebasket', as wisely advised by Bar-Hillel

---

[4] Note that Grice was special in that he took the view that the two schools of thought are not incompatible but complementary (see e.g. Recanati 2004b).

(1971: 405). The publication of Stephen Levinson's celebrated textbook *Pragmatics* in 1983 systematized the field and marked the coming of age of pragmatics as a linguistic discipline in its own right.

Since then, the field of inquiry has continued to expand and flourish. In the last two decades we have witnessed new developments such as Jay Atlas's, Laurence Horn's, and Stephen Levinson's neo-Gricean pragmatic theories, Dan Sperber and Deirdre Wilson's relevance theory, and important work by philosophers such as Kent Bach, Herman Cappelen, Ernest Lepore, Jason Stanley, and François Recanati. 'More recently', as the editors of a recently published *The Handbook of Pragmatics* declared, 'work in pragmatic theory has extended from the attempt to rescue the syntax and semantics from their own unnecessary complexities to other domains of linguistic inquiry, ranging from historical linguistics to the lexicon, from language acquisition to computational linguistics, from intonational structure to cognitive science' (Horn and Ward 2004: xi). To this, we can add the current, ongoing, heated debate about contextualism versus semantic minimalism, pragmatic intrusion into what is said, embedded implicature, unarticulated constituents, and politeness versus impoliteness in contemporary linguistics and the philosophy of language. One thing is now certain: the future of pragmatics is bright.

1.1.3. Two main schools of thought in pragmatics: Anglo-American versus European Continental

In contemporary pragmatics, two main schools of thought can be identified: the **Anglo-American** and the **European Continental** traditions. Within the Anglo-American conception of linguistics and the philosophy of language, pragmatics is defined as the systematic study of meaning by virtue of, or dependent on, language use. The central topics of inquiry include implicature, presupposition, speech act, deixis, and reference (see (1.1)). This is known as the **component** or '**pigeon-hole**' view of pragmatics. On this view, a linguistic theory consists of a number of core components: **phonetics** (the study of speech sounds), **phonology** (the study of sound systems), **morphology** (the study of the grammatical structure of words), syntax (the study of the grammatical relation between, or distribution of, words and other units within the sentence), and semantics (the study of meaning in abstraction from the speakers' intentions, their psychological states, and the cultural and social aspects of the context in which a linguistic expression is used). Each of these core components has a relatively properly demarcated domain of inquiry. Pragmatics, then, is just another core component placed in the same contrast set within a theory of language. By contrast, other 'hyphenated' branches of linguistics such as anthropological linguistics, educational linguistics, and sociolinguistics lie outside this set of core components. The component view of pragmatics is to some extent a reflection of the modular conception of the human mind, namely the claim that the mental architecture of *homo sapiens* is divided roughly into a central processor and a number of distinctive, specialised mental systems known as 'modules' (Fodor 1983).

Within the Continental tradition of linguistics and the philosophy of language, the view that pragmatics should be treated as a core component of a linguistic theory, in conjunction with phonetics, phonology, morphology, syntax, and semantics, is rejected. Instead, pragmatics is taken to present a functional perspective on all core components and 'hyphenated' areas of linguistics and beyond. According to Verschueren (1999: 7, 11), pragmatics constitutes a 'general functional (i.e. cognitive, social, and cultural) perspective on linguistic phenomena in relation to their usage in the form of behaviour'. Consequently, within the wider Continental tradition, the empirical orbit of pragmatics has been considerably widened, encompassing not only much that goes under the rubric of those non-core areas of linguistics such as sociolinguistics, educational linguistics, and discourse analysis, but also some that falls in the province of certain neighbouring social sciences. This represents the **perspective** view of pragmatics. This broader Continental demarcation of pragmatics is similar to the definition of pragmatics provided within the former **Soviet and East European tradition**. Under this approach, pragmatics (sometimes also called **pragmalinguistics**) is in general conceived of as a theory of linguistic communication, including how to influence people through verbal messages, that is, political propaganda (Prucha 1983).

Which of the two schools of thought, then, is conceptually more coherent and methodologically sounder? Interestingly enough, the Continental version is more faithful to the original view of pragmatics expressed by Morris. While Morris advocated the view that pragmatics constitutes a component, that is, '[s]yntactics, semantics and pragmatics are the components of a single science of semiotic but mutually irreducible components' (Morris 1938: 54), he did conclude that pragmatics should study 'the relation of signs to interpreters' and that 'since most, if not all, signs have as their interpreters living organisms, it is a sufficiently accurate characterization of pragmatics to say that it deals with the biotic aspects of semiosis, that is, with all the psychological, biological, and sociological phenomena which occur in the functioning of signs' (Morris 1938: 30).

In keeping with this broader Morrisian tradition, the Continental approach to pragmatics takes its cue not only from analytic philosophy, but also from a variety of research traditions as diverse as Prague school functionalism, Firthian linguistics, early pragmatic research conducted by German, Dutch, and Scandinavian scholars, the Paris-Geneva school of pragmatics, and Jürgen Habermas's universal pragmatics. Consequently, it adopts a much wider conception of pragmatics, 'perspectivizing' not only all the core components and 'hyphenated' areas of linguistics but also some fields of inquiry from certain neighbouring social sciences, with its research interests ranging from speech acts through medical communication to language and social struggle (Verschueren 1999, Mey 2001, see also issues of the *Journal of Pragmatics*, *Pragmatics*, and *Intercultural Pragmatics*, and entries in Verschueren et al.'s 1995 *Handbook of Pragmatics* and its periodic updates). Thus, pragmatics in the Continental sense appears to be a study of 'everything'. But a study of 'everything' is hardly a viable academic enterprise. Given the degree of overlap with the phenomena dealt with in other relatively well-established interdisciplinary fields of linguistics such as sociolinguistics, psycholinguistics, and neurolinguistics, it is rather difficult to see how a coherent research agenda of pragmatics can be made within the wider Continental tradition. 'Everything is pragmatics' amounts to saying that 'nothing is pragmatics'. Pragmatics delineated within such a conception seems too inclusive to be of much theoretical significance. It can at best serve as a flag of convenience under the auspices of which divergent branches of linguistic inquiry and beyond can momentarily find a common front in an intellectual coalition (see also Levinson 1987a). By way of contrast, the narrower Anglo-American, component view of pragmatics has a much more restricted research agenda. As mentioned above, it focuses on topics emerging from the principal concerns of the twentieth-century analytic philosophy, some of which stem from such eminent philosophers as Gottlob Frege, Bertrand Russell, Ludwig Wittgenstein, J. L. Austin, H. P. Grice, Peter Strawson, and John Searle. While it may be too restrictive, the Anglo-American school of pragmatics seems to delimit the scope of the discipline in a more coherent, systematic, and principled way than the

Continental tradition (Huang 2010d).[5] In this book, therefore, my discussion of pragmatics will largely be from the Anglo-American, component point of view.

1.2. Why pragmatics?

There are many reasons for including pragmatics in an integrated linguistic theory. Here, I shall discuss just two of them.

1.2.1. Linguistic underdeterminacy

It is now widely accepted that there is a huge gap between the meaning of a sentence and the messages actually conveyed by the uttering of that sentence. In other words, the linguistically encoded meaning of a sentence radically underdetermines the proposition a speaker expresses when he or she utters that sentence (see e.g. Austin 1962; Atlas 1977, 1989, 2005; Searle 1979, 1992, 1996; Travis 1981, 1997; Sperber and Wilson 1986; Recanati 1989, 1994, 2004a, 2004b; Bach 1997, 2005; Levinson 2000; Carston 2002;

---

[5] But two points should be noted here. First, there has recently been some convergence between the two camps. On the one hand, interesting work has been done on topics such as implicature, speech acts, and presupposition from a Continental, perspective point of view. On the other hand, research in the Anglo-American tradition has recently been extended to certain 'hyphenated' domains of linguistics such as computational linguistics, historical linguistics, and discourse analysis. Secondly, each side of the divide complements, and has much to learn from, the other side. Whereas the strength of the Anglo-American branch lies mainly in theory, and philosophical, cognitive, and formal pragmatics, the Continental tradition has much to offer in empirical work, and socio- (or societal), cross- (or inter-) cultural, and interlanguage pragmatics, to mention just a few examples. Consequently, a cross-fertilization in pragmatics of theory and empirical work on the one hand, and different approaches and methodologies on the other hand is highly desirable. Furthermore, looking at issues from different angles may not be a bad thing. Therefore, we should not only encourage both schools of thought to exist side by side peacefully but, more importantly, we should also promote dialogue and co-operation between them. Only in this way can the entire field of pragmatics, broadly construed, continue to flourish (Huang 2010d).

Horn 2004, 2009). This is generally known as the **linguistic underdetermi-nacy thesis**.[6] By way of illustration, consider (1.2)–(1.5).

(1.2)   You and you, but not you, stand up!

(1.3)   (Advice given by the British government during an outbreak of salmonella in the UK)
        Fried eggs should be cooked properly and if there are frail or elderly people in the house, they should be hard-boiled.

(1.4)   John is looking for his glasses.
        a. glasses = spectacles
        b. glasses = drinking vessels

(1.5)   (Cited in Levinson 2000: 174)
        They are cooking apples.
        a. What are they doing in the kitchen?
           They are cooking apples.
        b. What kind of apples are those?
           They are cooking apples.

The three uses of the pronoun *you*—called a deictic expression—in (1.2) can be properly interpreted only by a direct, moment-by-moment monitoring of the physical aspects of the speech event in which the sentence is uttered. In other words, the deictic parameter can be fixed only if the deictic expressions are accompanied by physical behaviour of some sort (such as a selecting gesture or an eye contact), which requires an extralinguistic physical context. I shall provide a detailed descriptive analysis of deixis in Chapter 5. Next, in (1.3), the preferred antecedent of the anaphoric pronoun *they* is *eggs* rather than *frail or elderly people*. The derivation of this reading is dependent on what the speaker is most likely to intend to mean and our real-world knowledge about who or what is or is not likely to be boiled. Finally, (1.4) is a case of lexical ambiguity, and (1.5), a case of syntactic ambiguity. In disambiguating them, contextual or real-world knowledge is needed to select the reading the speaker has intended. All this indicates that, frequently, conveyed meanings systematically supersede literal meanings through pragmatically based implication. Putting it another way, certain linguistic phenomena can be handled naturally only by recourse to extralinguistic, pragmatic factors such as context, real-world

---

[6] Bach (2005) called the linguistic underdeterminacy thesis the 'contextualist platitude'.

knowledge, and inference. In order to fill the gap created by linguistic underdeterminacy, pragmatics has to be included as a component in an overall theory of linguistic ability.

1.2.2. Simplification of semantics and syntax

The second reason why we need a pragmatic component is because its inclusion can effect a radical simplification of other core components, such as semantics and syntax, in an overall theory of linguistic ability.

Starting with semantics, it has been noticed at least since Aristotle that a sentence like (1.6) has two systematically distinct interpretations: a one-sided, lower-bounded 'at least' reading, as in (1.6a) and a two-sided, upper- and lower-bounded 'exactly' reading, as in (1.6b).

(1.6)   John has had nine girlfriends.
      a. John has had at least nine girlfriends.
      b. John has had exactly nine girlfriends.

How can a semanticist deal with sentences like (1.6)? Following the tradition initiated by Sir William Hamilton (1860), he or she has to treat these sentences as lexically or logically ambiguous. However, there is a serious problem at the very heart of this ambiguity analysis, namely, the account runs directly against the spirit of a metatheoretical principle known as 'Occam's razor', which dictates that entities are not to be multiplied beyond necessity. A particular version of Occam's razor, dubbed 'Occam's eraser' by Ziff (1960: 44) and 'modified Occam's razor' by Grice (1978, 1989: 47), is that senses or dictionary entries must not proliferate.[7] This has the consequence that, all things being equal, an account which has to suggest two lexical items is to be rejected in favour of an analysis which does not. Therefore, if we adopt the semantic analysis, we are forced to treat not just cardinal numbers like *nine*, but also adjectives like *warm*, quantifiers like *some*, and indeed most lexical items in English and other languages as ambiguous—clearly not an economic analysis.

[7] Cf. **Einstein's Chopper**, which says: 'The simpler a theory the more acceptable it is, provided that it accounts for all the facts; that is, don't invent more processes than you really need in an explanation.' See e.g. Botha (1989).

But if we have a pragmatic component in an integrated linguistic theory, things will be very different. As proposed in Horn (1972) and formalized in Gazdar (1979), the alternative analysis is to obtain the one-sided, lower-bounded 'at least' reading from semantics, and to derive the one-sided, upper-bounded 'at most' reading using a pragmatic enrichment called a **conversational implicature** (to be elaborated in Chapter 2).[8] In other words, on this account, a sentence like (1.6) asserts (or entails) the one-sided, lower-bounded reading 'at least nine girlfriends', conversationally implicates the one-sided, upper-bounded reading 'at most nine girlfriends', and the conjunction of the assertion and the implicature results in the corresponding two-sided, upper- and lower-bounded reading 'exactly nine girlfriends'. Such a division of labour between pragmatics and semantics allows us to avoid unnecessary semantic ambiguity and preserve semantic parsimony, thereby approximately halving the size of the English lexicon (Levinson 1983: 37–8; Horn 1988, 2004; Huang 2009). I shall discuss the relationship between pragmatics and semantics in Chapter 8.

We move next to the potential simplification of syntax by pragmatics. Within the principles-and-parameters theory and its minimalist descendent, Chomsky (1981, 1995) distinguished two types of abstract feature for NPs: anaphors and pronominals. An **anaphor** is a feature representation of an NP which must be referentially dependent and which must be bound within an appropriately defined minimal syntactic domain; a **pronominal** is a feature representation of an NP which may be referentially dependent but which must be free within such a domain. Interpreting anaphors and pronominals as two independent binary features, Chomsky hypothesized that we ideally expect to find four types of NP in a language—both overt and non-overt.

(1.7)   Chomsky's typology of NPs

		Overt	Empty
a.	[+anaphor, −pronominal]	lexical anaphor	NP-trace
b.	[−anaphor, +pronominal]	pronoun	*pro*
c.	[+anaphor, +pronominal]	—	PRO
d.	[−anaphor, −pronominal]	name	*wh*-trace/variable

---

[8]   The origin of this analysis can be traced back to the nineteenth-century English philosophers John Stuart Mill and Augustus De Morgan and the twentieth-century English philosopher H. P. Grice. See Chapter 2 for discussion.

Putting aside the four types of empty category,[9] the three lexically real-ized types of overt NP can be illustrated in (1.8).

(1.8) Overt NPs
    a. Lexical anaphors
      The composers admire *themselves/each other*.
    b. Pronouns
      He is Italian enough to understand the culture, and yet foreign enough to see its peculiarities.
    c. Names
      Jonathan Swift wrote an eighteenth-century satire called *Gulliver's Travels*.

Of the three types of overt NP listed in (1.8), anaphors, pronominals, and **r[eferential]-expressions** are subject to **binding conditions A, B, and C** respectively.

(1.9) Chomsky's binding conditions
    A. An anaphor is bound in a local domain.
    B. A pronominal is free in a local domain.
    C. An r-expression is free.

Binding is defined on anaphoric expressions in configurational terms, appealing to purely structural concepts like c-command, government, and locality. The binding theory accounts for the syntactic distribution of the three types of overt NP listed in (1.8). Consider, for example, (1.10) from English.

(1.10)   a. $Bach_1$ adored $himself_1$.
      b. $Bach_1$ adored him_2.
      c. $Bach_1$ adored $Bach_2$.

---

[9] The four types of empty category are illustrated below.

(i)   NP-traces
    Susan's brother was killed *t* in the Asian tsunami.
(ii) *pro*s (Spanish)
    Carreras sabe   que *pro* es estimado por Domingo.
    Carreras knows that   is esteemed by Domingo
    'Carreras knows that (he) is respected by Domingo.'
(iii) PROs
    John tried PRO to pass his driving test on the first attempt.
(iv) *wh*-traces/variables
    Who do you love *t*?
See e.g. Huang (1992a, 1992b, 1994, 1995, 2000a, 2007a) for comments on empty categories.

In (1.10a), *himself* is an anaphor in the Chomskyan sense. As such, it falls under binding condition A, according to which it is bound to its local antecedent *Bach*. Next, in (1.10b), *him*, being a pronominal, is subject to binding condition B. Given binding condition B, it cannot be bound in its local domain, and there is thus disjoint reference between it and *Bach*. Finally, in (1.10c), the second *Bach* is an r-expression. By binding condition C, it cannot be co-indexed with the first *Bach*. From examples like these, Chomsky concluded that the syntactic distribution of anaphors, pronominals, and r-expressions is accounted for by binding conditions A, B, and C, respectively. However, when confronted with a wider range of languages other than English, these binding conditions run into serious difficulties (see e.g. Huang 1991a, 1994, 2000a, 2004a, 2006c, 2007a for detailed discussion).[10]

In recent years, an alternative, neo-Gricean pragmatic theory of anaphora has been developed by Levinson (1987a, 1987b, 1991, 2000) and Huang (1991a, 1994, 2000a, 2000b, 2004a, 2006b, 2007a, 2010c, 2013c, 2014). On this account, binding conditions B and C are reduced to pragmatics. In somewhat simplified terms, this can be achieved in the following way. If binding condition A is taken to be grammatically specified in English, then binding condition B is the direct result of the application of a pragmatic principle called the Q-principle (to be discussed in detail in Chapter 2). Given this principle, the use of a semantically weaker pronoun where a semantically stronger reflexive could occur gives rise to a conversational implicature which conveys the negation of the more informative, coreferential interpretation associated with the use of the reflexive, as in (1.10b). By the same reasoning, binding condition C can also be eliminated. Wherever a reflexive could occur, the use of a semantically weaker proper name Q-implicates the non-applicability of the more informative, coreferential interpretation associated with the use of the reflexive. This is exactly what has happened in (1.10c). All this suggests that, as pointed out by Horn (1988: 115), 'an independently motivated pragmatic theory (or several such theories, on the compartmentalized view) should provide simplification and generalization elsewhere in the overall description of language'. I shall

---

[10] A current development in the Chomskyan, syntactic analysis of binding is to eliminate all the conditions that are specific to binding, and reduce them to some elementary, general, and independent principles of the computational system of language within Chomsky's minimalist program (see e.g. Reuland 2011). I shall discuss this development in Chapter 9.

return to the pragmatics of anaphora and binding in Chapter 9, where the relationship between pragmatics and syntax is to be addressed.

1.3. Some basic notions in semantics and pragmatics

So far, I have discussed what pragmatics is and why we need it. Next, I shall turn to a number of basic notions in semantics and pragmatics.

1.3.1. Sentence, utterance, and proposition

Let me begin with the distinction between sentence and utterance—a distinction that is of fundamental importance to both semantics and pragmatics. A **sentence** is a well-formed string of words put together by the grammatical rules of a language. As a unit of the language system, it is an abstract entity or construct defined within a theory of grammar. For example, (1.11) is a sentence in English, but (1.12) is not. (In this sub-section, a sentence is represented in italics, an utterance, between single quotation marks, and a proposition, in small capitals.)

(1.11)   *China suffered a lot during Mao's Cultural Revolution.*

(1.12)   *China a lot during Mao's Cultural Revolution suffered.

Sentence-meaning, then, refers to those aspects of meaning that are ascribed to a sentence in the abstract, that is, a sentence independent of its realization in any concrete form. The study of sentence-meaning normally belongs to semantics.

By contrast, an **utterance** is a particular piece of language—be it a word, a phrase, a sentence, or a sequence of sentences—spoken or written by a particular speaker or writer in a particular context on a particular occasion. In other words, it is a situated instance of language use which is partially contextually, culturally, and/or socially conditioned. It constitutes an occurrence of language behaviour on the part of a speaker or writer. For example, (1.13)–(1.16) are all utterances in English. (The quotation marks indicate that what is put between them is taken from a specific context on a specific occasion of use.)

(1.13)   'Hello!'

(1.14)   'A cappuccino, please.'

(1.15)   'China suffered a lot during Mao's Cultural Revolution.'

(1.16)   'Some books are to be tasted, others to be swallowed, and some few to be
chewed and digested; that is, some books are to be read only in parts; others
to be read but not curiously; and some few to be read wholly, with diligence
and attention. Some books also may be read by deputy, and extracts made
of them by others.' (Francis Bacon)

Of these, (1.15) is an instantiation of the sentence in (1.11). In such a case,
it is widely assumed (*à la* Bar-Hillel 1954) that an utterance is the pairing of
a sentence and a context, that is, the situation in which the sentence is
uttered (Levinson 1983: 18–19). **Utterance-meaning** or **speaker-meaning** (as
it is often called), then, is definable as what a speaker intends to convey by
making an utterance. The study of utterance-meaning normally falls under
pragmatics.

Finally, there is the notion of a **proposition**. A proposition is what is
expressed by a declarative sentence when that sentence is used to make a
statement, that is, to say something, true or false, about some state of affairs
in the external world. Put the other way round, a declarative sentence, when
uttered to make a statement, is said to convey a proposition. (1.19), for
example, is the proposition underlying both sentences (1.17) and (1.18).

(1.17)   *Liszt adored Chopin.*

(1.18)   *Chopin was adored by Liszt.*

(1.19)   LISZT ADORED CHOPIN

The **propositional content** of a sentence is that part of its meaning that can
be reduced to a proposition. This notion allows semanticists and pragmaticists to claim that different (types of) sentences may share the same propositional content, even though they differ in other aspects of meaning. For
example, the interrogative sentence in (1.20) is said to have the same
propositional content as the active declarative sentence in (1.17) and the
passive declarative sentence (1.18), namely (1.19). The difference is that
while in saying (1.17) and (1.18) the speaker asserts the corresponding
proposition, that is to say, he or she commits him- or herself to the truth
of the proposition, in uttering (1.20), the speaker questions its truth.

(1.20)   *Did Liszt adore Chopin?*

Propositions may be true or false (to be discussed below), may be known,
believed, or doubted, may be asserted or denied, and may be held constant

under paraphrase and translation. For example, (1.21) in Chinese, (1.22) in English, and (1.23) in Italian can be said to express the same proposition.

(1.21) *xia yu le.*

(1.22) *It is raining.*

(1.23) *Piove.*

Regarding the relationship between sentence and proposition, the same proposition can on the one hand be expressed by different sentences, as is attested by (1.17) and (1.18). On the other hand, the same sentence can be used to convey different propositions on different occasions. As a case in point, consider (1.24).

(1.24) *In his last years, my uncle fell victim to Alzheimer's disease.*

The sentence in (1.24), when uttered by different speakers, may say very different things about some state of affairs in the outside world. If (1.24) was said by Mary about her uncle John, she would have meant something quite different from what Henry would have meant if he had used it to talk about his uncle Albert. Thus, on these two different occasions, the use of the same sentence would have expressed two distinct propositions.

> Try putting these principles into practice by doing Exercise 1 at the end of this chapter.

Finally, the relationship between sentence, utterance, and proposition may schematically be represented in the tree diagram in (1.25) (adapted from Hurford and Heasley 1983: 23). What (1.25) basically says is that a proposition, being the most abstract of the three notions, can be expressed by different sentences. A given sentence, being the next most abstract of the three notions, can itself be instantiated by different utterances, which are the least abstract of the three notions.

(1.25) Relationship between sentence, utterance, and proposition

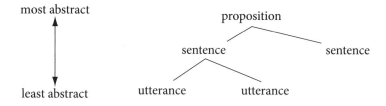

1.3.2. Context

We move next to context. **Context** is one of those notions that is used widely in the linguistics literature, but to which it is difficult to give a precise definition. From a relatively theory-neutral point of view, however, context may in a broader sense be defined as referring to any relevant features of the dynamic setting or environment in which a linguistic unit is systematically used. Furthermore, context can be seen as composed of three different sources—a view known as the 'geographic' division of context (Ariel 1990). In the first place, there is the **physical context**, which refers to the physical setting of the utterance. For example, the interpretation of (1.26) depends on the knowledge computable from the physical context of the utterance, that is, the spatio-temporal location of the utterance.

(1.26)   *He*'s not the chief executive; *he* is. *He*'s the managing director.

The second type is the **linguistic context**, which refers to the surrounding utterances in the same discourse. What has been mentioned in the previous discourse, for instance, plays a crucial role in understanding the elliptical construction used by Mary in (1.27).

(1.27)   John: Who gave the waiter a large tip?
         Mary: Helen.

Thirdly and finally, we have the **general-knowledge context**.[11] The information derivable from this type of context explains why (1.28a) is pragmatically well-formed but (1.28b) is pragmatically anomalous. This is because, given our real-world knowledge, we know that whereas there is a Forbidden City in Beijing, there is no such tourist attraction in Paris.

(1.28)   a. I went to Beijing last month. The Forbidden City was magnificent.
         b. ?I went to Paris last month. The Forbidden City was magnificent.

Clearly, what is involved here is a set of (true) background assumptions shared by the speaker and the addressee. Stalnaker (1974) called this **common ground**. The notion of common ground has been further developed by Clark (1996), who distinguished **communal** from **personal common ground**.

---

[11] Other terms include 'background', 'common-sense', 'encyclopaedic knowledge', and 'real-world knowledge context'.

The former refers to the set of background assumptions shared by members of a community and the latter, to the body of background knowledge two members of a community share from their past experience of each other.

Static versus dynamic conception of context
This is the traditional, and to some extent, **static** view of context, according to which, context is considered to consist of a set of variables (physical, linguistic, cognitive, cultural, social) that encircles an utterance or a stretch of discourse. Context of this type constitutes an *a priori*, static infrastructure of resources which are there for communicators to figure out the meaning of utterances at hand. In contrast to the traditional, static stance, there is the **dynamic** conception of context. On this view, context is not 'given'. Instead, it is established during the dynamic process of utterance production and comprehension. As soon as a linguistic expression such as a sentence is uttered, the current context for that utterance is set up, which becomes part and parcel of its environmental resources (Cap 2011). In other words, given the dynamic conception, context is regarded as a product of dynamic use of language, being interactionally construed, co-constructed, and negotiated, and imported and invoked. It relates language users and the language that they use in a dialectical manner. Put the other way round, to capture the dialectics of the dynamic nature of the construction of context, the use of language is seen as both context-dependent and context-creating (Fetzer (forthcoming), see also Roberts 2004 for a survey of the dynamic treatment of context in a number of formal semantic theories including Discourse Representation Theory (DRT), Dynamic Montague Grammar, and File Change Semantics). One point that is worth mentioning, however, is that the distinction between the static-dynamic view of context is a continuum: on the one hand, there are dynamic ingredients in a static conception of context; on the other, there are static elements in a dynamic treatment of context (see, e.g. Fetzer (forthcoming) for an overview of what she called the 'social and sociocultural', 'text-anchored', 'cognitive', and 'relational' approach to context, see also Finkbeiner et al. 2012).

1.3.3. Truth value, truth condition, and entailment

Finally, we come to the three central notions of truth value, truth condition, and entailment.

Truth value and truth condition

The notion of **truth value** is associated with that of proposition, and the notion of truth condition is linked to that of sentence.

As already mentioned, a proposition may be true or false. But the truth or falsity of a proposition may vary from utterance occasion to utterance occasion. For example, the proposition expressed by the sentence in (1.29), when uttered as a statement, is true in a situation in which the book is indeed on the desk, but is false in another situation in which the book is not on the desk. However, on a particular occasion, a proposition has a definite truth value, that is, it is either true or false in a standard, bivalent logic. It is true if and only if it corresponds to some state of affairs that obtains on that occasion, and it is false if and only if it does not. This is known variously as the 'correspondence', 'corresponding', 'realist', 'realistic', or 'simple' theory of truth.[12]

(1.29)   The book is on the desk.

On the other hand, while a sentence, outside particular uses, does not have a truth value, it does have **truth conditions**. What, then, are truth conditions? They are the conditions that the world must meet for the sentence to be true. A classic example, which originated with the Polish logician Alfred Tarski, is given in (1.30).

(1.30)   *Snow is white* is true if and only if snow is white.

What (1.30) tells us is under what conditions the English sentence *Snow is white* may be used to make a true statement about the external world. Or, putting it slightly differently, what is the condition that must hold of the

---

[12] Truth presents one of the most important issues in philosophy. The issue is concerned with the central question of how truth can be defined, that is, what it is to say that a sentence, statement, or proposition is true. The question is closely linked to many of the major issues in the philosophy of language, semantics, and pragmatics. A number of philosophical theories of truth have been developed, attempting to provide an answer to the question. In addition to the 'correspondence' theory mentioned here, there are also 'coherence', 'deflationalist', 'performative', 'semantic', and 'pragmatist' theories. There has been a tendency in recent research, especially with the development of the deflationalist theory of truth, to take truth as an undefined primitive concept governed by axioms (see Huang 2012a for the relevant entries and Burgess and Burgess 2011).

world, as it were, for the proposition expressed by the uttering of the English sentence *Snow is white* to be true.

Abstracting away from (1.30), we obtain the basic Tarskian formula for a theory of truth in (1.31).

(1.31)   *S* is true if and only if *p*,

where *S* is the name of a sentence in a language, and *p* is the set of conditions under which that sentence is true.

Let us now look at an illustration of how the notion of truth condition can contribute to sentence-meaning. Consider (1.32).

(1.32)   a. Only John$_1$ voted for John$_1$.
       b. Only John$_1$ voted for himself$_1$.

Assuming that John was not the only person who voted, the question that arises is whether (1.32a) and (1.32b) share the same truth conditions. The answer is negative. This is because for (1.32a) to be true, John must have received only one vote, namely, the vote from himself, but there is no such truth condition for (1.32b). For (1.32b) to be true, John could have received all the votes including the one from himself (e.g. Huang 2000a: 242). Therefore, the meanings of (1.32a) and (1.32b) are different simply because the truth conditions for (1.32a) and (1.32b) are different.

On the other hand, there are aspects of meaning that cannot be accounted for in terms of truth conditions. A simple example illustrating this point is given in (1.33).

(1.33)   a. We want peace and they want war.
       b. We want peace but they want war.

(1.33a) and (1.33b) share the exactly same truth conditions. However, the use of *but* in (1.33b) conveys a contrast between the information contained in the first conjunct and that contained in the second conjunct. Clearly, the meaning expressed by the use of *but* (standardly called a conventional implicature, about which more in Chapter 2) is not captured by the notion of truth condition.

Entailment
Next, the semantic relation of **entailment** can be defined in terms of truth as follows.

(1.34)   A proposition (or sentence expressing a proposition) p entails a proposition
(or sentence expressing a proposition) q if and only if the truth of p guaran-
tees the truth of q.

What (1.34) basically says is this: for p to entail q, whenever p is true, q is
also true. By contrast, if p is false, nothing is said about the truth value of q.
Defined thus, entailment represents a **truth-functional** relationship in the
sense that its function is to predict the truth value of a proposition from
what is known of the truth value of another. By way of illustration, let us
take a few examples.

(1.35)   a. The guerrillas killed the American ambassador.
          b. The American ambassador died.

In this pair of sentences, (1.35a) entails (1.35b). This is because if it is true
that the guerrillas killed a certain American ambassador, then it follows
ineluctably that the American ambassador died. The same story holds for
(1.36).

(1.36)   a. There's a horse on the grassland.
          b. There's an animal on the grassland.

Whenever there is some entity that is a horse, then it is necessarily the case
that this is also an animal, and hence (1.36a) entails (1.36b). Finally (1.37).

(1.37)   a. All of the company's employees got a pay rise.
          b. Some of the company's employees got a pay rise.

Again, in this pair, (1.37a) entails (1.37b). The reason is that if it is true
that all of the company's employees got a pay rise (provided that the
company in question does have employees), then there is no way to avoid
the conclusion that it is also true that some of the company's employees got
a pay rise.

Now try Exercise 2 at the end of this chapter.

Upward and downward entailment
In terms of direction, entailment can be divided into upward and downward
entailment. An **upward entailment** (also called **monotone increasing**, usually
represented MON↑) is one from a subset to a set. Putting it differently, the
direction of an upward entailment is from more to less specific, as in (1.38).
By contrast, a **downward entailment** (also termed **monotone decreasing**,
normally represented MON↓) is one from a set to a subset, In other

words, the direction of a downward entailment is from less to more specific, as in (1.39).

(1.38)   a. Every woman is roasting beef.
         b. Every woman is cooking.

(1.39)   a. No woman is cooking.
         b. No woman is roasting beef.

Note finally that one of the most important properties of an entailment is that it is not **defeasible**, that is, an entailment cannot disappear in any linguistic or non-linguistic context. This is why it must be seen as semantic in nature. In fact, a number of other semantic relations such as **equivalence** and **contradiction** can also be defined in terms of entailment (see also Huang 2011).

1.4. Organization of the book

The remainder of this book is divided into two parts. Part I covers those topics (except for reference) that are standardly included in a pragmatics textbook. Within this part, Chapter 2 is concerned with classical and neo-Gricean pragmatic theories of conversational and conventional implicature. The focus of Chapter 3 is on presupposition. Chapter 4 is devoted to speech act theory, concentrating on the classic work by Austin and Searle. Chapter 5 provides a detailed descriptive analysis of various types of deixis. Finally, Chapter 6 navigates around reference.

Part II deals with topics which represent new grounds in pragmatics, but which are under-represented in any of the existing pragmatics coursebooks. In particular, it focuses on various interfaces between pragmatics and other (core) areas of inquiry in linguistics. Chapter 7 discusses the pragmatics–cognition interface, concentrating on Sperber and Wilson's relevance theory. The interface between pragmatics and semantics is the topic of Chapter 8. Finally, Chapter 9 examines the interaction and division of labour between pragmatics and syntax, focusing on anaphora and binding.

Key concepts

pragmatics
syntax
semantics
ideal language philosophy
ordinary language philosophy
Anglo-American, component view (of pragmatics)
European Continental, perspective view (of pragmatics)
linguistic underdeterminacy thesis
Occam's razor
Occam's eraser or modified Occam's razor
sentence
sentence-meaning
utterance
utterance-meaning
speaker-meaning
proposition
propositional content
context
physical context
linguistic context
general-knowledge context
common ground
static conception (of context)
dynamic conception (of context)
truth value
truth condition
entailment
upward entailment
downward entailment

Exercises and essay topics

1. What is the propositional content of the following sentences?
    (i)   The shopkeeper had reduced the prices.
    (ii) The prices had been reduced by the shopkeeper.

    (iii)   It was the shopkeeper who had reduced the prices.
    (iv)   It was the prices that the shopkeeper had reduced.
    (v)   Had the shopkeeper reduced the prices?
    (vi)   Had the prices been reduced by the shopkeeper?
    (vii)   If only the shopkeeper had reduced the prices!
    (viii)   If only the prices had been reduced by the shopkeeper!

2. For each pair of sentences below, indicate whether the a sentence entails the b sentence.

    (i)   a. Susan is always complaining.
         b. Susan is often complaining.
    (ii)   a. Our neighbour's cat has caught a big mouse.
         b. Our neighbour's cat has caught a big animal.
    (iii)   a. It's raining.
         b. It's cold.
    (iv)   a. Everyone likes an apple.
         b. Everyone likes a piece of fruit.
    (v)   a. All birds should be protected by the law.
         b. All puffins should be protected by the law.
    (vi)   a. Some of my friends got promoted.
         b. Not all of my friends got promoted.
    (vii)   a. John was not cooking the fish.
         b. John was not frying the fish.
    (viii)   a. Henry and Jane are married.
         b. Henry and Jane are married to each other.

3. 'What a speaker conveys can fail to be fully determined by the (conventional) linguistic meaning of the sentence he utters' (Bach 1997). Do you agree?
4. Can you think of any other reasons why we need pragmatics in an integrated linguistic theory?
5. What are the differences, if any, between sentence and utterance?
6. What is context? Why is it so important to pragmatics?

Further readings

Huang (2013a).
Levinson (1983). Chapter 1.
Ariel (2010). Chapter 1.

Part I

Central topics in pragmatics

This part covers those topics (except for reference) that are standardly included in a pragmatics textbook. Chapter 2 is concerned with implicature (both conversational and conventional), focusing on classical and neo-Gricean pragmatics including a discussion of embedded (conversational) implicature. The focus of Chapter 3 is on presupposition. Chapter 4 is devoted to speech act theory, concentrating on the classic work by Austin and Searle. Chapter 5 provides an in-depth descriptive analysis of various types of deixis. Finally, Chapter 6 discusses reference.

2

Implicature

The concept of **implicature** (both **conversational** and **conventional**) has its origin in the work of the British philosopher H. P. Grice.[1] The central ideas were introduced by him in the William James lectures delivered at Harvard University in 1967 and were partially collected and published in Grice (1989). In these lectures, Grice presented a panorama of his thinking on meaning and communication—what he called his 'tottering steps' (Grice

---

[1] Though the Gricean notion has a long lineage. Some proto-Gricean ideas can go back at least as far as the first-century BC rhetorician Dionysius (de Jonge 2001) and the fourth-century rhetoricians Servius and Donatus. These ideas were later reiterated by the nineteenth-century English philosophers John Stuart Mill and Augustus De Morgan (Horn 2006). See also Chapman (2005).

1989: 4) towards a systematic, philosophically inspired pragmatic theory of language use, which has since come to be known as **Gricean pragmatics**. Since its inception, the Gricean paradigm has revolutionized pragmatic theorizing and to date remains one of the cornerstones of contemporary thinking in linguistic pragmatics and the philosophy of language.

This chapter is organized as follows. Section 2.1 discusses the classical Gricean theory of conversational implicature. In Section 2.2, I shall present two neo-Gricean pragmatic theories of conversational implicature. In Section 2.3, I shall mention some of the current debates about conversational implicature. The focus of Section 2.4 is on embedded (conversational) implicature. Finally, Section 2.5 examines the notion of conventional implicature, comparing and contrasting it with that of conversational implicature.

2.1. Classical Gricean theory of conversational implicature

2.1.1. Grice's notion of non-natural meaning or meaning$_{nn}$

On a general Gricean account of meaning and communication, there are two theories: a theory of non-natural meaning or meaning$_{nn}$ and a theory of conversational implicature. In his theory of meaning$_{nn}$, Grice (1957, 1969, 1989) emphasized the conceptual relation between **natural meaning (meaning$_n$)** in the external world and **non-natural, linguistic meaning (meaning$_{nn}$)** of utterances.[2] He developed a reductive analysis of meaning$_{nn}$ in terms of speaker intentions.

---

[2] According to Grice (1957, 1969, 1989), in the case of meaning$_n$, *x means that p* entails *p*. This explains why (ii) is semantically anomalous.

Grice (1989: 213)
(i)   Those spots meant measles.
(ii) *Those spots meant measles, but he hadn't got measles.

By comparison, in the case of meaning$_{nn}$, *x means that p* does not entail *p*. Now contrast (iii) and (iv) with (i) and (ii).

(Grice 1989: 214)
(iii) Those three rings on the bell (of the bus) mean that the bus is full.
(iv)   Those three rings on the bell (of the bus) mean that the bus is full. But it isn't in fact full—the conductor has made a mistake.

(2.1)   Grice's theory of meaning$_{nn}$
   S means$_{nn}$ p by 'uttering' U to A if and only if S intends:
   (i) A to think p,
   (ii) A to recognize that S intends (i), and
   (iii) A's recognition of S's intending (i) to be the primary reason for A thinking p.

where S stands for the speaker, A for the audience, U for the utterance, and p for the proposition (see also Levinson 2000: 13).

Defined thus, the essence of meaning$_{nn}$ is that it is communication which is intended to be recognized as having been intended. In other words, meaning$_{nn}$ or speaker-meaning is a matter of expressing and recognizing intentions (but see Gauker 2003 for a dissenting view). What is of theoretical interest here is that, as pointed out by Levinson (2000: 13), 'meaning$_{nn}$ (or something of the sort) draws an outer boundary on the communicational effects that a theory of communication is responsible for'.

2.1.2. Grice's co-operative principle and the maxims of conversation

In his theory of conversational implicature, Grice (1961, 1975, 1978, 1989) suggested that there is an underlying principle that determines the way in which language is used with maximum efficiency and effectively to achieve rational interaction in communication. He called this overarching dictum the **co-operative principle** and subdivided it into nine **maxims of conversation** classified into four categories: **Quality, Quantity, Relation**, and **Manner**. The names of the four categories are taken from the German philosopher Immanuel Kant (Grice 1989: 26). The co-operative principle and its set of associated conversational maxims ensure that in an exchange of conversation, the right amount of information is provided and that the interaction is conducted in a truthful, relevant, and perspicuous manner.

(2.2)   Grice's theory of conversational implicature
   a. The co-operative principle
      Make your conversational contribution such as is required, at the stage at which it occurs, by the accepted purpose or direction of the talk exchange in which you are engaged.
   b. The maxims of conversation
      Quality: Try to make your contribution one that is true.
      (i) Do not say what you believe to be false.
      (ii) Do not say that for which you lack adequate evidence.

Quantity:
  (i) Make your contribution as informative as is required (for the current purposes of the exchange).
  (ii) Do not make your contribution more informative than is required.
Relation: Be relevant.
Manner: Be perspicuous.
  (i) Avoid obscurity of expression.
  (ii) Avoid ambiguity.
  (iii) Be brief (avoid unnecessary prolixity).
  (iv) Be orderly.

The Gricean co-operative principle and its attendant maxims in (2.2) can be simplified in (2.3) (Huang 2000a: 206).

(2.3)   Grice's theory of conversational implicature (simplified)
  a. The co-operative principle
     Be co-operative.
  b. The maxims of conversation
     Quality/sincerity/truth/truthfulness: Be truthful.
       (i) Belief: Don't say what you believe to be false.
       (ii) Evidence: Don't say what you lack evidence for.
     Quantity/informativeness:
       (i) Don't say less than is required.
       (ii) Don't say more than is required.
     Relation: Be relevant.
     Manner/clarity: Express yourself clearly.
       (i) Avoid obscurity.
       (ii) Avoid ambiguity.
       (iii) Brevity: Be brief.
       (iv) Be orderly.

2.1.3. Relationship between a speaker and the maxims

What can a speaker do with regard to the maxims? First, he or she can straightforwardly **observe** the maxims. Secondly, he or she can **violate** a maxim. For example, he or she may breach Grice's first sub-maxim of Quality by telling a deliberate lie.[3] Thirdly, he or she can **opt out of** a maxim. This can be demonstrated by a speaker's use of **hedges**—linguistic expressions employed to express imprecision or qualification—in conversation.

---

[3] There are, of course, circumstances under which a speaker is not expected to follow the maxims. In a court of law, for example, witnesses are often not required to volunteer information, thereby violating Grice's maxim of Quantity.

(2.4)   Opting-out hedges in English
   a. Quality
      As far as I know,
      I'm not sure if this is true, but . . .
      I may be wrong, but . . .
   b. Quantity
      As you probably already know,
      I can't say any more,
      I probably don't need to say this, but . . .
   c. Relation
      Oh, by the way,
      I'm not sure if this is relevant, but . . .
      I don't want to change the subject, but . . .
   d. Manner
      I'm not sure if this is clear, but . . .
      I don't know if this makes sense, but . . .
      This may be a bit tedious, but . . .

There is thus evidence that speakers are not only aware of the maxims, but they are trying to follow them. Fourthly, a speaker can ostentatiously flout or exploit a maxim, to be illustrated shortly.

> At this point, have a go at Exercises 1 and 2 at the end of this chapter.

2.1.4. Conversational implicature$_O$ versus conversational implicature$_F$

What is a conversational implicature?

A **conversational implicature** is definable as a meaning or proposition expressed or implied by a speaker in the utterance of a sentence which is meant without being part of what is said in the strict sense. It is derived from the saying of what is said via Grice's co-operative principle and its component maxims of conversation. It provides an augmented, and sometimes, in 'flouts' cases, altered meaning to what is said. For example, when a speaker utters the sentence in (2.5a), he or she (*ceteris paribus*) conversationally implicates (2.5b).[4] (I use '+>' to stand for 'conversationally implicate'.)

---

[4] Strictly speaking, 'not hot' is what is conversationally implicated. 'The tea is not hot' is **what is communicated/conveyed/meant**, that is, the sum of what is said and

(2.5)   a. The tea is warm.

       b. +> The tea is not hot

Construed thus, a conversational implicature represents a relation between a speaker and a proposition produced by that speaker on the basis of the logic of conversation proposed by Grice. It constitutes, therefore, a component of speaker-meaning (but see note 6). In other words, a conversational implicature is part of what a speaker means, though not part of what a sentence means.

How, then, can the addressee work out a conversational implicature generated by the speaker on the basis of the evidence available? The answer provided by Grice is that utterances automatically raise certain expectations, and these speaker expectations guide the addressee to infer what is conversationally implicated by the speaker, given that both the speaker and the addressee are rational and co-operative agents. Of course, Grice formulated these speaker expectations in terms of his co-operative principle and its constituent conversational maxims. The co-operative principle and the maxims are essentially principles of language use based on the rational nature of human communication, and indeed any shared goal-oriented human activity (Grice 1989: 28). In other words, they are general communicative norms recognized jointly, though tacitly, by both the speaker and the addressee in order to communicate effectively and efficiently (Huang 2012b).

By way of summary, a conversational implicature is what is communicated/conveyed/meant minus what is said. It is beyond and above, and sometimes divergent from, what is said. A speaker implies or implicates, and the addressee infers. The addressee may or may not succeed in recovering the speaker's intended conversational implicature as an inference.[5]

what is conversationally implicated. In other words, put in the form of a formula, we have:

(i)   What is conversationally implicated = what is communicated/conveyed/ meant – what is said. Or

(ii) What is communicated/conveyed/meant = what is said + what is conversationally implicated.

In what follows, however, I shall not make the difference between what is communicated/conveyed/meant and what is conversationally implicated.

[5] When there are meaning discrepancies between utterance production (conversational implicature) and comprehension (inference), we have what Saul (2002) called an **'audience-implicature'**—a conversational implicature that is recognized

Nevertheless, it is the speaker's assumption about the inference that the addressee can reasonably be expected to draw that makes the production and comprehension of conversational implicature a rational, shared goal-oriented activity (Horn 2012).[6]

How is a conversational implicature engendered?

Assuming that Grice's co-operative principle and its associated maxims are normally adhered to by both the speaker and the addressee in a conversational interaction, Grice suggested that a conversational implicature can arise from either strictly observing or ostentatiously flouting the maxims. Let me call conversational implicatures that are generated by way of directly **observing** the maxims **conversational implicatures$_O$**. As an illustration, consider (2.6)–(2.9).

(2.6)   Quality
   Tim Berners-Lee invented the World Wide Web in 1989.
   +> The speaker believes that Tim Berners-Lee invented the World Wide Web in 1989, and has adequate evidence that he did

(2.7)   Quantity
   She [Ally] looked me right in the eye and said, 'I need to know how you feel about me.' I didn't say anything for a good time . . . 'I care deeply about you,' I said. 'But you don't love me?' 'I don't know.' She nodded. Tears streamed down her face. (Peter David Marks: A Bad Case of Puppy Love, *New York Times*)
   I care deeply about you.
   +> the speaker does not love the addressee

by the addressee but not intended by a speaker (see e.g. Thomas 1995: 58–61 and Gibbs 1999: 5–6 for exemplification). An audience-implicature contrasts with an **'utterer-implicature'**, that is, a conversational implicature that is intended by the speaker but not recognized by the addressee. Together, an audience- and an utterer-implicature are labelled a **'near-implicature'**.

---

[6] Currently, there is a split on the issue of whether a conversational implicature is a component of speaker-meaning or a pragmatic inference. Saul (2002) was of the view that Grice's main goal is to develop a theory of speaker-meaning, but not a theory of psychological processing. This view is echoed in Bach (2006a). Following Saul (2002) and Bach (2006a) and biting the bullet, Horn (2009) held that a conversational implicature is part of speaker-meaning rather than a pragmatic inference. By contrast, Sperber and Wilson (1986, 1995), Levinson (2000), and Atlas (2005), for example, are still treating a conversational implicature as a pragmatic inference.

(2.8)   Relation
        John: What's the time?
        Mary: The museum hasn't opened yet.
        +> It's at least before whenever the museum normally opens
(2.9)   Manner
        John went to a McDonald's and bought two hamburgers.
        +> e.g. John first went to a McDonald's and then bought two hamburgers

Given Grice's second sub-maxim of Quality, when a speaker makes an assertion, he or she conversationally implies that he or she believes it, hence the relevant conversational implicature in (2.6). This sub-maxim can account for '**Moore's paradox**', so-called by Wittgenstein (1953: 190). The paradox is concerned with the question why an utterance such as (2.10) is pragmatically anomalous. The answer is straightforward: (2.10) is a violation of the epistemic commitment of what a speaker asserts (Levinson 1983: 105; see also Grice 1989: 42; Austin 1962; Gazdar 1979; Atlas 1993; Bach 2004).

(2.10)   ?Tim Berners-Lee invented the World Wide Web in 1989, but I don't believe he did.

(2.7) exemplifies the fulfilment of Grice's first sub-maxim of Quantity. Since the speaker has used a semantically weaker expression (i.e. *care deeply about*), where a semantically stronger one (e.g. *love*) is available, he would contradict Grice's first sub-maxim of Quantity if the semantically stronger expression held. Consequently, he believes that the semantically stronger statement does not hold. Furthermore, he has not done anything to stop the addressee thinking that he so thinks, therefore he conversationally implicates that he does not love the addressee, although truth-conditionally, the utterance in (2.7) is not incompatible with the possibility that he loves her. Note next that this conversational implicature has been successfully figured out by the addressee, as indicated in her response 'But you don't love me' in the next turn of the conversation.

The conversational implicature arising in (2.8) results from the observation of Grice's maxim of Relation. If this maxim is to be satisfied, Mary's utterance has to be taken as relevant. Since John has asked a question, Mary should be providing an answer. Assuming that in saying what she has uttered, Mary is co-operatively answering John's question, we can infer that while Mary is not in a position to provide a straightforward answer, nevertheless she thinks that the museum's not being open yet might help John to get a partial answer, such as the one indicated above.

Finally, the conversational implicature in (2.9) is derived from Grice's fourth sub-maxim of Manner. By this sub-maxim, the speaker is expected to arrange the events in the order in which they took place, and the addressee is expected to draw the inference in such a way. (2.9) is also an instance of **iconicity**: the ordering of the linguistic elements iconically reflects—that is, mirrors—the temporal order of the reported events.

Secondly and more interestingly, conversational implicatures can be created by way of a speaker's deliberately **flouting** or **exploiting** the maxims. Let me call conversational implicatures thus induced **conversational implicatures$_F$**.

As mentioned above, the maxims of conversation, as postulated by Grice, may be overtly and blatantly breached. Faced with such a conspicuous flouting by the speaker, the addressee then has two options. One is to think that the co-operative principle has been abandoned as well. But he or she may—and characteristically does—choose a second option. He or she may assume that despite the speaker's apparent failure of co-operation, he or she is still observing the co-operative principle, and reasons roughly thus. If the speaker is still co-operative, and if he or she is exploiting a maxim in such a way that I should recognize the infringement, then he or she is doing so in order to convey some extra message, which is in keeping with the co-operative principle at some deeper level. Moreover, he or she knows that I am able to compute what that message is. A few examples will suffice to illustrate conversational implicatures$_F$.

(2.11) Quality
>   Tony Blair is no longer the Prime Minister of Britain, he is the Foreign Minister of the United States. (Nelson Mandela, quoted in Susie Dent, *Language Report* 2003: 62)
>   +> e.g. Tony Blair has followed the American foreign policies too closely

(2.12) Quantity
>   Back in the yard Boxer was pawing with his hoof at the stable-lad boy who lay face down in the mud, trying to turn him over. The boy did not stir. 'He is dead,' said Boxer sorrowfully. 'I had no intention of doing that. I forgot that I was wearing iron shoes. Who will believe that I did not do this on purpose?' 'No sentimentality, comrade!' cried Snowball, from whose wounds the blood was still dripping. 'War is war. The only good human being is a dead one.' (George Orwell, *The Animal Farm*)
>   War is war.
>   +> e.g. Terrible things always happen in a war. That's its nature, and it's no use lamenting the death of the stable-lad boy and blaming yourself

(2.13)   Relation

>   John: Susan can be such a cow sometimes!
>   (A moment of appalled silence)
>   Mary: Oh, what a lovely day today!
>   +> e.g. One shouldn't speak ill of people behind their back

(2.14)   Manner

>   a. John smiled.
>   b. The corners of John's lips turned slightly upward.
>   +> John did not exactly smile

When Mandela said (2.11), Tony Blair was the British Prime Minister, hence the utterance in (2.11) is patently false. (Notice that the head of the US government department that deals with foreign affairs is styled 'the Secretary of State' rather than 'the Foreign Minister'.) Mandela has clearly and openly flouted Grice's maxim of Quality. However, in order to preserve the assumption of co-operation, the addressee must assume that Mandela is trying to convey something rather different from what he has actually said, that is, the ironic reading which is opposite to the literal meaning of the sentence. A similar analysis can in principle be made for other types of 'figure of speech' such as metaphor, litotes, and hyperbole.

(2.12) is a tautology, and as such, is superficially uninformative. Confronted with this blatant breaking of Grice's maxim of Quantity, the addressee assumes that the speaker is actually co-operative and has to work out why he or she has made such an apparently uninformative utterance. The only way to do this is to interpret it as in fact highly informative. Hence the creating of the conversational implicature along the lines I have indicated.[7]

---

[7] According to Wierzbicka (1987, 1991), (2.12) cannot be used straightforwardly in French, German, Russian, Polish, Japanese, and Korean. On the basis of this observation, she claimed that tautological constructions like (2.12) are language-specific, and therefore cannot be universally accounted for in terms of the Gricean maxim of Quantity. But one of the anonymous referees has pointed out to me that tautological examples of the type illustrated by (2.12) are in fact possible in French, as in (i) and (ii).

(i)   La guerre, c'est la guerre.
      'War is war.'

(ii)   À la guerre comme à la guerre.
      'War is war.'

I can add (iii), which is the title of Chapter 33 of Antony Beevor and Artemis Cooper's *Paris after the Liberation 1944–1949* (London: Penguin Books, 1995).

What does Mary's response have to do with John's bad-mouthing Susan in (2.13), since it initially appears to infringe Grice's maxim of Relation? Clearly, if the assumption that Mary is still co-operative is to be maintained, we have to interpret her response as highly relevant at some non-superficial level. One of the possible ways to do so is to read it as conversationally implicating Mary's disapproval of John's bad-mouthing people behind their back.

The use of the prolix sentence (2.14b), where the simple sentence (2.14a) is available and would normally have been used, deviates sharply from Grice's third sub-maxim of Manner. But on the assumption that the speaker is co-operative, the conversational implicature is essentially that the speaker is not in a position to use the term *smile* here or that it is less than smile that he or she wants to communicate.

We thus have the first Gricean dichotomy between conversational implicature$_O$ and conversational implicature$_F$, namely, the distinction between those conversational implicatures that are generated from a simple assumption that the speaker is observing both the maxims and the co-operative principle, and those that are engendered in more complex ways on the basis of the speaker flouting a maxim but nevertheless following the co-operative principle. Grice's major achievement here is to have provided a unified analysis of both types.

> See whether you can now tackle Exercises 3, 4, and 5 at the end of this chapter.

(iii)   Paris sera toujours Paris.
        'Paris will always be Paris.'

Another anonymous referee has noted that the same holds for Russian. He or she has provided the following example, taken from a Russian grammar book.

(iv)   delo delom a ljubov' ljubov'ju.
       'Business is business and love is love.'

Finally, according to Mayumi Masuko (personal communication), the same construction is also used in Japanese.

(v)   Yakusoku-wa yakusoku.
      'A promise is a promise.'

See, for example, Meibauer (2008) for a neo-Gricean pragmatic analysis of tautologies.

2.1.5. Generalized versus particularized
conversational implicature

A second Gricean dichotomy, independent of the first, is between those conversational implicatures which arise without requiring any particular contextual conditions and those which do require such conditions. Grice called the first
kind **generalized conversational implicatures (GCIs)**, as in (2.15), and the second
kind **particularized conversational implicatures (PCIs)**, as in (2.16).

(2.15)   Most of John's friends believe in marriage.
         +> Not all of John's friends believe in marriage
(2.16)   John: Where's Peter?
         Mary: The light in his office is on.
         +> Peter is in his office

The implicature in (2.15) has a very general currency. Any utterance
of the form 'Most x are Y' will have the conversational implicature 'Not
all x are Y'. This conversational implicature will go through without
needing any particular contexts (see Ariel 2004 for further, detailed discussion of *most*). By contrast, the conversational implicature in (2.16) depends
crucially on its linguistic context. Mary's reply points to the possible connection between the light in Peter's office and his location, namely, if the
light in Peter's office is on, he may be in his office. Without such a specific
context, we will not have the conversational implicature under consideration. Needless to say, the distinction between GCIs and PCIs is a graded
concept. This is because a conversational implicature is more or less generalized or particularized depending on the amount of information provided
by the context that is needed to recover it. The theoretical importance of this
Gricean dichotomy has recently been subject to heated debates. Carston
(2002), for example, doubted whether such a distinction can be maintained.
On the other hand, Levinson (2000) put forward a rigorous defence of it. See
Grice (1975, 1981, 1989: 37–8) for further discussion. See Nicolle and
Clark's (1999) experimental evidence that when speakers are provided
with consistent criteria, they can make a distinction between GCIs and
PCIs. See also Doran et al. (2012) for a summary of the experimental
pragmatic works on GCIs.

Take a look at Exercise 6 at the end of this chapter.

2.1.6. Properties of conversational implicature

Conversational implicatures are characterized by a number of distinctive properties (Grice 1975, 1989; Sadock 1978; Levinson, 1983, 2000; Huang 1991a, 1994: 4–5, 2000a: 206–7, 2011). In the first place, there is **defeasibility** or **cancellability**—conversational implicatures can simply disappear in certain linguistic or non-linguistic contexts (but see Weiner 2006 and Section 2.4 and Chapter 8). How? They are cancelled if they are inconsistent with (i) semantic entailments, (ii) background assumptions, (iii) contexts, and/or (iv) priority conversational implicatures.[8] Let me take them one by one. (I shall postpone the discussion of (iv) until Section 2.2.3.)

First, conversational implicatures evaporate in the face of inconsistency with semantic entailments, as the utterances in (2.18) show. (I use '~ +>' to signify 'do not conversationally implicate'.)

(2.17)   John's wife is often complaining.
      +> John's wife is not always complaining
(2.18)   a. John's wife is often, in fact/indeed always, complaining.
      b. John's wife is often, and perhaps/maybe/possibly/even always, complaining.
      c. John's wife is not only often but always complaining.
      d. John's wife is often, or perhaps/maybe/possibly/even always, complaining.
      e. John's wife is often, if not always, complaining.
     ~ +> John's wife is not always complaining

All the utterances in (2.18) have the potential conversational implicature indicated in (2.17). However, all the sentences in (2.18) bear the semantic entailment that John's wife is always complaining due to the use of phrases such as *in fact always*, *perhaps always*, and *if not always*. Consequently, the potential conversational implicature is explicitly defeated by the inconsistent semantic entailment. This is called '**explicit defeasibility**'.

Next, conversational implicatures are suspended if they are not in keeping with background or ontological assumptions, often referred to as real-world knowledge. Compare and contrast (2.19) and (2.20).

---

[8] In addition, Q-implicatures can also be cancelled by metalinguistic negation. I shall discuss it in Section 2.2.2.

(2.19)   John and Mary bought an apartment near the Louvre in Paris.
+> John and Mary bought an apartment near the Louvre in Paris together, not one each

(2.20)   The Americans and the Russians tested an atom bomb in 1962.
~ +> The Americans and the Russians tested an atom bomb in 1962 together, not one each

The utterance of (2.20) has the potential 'togetherness' conversational implicature, as indicated in (2.19). However, this potential conversational implicature runs contrary to our background or ontological presumptions. Given our knowledge about history, it was impossible for the USA and the USSR to test an atom bomb together in 1962, because they were enemies at that time, thus the disappearance of the potential 'togetherness' implicature.

Thirdly, conversational implicatures are annulled when they run contrary to what the immediate linguistic context of an utterance tells us. Imagine the following exchange in a music shop.

(2.21)   John: This CD is eight euros, and I haven't got any money on me.
Mary: Don't worry, I've got eight euros.
~ +> Mary has got only eight euros

Here, given the immediate linguistic context of (2.21), Mary's response does not produce the usual conversational implicature that she has got only eight euros. This is because all the information needed here is whether or not Mary has got enough money for John to borrow and buy the CD rather than the exact amount of money she might in fact have. The cancellation of conversational implicature in (2.20) and (2.21) is a case of **implicit defeasibility**.[9] Notice that defeasibility is a necessary but not a sufficient condition for conversational implicatures (Horn 2007b).

A second property exhibited by conversational implicatures is **non-detachability**—any linguistic expression with the same semantic content tends to carry the same conversational implicature. (A principled exception is those conversational implicatures that arise via the maxim of Manner,

---

[9] Note that the following joke is based on the defeasibility of conversational implicatures (Leech 1983: 91).

(i)   Steven: Wilfrid is meeting a woman for dinner tonight.
Susan: Does his wife know about it?
Steven: Of *course* she does. The woman he is meeting *is* his wife.

about which later.) This is because conversational implicatures are attached to the semantic content, rather than the linguistic form, of what is said. Therefore, they cannot be detached from an utterance simply by replacing the relevant linguistic expressions with their synonyms. This is illustrated in (2.22), which indicates that the use of any linguistic expression that is synonymous with *almost* will trigger the same conversational implicature.

(2.22)   The film almost/nearly won/came close to winning an Oscar.
　　　　+> The film did not quite win an Oscar

Thirdly, **calculability**—conversational implicatures can transparently be derived via Grice's co-operative principle and its component maxims. Fourthly, **non-conventionality**—conversational implicatures, though dependent on the saying of what is coded, are non-coded in nature (Grice 1989: 39; Bach 1994a: 140). In other words, they rely on the saying of what is said but they are not part of what is said. They are associated with speakers but not sentences. Fifthly, **reinforceability**—conversational implicatures can be made explicit without producing too much of a sense of redundancy. This is because conversational implicatures are not part of the conventional import of an utterance. For example, the conversational implicature in (2.23) is made explicit in (2.24), and (2.24) is not judged to be semantically redundant.

(2.23)   John's girlfriend is pretty.
　　　　+> John's girlfriend is not beautiful
(2.24)   John's girlfriend is pretty, but not beautiful.

Next, there is **universality**—conversational implicatures tend to be universal, being motivated rather than arbitrary. Examples (2.25)–(2.29) from different languages all assert that some young people like pop music, and conversationally imply that not all young people like pop music. (2.30) from Malagasy asserts that some young people like famous songs, and conversationally implicates that not all young people like famous songs. All this shows that if a language has 'all' and 'some', the use of the semantically weaker 'some' will universally carry the conversational implicature 'not all'.

(2.25)   (Arabic)
　　　　ba'D   al-shabaab   yuHibbuun   al-muusiiqaa   al-Harakiyyah.
　　　　some   young people like-PL   the music   the moving-ADJ
　　　　'Some young people like pop music.'

(2.26)   (Catalan)
         A   alguns   joves   els   agrada   la   música   pop.
         To   some   young people   to them   like   the   music   pop
         'Some young people like pop music.'

(2.27)   (Chinese)
         yixie   nianqing   ren   xihuan   liuxing   yinyue.
         some   young   people   like   pop   music
         'Some young people like pop music.'

(2.28)   (Modern Greek)
         Se   merikus   neus   aresi   i   pop   musiki.
         to   some   young people   is pleasing   the   pop   music
         'Some young people like pop music.'

(2.29)   (Kashmiri)
         kanh-kanh   noujawan   chu   pop   musiki   pasabd karan.
         some   young people   be-3SG   pop   music   like
         'Some young people like pop music.'

(2.30)   (Malagasy)
         Misy   tanora   tia   ny   hira   malaza.
         exist   young   like   the   song   famous
         'Some young people like famous songs.'[10]

Finally, we have **indeterminacy**—conversational implicatures may sometimes be difficult to determine. Suppose Mary says (2.31), she may generate a range of indeterminate conversational implicatures.

---

[10]   It is generally acknowledged that the most well-known, apparent counterexample to the claim of universality for conversational implicatures is the one provided by Keenan (1976). In this work, Keenan claimed that the Malagasy-speaking culture of Madagascar is a speech community in which Grice's co-operative principle, and in particular his first sub-maxim of Quantity, is not adhered to. For example, in talking to her son, a Malagasy mother would use the following sentence to refer to her husband/the boy's father.

(i)   Mbola mator y ve ny olana?
      'Is the person still asleep?'
      +> the person in question is not the speaker's husband/the boy's father

This led Keenan to conclude that Grice's theory is culture-specific rather than universal. However, as pointed out by Brown and Levinson (1987: 288–9) and Horn (1988), if we examine the Malagasy fact more closely, we will find that it is not just in conformity with Grice's first sub-maxim of Quantity, it actually requires the existence of this sub-maxim for it to be interpreted. As Keenan herself was aware, Grice's

(2.31) John's boss is a machine.
  +> John's boss is cold
  +> John's boss is efficient
  +> John's boss is a workaholic
  +> ...

> You may now be ready to tackle Exercise 7 at the end of this chapter.

2.2. Two neo-Gricean pragmatic theories of conversational implicature

Since its inception, Grice's classical theory of conversational implicature has revolutionized pragmatic theorizing, giving rise to a large number of reinterpretations, revisions, and reconstructions. For example, the whole Gricean mechanism of the co-operative principle and its constituent maxims has been subject to various attempts at reduction. Early such attempts include Harnish (1976), in which Grice's maxims of Quality and Quantity are collapsed into a single maxim: make the strongest relevant claim justifiable by your evidence. Kasher (1976) argued that the entire Gricean machinery can be seen as following some sort of 'most effective, least effort' rationality principle. More recently, Welker (1994) has tried to make use of a super pragmatic principle, which requires the speaker to produce an utterance which brings the common ground closer to the conversational goals, and which is better than any other utterance the speaker could have

first sub-maxim of Quantity does generally hold for the Malagasy-speaking culture, as is attested by (2.30). (This was confirmed to me by Larry Horn, personal communication, who checked this fact with Keenan after her paper was published.) What Keenan showed was that in the Malagasy culture, Grice's first sub-maxim of Quantity may be overridden by some sociolinguistic principle such as the one of avoiding guilt. It is because of a particular Malagasy taboo on exact identification that the mother would avoid using a more informative term such as 'your father' to refer to her husband. If Grice's first sub-maxim of Quantity did not work at some deeper level, the boy would fail to recognize the intended referent. This is therefore a case of 'no deviation from the norm without a reason'. The deviation here is the Malagasy taboo on exact identification, but the norm is the universal first sub-maxim of Quantity proposed by Grice.

provided. However, of all the reductionist models, the most influential are the two-principled Hornian and the three-principled Levinsonian neo-Gricean pragmatic theories, to which I shall now turn.[11]

2.2.1. The Hornian system

Horn's Q- and R-principles
Horn (1984, 2004, 2012) suggested a bipartite model. On Horn's view, all of Grice's maxims (except the maxim of Quality) can be replaced with two fundamental and antithetical principles: the Q[uantity]-principle and the R[elation]-principle.

---

[11] Another influential reductionist model is, of course, Sperber and Wilson's (1986, 1995) relevance theory, which will be discussed in detail in Chapter 7. In a quite contrary spirit to the reductionist approach, Leech (1983) proposed that the Gricean maxims be revised upward, that is, to be proliferated. In particular, he argued that a **politeness principle** should be added to the Gricean mechanism, and that it should be taken as coordinate in nature to Grice's co-operative principle (see also Leech 2007). However, a number of arguments can be mounted against such an expansionist analysis. First, if we are allowed to invent a maxim for every regularity that is actually observed in language use, not only will we have an indefinite number of maxims, but pragmatic theory will be too unconstrained to be falsified. Secondly, the distribution of politeness (who has to be polite to whom) is socially controlled. By contrast, language usage principles of the Gricean sort are of a quite different status. Grice's co-operative principle defines an 'unmarked' or socially neutral (and indeed asocial) presumptive framework for communication, the essential assumption being 'no deviation from rational efficiency without a reason'. Politeness considerations are, however, just such principled reasons for deviation. Therefore, linguistic politeness is implicated in the classical way, with maximum theoretical parsimony, from Grice's co-operative principle. Thirdly, the assumption of co-operative behaviour is hard to undermine: tokens of apparent unco-operative behaviour tend to get interpreted as in fact co-operative at a 'deeper' level. Now, if politeness principles had maxim-like status, we would expect the same robustness: it should be hard to be impolite. But this is clearly counterintuitive (Brown and Levinson 1987: 4–5). To these, we can add that the expansionist approach is also inconsistent with the spirit of 'Occam's razor' (see Chapter 1), namely, the doctrine that theoretical entities are not to be multiplied beyond necessity (see also Huang 2004b). Politeness and impoliteness will be dealt with in Chapter 4.

(2.32) Horn's Q- and R-principles
   a. The Q-principle
      Make your contribution sufficient;
      Say as much as you can (given the R-principle).
   b. The R-principle
      Make your contribution necessary;
      Say no more than you must (given the Q-principle).

In terms of information structure, Horn's **Q-principle**, which collects Grice's Quantity$_1$, Manner$_1$, and Manner$_2$ maxims, is a lower-bounding pragmatic law which may be (and characteristically is) exploited to engender upper-bounding conversational implicatures: a speaker, in saying '... p ...', conversationally implicates that (for all he or she knows) '... at most p ...'. The *locus classicus* here is those conversational implicatures that arise from a semantic or lexical scale called a **Q-** or **Horn scale**.

Horn scales
There are two types of Horn scale: positive and negative. A **positive Horn scale** is defined in (2.33) (Horn 1972; Ducrot 1972; Grice 1975; Gazdar 1979; Atlas and Levinson 1981; Levinson 1987a, 1987b, 2000; see also Hawkins 1991; Matsumoto 1995).

(2.33) Positive Horn scales
      A set of linguistic alternates $<x_1, x_2, \ldots, x_n>$ such that $S(x_1)$ unilaterally entails $S(x_2)$, where S is an arbitrary simplex sentence-frame, and $x_1 > x_2$ and where $x_1, x_2, \ldots, x_n$ are
      a. equally lexicalized items, of the same word class, from the same register; and
      b. 'about' the same semantic relation or from the same semantic field.

A few examples of Horn scales are given in (2.34). (I use '< >' to represent a Horn scale.)

(2.34) a. Quantifiers
           <all, most, many, some>
        b. Connectives
           <and, or>
        c. Adjectives
           <beautiful, pretty, attractive>
        d. Adverbs
           <always, usually, often, sometimes>
        e. Cardinal numbers
           <n, ... 6, 5, 4, 3, 2, 1>

f. Articles
<the, a>
g. Modals
<must/have to, should/ought to, may/can>
<certain that p, probable that p, possible that p>
h. Verbs
<adore, love, like>

By way of illustration, take, for example, (2.34d). In this contrast set, *always* is semantically stronger than *usually*, which in turn is semantically stronger than *often*, which in turn is semantically stronger than *sometimes*. This is because a sentence containing *always* entails a sentence containing *usually,* which in turn entails a sentence containing *often*, which in turn entails a sentence containing *sometimes*, but not vice versa. The four adverbs are relatively equally lexicalized. All of them are adverbs of frequency, that is, they are from the same semantic field. More or less the same can be said of the rest of Horn scales in (2.34). In contrast, the sets in (2.35) are ruled out as Horn scales.

(2.35)   a. *<iff, if>
b. *<regret, know>
c. *<(p because q), (p and q)>

(2.35a) violates the equal lexicalization constraint specified in (2.33); there is no unitary lexeme in English, which standardly means the same as 'if and only if'. In other words, *iff* (which is in a special register) and *if* are not lexicalized to the same degree. Recently, Levinson (2000: 79) has further pointed out that the equal lexicalization condition is particularly relevant to the semantically stronger lexical expression in a Horn scale. Next, the reason why both (2.35b) and (2.35c) are excluded is that the two lexical expressions in each set are about different semantic relations, thus contradicting the same semantic relation constraint. For any two or more lexical expressions to constitute a Horn scale, they must be about the same semantic relation, and neither/none is allowed to introduce additional semantic fields (see also Huang 2004b).

We move next to a **negative Horn scale**, which is defined in (2.36) and exemplified in (2.37) (Levinson 2000: 82).

(2.36)   Negative Horn scales
For each well-formed positive Horn scale of the form $<x_1, x_2, \ldots, x_n>$, there will be a corresponding negative Horn scale of the form $<\sim x_n, \ldots, \sim x_2, \sim x_1>$, regardless of the relative lexicalization of the negation.

(2.37)   <not some, not many, not most, not all> i.e.
         <none, not many, not most, not all>

Given a Horn scale, if a speaker asserts a lower-ranked or semantically weaker alternate (i.e. a rightwards expression in the ordered set), then he or she conversationally Q-implicates that he or she is not in a position to assert any of the higher-ranked or semantically stronger ones (i.e. leftwards in the ordered set) in the same set. Thus, the use of the positive (2.38a) gives rise to the Q-implicature in (2.38b), and the assertion of the negative (2.39a) generates the Q-implicature in (2.39b).

(2.38)   a. Some of John's friends can speak Chinese.
         b. +> Not many/most/all of John's friends can speak Chinese

(2.39)   a. Not many of John's friends can speak Chinese.
         b. +> Not none of John's friends can speak Chinese; some of them can

These Q-implicatures are also called **Q$_{-scalar}$ implicatures** or **scalar Q-implicatures** (see Doran et al. 2009 for experimental evidence for the role played by scale types and discourse context on the interpretation of Q$_{-scalar}$ implicature).

Finally, an interesting point to note is that sometimes scalar expressions in the same semantic field form two Horn scales linked by a (sub-)contrary relationship rather than a single unified Horn scale, systematically engendering two opposite sorts of pragmatic enrichment (see e.g. Horn 1989: 239–40; Levinson 2000: 86–7; Israel 2004). This is illustrated by the paired Horn scales in (2.40). For example, in the 'evaluation' scalar domain, there are two opposite scales: a positive 'excellent' scale and a negative 'terrible/awful' scale.

(2.40)   a. Quantity
            <all, most, many, some> <none, hardly any, few>
         b. Frequency
            <always, usually, often, sometimes> <never, rarely, not always>
         c. Epistemic modality
            <necessary/certain, likely, possible> <impossible, unlikely, uncertain>
         d. Temperature
            <boiling, hot, warm>[12] <freezing, cold, cool, lukewarm>

---

[12] Notice that as pointed out by Doran et al. (2009), the scalar expressions that are higher-ranked than *hot* are lexicalized differently in different domains of temperature: *sweltering* for atmosphere and *scalding* for liquid.

    e. Preference

       <adore, love, like> <loathe, hate, dislike>

    f. Evaluation

       <excellent, good, all right/OK> <terrible/awful, bad, mediocre>

Finally, mention should be made of the fact that under certain circumstances, a Horn scale can be inverted. For example, the order of the cardinal numbers in the Horn scale in (2.41a) is reversed. Consequently, (2.41b) gives rise to the $Q_{\text{-scalar}}$ implicature in (2.41c).

(2.41)   a. $< \ldots 6, 7, 8, 9, 10, \ldots >$

       b. John has cut down his smoking to ten cigarettes a day.

       c. +> John hasn't cut down his smoking to less than ten cigarettes a day

However, as pointed out by Sadock (1984), this kind of scale-reversal seems to be restricted to cardinal numbers. Now contrast (2.41) with (2.42). Notice that the latter constitutes a negative Horn scale. The assertion of (2.42b) then generates the $Q_{\text{-scalar}}$ implicature in (2.42c).

(2.42)   a. $< \ldots \sim 12, \sim 11, \sim 10, \ldots >$

       b. John hasn't cut down his smoking to ten cigarettes a day.

       c. +> John has cut down his smoking to more than ten cigarettes a day

Of particular interest here is that the direction of $Q_{\text{-scalar}}$ implicatures engendered in an affirmative sentence like (2.41b) and in its negative counterpart like (2.42b) is exactly the opposite. The same is also true of the direction of **scalar** or **pragmatic entailments** here (see also Israel 2004).

Having discussed Horn's Q-principle and Horn scales, let me turn to his countervailing R-principle. The **R-principle**, which subsumes Grice's Quantity$_{-2}$, Relation, Manner$_{-3}$, and Manner$_{-4}$ maxims, is an upper-bounding pragmatic rule which may be (and systematically is) exploited to invite low-bounding conversational implicatures: a speaker, in saying '$\ldots p \ldots$', conversationally implicates that (for all he or she knows) '$\ldots$ more than $p \ldots$' (see also Atlas and Levinson 1981). This is exemplified in (2.43), adapted from Grice (1989: 38).

(2.43)   John broke a finger yesterday.

       +> The finger was one of John's own

Interaction of the Q- and R-principles

Viewing the Q- and R-principles as mere instantiations of Zipfian economy (Zipf 1949), Horn explicitly identified the Q-principle ('a hearer-oriented economy for the maximization of informational content') with Zipf's **Auditor's Economy** (the **Force of Diversification**) and the R-principle ('a speaker-oriented economy for the minimization of linguistic form') with Zipf's **Speaker's Economy** (the **Force of Unification**). Furthermore, Horn argued, quoting Martinet (1962: 139) as support, that the whole Gricean mechanism for pragmatic enrichment can be largely derived from the dialectic interaction (in the classical Hegelian sense) between the Q- and R-principles in the following way.[13]

(2.44) Horn's division of pragmatic labour
        The use of a marked (relatively complex and/or prolix) expression when a corresponding unmarked (simpler, less 'effortful') alternate expression is available tends to be interpreted as conveying a marked message (one which the unmarked alternative would not or could not have conveyed).

In effect, what (2.44) basically says is this: the R-principle generally takes precedence until the use of a contrastive linguistic form induces a Q-implicature to the non-applicability of the pertinent R-implicature (see also Huang 1991a, 1994, 2000a, 2007a, 2010a, 2012b).

2.2.2. The Levinsonian system

Horn's proposal to reduce Grice's maxims to the Q- and R-principles was called into question by Levinson (1987a, 1987b, 1991, 2000). On Levinson's view, Horn failed to draw a distinction between what Levinson called **semantic minimization** ('semantically general expressions are preferred to semantically specific ones') and **expression minimization** ('"shorter" expressions are preferred to "longer" ones').[14] Consequently, inconsistency arises

---

[13] It has been argued that the two counterbalancing forces at work are actually the ones which enjoin volubility and taciturnity, respectively. See Green (1995) for discussion about volubility.

[14] There is, of course, a strong tendency for the two distinct minimizations (or economies) to be conflated. This general correlation, in fact, follows directly from the Zipfian theory of economy. Zipf's **Principle of Economic Versatility** stipulates a direct correlation between a lexical item's semantic versatility and its frequency of use ('the more semantically general, the more use'); his **Law of Abbreviation** postulates an inverse relation between a lexical item's frequency of use and its length ('the more use, the shorter'). Taken jointly, the prediction is 'the more semantically general, the shorter' (Zipf 1949; Horn 1984; Haiman 1985a; Levinson 1987a,

with Horn's use of the Q- and R-principles. For example, in Horn's division of pragmatic labour (2.44), the Q-principle operates primarily in terms of units of speech production whereas elsewhere, in positive Horn scales (2.33), for instance, it seems to operate primarily in terms of semantic informativeness.

Considerations along these lines led Levinson to argue for a clear separation between pragmatic principles governing an utterance's surface form and pragmatic principles governing its informational content. He proposed that the original Gricean program (the maxim of Quality apart) be reduced to three neo-Gricean pragmatic principles: what he dubbed the Q[uantity]-, I[nformativeness]-, and M[anner]-principles. Each of the three principles has two sides: a speaker's maxim, which specifies what the principle enjoins the speaker to say, and a recipient's corollary or an addressee's maxim, which dictates what it allows the addressee to infer. The speaker's maxim is normally concerned with production and is a prohibition. By contrast, the recipient's corollary is usually about comprehension and is an obligation (see also Atlas 2005).

(2.45)   Levinson's Q-principle
The Q-principle
Speaker's maxim:
Do not provide a statement that is informationally weaker than your knowledge of the world allows, unless providing a stronger statement would contravene the I-principle.
Recipient's corollary:
Take it that the speaker made the strongest statement consistent with what he knows, and therefore that:

   (i) if the speaker asserted A(W), where A is a sentence frame and W an informationally weaker expression than S, and the contrastive expressions <S, W> form a Horn scale (in the prototype case, such that A(S) entails A(W)), then one can infer that the speaker knows that the stronger statement A(S) (with S substituted for W) would be false (or K~ (A(S)));

   (ii) if the speaker asserted A(W) and A(W) fails to entail an embedded sentence Q, which a stronger statement A(S) would entail, and <S, W> form a contrast set, then one can infer the speaker does not know whether Q obtains or not (i.e. ~K(Q) or equally {P (Q), P~(Q)}).

1987b; Huang 1994, 2007a). Considered from a slightly different perspective, the general correlation between semantic minimization and expression minimization may be seen as an instance of iconicity.

The Q-principle can be simplified as follows (e.g. Levinson 2000; Huang 2004b).

(2.46) The Q-principle (simplified)
        Speaker: Do not say less than is required (bearing the I-principle in mind).
        Addressee: What is not said is not the case.

The basic idea of the metalinguistic **Q-principle** is that the use of a linguistic expression (especially a semantically weaker one) in a set of contrastive semantic alternates (such as a Horn scale) Q-implicates the negation of the interpretation associated with the use of another expression (especially a semantically stronger one) in the same set. In other words, as mentioned already, the effect of this pragmatic strategy is to give rise to an upper-bounding conversational implicature: a speaker, in saying '... p ...', conversationally implicates that (for all he or she knows) '... at most p ...'. Seen the other way round, from the absence of a semantically stronger expression, one infers that the interpretation associated with the use of that expression does not hold. Hence, the Q-principle is essentially negative in nature.

Three types of Q-implicature can then be identified: (i) **Q-scalar** implicatures, (ii) **Q-clausal** implicatures, and (iii) **Q-alternate** implicatures. Q-scalar implicatures are derived from Horn scales. They are schematized in (2.47) and illustrated in, for example, (2.5), (2.15), (2.17), (2.38), and (2.39) (see also Huang 2010h). (The '~' is for negation.)

(2.47) Q-scalar : $<x, y>$
        $y +> Q\text{-scalar} \sim x$

Next, Q-clausal implicatures are enrichment of epistemic uncertainty. Like Q-scalar implicatures, Q-clausal implicatures also rest on a set of contrastive semantic alternates, but in this case, of a constructional kind. Wherever there is a construction $Y(p)$, where p is not entailed by $Y(p)$, and there is an alternative construction $X(p)$ semantically similar and of roughly equal brevity to $Y(p)$ except that $X(p)$ does entail p, then the use of the semantically weaker $Y(p)$ Q-implicates that the speaker does not know whether p obtains or not (Grice 1989: 8; Gazdar 1979: 59–62; Levinson 2000: 108–11, but see Atlas 1993 for a different view). Q-clausal implicatures are schematized in (2.48) and exemplified in (2.49)–(2.52).

(2.48) Q-clausal: $<X(p), Y(p)>$
        $Y(p) +> Q\text{-clausal } p, \sim p$

(2.49)   (Disjunction)
        <(p and q), (p or q)>
        Mary is a vegetarian or an environmentalist.
        +> Mary is perhaps a vegetarian, or perhaps not a vegetarian; perhaps an
        environmentalist, or perhaps not an environmentalist

(2.50)   (Conditional)
        <(since p then q), (if p then q)>
        If John wants to access the internet from home, he should buy a dial-up
        modem.
        +> John may want to access the internet from home, or he may not want to;
        he perhaps should buy a dial-up modem, or he perhaps should not

(2.51)   (Modal)
        <necessarily p, possibly p>
        It's possible that Buddhism is the world's oldest living religion.
        +> It's possible that Buddhism is the world's oldest living religion,
        and it's possible that Buddhism isn't the world's oldest living religion

(2.52)   (Verbal doublet)
        <(know that p), (believe that p)>
        Mary believes that Nigel has visited Kafka's house on Golden Lane in Prague.
        +> Nigel may have visited Kafka's house on Golden Lane in Prague, he
        may not have

In (2.49), while (p and q) entails its constituent sentences, (p or q) does not. This has the consequence that if the semantically weaker (p or q) is used, then the speaker Q-implies that he or she does not know whether it is p or not, and whether it is q or not, hence the conversational implicatures specified above. The same is true of (2.50). Here, (if p then q) is the non-entailing counterpart to (since p then q). Therefore the use of it will generate the Q-clausal implicature of epistemic uncertainty. Next, in (2.51), *necessarily p* is semantically stronger than *possibly p*. If the speaker avoids using it and instead opts for the semantically weaker *possibly p*, then he or she intends to Q-implicate that he or she does not know whether p obtains or not. Finally, in (2.52), (know that p) entails p but (believe that p) does not. By the same reasoning, the use of the latter will carry the Q-clausal implicature that the speaker does not know whether p is the case or not.

We move finally to Q-alternate implicatures. Roughly, we have two subtypes here. First, the lexical expressions in a set are informationally ranked, as in (2.53) and (2.54). Let me call Q-implicatures deriving from such a set **Q-ordered alternate** implicatures. By contrast, in the second subtype, the lexical expressions in the set are of equal semantic strength, as in (2.55) and (2.56). Let me term Q-implicatures thus induced **Q-unordered alternate** implicatures.

(2.53) Horn-like scales

<succeed, try>

a. In 1888, van Gogh tried to set up an artist's studio at Arles.

b. +> In 1888, van Gogh did not succeed in setting up an artist's studio at Arles

c. In 1888, van Gogh succeeded in setting up an artist's studio at Arles without even trying.

(2.54) Hirschberg scales

<divorce, separate>

a. John: Have they got divorced?

Mary: They have got separated.

b. +> They haven't got divorced yet

c. They have got divorced without separating.

(2.55) a. <white, red, blue, green, yellow, ... >

b. The flag is blue.

c. +> The flag is not, for example, white, red or green, or

+> The flag is not blue and red, or

+> The flag is only/all blue

(2.56) a. <French, German, Italian, Russian, Spanish, ... >

b. John: Do they teach any modern languages in that school?

Mary: They teach French, German, and Russian there.

c. +> They don't teach, for example, Italian and Spanish in that school

In (2.53), *succeed* is informationally stronger than *try*, but it does not entail *try*, as is attested by (2.53c). In other words, *succeed* and *try* form a contrast set, but the set is non-entailing. However, as in the case of $Q_{\text{-scalar}}$ implicatures arising from a Horn scale, the use of the infomationally weaker *try* in (2.53a) gives rise to a similar, $Q_{\text{-ordered alternate}}$ implicature. The same can be said of (2.54). But notice that there is a difference between the scale in (2.53) and that in (2.54). While the scale in (2.53) is given by the lexicon without requiring any specific context, the scale in (2.54) is provided by some general assumption about the world, context, and other pragmatic factors. In other words, whereas the former is a semantic or lexical scale that can be based on the different structures of the lexicon such as taxonomies, metonymies, and helices, that is, a Horn-like scale, the latter is essentially a nonce, pragmatic scale, that is, a contextually given *ad hoc* scale. Such a scale can be based on any partially ordered contrastive sets in a contextually salient way. Levinson (2000) called this kind of pragmatically defined set a **Hirschberg scale** (Hirschberg 1991; see also Fauconnier 1975; Harnish 1976; van Kuppevelt 1996; Coulson 2001).

Next, the lexical expressions in (2.55) are of equal informational strength, hence forming an unordered semantic or lexical scale. On the other hand, the scale in (2.56) constitutes an *ad hoc* pragmatic scale that is also based on an informational symmetry. In both cases, the use of any lexical expression in the set engenders a *weak* $Q_{\text{-unordered alternate}}$ implicature, namely the speaker is not in a position to use any other lexical expressions in this same scale. Finally, whereas Q-implicatures derivable from a Horn or Horn-like scale are generalized conversational implicatures (GCIs), those acting on a Hirschberg scale are particularized conversational implicatures (PCIs) (see also Huang 1991, 1994, 2000a, 2007a, 2010a, 2012b).[15]

Now try to do Exercises 8, 9, and 10 at the end of this chapter.

Metalinguistic negation

One of the interesting features of Q-implicatures is that they can be cancelled by **metalinguistic negation**[16]—a term introduced by Horn (1985) following Ducrot (1972). Metalinguistic negation is a device for rejecting a previous utterance on any grounds whatever including its morphosyntactic form, its phonetic realization, and its style or register. In other words, it represents the non-truth-functional use of negation and is concerned largely with the form rather than meaning of an utterance. Metalinguistic negation (in English) is characterized by a number of distinctive properties. In the first place, it consists of a negative clause/sentence followed by a rectifying one. Secondly, it is a rejoinder to a previous utterance, aspects of which it objects. Thirdly, taken descriptively, it constitutes a truth-conditional contradiction. In the fourth place, when spoken, it tends to occur with

---

[15] Note that there is another type of scale, in which the semantically strong expressions unilaterally entail the negation of the semantically weak ones, as in, for example, <<general, colonel, lieutenant, sergeant, corporal, private>>. Horn (2007a) called it a **rank order**.

[16] Other alternative terms include 'paradoxical', 'irregular', and 'pragmatic' negation.

a special, so-called contradiction intonation contour. Fifthly, it does not allow the use of negative polarity items like *any*. Sixthly, it does not permit negative incorporation. In the seventh place, its interpretation is frequently the outcome of a reanalysis. Finally, it is essentially an instantiation of quotation, mention, or representational use (Horn 1985, 1988, 1989: 363; Burton-Roberts 1989; Levinson 2000: 211–12; Carston 2002: 295). This non-truth-functional use of negation can be distinguished from standard, **descriptive**, truth-functional propositional negation. Consider (2.57).

(2.57)   a. Xiaoming was not born in Peking, he was born in Shanghai.
         b. Xiaoming was not born in Peking, he was born in Beijing.

(2.57a) represents the ordinary, truth-functional negation: what is negated is its truth-conditional semantic content. By contrast in (2.57b), we have metalinguistic negation. What is objected to is not its descriptive content (otherwise the two sentences would constitute a logical contradiction), but rather some property of the representation falling within the scope of negation. More specifically, the aspect that is objected to by the metalinguistic negation is the old-fashioned Wade phonetic spelling of Beijing. To see the difference more clearly, let us take a look at (2.58).

(2.58)   a. John doesn't have two BMWs, he has one.
         b. John doesn't have two BMWs, he has three.

Whereas the negation in (2.58a) is usually understood as denying the one-sided, lower-bounded reading that John has at least two BMWs, which is the putative logical form of the sentence, that in (2.58b) is computed as negating the corresponding, one-sided, upper-bounded or two-sided, lower- and upper-bounded interpretation that John has at most or exactly two BMWs. Thus, while the negation in the former is used in an unmarked, descriptive way, that in the latter is employed in a marked, metalinguistic way. Next, we have three more examples of metalinguistic negation in (2.59)–(2.61).

(2.59)   I didn't have nine euroes left, I had nine euros left.
(2.60)   They don't grow tom[a:touz] there, they grow tom[eiDouz] there.
(2.61)   We don't offer french fries here; we offer freedom fries here.[17]

---

[17] 'Freedom fries' was a term coined by the USA Congressman Walter Jones in 2003 in retaliation to France's refusal to join the USA in the Second Iraq War,

What is metalinguistically negated in (2.59) is a particular plural spelling form of *euro* in the previous utterance, what is rejected in (2.60) is a particular phonetic aspect of *tomatoes*, and finally what is objected to in (2.61) is a particular way of talking about fried potato chips.

Returning to Q-implicatures, it has been argued that the use of metalinguistic negation can cancel the Q-implicated upper-bounded reading that is potentially engendered. In addition to (2.58b), consider (2.62) and (2.63).

(2.62)   The mocha isn't warm; it's downright hot!
          (Compare: The mocha is warm. +> The mocha is not hot)
(2.63)   Charles: So John, how's that gorgeous girlfriend of yours?
          John: Ah, she's no longer my girlfriend.
          Charles: Oh, dear. Still I wouldn't get too gloomy about it. Rumour has it she never stopped bonking old Toby de Lisle in case you didn't work it out, heh.
          John: She is now my wife.
          (pause)
          Charles: Excellent, well ah... excellent, congratulations. (*Four Weddings and a Funeral*, 1994)
          <<wife, girlfriend>>
          Ah, she's no longer my girlfriend . . . She is now my wife.
          (Compare: Ah, she's my girlfriend. +> She's not my wife>

In (2.62), where *hot* and *warm* form a Horn scale, what is metalinguistically negated is the potential Q-implicated one-sided, upper-bounded or two-sided, lower- and upper-bounded interpretation, namely, the mocha is not hot.[18] The same holds for (2.63), where strictly speaking, *wife* and *girlfriend* constitute a

though french fries was originally a Belgian rather than a French food. In a similar way, after Turkey refused to allow an American infantry division to transit its territory to open up a second front in the north of Iraq, President Bush issued a second Executive Order decreeing that the term *Thanksgiving Turkey* should be relabelled as *Independence Bird*. There seems to be a tradition of renaming things that are from an unfriendly country in America. Witness, for instance, due largely to the anti-German sentiment in World War I, the substitution of 'hot dog' for 'frankfurter' (successful), 'liberty cabbage' for 'sauerkraut' (unsuccessful), and even 'liberty measles' for 'German measles'. In response to the restyling of 'french' to 'freedom', the American film director Woody Allen famously said that he would rather give his wife a french than a freedom, kiss (see e.g. <http://rationalwiki.org/wiki/Freedom_fries>).

[18] If words such as *just* and *only* are used in a scalar sentence, as in the following attested example, then we have a descriptive rather than a metalinguistic negation.

rank order. What is metalinguistically denied here is once again the potential Q-implied upper-bounded reading, namely, she is not the speaker's wife.

Note finally that the cancellation of potential Q-implicatures by metalinguistic negation is on a par with that by inconsistent semantic entailments. This can be shown by comparing (2.64) and (2.65).

(2.64) a. John's wife isn't often complaining; she's always complaining.
 b. Mary isn't a vegetarian or an environmentalist—she's both.
 c. It isn't possible John will become a great archaeologist—it's certain he will.
(2.65) a. John's wife is often complaining, in fact she's always complaining.
 b. Mary is a vegetarian or an environmentalist—perhaps she's both.
 c. Not only is it possible John will become a great archaeologist—it's certain he will.

> See whether you are now ready to do Exercise 11 at the end of this chapter.

Levinson's I-principle

(2.66) Levinson's I-principle
 Speaker's maxim: the maxim of minimization
 'Say as little as necessary', that is, produce the minimal linguistic information sufficient to achieve your communicational ends, (bearing the Q-principle in mind).
 Recipient's corollary: the rule of enrichment
 Amplify the informational content of the speaker's utterance, by finding the most specific interpretation, up to what you judge to be the speaker's m-intended point, unless the speaker has broken the maxim of minimization by using a marked or prolix expression.

(i) Doesn't she [Penelope Cruz] ever yearn for a less hectic life, maybe one where more time is spent in one place? She laughs hard as if the suggestion is quite ridiculous. 'Not at all. I love my life. I'm addicted to living like this and traveling all the time. I don't just like hotels, I love them. That's where I get my quiet time and quiet time is golden.' (Lesley O'Toole, *Lady Penelope. Sunday Express*, 14 March 2004)

 I don't just like hotels, I love them. (Compare: I just like hotels. +> I don't love hotels)

Specifically:
   (i) Assume the richest temporal, causal and referential connections between described situations or events, consistent with what is taken for granted.
   (ii) Assume that stereotypical relations obtain between referents or events, unless this is inconsistent with (i).
   (iii) Avoid interpretations that multiply entities referred to (assume referential parsimony); specifically, prefer coreferential readings of reduced NPs (pronouns or zeros).
   (iv) Assume the existence or actuality of what a sentence is about if that is consistent with what is taken for granted.

Setting aside its four instantiations, the I-principle can be simplified as follows (Levinson 2000; Huang 2004b).

(2.67) The I-principle
Speaker: Do not say more than is required (bearing the Q-principle in mind).
Addressee: What is generally said is stereotypically and specifically exemplified.

Mirroring the effects of his Q-principle, the central tenet of Levinson's I-principle is that the use of a semantically general expression I-implicates a semantically specific interpretation. In other words, as remarked above, the working of this pragmatic mechanism is to induce a lower-bounding conversational implicature: a speaker, in saying '...p...', conversationally implicates that (for all he or she knows) '...more than p...'. More accurately, in some cases, the conversational implicature engendered by the I-principle is one that accords best with the most stereotypical and explanatory expectation given our knowledge about the world. Schematically (I use '[ ]' to represent an I-scale):

(2.68) I-scale: [x, y]
     y +>$_1$ x

Some cases of I-implicature are given here.

(2.69) Conjunction buttressing
    p and q +> p and then q (temporal sequence)
              +> p therefore q (causal connectedness)
              +> p in order to cause q (teleology, intentionality)
    John pressed the spring and the drawer opened.
    +> John pressed the spring and then the drawer opened

+> John pressed the spring and thereby caused the drawer to open

+> John pressed the spring in order to make the drawer open[19]

(2.70)   Conditional perfection

if p then q +> iff p then q

If you give me a free Beethoven, I'll buy five Mozarts.

+> If and only if you give me a free Beethoven will I buy five Mozarts

(2.71)   Membership categorization

The toddler cried. The daddy gave her a cuddle.

+> The daddy was the father of the crying toddler

(2.72)   Mirror maxim

John and Mary bought a BMW.

+> John and Mary bought a BMW together, not one each

(2.73)   Frame-based inference

Mary pushed the cart to the checkout.

+> Mary pushed the cart full of groceries to the supermarket checkout in order to pay for them, and so on

(2.74)   Bridging-cross reference

John toured the Old Town Square in Prague. The Hus monument is magnificent.

+> There is a Hus monument in the Old Town Square in Prague

(2.75)   Inference to stereotype

Have you met our new nurse?

+> Have you met our new female nurse

(2.76)   Indirect speech act

Have you got a watch?

+> If you have got a watch and know the time, please tell me what it is

(2.77)   Definite reference

It's a Song vase and on the base of the vessel are four Chinese characters.

+> It's a Song vase$_1$ and on the base of the vase$_1$ are four Chinese characters

---

[19] Needless to say, *and* can also be I-implicated in other ways. Some examples follow.

(i)   It's summer in Auckland and it's winter in New York. (Contrast)

+> It's summer in Auckland and in contrast it's winter in New York.

(ii)   John sang a folk song and accompanied himself on the piano. (Simultaneity)

+> John sang a folk song and simultaneously accompanied himself on the piano.

(iii)   We spent a week in Boston and I visited Harvard University. (Containment)

+> We spent a week in Boston and during that week I visited Harvard University.

For further discussion, see Levinson (2000) and Carston (2002).

(2.78)   Lexical narrowing
John doesn't drink.
+> John doesn't drink alcohol

(2.79)   Negative raising
John didn't think that the government had used too much stick and too little carrot.
+> John thought that the government had not used too much stick and too little carrot

(2.80)   Negative strengthening
Maria doesn't like the English weather.
+> Maria positively dislikes the English weather

(2.81)   Noun-noun compound
a. the government's drugs campaign
+> the government's campaign against drugs
b. the government's safe-sex campaign
+> the government's campaign for safe sex

(2.82)   Specialization of spatial term
a. The nail is in the wood.
+> The nail is buried in the wood
b. The spoon is in the cup
+> The spoon has its bowl-part in the cup

(2.83)   Interpretation of possessive construction
a. John's father
+> the one to whom he is son
b. John's office
+> the one he works in
c. John's class
+> the one he attends
d. Newton's ideas
+> the ones originated from Newton
e. Halley's comet
+> the one named after Halley

(2.84)   Coreferential interpretation
John said that he had a reviving espresso after lunch.
+> John$_1$ said that John$_1$ had a reviving espresso after lunch

(2.85)   Proper name narrowing
Have you been to Shakespeare's birthplace?
+> Have you been to the birthplace of William Shakespeare, the English dramatist and poet?

(2.86)   Adjective interpretation
a. brown cow
+> most of its body surface is brown

      b. a brown book
      +> most of its cover is brown
      c. a brown newspaper
      +> all its pages are brown
      d. a brown crystal
      +> both its inside and outside are brown
      e. a brown paperbag
      +> the whole paperbag is brown
      f. a brown house
      +> only the outside of the house is brown
      g. a brown eye
      +> only the iris is brown

(2.87) Systematic ambiguity
      a. The whole nursery burnt down.
      +> The buildings of the whole nursery burnt down
      b. The whole nursery went on a country outing.
      +> The staff and children of the whole nursery went on a country outing

The class of I-implicatures is heterogeneous, but the implicatures in (2.69)–(2.87) share a number of properties, notably, first, they are more specific than the utterances that engender them. In other words, the utterances have been strengthened by the implicatures. For example, in (2.69), from the use of the semantically general *and*, we get the semantically more specific interpretation 'and then', and so on and so forth. In (2.78), the speaker uses the semantically general *drink*, and the addressee infers it as 'drink alcohol', which is semantically more specific. In (2.86), from *a brown cow*, we obtain the semantically more specific interpretation that most of the cow's surface body is brown. The same can be said of all the other examples. Secondly, unlike Q-implicatures, I-implicatures are positive in nature. Thirdly, in some cases, they are characteristically guided by socially or culturally stereotypical assumptions. This is the case, for instance, of (2.75). Fourthly, they are generally non-metalinguistic, in the sense that they make no reference to something that might have been said but was not (Levinson 2000: 119). Finally, they normally cannot be cancelled by metalinguistic negation (Horn 1989), as shown by (2.88)[20] (see also Huang 1991a, 1994, 2000a, 2007a, 2010a, 2012b).

---

[20] Of course, provided that metalinguistic negation is applicable. There are cases of I-implicatures in which metalinguistic negation does not seem to be pertinent, as in, for example, (2.71) and (2.74).

(2.88)   a. John didn't break a finger yesterday.

   ~ +> John broke a finger yesterday, but it wasn't one of his own

   b. John and Mary didn't buy a BMW.

   ~ +> John and Mary bought a BMW, but not together

   c. (Horn 1989: 388–9)

   John wasn't clever enough to solve the problem.

   ~+> John was clever enough to solve the problem, but he didn't do it

---

Try doing Exercise 12 at the end of this chapter.

Levinson's M-principle

(2.89)   Levinson's M-principle

Speaker's maxim:

Indicate an abnormal, non-stereotypical situation by using marked expressions that contrast with those you would use to describe the corresponding normal, stereotypical situation.

Recipient's corollary:

What is said in an abnormal way indicates an abnormal situation, or marked messages indicate marked situations.

Specifically:

Where S has said p containing marked expression M, and there is an unmarked alternate expression U with the same denotation D which the speaker might have employed in the same sentence frame instead, then where U would have I-implicated the stereotypical or more specific subset d of D, the marked expression M will implicate the complement of the denotation d, namely d' of D.

The M-principle can be simplified as follows (Levinson 2000; Huang 2004b).

(2.90)   The M-principle

Speaker: Do not use a marked expression without reason.

Addressee: What is said in a marked way conveys a marked message.

Unlike the Q- and I-principles, which operate primarily in terms of semantic informativeness, the metalinguistic **M-principle** operates primarily in terms of a set of alternates that contrast in form. The fundamental axiom upon which this principle rests is that the use of a marked linguistic expression M-implicates the negation of the interpretation associated with the use of an alternative, unmarked expression in the same set. Putting it another way, from the use of a marked linguistic expression, one infers that the stereotypical interpretation associated with the use of an alternative, unmarked linguistic expression does not obtain (see also Huang 1991, 1994, 2000a, 2007a, 2010a,

2012b; Horn 2004; Traugott 2004). Schematically (I use { } to represent an M-scale):

(2.91) M-scale: {x, y}

y +>M ~ x

M-implicatures are illustrated by the b sentences in (2.92)–(2.95), which are marked.

(2.92) a. The timetable is reliable.
+> The timetable is reliable to the stereotypical degree n
b. The timetable is not unreliable. (Double negation)
+> The timetable is reliable to a degree that is less than n

(2.93) a. John stopped the car.
+> John stopped the car in the usual manner
b. John caused the car to stop. (Verbal periphrasis or causative construction)
+> John stopped the car in an unusual manner, for example, by deliberately bumping into a wall

(2.94) a. John waited for the interview.
+> John waited for the interview for a stereotypical period of time, say, ten minutes
b. John waited and waited for the interview. (Repeated verb conjunct)
+> John waited for the interview for a considerably longer period of time, say, forty-five minutes[21]

---

[21] Another repeated construction is so-called '**contrastive focus reduplications (CFRs)**', also informally known as '**lexical cloning/clones**'. By contrastive focus reduplication or lexical cloning/clones is meant the phenomenon whereby there is a modifier reduplication of a lexical expression. Some examples follow.

(i) Frank is my COLLEAGUE-colleague. (Noun)
(ii) My car isn't MINE-mine, it's my parents'. (Pronoun)
(iii) I started a really worthless thread [...] well, actually, I didn't START-start it, but...(Verb)
(iv) I'm late but not LATE-late. (Adjective)
(v) I'm up, I'm just not UP-up. (Adverb)
(vi) A: I was sitting across from your husband at dinner.
B: Really?
A: Well, not ACROSS-across (but close-by) (Preposition)

See e.g. Ghomeshi et al. (2004) for further discussion of CFRs. See also Huang (2009) for a neo-Gricean analysis of it in terms of the interaction of the I- and M-principles. Notice further that at least some M-implicatures contribute to the truth conditions of a sentence.

(2.95)   a. Mary went from the bathroom to the bedroom.
         +> Mary went from the bathroom to the bedroom in the normal way
         b. Mary ceased to be in the bathroom and came to be in the bedroom.
         +> Mary went from the bathroom to the bedroom in an unusual way,
         for example, in a magic show, Mary had by magic been made to disappear
         from the bathroom and reappear in the bedroom

Go to the end of this chapter and attempt Exercise 13.

Interaction of the Q-, I- and M-principles

Given the above tripartite classification of neo-Gricean pragmatic principles, the question that arises next is how inconsistencies arising from
these potentially conflicting conversational implicatures can be resolved.
According to Levinson (1991, 2000), they can be resolved by an ordered set
of precedence, which encapsulates in part the Hornian division of pragmatic
labour, discussed in (2.44).

(2.96)   Levinson's resolution schema for the interaction of the Q-, I- and
         M-principles
         a. Level of genus: Q > M > I
         b. Level of species: e.g. $Q_{\text{-clausal}} > Q_{\text{-scalar}}$

   This is tantamount to saying that genuine Q-implicatures (where $Q_{\text{-clausal}}$
cancels rival $Q_{\text{-scalar}}$) precede inconsistent I-implicatures, but otherwise
I-implicatures take precedence until the use of a marked linguistic expression triggers a complementary M-implicature to the negation of the applicability of the pertinent I-implicature. By way of illustration, let us consider
(2.97)–(2.100).

(2.97)   Q > I
         If Bill Gates gave you a car for Christmas, it may have been a real one.
         (a) $Q_{\text{-clausal}}$ <(since p, q), (if p, q)>
             +> The car may or may not have been a real car
         (b) I [*car for Christmas*]
             +> The car was a toy car
         (c) Q > I
             +> Possibly the car was a real car

(2.98)   Q > M
         It is not unlikely that Oxford will win the next boat race, and indeed
         I think it likely.

(a) $Q_{\text{-clausal}}$ <know that p, think that p>
   +> It is possible that it is likely that Oxford will win the next boat race
(b) M{likely, not unlikely}
   +> It is less than fully likely that Oxford will win the next boat race
(c) Q > M
   +> It is likely that Oxford will win the next boat race

(2.99) M > I
   The corners of Mary's lips turned slightly upwards.
   (a) M
      +> Mary didn't exactly smile; she sort of smirked
   (b) I (Mary smiled.)
      +> Mary smiled in the normally way by producing a nice, happy facial expression
   (c) M > I
      +> Mary didn't exactly smile; she sort of smirked

(2.100) $Q_{\text{-clausal}} > Q_{\text{-scalar}}$
   If all of his friends don't love chocolate éclairs, then some of them do.
   (a) $Q_{\text{-clausal}}$ <(since p, q), (if p, q)>
      +> All of his friends may or may not love chocolate éclairs—the speaker doesn't know which
   (b) $Q_{\text{-scalar}}$ <all, some>
      +> Not all of his friends love chocolate éclairs
   (c) $Q_{\text{-clausal}} > Q_{\text{-scalar}}$
      +> Possibly all of his friends love chocolate éclairs

In (2.97), there is a $Q_{\text{-clausal}}$ implicature due to the use of (if p, q). But there is also a potential I-implicature to stereotype arising from the use of *the car for Christmas*. The two conversational implicatures are inconsistent with each other. Now given (2.96), the I-implicature is overridden by the Q-implicature. The same resolution mechanism is responsible for the cancellation of the M-implicature in (2.98). In this example, there is a $Q_{\text{-clausal}}$ implicature stemming from the use of the semantically weaker <think that p>. On the other hand, there is also a potential M-implicature associated with the use of the marked double negation *not unlikely*. Since the M-implicature is less powerful than the Q-implicature, it is blocked. Next in (2.99), there is a potential I-implicature generated by the use of *Mary smiled*. But since the speaker has avoided it and has instead opted for a marked form, an M-implicature is created. Again by (2.96), the I-implicature is neutralized by the M-implicature. Finally in (2.100), there is a $Q_{\text{-clausal}}$ implicature due to the use of the conditional (if p, q). But there is also a potential $Q_{-scalar}$ implicature due to the use of the semantically weaker quantifier *some*. Once again, given (2.96), the $Q_{-clausal}$ implicature defeats the inconsistent $Q_{-scalar}$ implicature. All this shows that a conversational implicature can also be cancelled if it is inconsistent with a priority conversational implicature, as specified in (2.96).

To sum up, conversational implicatures can be cancelled if they are inconsistent with (i) semantic entailments, (ii) background assumptions, (iii) contexts, and/or (iv) priority conversational implicatures. In addition, Q-implicatures can also be cancelled by metalinguistic negation.

The resolution schema in (2.96) can in fact be assimilated into a more general conversational implicature cancellation procedure put forward by Gazdar (1979). On Gazdar's view, the informational content of an utterance can be considered to be an ordered set of background assumptions, con-textual factors, semantic entailments, conversational implicatures, and so on and so forth. Each incrementation of the informational content of an utterance must be consistent with the informational content that has already existed, otherwise it will be cancelled according to the following hierarchy (adapted from Gazdar 1979, see also Huang 1991a, 1994, 2000a, 2003, 2007a, 2010a, 2010g, and Levinson 2000).

(2.101)   The conversational implicature cancellation procedure
        a. Background assumptions
        b. Contextual factors
        c. Semantic entailments
        d. Conversational implicatures
            (i) Q-implicatures
                (1) $Q_{-clausal}$ implicatures
                (2) $Q_{-scalar}$ implicatures
            (ii) M-implicatures
            (iii) I-implicatures

2.3. Some current debates about conversational implicature

At this point, it is useful to mention some of the current debates about conversational implicature. In the first place, the treatment of cardinal numbers as scalar expressions engendering $Q_{-scalar}$ implicatures is highly controversial (see e.g. Carston 2002; Bultinck 2005; Hurewitz et al. 2006;

Doran et al. 2009; Horn 2009; Huang et al. 2010 for arguments against, and Levinson 2000 for arguments for, the scalar analysis). Secondly, there is the issue of the epistemic strength of Q_{scalar} implicatures. This is concerned with the question of what it is a speaker Q_{scalar} implicates against. Two neo-Gricean pragmatic positions can be identified: the weak epistemic one represented by, for instance, Hirschberg (1991), Sauerland (2004), Geurts (2009), and Horn (2009), and the strong epistemic one advocated by, for example, Gazdar (1979) and Levinson (2000: 77–9). In the third place, a heated debate has been going on for the last decade or so, focusing on the nature of Gricean and neo-Gricean GCIs in general and Q_{scalar} implicatures in particular. One view is that they convey **default meanings** *sans* a conscious inferential process and irrespective of a particular context (see e.g. Levinson 2000 for strong defaultism and Horn 2009 for weak defaultism). This is called the **default inference theory**. Another, relevance-theoretic position is that they are essentially inferred contextually on a case-by-case basis (e.g. Sperber and Wilson 1986, 1995). This is labelled the **contextual inference theory**. In addition, a more recent, third view holds that the derivation of Q_{scalar} implicatures relies heavily on structural factors (e.g. Chierchia 2004, 2006, 2013; Chierchia et al. 2012). According to Chierchia and his associates, while a standard upper-bounding Q_{scalar} implicature arises from a positive Horn scale, it is quite weak and even blocked in a negative Horn scale and other downward entailing environments. On the basis of this claim, Chierchia argued that Q_{scalar} implicatures be computed compositionally. Furthermore, he devised an interpretation procedure, according to which Q_{scalar} implicatures are calculated locally in the tree diagram of a sentence and are integrated in the semantics where they occur. This has the consequence that the computation of Q_{scalar} implicatures falls under compositional semantics, hence part of grammar. This is known as the **structural inference theory** (see also the next section).[22] Furthermore, all the three models have recently been subject to studies in experimental pragmatics. While much of the relevance-theoretically oriented experimental work favours the contextual inference approach (e.g. Noveck and

---

[22] But, as pointed out by Levinson (2000) and Horn (2006, 2009), the alleged blockage of Q_{scalar} implicatures is due to the fact that a Horn scale is reversed under negation and other downward entailing operators, as in (2.36). Consequently, a different Q_{scalar} implicature is derived from the inverse scale, as in (2.39) (see also Huang 2010a and 2011).

Sperber 2007; Noveck and Reboul 2008), there is also evidence in support of the default inference theory (e.g. Grodner et al. 2007) and the structural inference view (e.g. Panizza and Chierchia 2008). See also Garrett and Harnish (2009). Next, in recent years, there has been an intense debate about (i) whether or not pragmatically enriched or inferred content can 'intrude' upon or enter the conventional, truth-conditional content of what is said, and (ii) if the answer to (i) is positive, then what the pragmatic intrusion under consideration is. I shall discuss this debate in Chapter 8. Finally, it is worth mentioning that there have been various attempts to integrate the classical and neo-Gricean pragmatic theories of conversational implicature with other current linguistic theories. These linguistic theories include decision theory (Merin 1999), Optimality theory including bidirectional Optimality theory (Blutner and Zeevat 2004), and game theory (Benz et al. 2006). See also Blutner (forthcoming).

2.4. Embedded (conversational) implicature

All of the conversational implicatures I have discussed so far are generated at the sentential level. In this section, I turn to so-called 'embedded (conversational) implicatures'. Recently, embedded implicatures and especially embedded Q$_{\text{-scalar}}$ implicatures have attracted a growing amount of attention from both philosophers of language and linguistic semanticists and pragmaticists.

2.4.1. What is an embedded implicature?

An **embedded implicature** is a seeming conversational implicature that is engendered locally at the sub-sentential level, typically occurring in a clause that is embedded under a logical operator such as a propositional attitude verb, a conditional, and a comparative.

(2.102)   a. John believes that some of his colleagues are afraid of spiders.
    b. +> John believes that not all of his colleagues are afraid of spiders
    Or the weaker
    c. +> John does not believe that all of his colleagues are afraid of spiders

(2.103)   Parents are less happy if their children go to bed and brush their teeth.
          +> Parents are less happy if their children go to bed first and then brush
          their teeth
(2.104)   John knows that the train timetable is not unreliable.
          +> John knows that the train timetable is less reliable than the uttering of
          the sentence 'John knows that the train timetable is reliable' suggests

In the belief report (2.102), the use of *some* seems to create a $Q_{\text{-scalar}}$
implicature arising locally in the clause embedded under the propositional
attitude verb *believe* (with the epistemic part of the speaker omitted). In
(2.103), the apparent I-implicature stemming from the use of *and* occurs
within the scope of the conditional. Note further that this conversational
implicature *cannot* normally be cancelled. Finally, (2.104) contains the
factive verb *know*, embedded under which is the clause where the use of
less reliable generates a seeming M-implicature.

2.4.2. The main problem

Cohen (1971) was perhaps the first to bring the phenomenon of embedded
implicature to the attention of philosophers and linguists. His examples are
given in (2.105) and (2.106).

(2.105)   a. The old king has died of a heart attack and a republic has been declared.
          b. +> The old king has died of a heart attack first and then a republic has
             been declared.
(2.106)   a. A republic has been declared and the old king has died of a heart attack.
          b. +> A republic has been declared first and then the old king has died of a
             heart attack.

On a standard Gricean account, the sentences in (2.105a) and (2.106a)
have exactly the same truth-conditional content, even though they differ in
the temporal sequence of events. This difference in conveyed meaning,
which was also observed by, for example, Strawson (1952), Ryle (1954),
and Urmson (1956), is accounted for in terms of a GCI, namely, a neo-
Gricean I-implicature, as indicated by the relevant conversational implicatures in (2.105b) and (2.106b).

However, according to Cohen, this analysis of Grice's is untenable. If the
sentences in (2.105a) and (2.106a) really have the same truth-conditional
content and differ only in conversational implicatures, then when they are

embedded in the antecedent of a conditional, as in (2.107) and (2.108), given Grice's analysis of *if*, they should also have the same truth-conditional content.

(2.107)   If the old king has died of a heart attack and a republic has been declared, then Tom will be quite content.

(2.108)   (Adapted from Cohen 1971)
If a republic has been declared and the old king has died of a heart attack, then Tom will not be content at all.

But (2.107) and (2.108) are not truth-conditionally equivalent. The pragmatically enriched temporal relation, which holds between the conjuncts in (2.105b) and (2.106b), is an integral part of the antecedents of the conditionals in (2.107) and (2.108). With one temporal sequence of events, Tom will be happy; with the other temporal sequence of events, Tom will be unhappy (see also Cohen 1977). This indicates that the pragmatically enriched temporal relation falls within the scope of the conditional—a logical operator. However, given the classical Gricean mechanism, this is simply not possible (but see Walker 1975 for a defence of the Gricean analysis). The reason is that conversational implicatures can only be derived on the basis of a full speech act, namely, the speech act of saying something performed by a speaker. Consequently, they can arise only at the speech act or sentential level but not at the sub-speech act or sub-sentential level (see also Geurts 2010 for other problems in relation to Q-scalar implicature).[23]

2.4.3. Analyses

Currently, the study of embedded implicatures is largely restricted to a subtype of conversational implicature, namely Q-scalar implicatures. With regard to embedded Q-scalar implicatures, there are roughly two approaches: grammatical and pragmatic. Within the first, grammatical camp, which is

---

[23] According to Recanati (2010), this argument was also made independently by Ducrot (1973) (see also Wilson 1975 and King and Stanley 2005). But there are scholars like Green (1998) who are of the view that a generalized conversational implicature is *eo ipso* embeddable. His **embedded implicature hypothesis** runs like this: 'If assertion of a sentence *S* conveys the implicatu[re] that *p* with nearly universal regularity, then when *S* is embedded the content that is usually understood to be embedded for semantic purposes is the proposition (*S* & *p*)'.

called **conventionalism** by Geurts (2010), there are two varieties: **lexicalist conventionalism** and **syntax-based/driven conventionalism**.[24] The central idea underlying both versions of conventionalism is that a so-called embedded Q_{scalar} implicature is part of the lexico-grammatical content of a sentence. In other words, it is part of the conventional, truth-conditional meaning rather than a pragmatic enrichment of a sentence. More specifically, according to conventionalism, embedded Q_{scalar} implicatures 'are not implicatures at all, but rather **soft entailments** projected from the lexicon or the grammar' (Geurts 2010: 134, my boldtype). They are soft entailments because they can be defeated. With regard to lexicalist conventionalism, an embedded Q_{scalar} implicature is 'hard-wired into the lexical entries' of an implicature trigger (Geurts 2010: 145). Given that it is defeasible, it is not part of the lexical meaning of the linguistic expression involved. Nevertheless, it is part of the lexical content or lexical inference of that expression. Consequently, an embedded Q_{scalar} implicature can be accounted for in terms of a default implicature. This approach is represented by Cohen (1971, 1977), Chierchia (2004), and especially Levinson (2000). Next, according to the syntax-based conventionalism, the grammar of a language is equipped with a covert or hidden exhaustivity (EXH) operator, whose meaning is akin to 'only' in English. This syntactic operator can be freely inserted into the tree diagram of a sentence. In other words, under the syntactic approach, an embedded Q_{scalar} implicature is generated by the computational system of grammar. It is calculated and integrated locally in a compositional way (see e.g. Fox 2007; Chierchia 2006, 2013; Chierchia et al. 2012; and see also Gajewski and Sharvit 2012). Construed thus, this **localist** or **localistic** model is too powerful in that the covert EXH operator engenders more readings than is desired for any given sentence. This over-generation has to be constrained in one way or another. The most popular proposal within the syntax-based camp is to adopt (a version of) the '**Power Principle**', namely, the idea that out of two readings x and y, where x is stronger than y, x should be the preferred reading. From an experimental point of view, conventionalism has received support from Clifton Jr. and Dube (2010) and Chemla and Spector (2011) (but see Geurts and van Tiel 2013 for a critique).

We move next to the pragmatic approach. One variety is to defend the Gricean **globalist** account of Q_{scalar} implicature. This is represented by

---

[24] Conventionalism is also called the 'semanticization' of embedded implicatures by Recanati (2010).

Sauerland (2004), van Rooij and Schulz (2004), Horn (2006, 2009), Spector (2006), Russell (2006), and especially Geurts (2009, 2010). On this view, contrary to the conventionalist **continuity hypothesis** or stance that the upper-bounded reading of a $Q_{-scalar}$ implicature occurs across the board, be it at the sentential level (unembedded) or at the sub-sentential level (embedded) and that it 'occurs systematically and freely in arbitrarily embedded positions' (Chierchia et al. 2012), an embedded $Q_{-scalar}$ implicature requires special linguistic marking such as a contrastive stress. It is marginal and rare and sometimes the upper-bounded reading has to be forced. In other words, an embedded $Q_{-scalar}$ implicature constitutes an exceptional and marked case (see also Ippolito 2010). Furthermore, the use of embedded and unembedded scalar expressions is computed differently. While the use of unembedded scalar expressions give rise to $Q_{-scalar}$ implicatures, the use of embedded ones does not. Moreover, embedded scalar expressions are frequently dealt with on a case-by-case basis. In the case of the belief report in (2.102), for example, (2.102b) is not treated as a locally engendered $Q_{-scalar}$ implicature. Rather, it is analysed as *following from* a $Q_{-scalar}$ implicature licensed by (2.102a) (Geurts and van Tiel 2013). This version of Gricean globalist account is experimentally supported by Geurts and Pouscoulous (2009) (but see Clifton Jr. and Dube 2010 for criticism) and Geurts and van Tiel (2013).

Another pragmatic account is developed by Recanati (2003, 2010) (see also Bach 1994a,b). Under this truth-conditional pragmatic approach, an embedded $Q_{-scalar}$ implicature is explained in terms of a **primary pragmatic process** of modulation, in particular free enrichment. By **modulation** is meant a primary pragmatic process that is pragmatically controlled or contextually driven (top-down), optional, and produced locally. It intersperses with the compositional determination of the truth-conditional content of a sentence uttered. In other words, modulation takes the meaning of a linguistic expression as input and yields as output a pragmatically enriched meaning, which functions as a compositional value. **Free enrichment**, according to Recanati, is the most typical and pervasive subtype of modulation. Under free enrichment, the meaning of a linguistic expression can be contextually strengthened, that is, it can be contextually given a more specific reading than is literally encoded by that expression. This is the case for embedded $Q_{-scalar}$ implicatures. For example, the meaning of the scalar expression *some* in (2.102a) is freely enriched to 'some but not all'.

Finally, Recanati is of the view that the grammatical and pragmatic approaches to embedded $Q_{-scalar}$ implicatures may complement each other.

The heated debate is still going on. According to Geurts and van Tiel (2013), the broad consensus reached between the grammatical and pragmatic camps is that there are two mechanisms that underwrite the upper-bounded reading (or **upper-bounded construal (UBC)** in their terminology) of the use of scalar expressions: $Q_{-scalar}$ implicatures and **truth-conditional narrowing**. What is at stake is the issue of how to make the division of labour between the two mechanisms. I shall return to some cases of embedded implicature in Chapter 8.

2.5. Conventional implicature

2.5.1. What is conventional implicature?

In the last four sections, I have discussed conversational implicature. In this section, I shall examine the second category of implicature put forward by Grice, namely, conventional implicature.

The German mathematician, logician, and philosopher Gottlob Frege was perhaps the first modern scholar to take note of conventional implicature. His analysis of the *Andeutung* relation can be taken as a direct precursor of Grice's concept of conventional implicature (see Frege 1892 and 1918–19; see also Bach 1999; Horn 2007b; Feng 2010). An *Andeutungen* or **conventional implicature** is a non-truth-conditional meaning which is not derivable in any general considerations of co-operation and rationality from the saying of what is said, but arises solely because of the conventional features attached to particular lexical items and/or linguistic constructions. A number of standard examples follow (I use '+>>' to stand for 'conventionally implicate')

(2.109) *p* therefore *q* +>> *q* follows from *p*
         He is a Chinese; he, therefore, knows how to use chopsticks.
(2.110) *p* but *q* +>> *p* contrasts with *q*
         John is poor but he is honest.
(2.111) Even *p* +>> contrary to expectation
         Even his wife didn't think that John would win the by-election.
(2.112) *p* moreover *q* +>> q is in addition to p
         Xiaoming can read German. Moreover, he can write poems in the language.

(2.113)   *p* so *q* +>> *p* provides an explanation for *q*

Mary is taking Chinese cookery lessons. So her husband has bought her a wok.

In (2.109), the conventional implicature triggered by the use of *therefore* is that being Chinese provides some good reason for knowing how to use chopsticks. In (2.110), there is a conventional implicature of contrast between the information contained in *p* and that contained in *q*[25] (Grice 1989: 25, 88). In (2.111), *even*, being epistemic in nature, conventionally implicates some sort of unexpectedness, surprise, or unlikeness (see e.g. Kempson 1975; Karttunen and Peters 1979; Kay 1990; Barker 1991; Lycan 1991; Farncescotti 1995). In (2.112), the use of *moreover* brings in the conventional implicature that the statement made in *q* is additional to the statement made in *p* (Grice 1989: 121). Finally in (2.113), the conventional implicature contributed by *so* is that the fact that Mary is learning how to cook Chinese food explains why her husband has bought her a wok. Other representative lexical items that are considered to engender

[25] It should be pointed out here that *but* seems to have a number of uses including (i) denial of expectation, which is usually asymmetric, as in (2.110); (ii) contrastive, which is typically symmetric, as in (i) (due first to Lakoff 1971); and (iii) correction, as in (ii) (see e.g. Fraser 2010 and Zeevet 2012 for other uses of *but*; see also Blutner forthcoming).

(i)   Our sales have gone up and theirs have gone down.
(ii) That's not my father but my uncle.

The same can be said of *mais* in French (e.g. Anscombre and Ducrot 1977). On Horn's (1989) view, the distinction is mainly one of semantic ambiguity. This analysis can be supported by the fact that there are languages in which the different uses of *but* are lexicalized. For example, German uses *aber* for the denial of expectation/contrastive *but* and *sondern* for the correction *but*. The two 'but's in Finnish, Spanish, and Swedish differ essentially in the same way. In Finnish, the denial of expectation/contrastive *but* is translated as *mutta* and the correction *but* as *vaan*. Spanish utilizes *pero* for the former and *sino* for the latter. Swedish has *men* and *utan*, respectively (Horn: 1989: 406–9). Finally, there are also two 'but's in Russian: *no* and *a*, the latter serving the function of marking discontinuity in discourse. Furthermore, as pointed out by Anscombre and Ducrot (1977) for *mais* in French, the denial of expectation/contrastive *but* and the correction *but* have complementary syntactic distributions.

conventional implicatures in English include *actually, also, anyway, barely, besides, however, manage to, on the other hand, only, still, though, too,* and *yet.*

See whether you can tackle Exercise 14 at the end of this chapter.

2.5.2. Properties of conventional implicature

Properties of conventional implicatures can best be characterized in contrast to those of conversational implicatures, discussed above (Grice 1975; Levinson 1983: 127–8; Horn 1988).

The main similarity between conventional and conversational implicature is that neither makes any contribution to truth conditions (but see Section 2.4 and Chapter 8). Recall (1.33) in Chapter 1, repeated here as (2.114) for ease of exposition.

(2.114)   a. We want peace and they want war.
           b. We want peace but they want war.

As mentioned in Section 1.3.3 of Chapter 1, (2.114b) shares the same truth condition as (2.114a), though it contains the conventional implicature of contrast triggered by the use of the connective *but.* This indicates that like a conversational implicature, a conventional implicature does not contribute to the truth condition of its corresponding sentence. A second similarity is that both conventional and conversational implicatures are associated with speaker or utterance rather than sentence.

On the other hand, there are a number of important differences between conventional and conversational implicatures. First of all, conventional implicatures are not derived from Grice's co-operative principle and its component maxims, but are attached by convention to particular lexical items or linguistic constructions. They are therefore an arbitrary part of meaning, and must be learned *ad hoc.* By contrast, conversational implicatures are derived from the co-operative principle and its attendant maxims. Hence, they are non-conventional by definition, that is, they are motivated rather than arbitrary.

Secondly, conventional implicatures are not calculable via any natural procedure, but are rather given by convention, thus they must be stipulated. By comparison, conversational implicatures are calculable using pragmatic principles, contextual knowledge, and background assumptions.

Thirdly, conventional implicatures are not cancellable, that is, they cannot be defeated. On the contrary, conversational implicatures are cancellable. Fourthly, conventional implicatures are (arguably) detachable,[26] because they depend on the particular linguistic items used. By comparison, conversational implicatures (except those arising from the M-principle) are non-detachable, because they are attached to the semantic content, but not to the linguistic form, of what is said. Fifthly, conventional implicatures tend not to be universal. By contrast, conversational implicatures tend to be universal.

Now, it should be pointed out that unlike the notion of conversational implicature, the notion of conventional implicature may not seem to be a very coherent one. Even Grice himself (1989: 46) warned that 'the nature of conventional implicature needs to be examined before any free use of it, for explanatory purposes, can be indulged in'. Horn (2004: 6), himself a neo-Gricean pragmaticist, went a step further by claiming that 'the role played by conventional implicature within the general theory of meaning is increasingly shaky'. Since its inception, conventional implicature has been subject to numerous attempts to reduce it to semantic entailment, conversational implicature, and presupposition (Levinson 1983: 128), and more recently, to part of what is said (Bach 1999, but see Barker 2003 for a different view), part of tacit performatives (Rieber 1997), vehicles for performing second-order speech acts (Bach 1999), and procedural meaning in relevance theory (Blakemore 2002, 2004).

But recently, Potts (2005) has made a brave attempt to resurrect the concept of conventional implicature. He 'retain[ed] Grice's brand name but alter[ed] the product' (Horn 2007b) by focusing on expressive expressions like epithets, attributive adjectives, and honorifics, and supplements like non-restrictive relatives, parentheticals, and appositives rather than lexical items such as *but*, *therefore*, and *even*. He isolated four essential properties of conventional implicature. The first of these properties is **conventionality**—conventional implicatures are part of the conventional meaning of the linguistic expressions involved. The second property is **commitment**—conventional implicatures are commitments, and thus they engender entailments. The third property is **speaker orientation**—the commitments are made by the speaker of an utterance. The final property is

---

[26] Cf. We want peace. *However/nevertheless/on the other hand*, they want war.

independence—conventional implicatures are logically and compositionally independent of what is said (see also von Heusinger and Turner 2006). Taking the view that conventional implicature is semantic in nature, Potts developed a logic of the notion by modelling it with a type-driven multi-dimensional semantic translation language (see Horn 2007b and Feng 2010 for criticisms of this analysis). Feng (2010) presented another development of Grice's concept of conventional implicature. The properties extracted by him for conventional implicatures are (i) **non-truth-conditionality**, (ii) speaker orientation, (iii) **infallibility**, (iv) **occurrency**, (v) **dependency**, and (vi) **context-sensitivity**. He further argued that properties (i)–(iv) are intimately associated with **subjectivity**. Finally, contrary to Potts's view, Horn (2007) maintained that conventional implicature has both a semantic and pragmatic character. This is why a conventional implicature is so named by Grice. According to Horn (2007b: 50), '[conventional implicature] is semantic insofar as it involves an aspect of the conventional meaning of a given expression rather than being computable from general principles of rational behavior or communicative competence, but it is pragmatic insofar as it involves considerations of appropriateness rather than truth of the sentence in which it appears.' Whether belonging to semantics or balancing on the edge between semantics and pragmatics, Potts's, Feng's, and Horn's recent works have shown that the Fregeo-Gricean concept of conventional implicature is, after all, not that incoherent.

By way of summary, meaning$_{nn}$/speaker-meaning or the total significa-tion of an utterance in a Gricean system may be represented schematically as follows (Levinson 2000: 13, but see Davis 1998 for a critique of Gricean pragmatics).

(2.115)

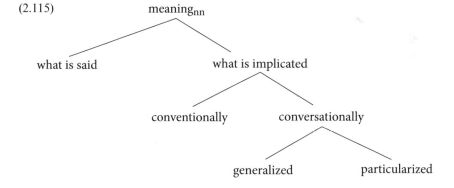

2.6. Summary

In this chapter, I have considered implicature. Section 2.1 discussed the classical Gricean theory of conversational implicature. Section 2.2 presented the latest developments first of the Hornian and then of the Levinsonian neo-Gricean pragmatic theories of conversational implicature. In Section 2.3, I took a look at some of the current debates about conversational implicature. Next, in Section 2.4, I examined embedded (conversational) implicature. Finally, the focus of Section 2.5 was on the notion of conventional implicature including a comparison and contrast between conventional and conversational implicature.

Key concepts

implicature

$meaning_{nn}$

co-operative principle

maxims of conversation (Quality, Quantity, Relation, Manner)

conversational implicature

$conversational\ implicature_O$

$conversational\ implicature_F$

generalized conversational implicature (GCI)

particularized conversational implicature (PCI)

properties of conversational implicature (cancellability/defeasibility, non-detachability, calculability, non-conventionality, reinforceability, universality, indeterminacy)

Q-principle (Horn)

Horn scale

positive Horn scale

negative Horn scale

R-principle

division of pragmatic labour

Q-principle (Levinson)

$Q_{-scalar}$ implicature

$Q_{-clausal}$ implicature

$Q_{-alternate}$ implicature

$Q_{\text{-ordered alternate}}$ implicature

$Q_{\text{-unordered alternate}}$ implicature

Hirschberg scale

rank order

metalinguistic negation

I-principle

M-principle

interaction of Q-, I-, and M-principles

default inference theory (of $Q_{\text{-scalar}}$ implicature)

contextual inference theory (of $Q_{\text{-scalar}}$ implicature)

structural inference theory (of $Q_{\text{-scalar}}$ implicature)

embedded (conversational) implicature

grammatical approach (to embedded implicature)

conventionalism (of embedded implicature)

lexicalist conventionalism (of embedded implicature)

syntax-based conventionalism (of embedded implicature)

(Gricean) pragmatic approach (to embedded implicature)

conventional implicature

properties of conventional implicature

Exercises and essay questions

1. Children with pragmatic disorders may often fail to observe the maxims. In the following conversation (adapted from Bishop 1997: 183, cited in Peccei 1999: 29), which maxim did the child violate?
   Speech therapist: So you like ice cream. What are your favourite flavours?
   Child with a pragmatic disorder: Hamburger . . . fish and chips.
2. Which maxims does the speaker intend to opt out from by using the following hedges?
     (i) I don't think I have sufficient evidence for this, but . . .
    (ii) I'm not at liberty to say any more.
   (iii) I know this is irrelevant, but . . .
    (iv) Apparently, . . .
     (v) This is a bit confused, but . . .
    (vi) This may be just a rumour, but . . .
   (vii) So, to cut a long story short,
  (viii) Not to change the topic, but . . .
    (ix) I'm sure you already know this, but . . .
     (x) People say . . .

3. Joe and Irving are the two characters in a computer program called Tale-Spin, cited in Mey (2001: 88). In the following passage, what is the conversational implicature Joe failed to work out? Is it a conversational implicature$_O$ or conversational implicature$_F$?

   One day Joe Bear was hungry. He asked his friend Irving Bird where some honey was. Irving told him there was a beehive in the oak tree. Joe threatened to hit Irving if he didn't tell him where some honey was.

4. What is the conversational implicature of Mary's reply in the following conversation? Is it a conversational implicature$_O$ or conversational implicature$_F$? If it is a conversational implicature$_F$, which maxim is flouted?

   (i) John: India is the most populous country in the world, isn't it?
      Mary: I'm the Queen of Sheba.

   Next, how about the clergyman's reply in the following passage from C. P. Snow's *Variety of Men*?

   (ii) He (Lord Rutherford) said in a speech: 'As I was standing in the drawing-room at Trinity, a clergyman came in. And I said to him: "I'm Lord Rutherford." And he said to me: "I'm the Archbishop of York."'

5. Twenty-two months after the Berlin Wall was erected, President J. F. Kennedy announced in German at a West Berlin rally that he was a Berliner. What he should have said was *Ich bin Berliner* ('I'm a Berliner'), but due to his speech writer's limited knowledge of German, he managed instead to say *Ich bin ein Berliner*, which means that he was a jam doughnut (e.g. William J. Miller, *New York Times*). (Another, less widely-held version is that this is simply a misconception; *Ich bin ein Berliner* was not only correct, but the only way to express what President Kennedy wanted to say (e.g. *Wikipedia*). However, despite his mistake, his audience did not fail to compute the conversational implicature of what he said. What is the conversational implicature in question? Which maxim is flouted?

6. Of the following two conversational implicatures, which is the generalized one, and which is the particularized one?

   John: How did yesterday's guest lecture go?
   Mary: Some of the faculty left before it ended.
   +> (a) Not all of the faculty left before it ended
   +> (b) The lecture didn't go well

7. In the following passage taken from a novel set on a Navajo reservation (Tony Hillerman, *Skinwalkers*, cited in Thomas 1995: 76), the speaker is the daughter of a murdered man. She is talking to Officer Jim Chee of the Navajo Tribal Police. Why does she use the vague terms 'the one who got killed' and 'that man' to refer to her father? Is this a real counterexample to the claim of universality for Grice's first sub-maxim of Quantity?

   'Last time you were with the FBI man—asking about the one who got killed,' she said, respecting the Navajo taboo of not speaking the name of the dead. 'You find out who killed that man?'

8. What are the Q-implicatures of the following? Which type of Q-implicatures do they belong to?
   (i) <Mary's husband, a man>
       Mary is chatting with a man by the lake.
   (ii) <realize, think>
       (The title of a 2007 comedy film)
       I think I love my wife.
   (iii) <roast, stir-fry, boil, steam, bake, . . . >
       Please stir-fry the bean sprouts.
   (iv) <loathe, hate, dislike>
       Xiaoming dislikes cheese.
   (v) <president, prime minister>
       Her uncle is the prime minister.
   (vi) <marry, engage>
       The Smiths have got engaged.
   (vii) <and, or>
       John will send it either as an e-mail or as an attachment.
   (viii) <Barack Obama's autograph, Hillary Clinton's autograph>
       My brother has got Hillary Clinton's autograph.
   (ix) <identical, similar>
       The two impressionist paintings are similar.
   (x) <not (*p* or *q*), not (*p* and *q*)>
       Peter is not both a chief and a gardener.

9. What are the Q-implicatures of the following?
   (i) The sprinter can run 100m in 9.8 seconds.
   (ii) The sprinter can't run 100m in 9.8 seconds.

10. As discussed with respect to examples in (2.40), *boiling, hot, warm, lukewarm, cool, cold*, and *freezing* form two Horn scales, that is, <boiling, hot, warm> and <freezing, cold, cool, lukewarm>. Why is this the case? What evidence can you adduce to substantiate the analysis that *lukewarm* should be grouped with the 'coldness' rather than 'hotness' scale?

11. Can you distinguish metalinguistic from descriptive negation in the following?
    (i) John didn't graduate from Oxford. He graduated from Cambridge.
    (ii) John didn't have two monGEESE, he had two monGOOSES.
    (iii) He isn't a taxi driver, he is a bus driver.
    (iv) He's not my dad, he's my father.
    (v) They don't speak [seltic], they speak [keltic].
    (vi) Mary doesn't like house sparrows, she likes bullfinches.
    (vii) We didn't have the party at the cyber café, we had it in the students' common room.
    (viii) Barack Obama isn't the first President of the United States of America who is African-American. He is the first African-American President of the United States of America.

    (ix) They don't need six new computer mouses, they need six new computer mice.

    (x) Susan didn't marry three times, she married four times.

12. What are the I-implicatures of the following?

    (i) John is reading two modern languages at Oxford University.

    (ii) If you let me see the manuscript, I'll make a donation to the library.

    (iii) The children ate the cake and apples after dinner.

    (iv) His secretary talked learnedly about the internet.

    (v) The police moved in and the suspects were arrested.

    (vi) John and Mary scrubbed the carpet afresh.

    (vii) I have no idea if John's in a relationship.

    (viii) a. The apple is red.

        b. The watermelon is red.

        c. The pencil is red.

        d. The book is red.

        e. The house is red.

    (ix) I usually have an egg for breakfast in the morning.

    (x) Something smells here.

13. What are the M-implicatures of the b utterances of the following?

    (i) a. John went to university.

       b. John went to the university.

    (ii) a. John stopped the alarm.

       b. John got the alarm to stop.

    (iii) a. Mary has a pink dress.

       b. Mary has a pale red dress.

    (iv) a. John could swim the English Channel.

       b. John had the ability to swim the English Channel.

    (v) a. John drank glasses of Pinot Noir for dinner yesterday evening.

       b. John drank glasses and glasses of Pinot Noir for dinner yesterday evening.

    (vi) a. That's his father.

       b. That's his mother's husband.

    (vii) a. Peter is a rich businessman.

       b. Peter is a RICH-rich businessman.

    (viii) a. Their new boss is a friendly person.

       b. Their new boss is not an unfriendly person.

14. What are the conventional implicatures of the following?

    (i) John hasn't finished his thesis *yet*.

    (ii) *Actually* the two families live opposite each other.

    (iii) *Even* his sister belly-danced in a Lebanese restaurant two nights a week.

    (iv) Mike forgot to ring the client, *too*.

    (v) The VIPs have *still* not arrived.

(vi) Mary was born in London. *On the other hand*, her husband was an immigrant from Pakistan.

(vii) John *managed to* complete his thesis on virtual reality technology.

(viii) (French)

Mary: Pardon, Monsieur, pour aller à le parc?

Pierre: *Vous* allez jusqu'au bout de la rue.

Mary: 'Excuse me, Sir, how to get to the park?'

Pierre: 'You go to the end of the road.'

15. What is a conversational implicature? What are the essential properties of a conversational implicature? Discuss with illustrations.

16. What are the Q-, I-, and M-principles? Exemplify with your own examples.

17. To what extent can the Q- and I-principles be distinguished?

18. What is metalinguistic negation? How can it be distinguished from descriptive negation?

19. Apart from taboo, which other sociopragmatic factors do you think can override conversational implicature? Can you substantiate your arguments with examples?

20. What is embedded implicature? What is the main problem it has posed for the classical Gricean account of conversational implicature?

21. Which approach to embedded implicature do you prefer, grammatical or Gricean pragmatic? Why?

22. What are the similarities and differences between conversational and conventional implicatures?

Further readings

Grice (1989). Part I and Retrospective Epilogue.

Levinson (2000). Chapters 1 and 2.

Horn (2012).

Geurts (2010). Chapters 7 and 8.

3

Presupposition

Presupposition is another topic in pragmatics that originates within the tradition of the philosophy of language. The German mathematician, logician, and philosopher Gottlob Frege is generally recognized as the first scholar in modern times who (re)introduced the philosophical study of presupposition into philosophy and linguistics (see especially Frege 1892, who pointed out that *Kepler died/did not die in misery* presuppose '*voraussetzen*' that *Kepler* denotes something), though the notion of presupposition may be traced back at least as far as the medieval philosopher Petrus Hispanus (Horn 1996).

Since its (re)introduction, presupposition has attracted an ever-growing amount of attention from both philosophers and linguists. In the philosophy of language, the study of presupposition has largely been confined to debates about the nature of reference and (singular) referring expressions (see e.g. the classical works of Frege 1892, Russell 1905, and Strawson 1950).[1] In linguistics,

---

[1] For discussion about the philosophical background of presupposition, see, for example, Levinson (1983), Soames (1989), Horn (1996), and Atlas (2004, 2005). I shall examine reference in Chapter 6.

on the other hand, the investigation of presupposition is concerned with a much wider range of phenomena, centring around the general debates over the interaction and division of labour between semantics and pragmatics.

The organization of this chapter is as follows. Section 3.1 discusses the general phenomenon of presupposition. Next, Section 3.2 examines the properties of presupposition, covering constancy under negation in Section 3.2.1, defeasibility in Section 3.2.2, and the projection problem in Section 3.2.3. Finally, Section 3.3 presents an overview of three influential accounts of presupposition, namely, the filtering-satisfaction analysis (3.3.2), the cancellation analysis (3.3.3), and the accommodation analysis (3.3.4).

3.1. Phenomena of presupposition

3.1.1. What is presupposition?

Presupposition can be informally defined as a piece of information or a proposition whose truth is taken for granted in the utterance of a sentence. Its main function is to act as a precondition of some sort for the appropriate use of that sentence. This background assumption will remain in force when the sentence that contains it is negated. Furthermore, three conceptions of presupposition can be identified. First, presupposition is definable as a relation between sentences or statements. This is **semantic presupposition**, also called **conventional, sentence**, or **statement presupposition**. The conception of semantic presupposition is usually attributed to the British philosopher Peter Strawson, though it may be traced back to Frege (1892). Secondly, presupposition can by contrast be defined as a belief a speaker takes for granted in making an assertion. On this view, a speaker presupposes in uttering a sentence rather than a sentence itself presupposes. In other words, it is speakers or utterances but not sentences or statements that carry presupposition. Presupposition normally represents given information in one sense or another, and is part of the (relevant) context (or common ground), and in particular, the **speaker's commitment slate** in which the sentence is uttered. This is the concept of **pragmatic presupposition**, also known as **conversational, speaker**, or **utterance presupposition**. The champion of this pragmatic approach to presupposition is the American philosopher Robert Stalnaker. In addition, there is also a third, in between, conception of presupposition, which involves both linguistic forms (sentences) and language users (speakers). This **semantico-pragmatic** concept of presupposition, also called '**utterance presupposition**', is put forward by Kattunen (1973) and Soames (1982) (see e.g. Beaver and Geurts 2011, 2012 for further discussion of the third conception).

3.1.2. Some representative examples of presupposition

Presupposition is usually generated by the use of particular lexical items and/or linguistic constructions. Lexical items and linguistic constructions that engender presuppositions are called **presupposition triggers**. While presupposition has in general been regarded as 'a heterogeneous collection of quite distinct and different phenomena' (Levinson 1983: 217), since Karttunen (1973, 1974) and Karttunen and Peters (1979), a list of its representative examples may be given below (see e.g. Levinson 1983: 181–5; Soames 1989; Geurts 1999: 2; Beaver 2001: 10–12; Atlas 2004, 2005: 119; Beaver and Geurts 2011, 2012). (I use the symbol '>>' to stand for 'presuppose'. The positive and negative versions of a sentences are separated by /, and the lexical presupposition triggers are italicized here.)

(3.1)   Definite descriptions (Russell 1905)
        The (present) king of France is/isn't bald.
        >> There is a (present) king of France

(3.2)   Factive predicates
        a. Epistemic or cognitive factives
           John *knows*/doesn't *know* that Baird invented television.
           >> Baird invented television
        b. Emotive factives
           John *regrets*/doesn't *regret* that he has said the unsayable.
           >> John has said the unsayable

(3.3)   Aspectual/change of state predicates
        a. Bart: Man, are you illin'?
           Lisa: Rappers *stopped* saying illin' twelve years ago!
           Bart: I'm keepin' it real!
           Lisa: They *stopped* saying keepin' it real three years ago!
           Bart: Mom, Lisa's dissin' me!
           Marge: Dissin'? Do rappers still say that?

(*The Simpsons*)

Rappers *stopped* saying illin' twelve years ago!

>> Rappers had been saying illin'

They *stopped* saying keepin' it real three years ago!

>> They had been saying keepin' it real

b. Mary has/hasn't *stopped* beating her boyfriend.

>> Mary has been beating her boyfriend

(3.4) Iteratives

a. Iterative verbs

John *returned*/didn't *return* to Cambridge.

>> John was in Cambridge before

b. Iterative adverbs

The boy cried/didn't cry wolf *again*.

>> The boy cried wolf before

c. Iterative prefixes

Jane *re*married/never *re*married.

>> Jane married before

(3.5) Implicative predicates

John *managed*/didn't *manage* to give up smoking.

>> John tried to give up smoking

(3.6) Quantifiers

The committee interviewed/didn't interview *all* the short listed candidates for the post.

>> There were candidates

(3.7) Temporal clauses

After she shot to stardom in a romance film, Jane married/didn't marry a millionaire entrepreneur.

>> Jane shot to stardom in a romance film

(3.8) Cleft sentences

a. Clefts

It was/wasn't Baird who invented television.

>> Someone invented television

b. Pseudo-clefts

What Baird invented/didn't invent was television

>> Baird invented something

(3.9) Counterfactual conditionals

If an ant was as big as a human being, it could/couldn't run five times faster than an Olympic sprinter.

>> An ant is not as big as a human being

In (3.1), the presupposition trigger is the definite description *the (present) king of France* and the presupposition is called '**existential presupposition**'.

The class of definite descriptions may include proper names, possessives, and certain *wh*-phrases. In (3.2), the indicators of the presuppositions are the factive verbs, and both presuppositions are known as '**factive presuppositions**'. Factive presuppositions can further be divided into two subtypes: those triggered by the use of epistemic or cognitive factives like *know* (which concern knowledge of fact) and those produced by emotional factives such as *regret* (which are concerned with emotional attitude towards fact). Occasionally, factive presuppositions may arise from the use of factive NPs like *the fact/knowledge*, *the realization*, and *the regret*. This is illustrated by (3.10) and (3.11).

(3.10)   The police came/didn't come to *the realization* that a ladder had been placed by the burglars.
>> A ladder had been placed by the burglars.

(3.11)   a.   It's in my nature to dwell on regrets and if onlys, things I wish I'd done, things I wish I hadn't. Indeed one of my regrets is that I'm the type of person who has a lot of regrets. (Robert Crampton, *Times Magazine*, 14 June 2008)
Indeed *one of my regrets* is that I'm the type of person who has a lot of regrets.
>> The speaker is the type of person who has a lot of regrets

b.   J. K. Rowling has the world at her fingertips and more money than she can spend, but her greatest regret is that her mother died from multiple sclerosis without knowing about her success. (*The Daily Telegraph*, Tuesday, 10 January 2006)
[H]er greatest regret is that her mother died from multiple sclerosis without knowing about her success.
>> [H]er mother died from multiple sclerosis without knowing about her success.

The epistemic factive presupposition in (3.10) is triggered by the epistemic factive NP *the realization*, the emotional factive presupposition in (3.11a), by the emotive factive NP *one of my regrets,* and that in (3.11b), also by the emotive factive NP *her greatest regret*. Next, the presupposition in both (3.3a) and (3.3b) is introduced by the aspectual/change-of-state verb *stop*. The presupposition triggers in (3.4) are the three iteratives, and the presupposition-inducing lexical expression in (3.5) is the implicative verb *manage*. The presupposition in (3.6) is due to the universal quantifier *all*. Notice that the presupposition triggers in (3.1)–(3.6) are **lexical triggers**. By contrast, those in (3.7)–(3.9) are **constructional** or **structural triggers**. The presupposition in (3.7) is triggered by a temporal clause, the presuppositions in (3.8), by the cleft sentence including both clefts and pseudo-clefts, and the presupposition in (3.9), by a counterfactual conditional.[2]

Have a look at Exercises 1, 2, and 3 at the end of this chapter.

3.2. Properties of presupposition

Presuppositions exhibit a number of distinctive properties, notably, (i) constancy under negation, and (ii) defeasibility or cancellability. In addition, certain cases of defeasibility give rise to what is known as the projection problem.

3.2.1. Constancy under negation

By **constancy under negation** is meant that a presupposition generated by the use of a lexical item or a syntactic structure remains the same when the sentence containing that lexical item or syntactic structure is negated.[3] Using constancy under negation as a diagnostic, presuppositions can be more formally defined in (3.12) (see also Beaver 1997, 2001 and Beaver and Geurts 2011, 2012 for a number of non-theory-neutral formal definitions).

---

[2] One interesting point to note is that when a presupposition is queried, the relevant lexical presupposition trigger is frequently queried in an explicit way. Some examples follow.

(i)   a. *The (present) king of France* is bald.
      b. *The (present) king of France*? But is France not a republic?
(ii) a. The boy cried wolf *again*.
      b. What do you mean by *again*? Did the boy cry wolf before?
(iii) a. John *regrets* that he has said the unsayable.
      b. Did you use the word *regret*? John has never said the unsayable.

[3] In addition, presuppositions are also preserved under questions, modals, and conditionals. See, for example, Soames (1989), Chierchia and McConnell-Gent (2000), and Atlas (2004, 2005) for exemplification and discussion. Generalizing, we can say that presuppositions tend to escape from, or project out of, any embedded position, that is, any position that is embedded under a logical operator such as a negation, a modal, and a conditional (but see the discussion of examples 3.33 and 3.34 below).

(3.12)   An utterance of a sentence *S* presupposes a proposition *p* if and only if
a. if *S* is true, then *p* is true
b. if *S* is false, then *p* is still true

What (3.12) basically says is this: for utterance of *S* to presuppose *p*, whenever *S* is true, *p* is also true, and whenever *S* is false, *p* is still true.

There are, however, problems at the very heart of this **negation test**. On the one hand, constancy under negation may not be necessary. For example, there is a class of sentences which is hard, if not impossible, to negate, yet they bear presuppositions, as in (3.13) (e.g. Green 1996). On the other hand, constancy under negation may not be sufficient. This is shown by (3.14) and (3.15). Although (3.14) and (3.15) satisfy the negation test, the pragmatically enriched information in the former is standardly analysed as a felicity condition on the speech act of requesting (about which in Chapter 4), and that in the latter, as a conventional implicature (see Chapter 2).

(3.13)   Long live the (present) king of France!
>> There is a (present) king of France
(3.14)   Do/don't bring the digital camera here.
?>> The digital camera is not here
(3.15)   (Chinese)

nin	xiawu	lai	bu	lai.
you-HON	afternoon	come	not	come

'Will you come this afternoon?'
?>> The addressee is socially superior to or distant from the speaker

---

Now see whether you can tackle Exercise 4 at the end of this chapter.

3.2.2. Defeasibility

Like conversational implicatures, but unlike semantic entailments, presuppositions are **defeasible** or **cancellable**. They are nullified if they are inconsistent with (i) background assumptions, (ii) conversational implicatures, and (iii) certain discourse contexts. Furthermore, they can also drop out in certain intrasentential contexts, some of which give rise to the projection problem of presupposition. Defeasibility has in general been taken as the second most important property of presupposition.

In the first place, presuppositions can disappear in the face of inconsistency with background assumptions or real-world knowledge. Contrast (3.16) and (3.17) (I use '~ >>' to stand for 'does not presuppose').

(3.16)   John got an assistant professorship before he finished his PhD.
   >> John finished his PhD
(3.17)   John died before he finished his PhD.
   ~ >> John finished his PhD

While the uttering of (3.16) presupposes that John finished his PhD by virtue of the temporal clause, (3.17) does not carry that presupposition. This is because the putative presupposition conflicts with our real-world knowledge that after one dies, one cannot do anything. Consequently, the unwanted presupposition vanishes.[4]

Secondly, presuppositions can be cancelled by inconsistent conversational implicatures. This is illustrated in (3.18).

(3.18)   If John is organizing a stag night, Mary will be angry that he is doing so.
   +> perhaps John is organizing a stag night, perhaps he isn't
   ~ >> John is organizing a stag night

The use of the factive predicate *angry* in (3.18) should generate the potential presupposition that John is organizing a stag night. However, there is also a $Q_{\text{-clausal}}$ conversational implicature due to the use of the conditional in

---

[4] Compare (3.17) with (i).
(i) John died before he reached the hospital's accident and emergency department.
  >> John reached the hospital's accident and emergency department

(i) has the presupposition indicated above only on the understanding that *he* means John's body.

More importantly, David Cram has pointed out to me that for some native speakers of English including himself, the presupposition of (3.17) cannot be cancelled. For this group of speakers, only the non-finite alternative of (3.17) allows the presupposition to be defeated. This is given in (ii).

(ii)   John died before finishing his PhD.
   ~ >> John finished his PhD

Furthermore, David Cram has offered a neo-Gricean pragmatic explanation along the following lines: if the speaker had intended the presupposition to be suspended, he or she would have used (ii). If (ii) is not used, but (3.17) is employed instead, then a pragmatic enrichment can be drawn, namely, the speaker does not intend the presupposition to be cancelled.

(3.18), namely, perhaps John is not organizing a stag night (see Chapter 2). In the face of the contradictory conversational implicature, the putative presupposition here is defeated.

Thirdly, presuppositions are contextually cancellable, that is, they can evaporate if they run contrary to what the immediate discourse context tells us. Consider first (3.19), where the putative presupposition is defeated by the inconsistent proposition that is already established in the immediate discourse background.

(3.19)   There is no (present) king of France. Therefore the (present) king of France isn't bald.
~ >> There is a (present) king of France

In (3.19), the use of the second sentence should presuppose that there is a (present) king of France. The reason it does not is because such a putative presupposition is inconsistent with the preceding proposition, already established in the immediate discourse background, namely, there is no (present) king of France. As a result, the unwanted presupposition fails to survive.[5]

Next, presuppositions can be suspended by so-called '**reduction arguments**'— arguments that proceed by eliminating each of the possibilities—in a discourse. This is exemplified by (3.20), cited from Chierchia and McConnell-Ginet (2000).

(3.20)   A, noticing the open door: Was it you who opened the door to the porch? I closed it at lunch time.

---

[5] Contrast (i) and (ii).

(i)   John doesn't/didn't/You don't/didn't know that Baird invented television.
>> Baird invented television
(ii)   I don't know that Baird invented television
~ >> Baird invented television

Here, there is a contrast between the use of a third-second-person subject and that of a first-person subject in a negative sentence containing the factive verb *know*: while the presupposition in the former gets through, that in the latter (sometimes) drops out. In other words, the use of *know* triggers a presupposition only in some person and tense forms, which led Karttunen (1971) to call *know* a '**semifactive**'. The reason why (ii) does not carry the presupposition is because what is presupposed in (ii) is precisely what is denied by what is explicitly said about the speaker's knowledge or beliefs (see Gazdar 1979: 142, 153–4 for an analysis of how the presupposition in (ii) but not (i) is correctly cancelled).

B: Well, it wasn't me who opened it, because I've been gone all afternoon, and it wasn't Joan who opened it, because she was with me, and it wasn't any of the kids who opened it, because they're on a field trip, and I strongly suspect that nobody opened it—there was a lot of wind this afternoon, you know.
~ >> Someone opened the door to the porch

In this passage, the utterance of each of the cleft sentences should engender the presupposition that someone opened the door to the porch. However, as pointed out by Levinson (1983: 189) for a similar example, the whole purpose of B's utterance in (3.20) is to convince the addressee that no one opened it. This has the consequence that the presupposition is overridden; 'it was adopted as a counterfactual assumption to argue [for] the untenability of such an assumption' (Levinson 1983: 189).

Finally, presuppositions can disappear in a discourse where evidence for their truth is being weighed and rejected, as in (3.21), due to Levinson (1983: 189).

(3.21) A: Well we've simply got to find out if Serge is a KGB infiltrator.
    B: Who if anyone would know?
    C: The only person who would know for sure is Alexis; I've talked to him and he isn't aware that Serge is on the KGB payroll. So I think Serge can be trusted.
    ~ >> Serge is on the KGB payroll

C's utterance *he isn't aware that Serge is on the KGB payroll* contains the epistemic factive predicate *aware*. Although the use of factive predicates typically presupposes the truth of their complements, the use of it in this example does not. This is because the presupposition clashes with the whole point of C's argument, namely, that since Alexis is not aware that Serge is on the KGB payroll, he is not a KGB infiltrator. When this happens, the unwanted presupposition is again blocked.

In the fourth place, presuppositions can be blocked in certain **intrasentential contexts**, that is, they can be defeated by using other clauses in the same complex sentence to increment the local, intrasentential context. Three cases are of particular interest. The first of these is that a presupposition of a sentence can be **overtly denied** in a (coordinate) clause without any apparent contradiction. This is exemplified in (3.22)–(3.24).

(3.22) The president doesn't regret vetoing the bill because in fact he never did so!
    ~ >> The president vetoed the bill
(3.23) John didn't manage to open an e-savings account, in fact he didn't even try!
    ~ >>John tried to open an e-savings account
(3.24) The (present) king of France isn't bald—there is no (present) king of France!
    ~ >> There is a (present) king of France

Notice that in many cases, outright denial of presupposition is not possible with positive sentences. Contrast (3.22)–(3.24) with (3.25)–(3.27).

(3.25)   *The president regrets vetoing the bill because in fact he never did so!
(3.26)   *John managed to open an e-savings account, in fact he didn't even try!
(3.27)   *The (present) king of France is bald—there is no (present) king of France!

There is thus, at least in these cases, an asymmetry between negative and positive sentences with regard to defeasibility. This asymmetry has led to an entailment analysis for positive sentences, namely, the argument that what is allegedly presupposed in these sentences is actually what is entailed. Since semantic entailments cannot be overtly denied without producing semantic anomaly, the anomaly displayed in (3.25)–(3.27) is entirely expected. A second point to note is that the negation involved in overt denial of presupposition in (3.22)–(3.24) is generally considered as a metalinguistic negation (see Chapter 2). See for example, Horn (1985, 1989) and Burton-Roberts (1989) for further arguments, but see Carston (2002), Geurts (1998, 1999: 71–2), and Atlas (2004) for scepticism, though for different reasons.

Next, a presupposition of a sentence can be **explicitly suspended** in an *if* clause that follows. Witness (3.28)–(3.30).[6]

(3.28)   John clearly doesn't regret being an anti-austerity campaigner, if he actually ever was one.
    ~ >> John was an anti-austerity campaigner
(3.29)   John didn't tamper with their computers again, if indeed he ever did.
    ~ >> John tampered with their computers before
(3.30)   I'm sure John's wife is beautiful, if he has a wife.
    ~ >> John has a wife

Finally, presuppositions can disappear with certain **verbs of saying** such as *say, mention, tell, ask*, and *announce* and certain **verbs of propositional attitude** such as *believe, think, imagine, dream*, and *want*.

(3.31)   a. John said/mentioned/told Bill that Mary managed to speak with a broad Irish accent.
    ~ >> Mary tried to speak with a broad Irish accent
(3.32)   a. Mr Wang believed/dreamed/imagined that he is the emperor of China.
    ~ >> there is an emperor of China

---

[6] The explicit suspension of a presupposition in examples like (3.28)–(3.30) may be regarded as a special case of presuppositional heritability in conditionals of this sort.

As pointed out by Green (1996: 77–8), these are 'world-creating' verbs. They can define worlds other than our real world, which has been taken for granted as relevant for the evaluation of the pertinent presuppositions. The use of these verbs can lead to the evaporation of presuppositions.

Examples (3.22)–(3.24) and (3.28)–(3.32) form part of what Langendoen and Savin (1971) first called the projection problem of presupposition, namely, to state and explain the presuppositions of complex sentences (as 'wholes') in terms of the presuppositions of their component simple sentences (as 'parts'), to which we now turn.

> See whether you are ready to do Exercise 5 at the end of this chapter.

3.2.3. The projection problem

It is in general expected that the presuppositions of a simple sentence will ascend to become the presupposition of the complex sentence of which the simple sentence is a part. Put the other way round, a complex sentence is generally expected to presuppose the conjunction of the presuppositions of all its constituent, simple sentences. This is known as the '**cumulative hypothesis**'. Characterized thus, the **projection problem** of presupposition can be seen as a special case of the **Fregean principle of compositionality**, which dictates that the meaning of a compound expression is a function (i.e. combination) of the meanings of its parts and their syntactic mode of combination (see e.g. Janssen 1997 for an overview of compositionality). The projection problem manifests itself in two opposite directions. On the one side of the projection coin, the presuppositions of a component sentence may fail to be projected onto, and hence inherited by, the whole complex sentence. On the other side, the presuppositions of a component sentence may be preserved when that constituent sentence becomes part of a more complex sentence.

Recollect now examples (3.22)–(3.24) and (3.28)–(3.32), which point to three cases where presuppositions disappear by virtue of intrasentential context. In (3.22)–(3.24), the presuppositions are overtly denied by the adding of a coordinate clause, in (3.28)–(3.30), they are explicitly suspended by the adding of an *if* clause, and finally in (3.31) and (3.32) they are cancelled in saying and belief contexts. But what is common to all the three cases is that the presuppositions of a lower clause are blocked in the whole sentence. The same is true of presuppositions in complex or compound sentences formed with connectives such as *and*, *or*, and *if...then*. Consider (3.33) and (3.34).

(3.33)   If the bishop promotes the politically incorrect, then he will regret doing so.
        ~ >> The bishop will promote the politically incorrect

(3.34)   Either the bishop will not promote the politically incorrect, or he will regret doing so.
        ~ >> The bishop will promote the politically incorrect

In both (3.33) and (3.34), the second clause alone would carry the presupposition that the bishop will promote the politically incorrect. However, this putative presupposition evaporates in the whole of the conditional in (3.33) and in the whole of the disjunction in (3.34). The reason the presupposition does not get through in either example is that in (3.33), it 'is mentioned in the first clause and is thus made hypothetical', and in (3.34), 'the alternative expressed in the first clause is the negation of the presupposition of the second clause' (Levinson 1983: 196). Once again, the presupposition of a part fails to project onto the whole.

We move next to the other side of the projection coin, namely, the survival of the presuppositions of a part as those of the whole in various contexts. The first of these in which a presupposition can survive is, as already mentioned, under negation. Apart from examples (3.1)–(3.10), there is (3.35).

(3.35)   It was/wasn't John who hadn't been out of his house for a month.
        >> Someone hadn't been out of his house for a month

The second kind of context in which presuppositions percolate is when the sentences with presupposition triggers are embedded in modal operators such as *it's possible that, it's likely that, ought to, should*, and *may*. This is illustrated in (3.36)–(3.37).

(3.36)   It's possible/there's a chance that the nursery teacher sold nine Christmas raffle tickets.
        >> There is a nursery teacher

(3.37)   The nursery teacher could/should/ought to have sold nine Christmas raffle tickets
        >> There is a nursery teacher

In both (3.36) and (3.37), the presupposition of the embedded sentence *The nursery teacher sold nine Christmas raffle tickets* gets through unblocked when the sentence is embedded under the various modal operators.

> Your final exercise in this chapter is Exercise 6 at the end of this chapter.

Finally, let us turn to compound sentences formed by connectives again. We saw above that in some such sentences (i.e. (3.33)–(3.34)), presuppositions fail to be projected from the part to the whole. However, there are other compound sentence types within which presuppositions of a component part can indeed be inherited by the complex whole. As an illustration, consider (3.38) and (3.39).

(3.38)   If Susan returned to England, (then) she would be arrested.
            >> Susan was in England before
(3.39)   Either Susan returns to England, or she will flee to Spain.
            >> Susan was in England before

Taken in isolation, the sentence *Susan returned/s to England* presupposes that Susan was in England before. Now, when it is embedded in the conditional (3.38) or the disjunction (3.39), the presupposition of the embedded clause percolates up a higher level unblocked.

The projection problem has in general been regarded as 'the curse and the blessing of modern presupposition theory' (Beaver 2001: 13). It is a curse because it has proven so resistant to a solution, and in the meantime, it is a blessing because 'it provides an objective basis for the claim that there is a distinct presuppositional component to meaning, and a way of identifying presuppositional construction' (Beaver 2001: 13, but see e.g. Atlas 2004, 2005 for a different view).

3.3. Analyses

There is a large variety of theoretical approaches to presupposition ranging from treating presupposition and anaphora in a parallel way[7] (e.g. Soames

[7] In this type of analysis, on the basis of some similarities between presupposition projection and anaphoric binding (Soames 1989; Kripke 2009), it has been argued that on the one hand, presupposition be analysed as anaphora (e.g. van der Sandt 1992), and on the other, anaphora be taken as a special case of presupposition (e.g.

1989; van der Sandt 1992; Geurts 1998, 1999; Krahmer 1998; Kripke 2009), through a probabilistic and deterministic account (Merin 2003), to a cognitive, experiential analysis (e.g. Marmaridou 2000). Furthermore, little if any current work has advanced a purely semantic account of presupposition (see e.g. Kempson 1975, Wilson 1975, Böer and Lycan 1976, Gazdar 1979, Levinson 1983, and van der Sandt 1988 for early critiques of semantic analyses).[8] In what follows, I shall discuss the three main issues surrounding presupposition first, and then concentrate on the three analyses I judge to be the most important and influential in the study of presupposition.

3.3.1. Three main issues

As pointed out by Geurts (1999: 1) and Beaver and Geurts (2011), there are three main theoretical issues in accounting for presupposition. The first and oldest one is concerned with **presupposition failure**. If a statement presupposes something which does not exist, what are the consequences for that statement? As we have already seen, a much quoted Russellian example of statements of this sort is the positive part of (3.1), repeated here as (3.40).

(3.40)   The (present) king of France is bald.

Given that there is no (present) king of France, the question boils down to this: what is the truth status of the sentence? Frege's (1892) view was that if *the (present) king of France* generates a presupposition failure, then (3.40) does not have a truth value. But this position was rejected by Russell (1905). On Russell's view, since (3.40) asserts both that there is a (present) king of France and that he is bald, if the (present) king of France does not exist, the sentence is false. (I shall have more to say about Russell's analysis in Chapter 6, where reference is to be discussed.) Russell's theory remained unchallenged for almost half a century. In 1950, in an attempt to resurrect Frege's idea, the British philosopher Peter Strawson published an article to

---

Geurt 1999). I am not sure if the presupposition as anaphora account can provide a unified analysis of all cases of presupposition.

[8] However, a recent, neo-Strawsonian semantic analysis can be found in Burton-Roberts (1989, 1999), which appeals to, among other things, a cognitive tendency to bivalence. But as we have already seen, Burton-Roberts has to utilize the pragmatic concept of metalinguistic negation in an attempt to avoid arguing for a lexical ambiguity analysis of negation. See also Seuren (2000).

argue that Russell's account is wrong. According to Strawson (1950), Russell failed to make a distinction between a sentence and the use of a sentence (via an utterance) on a particular occasion. In using (3.40), a speaker does not assert but merely **presupposes** the existence (and unique-ness) of a (present) king of France and uses the definite description *the (present) king of France* to refer to that individual and predicate his bald-ness. If there is no (present) king of France, the statement made by the speaker in (3.40) is not successful. In other words, there is a presupposition failure. Consequently, (3.40) is neither true nor false: there is simply a **truth-value gap**, or to use Horn's (1996) metaphor, a truth-functional black hole.[9,10] In contrast to this semantic analysis, a pragmatic approach inspired by Stalnaker (1998) claims that in uttering (3.40), a speaker believes that there exists a (present) king of France. If the belief turns out to be false, then the utterance would be somewhat inappropriate. But contrary to what Strawson argued, the sentence uttered does not lack a truth value. As a consequence, no truth-value gaps are needed. Put slightly differently, on this pragmatic characterization of presupposition, if someone says (3.40), then since there is no (present) king of France, the utterance is simply 'infelici-tous'. Secondly, there is the now familiar projection problem. Thirdly and finally, we have the **triggering problem,** namely, the problem of explaining the origin or source of presupposition. Where do presuppositions come from? Or, put slightly differently, why do presuppositions take place in the first place? The standard, though imperfect semantic answer to this question is that presuppositions are engendered by certain presupposition-inducing lexical expressions and/or syntactic constructions. However, given that

---

[9] Notice that in his subsequent work, while sticking with his initial analysis of (3.40), Strawson (1964) showed some doubt about his original position that presup-position failure will inevitably lead to lack of a truth value. As an illustration, consider (i).

(i)   Last week, the school was visited by the (present) king of France.

According to Strawson (1964), since there is no (present) king of France, (i) was false. His explanation was that unlike in (3.40), *the (present) king of France* in (i) is not the topic of the sentence and non-topical definite descriptions are non-presuppositional.

[10] It is interesting to note how Russell reacted to Strawson's (1950) criticisms. In a stinging rebuttal, Russell declared: 'I am totally unable to see any validity whatever in any of Mr Strawson's arguments' (Russell 1957: 385).

much current research on presupposition centres round the projection problem utilizing a formal semantico-pragmatic model, my discussion below will
also reflect this emphasis.

3.3.2. The filtering-satisfaction analysis

The central idea of the **filtering-satisfaction** (or **Karttunen-Stalnaker**) ana-
lysis is that a presupposition, which is assumed not to be cancellable, has to
be entailed (or '**satisfied**', as Karttunen put it) in its local context of evaluation in which the presupposition trigger is evaluated. A **local context** is the
context against which (a part of) a sentence/clause is assessed. It is conceived
of as a set of propositions. It may be more informative than a **global
context**—the context against which a sequence of sentences/clauses is evaluated. For instance, when assessing a conjunction, the second conjunct is
evaluated in a local context, which consists of not only the information
given in the global context but also that provided in the first conjunct
(Beaver and Geurts 2011). Furthermore, a local context of interpretation
is constructed in a dynamic way, being developed online. This makes it
possible for an unwanted presupposition to be filtered out during the
derivation of a sentence in a bottom-up manner (see e.g. Karttunen 1973,
1974; Karttunen and Peters 1979; Stalnaker 1973, 1974, 1978, 1999; and see
also Beaver 2008 and Schlenker 2008).

In order to handle the projection problem, Karttunen (1973) classified
presupposition predicates and operators into three types: (i) **plugs**, which
block off all the presuppositions of the lower clauses, (ii) **holes**, which let all
such presuppositions ascend to become presuppositions of the matrix sentence, and (iii) **filters**, which prevent some but not all such presuppositions
from being projected to the matrix sentence. Examples of plugs include verbs
of saying and verbs of propositional attitudes, and perhaps presupposition-
cancelling metalinguistic negation (Horn 1996: 307) (see Chapter 2). By
contrast, factive verbs and modal operators are treated as holes. Descriptive
negation is also taken as a hole with respect to presuppositions. Finally,
binary logical connectives are filters. As remarked above, they allow some
presuppositions to ascend to become presuppositions of the whole but not
others. Further examples of each of the three types of presupposition predicates and operators are given here.

(3.41) Plugs

    a. John said/thought that Peter had started buying blue-chip shares.

      $\sim$ >> Peter hadn't been buying blue-chip shares

    b. John doesn't regret running the red light, because in fact he never did so.

      $\sim$ >> John ran the red light

(3.42) Holes

    a. John knows that George Orwell is the pseudonym of Eric Arthur Blair.

      >> George Orwell is the pseudonym of Eric Arthur Blair

    b. It's unlikely that John will play the piano again.

      >> John played the piano before

    c. The President didn't die of SARS.

      >> There was a President.

(3.43) Filters

    a. John has three children, and all his children are intelligent.

      $\sim$ >> John has children

    b. John has three children, and he regrets that he didn't study developmental psychology in university.

      >> John didn't study developmental psychology in university

In (3.41) the plugs, that is, the verbs *say* and *think*, and the metalinguistic negation block the presuppositions of the (embedded) clauses from ascending to the whole sentence. By contrast, in (3.42) the presuppositions under the holes, that is, the verb *know*, the modal operator *unlikely*, and the descriptive negation, get through unblocked. Finally, filters let presuppositions go through only discriminately. While in (3.43a), the putative presupposition of the second conjunct is cancelled by the filter; in (3.43b), it is projected onto the whole conjunction.

Regarding filters, the question that arises next is under what circumstances a presupposition will be, and under what conditions it will not be, filtered out. The answer provided by Karttunen (1973) is as follows:

(3.44)   In a sentence of the form 'if p then q', the presuppositions of the parts will be inherited by the whole unless q presupposes r and p entails r.

(3.45)   In a sentence of the form 'p & q', the presuppositions of the parts will be inherited by the whole unless q presupposes r and p entails r.

(3.46)   In a sentence of the form 'p or q', the presuppositions of the parts will be inherited by the whole unless q presupposes r and $\sim p$ entails r.

What the filtering condition (3.44) says is this: in the case of a conditional, if the presupposition that would have been engendered by the second clause is entailed by the first clause, then the presupposition will be filtered out, as in (3.33). Otherwise, it will survive to be projected to the whole sentence, as in

(3.38).The same is true of a conjunction, as stated in the filtering condition (3.45). This is illustrated in (3.43a) and (3.43b), respectively. In (3.43a), the putative presupposition of the second conjunct fails to be inherited by the whole sentence, because the first conjunct entails what the second presupposes. This has the consequence that (3.43a) does not presuppose but rather asserts or entails that John has children. By comparison, in (3.43b), since the first conjunct does not entail what the second presupposes, the presupposition of the second conjunct is projected to become the presupposition of the whole sentence. Finally, in the case of a disjunction, the putative presupposition of the second clause will be ruled out if it is entailed by the negation of the first clause. This is the case of (3.34). Otherwise it will percolate up to the whole sentence, as in (3.39).[11]

The filtering-satisfaction analysis represents the first systematic study of presupposition within the context of modern linguistics. As a consequence, it has set the critical background for all subsequent accounts of this important topic in theoretical pragmatics, prefiguring much of the later work such as Gazdar (1979), Heim (1983, 1992), and Beaver (2001). However, there are problems for this analysis. From a conceptual point of view, the positing of plugs, holes, and filters seems largely to be arbitrarily stipulated rather than independently motivated, thus lacking explanatory power. Somewhat related is the problem that under this analysis, negation is forced to be treated as ambiguous: descriptive negation as a hole but metalinguistic

---

[11] Faced with examples like (i) and (ii), Karttunen (1974) had to modify (3.44) and (3.45) by replacing 'entail' with 'entail in context', thus allowing access to real-world knowledge.

(i)   Geraldine is a Mormon and she has given up wearing her holy underwear!
(ii) If Geraldine is a Mormon, she has given up wearing her holy underwear!
(iii) >> Geraldine used to wear her holy underwear

Here, the second clause in (i) and (ii) presupposes (iii) by virtue of the use of the change-of-state verb *give up* (ignoring another presupposition arising due to the use of the definite description *her holy underwear*, namely, Geraldine has/had a holy underwear). But whether this presupposition can percolate up unfiltered depends on our beliefs about what Mormons wear. If we have no knowledge whatsoever about what they wear, then this presupposition will get through. On the other hand, if we assume that only Mormons habitually wear holy underwear, then this presupposition inheritance will be blocked. This is because in this context, the presupposition of the second clause is (indirectly) entailed by the first clause.

negation as a plug. Clearly this runs against the spirit of Occam's razor (see Chapter 2).

Turning next to empirical considerations, counterexamples are not difficult to find. First of all, a presupposition embedded under a plug, for example, can sometimes survive unscathed, contra the predictions of the filtering-satisfaction analysis. This is the case of (3.47).

(3.47)   (Levinson 1983: 196)
Churchill said that he would never regret being tough with Stalin.
>> Churchill was tough with Stalin

In this example, as pointed out by Levinson (1983: 196), in spite of the presence of the verb *say*, which is a plug in Karttunen's analysis, the presupposition of the embedded clause is inherited by the whole sentence. Next, the filtering conditions also make wrong predictions. Consider (3.48), due to Gazdar (1979).

(3.48)   It's possible that John has children and it's possible that his children are away.
~ >> John has children

The use of *his children* in the embedded clause of the second conjunct presupposes that John has children, and this presupposition is inherited by the second conjunct as a whole, *possible* being a hole. However, the presupposition is not locally satisfied in (3.48) because it is not entailed by the first conjunct. This has the consequence that, given the filtering condition for conjunction (3.45), (3.48) should presuppose that John has children—a prediction that is intuitively incorrect (see e.g. Gazdar 1979; Levinson 1983: 209–10; Kadmon 2001: 134; see also Levinson 1983: 210–11 for further counterexamples to the filtering conditions). Finally, the filtering-satisfaction theory cannot accommodate defeasibility of presupposition—the second most important property of presupposition. This is particularly true of those putative presuppositions that are contextually defeated, as exhibited in examples such as (3.19)–(3.21). Take, for example, (3.19) as an illustration. As we have already seen, the sentence *Therefore the (present) king of France isn't bald* does not here presuppose that there is a (present) king of France because the putative presupposition is defeated by the contradictory proposition that there is no (present) king of France, which has already been established in the immediate discourse context. But under the filtering-satisfaction theory, on the assumption that descriptive negation is a hole, the unwanted presupposition is wrongly predicted to get through (for some recent, more technical critiques of the filtering-satisfaction analysis, see e.g. van der Sandt 1988 and Geurts 1999).[12]

3.3.3. The cancellation analysis

In contrast to the filtering-satisfaction analysis, inspired in part by Stalnaker's account of semifactives, underlying Gazdar's (1979) **cancellation analysis** is the crucial assumption that a presupposition is cancellable (see also Soames 1979, 1982). On this theory, what a presupposition trigger engenders is merely a **potential presupposition**. A potential presupposition will become an **actual presupposition**, unless it is defeated. With respect to the projection problem, what the cancellation analysis predicts is that each and every presupposition of the embedded clause will become an actual presupposition of the complex sentence, unless it is nullified by certain linguistic and non-linguistic factors.

How, then, can a potential presupposition be cancelled? Like a conversational implicature, a potential presupposition is defeated if it is inconsistent with (i) background assumptions, (ii) contextual factors, and (iii) semantic entailment (see also Chapter 2). In addition, a potential presupposition is cancelled if it clashes with conversational implicatures.

In the first place, a potential presupposition is cancelled if it is inconsistent with background assumptions or real-world knowledge. Recollect (3.17) and consider (3.49).

(3.49)   John hasn't discovered that Angola is in Asia.
         ~ >> Angola is in Asia

The use of the factive verb *discover* should give rise to the potential presupposition that Angola is in Asia. But this proposition runs against our real-world knowledge that Angola is an African country. Consequently the unwanted presupposition is defeated by the contradictory real-world knowledge.

---

[12] On the basis of the presuppositional behaviour of *even*, *too*, and *manage to*, Karttunen and Peters (1979) took the view that all kinds of presupposition are conventional implicatures in the sense articulated by Grice (see Chapter 2). One problem for such an analysis is that many types of presupposition are cancellable (e.g. Levinson 1983: 210; Soames 1989: 581, 603).

Secondly, a potential presupposition is defeated if it is at variance with contextual factors. In addition to (3.19), there is (3.50).

(3.50) John: I don't have a car.
Mary: So at least you don't need to worry about where to park your car.
~ >> John has a car

The potential presupposition that John has a car is in contradiction to the assertion that has already been put in the context. Since the assertion in the context is more powerful, the inconsistent potential presupposition fails to become an actual presupposition.

Next, a potential presupposition disappears if it is not in keeping with semantic entailments. Consider (3.22)–(3.24) and (3.51).

(3.51) John doesn't know that Mary is a hay fever sufferer: she isn't.
~ >> Mary is a hay fever sufferer

In (3.51), for instance, there should be a potential presupposition, namely, Mary is a hay fever sufferer. But there is also a conflicting semantic entailment, namely, Mary is not a hay fever sufferer. Now, given that a potential presupposition has to be consistent with any existing semantic entailment, the potential presupposition vanishes.

Finally, a potential presupposition is abandoned if it clashes with a conversational implicature. We have already seen an example in (3.18). Another example is given here.

(3.52) (Gazdar 1979 crediting Karttunen)
If I realize later that I haven't told the truth, I will confess it to everyone.
+> I will not realize later that I haven't told the truth
~ >> I haven't told the truth

The whole sentence in (3.52) carries a potential presupposition that the speaker hasn't told the truth. But (3.52) also has a conversational implicature to the effect that the speaker doesn't know that he hasn't told the truth (Gazdar 1979: 150, 153–4; Soames 1989; see also Stalnaker 1974). As a result of this conflict, the potential presupposition is defeated by the inconsistent conversational implicature. Notice further that presupposition-cancelling conversational implicatures are usually $Q_{\text{-clausal}}$ ones.

It should be mentioned at this point that there are two important characteristics of Gazdar's presupposition cancellation mechanism. First, a potential presupposition is overridden if it conflicts with any of the factors we have discussed above, but the cancellation must proceed in a fixed order of priority, which is stated in (3.53) (cf. Chapter 2).

(3.53)   Gazdar's presupposition cancellation procedure
  a. Background assumptions
  b. Contextual factors
  c. Semantic entailments
  d. Conversational implicatures
  e. Presuppositions

Put the other way round, the augmentation of the Gazdarian context (i.e. the common ground), which consists of a set of non-controversial propositions, runs according to the following order of priority: first the relevant background assumptions are placed in the context, then the contextual information is added, then the entailments of what is said, then the conversational implicatures, and only finally the presuppositions. The second, related point is that at each step in the process of augmentation, the additional proposition can be added only if it does not contradict any proposition that is already put in the context (see Gazdar 1979 for further discussion).

From a conceptual point of view, the cancellation analysis is preferable to the filtering-satisfaction analysis. There is no need to postulate arbitrary notions such as plugs, holes, and filters on Gazdar's theory. Next, empirically speaking, many of the counterexamples to the filtering-satisfaction analysis, as we have already seen, fall out naturally from the cancellation theory. Recollect (3.48). In that example, the presupposition of the second conjunct that John has children is not projected onto the whole sentence. On Gazdar's analysis, this is correctly accounted for by the fact that (3.48) bears a $Q_{\text{-clausal}}$ conversational implicature, namely, the speaker is not sure whether John has children or not. This implicature, which is inconsistent with the potential presupposition, is added to the context prior to the potential presupposition, thus ensuring the loss of the latter. The same story can be told of (3.19). Since the entailment that there is no (present) king of France is already present in the immediate discourse context, given Gazdar's cancellation mechanism, the inconsistent potential presupposition that there is a (present) king of France cannot be added to the context, which correctly explains why the potential presupposition is cancelled.

Despite its conceptual simplicity and elegance and its empirical coverage, the cancellation analysis, however, is not without its own problems. Conceptually, given that presuppositions are commonly taken to be more conventional than conversational implicatures, why should they be defeated by the latter? In other words, why should presuppositions be the last to be added in the process of updating the common ground? In an attempt to avoid this problem, van der Sandt (1988) suggested that Gazdar's cancellation procedure in (3.53) be reordered and, more specifically, presuppositions be fronted to the beginning of a sentence provided that it does not run counter to any Gricean and neo-Gricean conversational maxims or principles. The *raison d'être* behind the proposal is that, as mentioned above, 'presuppositions are given information, and in this sense "precede" their carrier sentences, if not *de facto* then at least *de jure*' (Beaver and Geurts 2011). Next, from an empirical perspective, there are counterexamples. As an illustration, consider (3.54), which represents the class of examples on which the cancellation theory fails. This set of counterexamples was first pointed out by Soames (1982).

(3.54)   If someone in the linguistics department won the research grant, it was John who won it.

~ >> someone won the research grant

The problem is this: the consequent of (3.54) bears the potential presupposition that someone won the research grant, but this presupposition is not inherited by the whole conditional, as correctly predicted by the filtering-satisfaction theory. By contrast, under any cancellation theory, the disappearance of the potential presupposition is dependent on the cancelling conversational implicature generated by the *if* clause. But the relevant conversational implicature here is that the speaker is not sure that someone in the linguistics department won the research grant, and as such it is not inconsistent with the potential presupposition under consideration (because someone outside the linguistics department might have won the grant), hence the failure to prevent the potential presupposition from becoming the actual presupposition—an incorrect outcome (see Heim 1983, Landman 1986, and van der Sandt 1988 for other counterexamples).[13]

On the basis of counterexamples like (3.54), and of the observation that the filtering-satisfaction and cancellation analyses are complementary in their coverage of data, Soames (1982) suggested a synthesis of the two theories, arguing that a correct account of presupposition projection requires both Karttunen's local filtering and Gazdar's global cancelling mechanisms. Two models of incorporation are then considered: (i) filter

---

[13] One solution proposed by Landman (1986) is to strengthen conversational implicature further so that it can cancel the unwanted presupposition. But such a proposal may create more problems than it solves.

first and cancel afterwards and (ii) cancel first and filter afterwards. Soames adopted the second alternative (see also Soames 1989, Beaver, 2001: 70–72, and Kadmon 2001: 139–42 for further discussion).

3.3.4. The accommodation analysis

In an attempt to combine the strengths of both the filtering-satisfaction and cancellation theories, Heim (1983, 1992) developed a particular version of the filtering-satisfaction model, couched in her dynamic semantic theory of context change (see also van der Sandt 1992).[14] Her semantic theory is 'dynamic' in the sense that it does not take a sentence as an isolated statement with truth conditions or a proposition with truth values. Instead, it treats the sentence in terms of what contributions it can potentially make to a discourse, that is, the sentence's context change potential. Let me dub this model of presupposition the **accommodation analysis**.

On Heim's view, the meaning of a linguistic expression, including the presupposition of a sentence, is its context change potential. The notion of **accommodation** is generally attributed to Lewis (1979), but it was originated by Strawson (1950, 1971). Other scholars who made important contributions to the concept before Lewis include Karttunen (1974), Stalnaker (1974), and Ballmer (1975, 1978). Simply put, accommodation provides an explanation for how a missing proposition required by what a speaker has said is supplied by the addressee so that what has been said by the speaker can be accepted. In other words, the addressee accommodates to the speaker (see also Levinson 2000: 60–1 and Huang 2000a: 239). Thus, in the case of presupposition, a presupposition has to be satisfied in its local context, and if it is not, it has to be accommodated. Thus, accommodation offers a dynamic process of 'repair' in discourse, whereby a 'tacit extension' is made by the addressee to the discourse context to allow for update with

---

[14] While Heim's model is in general considered to represent the first systematic, dynamic approach to presupposition, the background for the perspectival shift from static to dynamic analyses was set in Karttunen (1973) and the change was implemented in Karttunen (1974). Consequently, both Karttunen and Stalnaker's filtering-satisfaction and Gazdar's cancellation accounts can also be said to be dynamic. In fact, almost all of the modern/contemporary approaches to presupposition are dynamic in nature. One advantage of Heim's approach, however, is that it can handle presupposition projection below the level of the clause.

otherwise unfulfilled presuppositions (Beaver 2001).[15] As an illustrating example, consider (3.55), due to Gazdar (1979: 106), when uttered by John who is late for a meeting.

(3.55)   I'm sorry I'm late, my car broke down.
>> The speaker has a car and he came by car

Even if no one in the audience previously knew the presupposition of (3.55), they will let the proposition get through unblocked, that is, they will accommodate to the assumption that the speaker has a car and he came by car. What seems to happen here is that the presupposition in question is simply added to the discourse context as if it had already been there all along. As a consequence, a deviant usage is brought back into line with expectations by a co-operative audience.

Needless to say, accommodation is constrained by certain conditions, one of which is 'bridging', mentioned above (see note 15), namely the requirement that the new information added to the discourse context has to be related in one way or another to the information already there. Another, more important constraint on accommodation is that what is accommodated to must be non-controversial and be consistent with all the propositions already placed in the context (see e.g. Soames 1979, 1989: 567; Atlas 2004). Suppose that John had uttered (3.56) (due to Levinson 1983: 205) instead of (3.55) in the above scenario.

(3.56)   I'm sorry I'm late, my fire-engine broke down.
?>> The speaker has a fire-engine and he came by fire-engine

The reason that the required presupposition of (3.56) would probably be much more difficult to accommodate is that it runs contrary to our real-world knowledge that an average person usually does not own a fire-engine

---

[15] According to Beaver and Geurts (2011), accommodation can be defined both broadly and narrowly. On a broad definition, accommodation is bridging involving real-world knowledge (see Chapter 2). By contrast, if accommodation is construed more strictly, it has nothing to do with real-world knowledge. In such a case, there may be an **'accommodation module'**. In the following example, for instance, while on a broad understanding of accommodation, both (ii) and (iii) are accommodated; on a strict construal, only (ii) is. (iii) is a bridging inference.

(i)   John read a book about Schubert and wrote to the author.
(ii)   There is an author
(iii) The said author wrote a book about Schubert read by John

and does not drive a fire-engine to a meeting. All this shows that new information can, and frequently will, be conveyed by way of presupposition and that accommodation is essentially a mechanism to increment the discourse context with new, non-controversial assumptions.[16] Looked at this way, accommodation can be regarded as a special case of the exploitation of the Gricean machanism: the speaker exploits the maxims of conversation to engender pragmatic enrichments (see Chapter 2) (Stalnaker 1974; Horn 1996; see also Thomason 1990.).[17]

On Heim's analysis, two types of context are identified, corresponding to two types of accommodation: (i) global context, namely the context against which a sequence of sentences/clauses is evaluated, and (ii) local context, namely the context against which (a part of) a sentence/clause is assessed (see Section 3.3.2). The former gives rise to **global** (or in Soames' 1989 terms, *de facto*) **accommodation**, and the latter creates **local** (or again to use Soames' 1989 terminology *de jure*) **accommodation**.[18] By way of illustration, take (3.57).

(3.57)   The (present) king of France isn't bald.
         >> there is a (present) king of France

In performing global accommodation, we amend the initial context to a new context that contains the assumption that France has a (present) king. This

[16] Somewhat related to the constraints are the observation made by van der Sandt (1992) that presuppositions whose triggers' descriptive content is relatively poor are more difficult to be accommodated, as is illustrated by the presupposition triggered by *the guy* in *She has almost given up hope of finding the guy*. For further discussion, see Beaver and Geurts (2011).

[17] As pointed out by Horn (1996), the connection between accommodation and exploitation is forged by Grice himself, as can be seen from the following passage by Grice (1989: 274): '[I]t is quite natural to say to somebody, when we are discussing some concert, *My aunt's cousin went to that concert*, when we know perfectly well that the person we are talking to is very likely not even to know that we have an aunt, let alone know that our aunt has a cousin. So the supposition must be not that it is common knowledge but rather that it is noncontroversial, in the sense that it is something that we would expect the hearer to take from us (if he does not already know)'.

[18] According to Soames (1989: 578), in global or *de facto* accommodation, apparent violations of presuppositional requirements are accommodated by adjusting the existing conversational facts to fit the requirements. By contrast, in local or *de jure* accommodation, these violations are accommodated by adjusting the requirements to fit the conversational facts.

leads to the interpretation that there is a (present) king of France and he is not bald, thus retaining the expectable presupposition. By contrast, in performing local accommodation, we don't amend the initial context in a global way. Instead we amend it only at the point where it has to be amended. This gives rise to the interpretation to the effect that it is not the case that there is a (present) king of France and he is bald.

The question that comes up next is when global accommodation is used and when local accommodation is employed? The answer provided by Heim (1983) is that global accommodation is *ceteris paribus* preferred over local accommodation. This is captured in Heim's **preference for global accommodation (PGA)** in (3.58).

(3.58)   The preference for global accommodation (PGA)
         Global accommodation is preferred to non-global accommodation.

In other words, global accommodation is normally performed unless it is forced out by, say, threat of contradiction. Only in the latter case is local accommodation performed (see also van der Sandt 1992).[19] This can be illustrated by a consideration of (3.59).

(3.59)   John: Auntie Anna doesn't have a cat.
         Mary: So at least you don't have to look after her cat when she is on holiday.
         ~ >> Auntie Anna has a cat

Here, if we employ the strategy of global accommodation, that is, if we make the global assumption that Auntie Anna has a cat, the proposition will clash directly with what is already in the context engendered by John's utterance in the previous turn in the mini-conversation, namely, Auntie Anna does not have a cat. Consequently, global accommodation is forced out, and local accommodation is performed. The latter will produce an interpretation to the effect that Auntie Anna does not have a cat and John

---

[19] In van der Sandt's (1992) accommodation analysis, which is formulated within the framework of Discourse Representation Theory (DRT), in addition to global and local accommodations of presupposition, there is a third, in-between type of accommodation, labelled '**intermediate accommodation**'. Intermediate accommodation arises in a context that lies between the global and local context. One such context may be one in which a presupposition contains a variable bound by a quantifier, as in (i).

(i)   Most Americans walk their dogs after work.

But see e.g. Beaver and Geurts (2011) for the arguments that there is nothing like intermediate accommodation.

does not have to look after her cat when she is on holiday, hence the disappearance of the putative presupposition—an empirically correct prediction.[20]

There are, however, problems at the very core of the accommodation analysis. One main problem centres on the relationship between global and local accommodation. In the first place, as pointed out by Soames (1989: 601), the preference for global accommodation will make the wrong prediction that (3.60) presupposes that someone solved the problem.

(3.60)   Either it was Susan who solved the problem, or no one at the conference did.
         ~ >> someone solved the problem

Secondly, following Roberts (1996), Kadmon (2001: 172) argued that on the assumption that (3.61) does not bear the presupposition that Sue smoked, both global and local accommodations are possible.

(3.61)   If Sue stopped smoking yesterday, for example, that would explain why she is chewing candy all the time today.
         ~ >> Sue smoked

If this is correct, then the argument that local accommodation is legitimate only if global accommodation is not plausible has to be abandoned (see. e.g. Soames 1989, Guerts 1999 for further arguments against the accommodation analysis, and Asher and Lascarides 1998 for an attempt to replace accommodation with discourse update through rhetorical links; see also Bauerle, Reyle, and Zimmerman 2003).[21]

---

[20] One attempt at providing an explanation for the PGA can be found in what Beaver (2001) called the **Atlas principle** (Atlas 1977), which goes like this: One accommodation alternative is preferred to another if the former yields a stronger meaning than the latter (i.e. if the first meaning unilaterally entails the second). From the perspective of an addressee, the principle seems to resemble Grice's second sub-maxim of Quantity or Levinson's I-principle (see Chapter 2). According to Beaver and Geurts (2011), however, there are some doubts that in general an addressee prefers a stronger reading to a weaker one.

[21] Mention should be made here of another important analysis of presupposition, namely, the (neo-)Gricean approach. Deriving ultimately from the ideas of Grice (1981), the central tenet of the (neo-)Gricean analysis in its broad sense is to reduce presupposition to various combinations of an entailment and a conversational implicature, utilizing the Gricean machinery (see Chapter 2). Early attempts along this line include Atlas (1975), Kempson (1975), Wilson (1975), Böer and Lycan (1976), and Atlas and Levinson (1981). Various contemporary advances of the

3.4. Summary

In this chapter, I have examined presupposition. I discussed the general phenomena of presupposition in Section 3.1. I proceeded to consider the properties of presupposition in Section 3.2. Finally, in Section 3.3, I surveyed three important analyses of presupposition.[22]

One consensus to be reached is that, as so nicely summed up by Soames (1989: 556, 606), 'presupposition may not be a single phenomenon with a unitary explanation, but rather a domain of related issues involving the interaction of several semantic and pragmatic principles', and therefore 'theories of presupposition are neither exclusively semantic nor exclusively pragmatic, but rather require the integration of both kinds of information'.

One main weakness can also be identified. There has been virtually no cross-linguistic study of presupposition. It is not unreasonable to speculate that while presupposition exhibits universal properties, it could also display language-specific ones. In my view, a better understanding of presupposition can be attained only if the phenomena are approached from a cross-linguistic perspective.

Finally, there is a current debate over the various reformulations and applications of Heim's (1991) principle of **maximize presupposition**, the central idea of which is that lexical items or sentences are ordered on a presupposition strength scale, and those lexical expressions or sentences with stronger presuppositions are preferred over those with weaker ones. Furthermore, given the principle, it is predicted that the use of a presuppositionally weaker lexical item or sentence (for example, one without any presupposition triggers) will result in a specific pragmatic inference dubbed '**antipresupposition**' or '**implicated presupposition**'—namely, the presupposition is not true (Bade 2013). The interested reader is referred to, for example, Chemla (2008), Margi (2009), and Schlenker (2012).

---

analysis can be found in Atlas (2004, 2005), Abbott (2006), Simons (2003, 2014), and Schlenker (2007, 2008). The (neo-)Gricean theory of presupposition may be seen as an instantiation of what Levinson (1983: 216–17) dubbed the 're-allocation programme'.

[22] One topic I have omitted in this chapter is presuppositions and attitudes. For a useful discussion, see e.g. Beaver and Geurts (2011). See also Chemla and Schlenker (2012) for an experimental approach to presupposition projection.

Key concepts

presupposition
semantic presupposition
pragmatic presupposition
semantico-pragmatic presupposition
presupposition trigger (lexical trigger, constructional/structural trigger)
properties of presupposition (constancy under negation, defeasibility)
presupposition projection problem
plug
hole
filter
filtering condition (for conditional)
filtering condition (for conjunction)
filtering condition (for disjunction)
potential presupposition
actual presupposition
presupposition cancellation procedure
accommodation
global accommodation
local accommodation
intermediate accommodation

Exercises and essay questions

1. What does a speaker presuppose in the utterance of the following sentences? (Lexical presupposition triggers are italicized here.)
    (i)   The burglar *realized* that he had been filmed on closed circuit television.
    (ii)   John *forgot* to do the washing up.
    (iii) John hasn't driven a car *since* he had the accident.
    (iv)   Professor Matthews was *glad* that he had solved one of evolution's great mysteries.
    (v)   John isn't off cigarettes *again*.
    (vi)   It wasn't John who moved to Spain.
    (vii) Miriam *discovered* that her husband was having an affair.
    (viii) Mary *started* emptying the shopping bags.
    (ix)   It's *odd* that John doesn't know how to use an iPad.

    (x)   Susan has fed *every* cat.

    (xi)   If John hadn't missed the interview, he would have got the job.

    (xii)   John hasn't *found out* that his brother used all the printer paper.

    (xiii)   (Proper names)

          The poet wasn't *William Shakespeare.*

    (xiv)   (Focus or contrast elements)

          HE gave her a rose.

    (xv)   (Possessive NPs)

          Helen has been cruel to *her mother-in-law.*

    (xvi)   (Additive particles)

          Looked at economically, the problem is easy to solve, *too.*

2. Can you work out the presuppositions of the following utterances?

    (i)   John *pretended* that he was a professional footballer.

    (ii)   John, who read mathematics at Harvard University, was a friend of mine.

    (iii)   John *accused* Bill of cheating in the final exam.

    (iv)   That John hadn't had a bath for more than three weeks bothered Susan.

    (v)   (Comparisons of equality)

          John isn't as rich as Peter.

    (vi)   John *criticized/reproached* Susan for wearing a fur coat.

    (vii)   (Manner adverbs)

          Jamie walked *slowly* into the study.

    (viii)   (Comparatives)

          Mary is a far more successful lawyer than Susan.

3. In 2009, there was a referendum on the smacking law in New Zealand. 87% of those who took part in the referendum voted no on the question: 'Should a smack as a part of good parental correction be a criminal offence in New Zealand?' Take a careful look at the wording of the referendum question and explain why the vast majority of the voters said no.

4. In each of the following sentences/utterances, I have identified an inference in (b). Using constancy under negation as a diagnostic, can you tell which inference is a presupposition and which is not?

    (i)   a. John has three girlfriends.

          b. John does not have, for example, four girlfriends

    (ii)   a. John understands that raised cholesterol level will increase the risk of heart disease.

          b. Raised cholesterol level will increase the risk of heart disease

    (iii)   a. It was in August that John found his brother.

          b. John found his brother sometime

    (iv)   a. Even John's mother likes surfing the net.

          b. Others, besides John's mother, likes surfing the net; and of those under consideration, John's mother is among the least likely to do so

(v) a. Please open the window.

b. The window is not open

(vi) a. All of her children believe in marriage.

b. Some of her children believe in marriage

(vii) (French)

a. Vous êtes en vacances?

'You are on holiday?'

b. The addressee is socially superior to or distant from the speaker

(viii) a. John is rich but humble.

b. There is a contrast between being rich and being humble

5. What are the putative presuppositions of the following? How is each of them cancelled?

(i) Manchester United didn't regret losing the game, because in fact they won!

(ii) Dr Smith left the university before being promoted to an associate professor.

(iii) You say that somebody in this room fancies Henry. Well, it isn't Mary who fancies Henry, it isn't Lucy, and it certainly isn't Jane. In fact, nobody in this room fancies Henry!

(iv) Charles stumbled and sprained his ankle before he finished running the 400 metres.

(v) John doesn't know that Neil Armstrong was the first man to travel in space.

(vi) John was in his office when the news was announced, if it was in fact ever announced.

(vii) He is proud that he is the Tsar of Russia, but of course there isn't any such Tsar anymore!

(viii) If Cambridge wins the boat race, John will be happy that Cambridge is the winner.

(ix) Luckily, Rosemary managed to catch the vase before it fell to the ground and broke.

(x) The real estate agent believed that there would be a buoyant demand for homes soon.

(xi) Alice: '[I]t would not be possible to have another cup of tea as she had not yet had any tea at all. (*Alice in Wonderland*)

(xii) I don't know that his father was an infamous Red Guard during Mao's Cultural Revolution in China.

6. If (i) is negated, or put in modal contexts, will its entailment survive? (I use '||-' to stand for 'entail'.) Contrast it with the behaviour of presuppositions under the same circumstances, as shown in (3.35)–(3.37). What conclusions can you reach?

(i) The nursery teacher sold nine Christmas raffle tickets.

||- The nursery teacher sold eight Christmas raffle tickets

7. What is presupposition? What is semantic, what is pragmatic, and what is semantico-pragmatic presupposition?
8. What are the essential properties of presupposition?
9. To what extent is presupposition a pragmatic phenomenon?
10. What is the projection problem for presupposition?
11. What are the similarities and differences between conversational implicature and presupposition?
12. Critically assess one of the three analyses of presupposition discussed in this chapter.

Further readings

Karttunen (1973).
Gazdar (1979).
Atlas (2004) or Atlas (2005). Chapter 4.
Beaver and Geurts (2011).

4

Speech acts

Speech act theory, though foreshadowed by the Austrian-born British philosopher Ludwig Wittgenstein's views about **language games**, is usually attributed to the British philosopher J. L. Austin.[1] The basic ideas, which were formed by him in the late 1930s, were presented in his lectures given at Oxford University in 1952–4, and later in his William James lectures delivered at Harvard University in 1955. These lectures were eventually published posthumously as *How to do things with words* in 1962. After his death in 1960, Austin's ideas were refined, systematized, and advanced

---

[1] For a brief discussion of the history of speech act theory from ancient Greek philosophers through Frege and Wittgenstein to Austin and Grice, see e.g. Sbisà (2009). See also Smith (1990).

especially by his Oxford pupil, the American philosopher John R. Searle. Simply stated, the central tenet of speech act theory is that the uttering of a sentence is, or is part of, an action within the framework of social institutions and conventions. Put in slogan form, saying is (part of) doing, or words are (part of) deeds.

In Section 4.1, I shall discuss Austin's dichotomy between performatives and constatives. The focus of Section 4.2 is on his felicity conditions on performatives. In Section 4.3, I shall examine Austin's tripartite distinction between locutionary, illocutionary, and perlocutionary acts. In Section 4.4, I shall proceed to take a look at Searle's felicity conditions on speech acts. Then, in Section 4.5, I shall present Searle's classification of speech acts. Next, in Section 4.6, I shall consider indirect speech acts including a discussion of politeness and impoliteness. Finally, Section 4.7 undertakes to discuss some cultural aspects of speech acts.

4.1. Performatives versus constatives

4.1.1. The performative-constative dichotomy

In the 1930s, a very influential movement in philosophy was **logical positivism**. Inspired by empiricism and verificationism, logical positivism was developed by a group of philosophers, mathematicians, and physicists principally in Vienna between the 1920s and 1940s. One of the central doctrines of logical positivism is what is now called the **descriptive fallacy**, namely, the view that the only philosophically interesting function of language is that of making true or false statements. A particular version of the descriptive fallacy is the so-called **verificationist thesis** of meaning, namely, the idea that 'unless a sentence can, at least in principle, be verified (i.e. tested for its truth or falsity), it was strictly speaking meaningless' (Levinson 1983: 227, see also Lyons 1995: 173). In other words, according to the proponents of logical positivism, the meaning of any statement is its method of verification by means of empirical observation. This has the consequence that they reject as meaningless many statements of religion, aesthetics, morality, literature, and metaphysics. For example, statements like those in (4.1) are simply meaningless, because they are not used to make propositions that are testable or falsifiable, and therefore verifiable. Instead, they express subjective judgements.

(4.1)   a. Shouting and screaming at your children is wrong.
        b. Elizabeth is more beautiful than Mary.
        c. Getting married and having children is better than having children and getting married.

It was against this philosophical background that Austin set about developing his theory of speech acts (Austin 1962). He made two important observations. First, he noted that some ordinary language sentences such as those in (4.2) are not employed to make a statement, and as such they cannot be said to be true or false.

(4.2)   a. Good morning!
        b. Is she a vegetarian?
        c. Put the car in the garage, please.

Secondly and more importantly, Austin observed that there are ordinary language declarative sentences that resist a truth-conditional analysis in a similar fashion. The point of uttering such sentences is not just to say things, but also actively to do things. In other words, such utterances have both a descriptive and an effective aspect. Accordingly, Austin called them **performatives**, and he distinguished them from assertions, or statement-making utterances, which he called **constatives**. Put slightly differently, in Austin's view, an initial distinction was made between performatives and constatives. Performatives are utterances that are used to do things or perform acts, as in (4.3). By contrast, constatives are utterances that are employed to make assertions or statements, as in (4.4).

(4.3)   a. I christen/name this ship the Princess Elizabeth.
        b. I now pronounce you man/husband and wife.
        c. I sentence you to ten years in prison.
        d. I promise to come to your talk tomorrow afternoon.
        e. I command you to surrender immediately.
        f. I apologize for being late.
(4.4)   a. My daughter is called Elizabeth.
        b. The children are chasing squirrels in the park.
        c. Maurice Garin won the first *Tour de France* in 1903.

Unlike those in (4.4), the declarative sentences in (4.3) have two characteristics: (i) they are not used intentionally to say anything, true or false, about certain states of affairs in the external world, and (ii) their use constitutes (part of) an action, namely, that of christening/naming a ship in (4.3a), that of pronouncing a couple married in (4.3b), that of sentencing a convicted criminal in (4.3c), that of promising in (4.3d), that of ordering in (4.3e), and finally that of apologizing in (4.3f). In addition, as pointed out in Huang (2006a), there are two further differences between (4.3a)–(4.3c) and (4.3d)–(4.3f). The first is that while (4.3a)–(4.3c) are part of a conventional or ritual behaviour supported by institutional facts (see also Strawson 1964), (4.3d)–(4.3f) are not. Secondly, while the **performative verb**, that is, the verb naming the action while performing it in (4.3a)–(4.3c), is in general an essential element and cannot be omitted, it can in (4.3d)–(4.3f). In other words, whereas, for example, we cannot christen/name a ship without using the verb *christen* or *name*, we can make a promise without using the verb *promise*, as in (4.5).

(4.5)   I'll come to your talk tomorrow afternoon.

> This would be a good point at which to attempt Exercise 1 at the end of this chapter.

Explicit versus implicit performatives

Performatives can further be divided into two types: explicit and implicit, or in Austin's (1962: 69) term, primary. **Explicit performatives** are performatives which contain a performative verb that makes explicit what kind of act is being performed. By contrast, **implicit performatives** are performatives in which there is no such a verb. This contrast is illustrated by the explicit performatives in (4.3) and the implicit performatives in (4.5) and (4.6).

(4.6)   a. Surrender immediately.
          b. How about going to New York on Saturday?
          c. Leave me alone, or I'll call the police.

> Now go to the end of this chapter and try Exercise 2.

Syntactic and semantic properties of explicit performatives

Austin also isolated a number of syntactic and semantic properties of explicit performatives in English. They are: (i) explicit performatives contain a performative verb,[2] (ii) the performative nature of such a verb can be

---

[2] Cross-linguistically, the size of the inventory of performative verbs varies from language to language. English is extremely rich in performative verbs. According to

reinforced by adding the adverb *hereby*, and (iii) explicit performatives occur in sentences with a first person singular subject of a verb in the simple present tense, indicative mood, and active voice.

However, as Austin himself was aware, there are exceptions. Explicit performatives can sometimes take a first-person plural subject, as in (4.7); a second-person singular or plural subject, as in (4.8); and a third-person singular or plural subject, as in (4.9). In addition, there are cases where the explicit performative verb is 'impersonal', that is, it does not refer to the speaker, as in (4.10). Furthermore, as (4.8), (4.9), (4.10a), (4.10c), and (4.11b) show, explicit performatives can also occur in sentences with the verb in the passive voice. Finally, as the attested examples in (4.11) indicate, they can also occur in sentences of present progressive aspect.

(4.7)   We suggest that you go to the embassy and apply for your visa in person.

(4.8)   You are hereby warned that legal action will be taken.

(4.9)   Passengers are hereby requested to wear a seat belt.

(4.10)   a. *Taken from a company's AGM notice*
             Notice is hereby given that the Annual General Meeting of O2 plc will be held at The Hexagon, Queens Walk, Reading, Berkshire RG1 7UA on Wednesday, 27 July 2005 at 11.00 am for the following purposes: . . .

          b. (Hurford and Heasley 1983: 239)
             The management hereby warns customers that mistakes in change cannot be rectified once the customer has left the counter.

          c. (Levinson 1983: 260)
             It is herewith disclosed that the value of the estate left by Marcus T. Bloomingdale was 4,785,758 dollars.

(4.11)   (Thomas 1995: 45)

          a. *A radio journalist is interviewing the Chairman of Railtrack during a strike by signal workers.*
             A: Are you denying that the Government has interfered?
             B: I am denying that.

          b. *Taken from a naval disciplinary hearing*
             You are being discharged on the grounds of severe temperamental unsuitability for service in the Royal Navy.

Lyons (1995), there are hundreds, if not thousands, of such verbs in the language. By contrast, Russian is a language that contains a much smaller number of such verbs.

Notice next that performative verbs can also be used descriptively. In this usage, they behave like non-performative verbs.

(4.12)   a. I baptized John's baby last Sunday.
         b. You are always promising to do housework, but you never do it.
         c. It's the Head of Department who authorized John to work in our lab.

See whether you can do Exercises 3 and 4 at the end of this chapter.

4.1.2. The performative hypothesis

In order to account for implicit performatives, an analysis known as the **performative hypothesis** was put forward in the 1970s. The basic idea of the hypothesis is that underlying every sentence there is a 'hidden' matrix performative clause of the form given in (4.13).

(4.13)   I (hereby) Vp you (that) S

where Vp is a performative verb, and S is a complement clause. The performative verb, which is in the indicative mood, active voice, and simple present tense (see above), will always make explicit what is implicit, though the matrix performative clause can be deleted without meaning being changed (see e.g. Ross 1970; Lakoff 1972; Sadock 1974; see Gazdar 1979 and Levinson 1983 for a more detailed formulation of the hypothesis; see also Sadock 2004 for further discussion). Thus, according to this hypothesis, the performative matrix clause in deep or underlying structure of (4.14) shows up overtly in (4.15).

(4.14)   Stand up.
(4.15)   I hereby request that you stand up. Or,
         I hereby order you to stand up.

There are, however, problems at the very heart of this analysis. One such problem is that there are many cases of implicit performatives which do not have an explicit performative version, even though the relevant verb can be used in a descriptive way. As an illustration, consider (4.16).

(4.16)   a. You're a stupid cow.
         b. ?I hereby insult you that you're a stupid cow.
         c. John insulted Mary by saying that she was a stupid cow.

Intuitively (4.16a) is most naturally interpretable as an insult, but contrary to the prediction of the performative hypothesis, it does not seem to have an explicit performative equivalent, as is shown by the oddness of (4.16b). On the other hand, as (4.16c) indicates, the verb *insult* can be used descriptively without any problem. More or less the same can be said of such acts as lying, threatening, and punishing. Faced with this and a variety of other syntactic, semantic and pragmatic difficulties (see e.g. Levinson 1983: 243–78; Yule 1996: 52–3; Marmaridou 2000: 187; Sadock 2004), the performative hypothesis has long been abandoned.

4.2. Austin's felicity conditions on performatives

On Wednesday 21 January 2009, President Obama even managed to squeeze in one small but pressing matter—retaking his oath of office. Chief Justice John Roberts inadvertently switched a word while administering it on Tuesday 20 January 2009. In other words, Obama was sworn in for a second time for his first term of office.

As already mentioned, it makes no sense to call a performative true or false. Nevertheless, Austin noticed that for a performative to be 'felicitous' or successful, it must meet a set of conditions. For example, one such condition for performing the act of naming is that the speaker must be recognized by his or her community as having the authority to do it; for performing the act of ordering, the condition is that the speaker must be in authority over the addressee, and finally, for performing the act of promising, one condition is that what is promised by the speaker must be something the addressee wants to happen. Austin called these conditions **felicity conditions**. In other words, felicity conditions are conditions under which words can be used properly to perform actions. Moreover, Austin (1975: 14–15) distinguished three different types of felicity condition.

(4.17)   Austin's felicity conditions on performatives
      A. (i) There must be a conventional procedure having a conventional effect.
          (ii) The circumstances and persons must be appropriate, as specified in the procedure.
      B. The procedure must be executed (i) correctly and (ii) completely.
      C. Often
          (i) the persons must have the requisite thoughts, feelings, and intentions, as specified in the procedure, and
          (ii) if consequent conduct is specified, then the relevant parties must so do.

Violation of any of the conditions in (4.17) will render a performative infelicitous or 'unhappy'. If conditions A or B are not observed, then what Austin described as a **misfire** takes place. For instance, in England, a registrar conducting a marriage ceremony in an unauthorized place will violate condition A (i), thus committing a misfire. The same is true for a clergyman baptizing the wrong baby, because in this case, condition A (ii) is not fulfilled. Next, as an illustration of a violation of condition B (i), consider the case of a bridegroom not saying the exact words that are conventionally laid down at a marriage ceremony.[3] As to condition B (ii), it dictates that the procedure must be complete. Thus, in making a bet, the bet is not 'on' unless *You are on* or something with the same effect is uttered by the addressee. In Austin's terminology, this counts as a satisfactory **uptake**,[4] the absence of which will again cause a misfire. Finally, if condition C is not met resulting in insincerities, then an **abuse** is the outcome. Examples of an abuse include congratulating someone when one knows that he or she passed his or her examination by cheating (condition C (i)), making a promise when one already intends to break it (condition C (ii)), and marrying without intending to consummate the marriage (see also Sadock's 2004 discussion of these conditions in terms of misinvocation, misexecution, and abuse). One of the problems of these felicity conditions is that as pointed out by Strawson (1964), they are over-impressed with ritualized or institutionalized acts. I shall return to the question of felicity conditions when we come to Searle's work later.

> Now have a go at Exercise 5 at the end of this chapter.

---

[3] The standard formula at a Church of England wedding has variants:

(i) The Book of Common Prayer version
Curate: Wilt thou have this woman to thy wedded wife, ...
Bridegroom: I will.
(ii) The Alternative Service Book version
Curate: (Name), will you take (Name) to be your wife ...
Bridegroom: I will.
In America, the following is also used.
(iii) Curate: Do you take this woman ...
Bridegroom: I do.

[4] Thomas (1995: 40–1) called performatives like betting '**collaborative**' **performatives**, because their success depends on particular uptake of another person. Other collaborative performatives include bequeathing and challenging.

4.3. Locutionary, illocutionary, and perlocutionary acts

The initial distinction made by Austin between performatives and constatives was soon to be rejected by him in favour of a general theory of speech acts. In fact, as pointed out by Levinson (1983: 231), there are two internal shifts in Austin's arguments. First, there is a switch from the view that performatives are a special class of sentences/utterances with peculiar syntactic and semantic properties to the view that there is a general class of performatives that encompasses both explicit and implicit performatives, the latter including many, if not all, other types of sentence/utterance. The second shift is from the performative/constative dichotomy to a general theory of illocutionary acts, of which the various performatives and constatives are just special subcases.

What led Austin to abandon the performative/constative dichotomy? In the first place, he noted that like performatives, constatives are also subject to the felicity conditions stated in (4.17). Recollect so-called 'Moore's paradox' discussed in Chapter 2, as illustrated by (4.18).

(4.18)   ?Princess Diana died in a fatal car crash in Paris with Dodi Al Fayed, but I don't believe it.

This utterance is infelicitous because it violates condition C (i) in (4.17). In the same vein, if someone utters (4.19) when he or she knows that John does not in fact have a wife, then its presupposition will not go through (see Chapter 3). The reason the presupposition fails to carry through is that condition A (ii) in (4.17) is not adhered to.

(4.19)   I'm sure John's wife is a feminist.

Secondly, Austin observed that performatives and constatives may be impossible to distinguish even in truth-conditional terms. On the one hand, there are '**loose**' constatives that may not be assessed strictly by means of truth conditions, as in (4.20).

(4.20)   a. (Austin 1962)
                France is hexagonal.
           b. John is bald.
           c. London is sixty miles from where I live.

France is not, strictly speaking, hexagonal. John still has quite a few wispy strands of hair on his head. London may not be exactly sixty miles from where the speaker lives. Thus, statements like those in (4.20) can only be said to be more or less or roughly true. On the other hand, there are utterances like those in (4.21) that pass the *hereby* test, and therefore are performatives by definition, but that nevertheless are used to assert or state. In these cases, the performatives must be counted simultaneously as constatives.

(4.21) a. I hereby state that John is growing GM crops.
      b. I hereby tell you that the prime minister is not going to stand down.
      c. I hereby hypothesize that there is water on Mars.

On the basis of such evidence, Austin concluded that constatives are nothing but a special class of performatives, and that the two-way distinction between performatives as action-performers and constatives as truth-bearers can no longer be maintained.

Consequently, Austin claimed that all utterances, in addition to meaning whatever they mean, perform specific acts via the specific communicative force of an utterance. Furthermore, he introduced a threefold distinction among the acts one simultaneously performs when saying something.

(4.22) Three facets of a speech act
      (i) Locutionary act: the production of a meaningful linguistic expression.
      (ii) Illocutionary act: the action intended to be performed by a speaker in uttering a linguistic expression, by virtue of the conventional force associated with it, either explicitly or implicitly.
      (iii) Perlocutionary act: the bringing about of consequences or effects on the audience through the uttering of a linguistic expression, such consequences or effects being special to the circumstances of the utterance.

A **locutionary act** or **locution** is the basic act of speaking, which itself consists of three related subacts. They are (i) a **phonic** act of producing an utterance-inscription, (ii) a **phatic** act of composing a particular linguistic expression in a particular language, and (iii) a **rhetic** act of contextualizing the utterance-inscription (Austin 1962; Lyons 1995: 177–85). In other words, the first of these three subacts is concerned with the physical act of making a certain sequence of vocal sounds (in the case of spoken language) or a set of written symbols (in the case of written language). The second refers to the act of constructing a well-formed string of sounds/symbols, be it a word, phrase, or sentence, in a particular language. The third subact is responsible for tasks such as assigning reference, resolving deixis, and disambiguating the utterance-inscription lexically and/or grammatically. These three subacts correspond broadly to the three distinct levels and modes of explanation in linguistic theory, namely, phonetics/phonology, morphology/syntax, and semantics/pragmatics.

When we say something, we usually say it with some purpose in mind. This is the illocutionary act or illocution. In other words, an **illocutionary act** or **illocution** refers to the type of function the speaker intends to fulfil or the type of action the speaker intends to accomplish in the course of producing an utterance. It is an act defined within a system of social conventions. In short, it is an act accomplished in speaking. Examples of illocutionary acts include accusing, apologizing, blaming, congratulating, giving permission, joking, nagging, naming, promising, ordering, refusing, swearing, and thanking. Whereas in some cases (such as stating, advising, and promising), the performance of an illocutionary act is entirely linguistic, in other cases (such as appointing, naming, and protesting), it may involve extralinguistic behaviour as well. The functions or actions that have been just mentioned are also commonly referred to as the **illocutionary force** of the utterance. Illocutionary force is frequently conveyed by what Searle (1969) called an **illocutionary force indicating device (IFID)**, the most direct and conventional type of which is an explicit performative in the form of (4.13). Indeed, the term 'speech act' in its narrow sense is often taken to refer specifically to illocutionary acts.

It should be mentioned at this point that the same linguistic expression can be used to carry out a wide variety of different speech acts, so that the same locutionary act can count as having different illocutionary forces in different contexts. Depending on the circumstances, (4.23) could be a predication, promise, offer, warning, or threat.[5]

(4.23)   I'll be there this afternoon.

In fact, Alston (1994) argued that the meaning of a sentence consists in its having a certain **illocutionary act potential (IAP)** that is closely and

---

[5] Notice that the following joke is based on the misunderstanding of the illocutionary force of the act performed by the customs officer. A request to declare goods on which tax should be paid is misinterpreted as an offer.

(i)   (At the customs of an international airport)
      Customs officer: Cigarettes, brandy, whisky...
      Foreign tourist: How nice you are in this country. Can I have a bottle of brandy?

conventionally associated with its form. On this view, to know what a sentence means is to know what range of illocutionary acts it can be conventionally used to perform (see also Recanati 2004b).

Conversely, the same speech act can be performed by different linguistic expressions, or the same illocutionary force can be realized by means of different locutionary acts. The utterances in (4.24), for example, illustrate different ways of carrying out the same speech act of requesting.

(4.24)   (At the ticket office in a railway station)
     a. A day return ticket to Oxford, please.
     b. Can I have a day return ticket to Oxford, please?
     c. I'd like a day return ticket to Oxford.

Roughly, three approaches to illocutionary acts (or speech acts in its narrow sense) can be identified: (i) **intentional**, (ii) **normative**, and (iii) **interactional**. While all three accounts take to some extent as a point of departure the received analysis of illocutionary acts made by Austin (1962) in terms of conventional procedures, and by Searle (1969) in terms of constitutive rules, the central tenet of the first perspective is that an illocutionary act is considered to be an expression of a speaker's intention and the addressee's recognition of it (e.g. Grice 1957, 1989; Strawson 1964; Bach and Harnish 1979; and see also Sadock 2004).[6] Next, on a normative view, with an illocutionary act, the speaker takes up certain commitments (e.g. Alston 2000). Finally, given the interactional position, it is assumed that an illocutionary act is explained in terms of a possibly tacit intersubjective agreement reached by interlocutors in the course of an interaction (e.g. Sbisà 2009). It is possible that the three approaches can to some extent be made complementary.

Finally, a **perlocutionary act** or **perlocution** concerns the effect an utterance may have on the addressee. Put slightly more technically, a perlocutionary act is the one by which the performance of an illocutionary act

---

[6] At this point, it should be mentioned that both Grice's theory of meaning$_{nn}$ or speaker-meaning and his theory of conversational implicature (Chapter 2) have greatly influenced the development of speech act theory, especially after the death of Austin. The former has brought to the fore the vital role that a speaker's intention plays in the production of a speech act, and the latter has been employed in speech act theory to account for how the addressee comprehends a speech act on the basis of pragmatic inference. I shall discuss the interpretation of indirect speech acts in Section 4.6.2.

produces a certain effect in or exerts a certain influence on the addressee. Still another way to put it is that a perlocutionary act represents a consequence or by-product of speaking, whether intentional or not. It is therefore an act performed by speaking. For example, in an armed bank robbery, a robber may utter (4.25) to get the cashier to open the safe. This effect of the act performed by speaking is also generally known as the **perlocutionary effect**.

(4.25)   My gun is loaded.

While there are unclear cases, the main differences between illocutionary acts and perlocutionary effects can be summed up as follows. In the first place, illocutionary acts are intended by the speaker, while perlocutionary effects are not always intended by him or her. Secondly, illocutionary acts are under the speaker's full control, while perlocutionary effects are not under his or her full control. Thirdly, if illocutionary acts are evident, they become evident as the utterance is made, while perlocutionary effects are usually not evident until after the utterance has been made (Hurford and Heasley 1983: 247). Fourthly, illocutionary acts are in principle determinate,[7] while perlocutionary effects are often indeterminate. Finally, illocutionary acts are more, while perlocutionary effects are less, conventionally tied to linguistic forms (see also Sadock 2004).

> At this point, see whether you can tackle Exercise 6 at the end of this chapter.

4.4. Searle's felicity conditions on speech acts

Recall our discussion of the felicity conditions specified by Austin in Section 4.2. Just as its truth conditions must be met by the world for a

---

[7] But there are situations in which an illocutionary act is not determinate, as the following example shows.
(i)   Employer: I'll come back to see how the work is progressing the day after tomorrow.
      Union representative: Is that a promise or a threat?

sentence to be said to be true (see Chapter 1), its felicity conditions must be fulfilled by the world for a speech act to be said to be felicitous. Searle (1969) took the view that the felicity conditions put forward by Austin are not only ways in which a speech act can be appropriate or inappropriate, but they also jointly constitute the illocutionary force. Put in a different way, the felicity conditions are the **constitutive rules**—rules that create the activity itself—of speech acts. On Searle's view, to perform a speech act is to obey certain conventional rules that are constitutive of that type of act. On the basis of the original Austinian felicity conditions, Searle formulated a new set of felicity conditions in terms of four basic categories, namely, (i) the propositional content, (ii) the preparatory condition, (iii) the sincerity condition, and (iv) the essential condition. As an illustration of these conditions, consider (4.26) and (4.27)

(4.26)   Searle's felicity conditions for promising
      (i) Propositional content: future act A of S
      (ii) Preparatory: (a) H would prefer S's doing A to his not doing A, and S so believes (b) It is not obvious to both S and H that S will do A in the normal course of events
      (iii) Sincerity: S intends to do A
      (iv) Essential: the utterance of e counts as an undertaking to do A

where S stands for the speaker, H for the hearer, A for the action, and e for the linguistic expression.

(4.27)   Searle's felicity conditions for requesting
      (i) Propositional content: future act A of H
      (ii) Preparatory: (a) S believes H can do A (b) It is not obvious that H would do A without being asked
      (iii) Sincerity: S wants H to do A
      (iv) Essential: the utterance of e counts as an attempt to get H to do A

Let us now work through these conditions one by one. The **propositional content condition** is in essence concerned with what the speech act is about. That is, it has to do with specifying the restrictions on the content of what remains as the 'core' of the utterance (i.e. Searle's **propositional act**) after the illocutionary act part is removed. For a promise, the propositional content is to predicate some future act of the speaker, whereas in the case of a request, it is to predicate some future act of the addressee. The **preparatory conditions** state the real-world prerequisites for the speech act. For a promise, these are roughly that the addressee would prefer the promised action to be accomplished, that the speaker knows this, but also that it is clear to both the speaker and the addressee that what is promised will not happen in the normal course of action. In the case of a request, the preparatory conditions are that the speaker has reason to believe that the addressee has the ability to carry out the action requested, and that if the addressee is not asked, he or she would not of themselves perform the action. Next, the **sincerity condition** must be satisfied if the act is to be performed sincerely. Thus, when carrying out an act of promising, the speaker must genuinely intend to keep the promise. When making a request, the speaker must want the addressee to do the requested action. Notice that if the sincerity condition is not fulfilled, the act is still performed, but there is an abuse, to use Austin's term. Finally, the **essential condition** defines the act being performed in the sense that the speaker has the intention that his or her utterance will count as the identifiable act, and that this intention is recognized by the addressee. Thus in the case of a promise, the speaker must have the intention to create an obligation to act, and for a request, the speaker must intend that his or her utterance counts as an attempt to get the addressee to do what is requested. Failure to meet the essential condition has the consequence that the act has not been carried out. One of the achievements of Searle's facility conditions is that they have avoided the over emphasis on institutionalized speech acts as shown by the original Austinian ones.

Now see what you make of Exercise 7 at the end of this chapter.

4.5. Searle's typology of speech acts

Can speech acts be classified, and if so, how? Austin (1962) grouped them into five types: (i) **verdictives**—giving a verdict, (ii) **exercitives**—exercising power, rights, or influence, (iii) **commissives**—promising or otherwise undertaking, (iv) **behabitives**—showing attitudes and social behaviour, and (v) **expositives**—fitting an utterance into the course of an argument or conversation. Since then, there have been many attempts to systematize, strengthen, and develop the original Austinian taxonomy. Some of these new classifications are formulated in formal/grammatical terms, others, in semantic/pragmatic terms, and still others, on the basis of the combined formal/grammatical and semantic/pragmatic modes (see e.g. Sadock 2004 for a review). Of all these (older and newer) schemes, Searle's (1975a) **typology of speech acts** remains the most influential. This is because it rests upon a clear and rich conceptual framework.

Under Searle's taxonomy, speech acts are universally grouped into five types along four dimensions: (i) **illocutionary point** or purpose of the type of act, which is a component of illocutionary force, (ii) **direction of fit** or relationship between words and world, (iii) **expressed psychological state**, and (iv) propositional content (see also Searle 1979, 2002, but see Section 4.7.1). The five types of speech acts are further explained below.

(i) **Representatives** (or **assertives**; the constatives in the original Austinian performative/constative dichotomy) are those kinds of speech acts that commit the speaker to the truth of the expressed proposition, and thus carry a truth-value. They express the speaker's belief. Paradigmatic cases include asserting, claiming, concluding, reporting, and stating. In performing this type of speech act, the speaker represents the world as he or she believes it is, thus making the words fit the world of belief. Representatives are illustrated in (4.28).

(4.28)   a. Chinese characters were borrowed to write other languages, notably Japanese, Korean, and Vietnamese.
         b. Francis Crick and Jim Watson discovered the double helix structure of DNA.
         c. The soldiers are struggling on through the snow.

(ii) **Directives** are those kinds of speech acts that represent attempts by the speaker to get the addressee to do something. They express the speaker's desire/wish for the addressee to do something. Paradigmatic cases include advice, commands, orders, questions, and requests. In using a directive, the speaker intends to elicit some future course of action on the part of the addressee, thus making the world match the words via the addressee. Directives are exemplified in (4.29).

(4.29)   a. Turn the TV down.
         b. Please don't use my electric shaver.
         c. Could you please get that lid off for me?

(iii) **Commissives** are those kinds of speech acts that commit the speaker to some future course of action. They express the speaker's intention to do something. Paradigmatic cases include offers, pledges, promises, refusals, and threats. In the case of a commissive, the world is adapted to the words via the speaker him- or herself. Examples of commissives are presented in (4.30).

(4.30)   a. I'll be back in five minutes.
       b. We'll be launching a new policing unit to fight cyber crime on the internet soon.
       c. I'll never buy you another computer game.

(iv) **Expressives** are those kinds of speech acts that express a psychological attitude or state of the speaker such as joy, sorrow, and likes/dislikes. Paradigmatic cases include apologizing, blaming, congratulating, praising, and thanking. There is no direction of fit for this type of speech act.[8]

(4.31)   a. Well done, Elizabeth!
       b. I'm so happy.
       c. Wow, great![9]

(v) **Declarations** (or **declaratives**) are those kinds of speech acts that effect immediate changes in some current state of affairs. Because they tend to rely on elaborate extralinguistic institutions for their successful performance, they may be called '**institutionalized performatives**'. In performing this type of speech act, the speaker brings about changes in the world; that is, he or she effects a correspondence between the propositional content and the world. Paradigmatic cases include bidding in bridge, declaring war, excommunicating, firing from employment, and nominating a candidate. As to the direction of fit, it is both words-to-world and world-to-words.[10]

---

[8] Alternatively, one might claim, as Yule (1996: 55) did, that in performing the speech act of an expressive, the speaker makes known what he or she feels, thus rendering the words to fit the world of feeling.

[9] In many languages including English, sentences with the import of the following are often used to express one's strong emotions.

(i)   a.   I simply don't know what to say!
     b.   I'm absolutely speechless!
     c.   No words can express my . . . !

[10] Notice that some performative verbs in English can fit into more than one of Searle's categories. They include *advise, confess, suggest, tell,* and *warn.*

(i)   I warn you not to dance/against dancing on the table. (directive)
(ii)   I warn you that there are no train services on Sundays. (assertive)

(4.32) a. President: I declare a state of national emergency.
   b. Chairman: The meeting is adjourned.
   c. Jury foreman: We find the defendant not guilty.

Speech act types, illocutionary points, directions of fit, and expressed psychological states can be summarized in (4.33) (SOA = state of affairs) (see Vanderveken 1994 for a formalization in terms of illocutionary logic).[11]

(4.33)

Speech act type	Illocutionary point	Direction of fit	Expressed psychological state
Representative	presenting a true SOA	words-to-world	belief (speaker)
Directive	attempting to get someone to bring about an SOA	world-to-words	desire (addressee)
Commissive	committing to bring about an SOA	world-to-words	intention (speaker)
Expressive	communicating an attitude or emotion about an SOA	none	variable (speaker)
Declaration	bringing about an SOA	both	none (speaker)

Now attempt Exercise 8 at the end of this chapter.

4.6. Indirect speech acts

4.6.1. What is an indirect speech act?

Most of the world's languages have three basic sentence types: (i) declarative, (ii) interrogative, and (iii) imperative.[12] In some languages, the three

---

[11] In Searle (1983), there were also three directions of fit between mind and the world: (i) the mind-to-world direction of fit, (ii) the world-to-mind direction of fit, and (iii) the empty direction of fit. De Sousa Melo (2002) argued that a fourth direction of fit—the double direction of fit—be added to Searle's typology, paralleling the four directions of fit between words and the world.

[12] There are languages in the world that lack a genuine declarative. One such language is Hidatsa, as described in Sadock and Zwicky (1985).

major sentence types are distinguished morphologically and/or syntactically. Somali provides an example of such a language.

(4.34)   (Saeed 2003: 237)
    a. Warkii   waad   dhegeysatay.
       news the DECL-you listen to-2SG-PAST
       'You listened to the news.'
    b. Warkii   miyaad dhegeysatay.
       news the Q-you   listen to-2SG-PAST
       'Did you listen to the news?'
    c. Warkii   dhegeyso.
       news the listen to-2SG-IMPV
       'Listen to the news.'

In (4.34), the declarative format is marked by *waa*, the interrogative format
is indicated by *ma*, and the imperative format is indicated with a zero
marking (Saeed 2003: 237). Another example is provided by Greenlandic.

(4.35)   (Sadock and Zwicky 1985)
    a. Igavoq.
       cook-INDIC-3SG
       'He cooks.'
    b. Igava.
       cook-Q-3SG
       'Does he cook?'

In (4.35), the declarative and interrogative are differentiated by means of
separate personal suffixes (Sadock and Zwicky 1985). Finally, in Lakhota,
the difference between a 'declarative' with an indefinite pronoun and an
interrogative with an interrogative pronoun is marked by the adding of a
sentence-final question particle. (Notice that the indefinite and interrogative
pronouns are identical.) This is illustrated in (4.36).

(4.36)   (Croft 1994)
    a. Mniluzahe Othuwahe ekta tuwa ya.
       Rapid   City   to   who go-3SG
       'Someone went to Rapid City.'
    b. Mniluzahe Othuwahe ekta tuwa ya   he?
       Rapid   City   to   who go-3SG Q
       'Who went to Rapid City?'

Moreover, the three major sentence types are typically associated with the
three basic illocutionary forces, namely, asserting/stating, asking/questioning,

and ordering/requesting, respectively. Thus, the three Somali sentences in (4.34), for instance, may be paraphrased using explicit performatives.

(4.37) a. I (hereby) state that you listened to the news.
      b. I (hereby) enquire whether you listened to the news.[13]
      c. I (hereby) order you to listen to the news.

Now, if there is a direct match between a sentence type and an illocutionary force, we have a **direct speech act**. In addition, explicit performatives, which happen to be in the declarative form, are also taken to be direct speech acts, because they have their illocutionary force explicitly named by the performative verb in the main part (or 'matrix clause') of the sentence. On the other hand, if there is no direct relationship between a sentence type and an illocutionary force, we are faced with an **indirect speech act**. Thus, when an explicit performative is used to make a request, as in (4.38), it functions as a direct speech act; the same is the case when an imperative is employed, as in (4.39). By comparison, when an interrogative is used to make a request, as in (4.40), we have an indirect speech act.

(4.38) I request you to pass the salt.
(4.39) Pass the salt.
(4.40) Can you pass the salt?

In short, the validity of the distinction between direct and indirect speech act is dependent on whether or not one subscribes to what Levinson (1983: 264, 274) called the **literal force hypothesis**—the view that there is a direct structure–function correlation in speech acts and that sentence forms are by default direct reflexes of their underlying illocutionary forces.

There are, however, problems at the very heart of the literal force hypothesis. One is that there are cases of speech acts where even the direct link between performative verbs and speech acts breaks down. Consider (4.41).

---

[13] Some native speakers of English may find sentences like (4.37b) odd (e.g. Sadock and Zwicky 1985). For this group of speakers, the interrogative is a sentence type for which there is no explicit performative equivalent. A better example may be provided by the exclamation in English.

(i) a. What a beautiful girl she is!
     b. ?I (hereby) exclaim what a beautiful girl she is.
     c. I exclaimed what a beautiful girl she was.

As shown by (ia) and (ib), the exclamation in English does not have a corresponding explicit performative, though the verb *exclaim* can be used descriptively.

(4.41)   I promise to sack you if you don't finish the job by this weekend.

In (4.41), the performative verb is *promise*, but the illocutionary force that is most naturally ascribed to this speech act is that of either a threat or a warning. This shows that contrary to the main prediction of the literal force hypothesis, we cannot always identify speech acts even with sentences that contain a performative verb.

Secondly and more importantly, as pointed out by Levinson (1983: 264), most usages are indirect.[14] The speech act of requesting, for example, is very rarely performed by means of an imperative in English. Instead, it is standardly carried out indirectly. Furthermore, there are probably infinitely many varieties of sentence that can be used to make a request indirectly, as shown in (4.42) (adapted from Levinson 1983: 264–5, see also Bertolet 1994 and Holdcroft 1994).

(4.42)   a. I want you to close the window.
      b. Can you close the window?
      c. Will you close the window?
      d. Would you close the window?
      e. Would you mind closing the window?
      f. You ought to close the window.
      g. May I ask you to close the window?
      h. I wonder if you'd mind closing the window.

> See whether you can tackle Exercise 9 at the end of this chapter now.

4.6.2. How is an indirect speech act analysed?

Roughly, there are three main approaches. The first is to assume the existence of a **dual illocutionary force**, as proposed by Searle (1975b). On this assumption, an indirect speech act has two illocutionary forces, one literal or direct and the other non-literal or indirect. While the literal/direct force is secondary, the non-literal/indirect force is primary. Next, whether an utterance can be used to perform an indirect speech act has to do with the relevant felicity conditions. For example, (4.40) both infringes the felicity

---

[14] As we will shortly see in Section 4.7, the degree of directness/indirectness may vary cross-linguistically. See also note 18.

condition for the act of questioning and queries the preparatory condition for the act of requesting. This explains why it can function as an indirect speech act whereas (4.43), for example, cannot. The reason is that in the case of (4.43), the felicity conditions are irrelevant.

(4.43) (Searle 1975b)
        Salt is made of sodium chloride.

Finally, on Searle's view, a speaker's performing and an addressee's understanding of an indirect speech act always involves some kind of inference, along the general lines of the rational, co-operative model of communication articulated by Grice (see Chapter 2 and note 6).[15]

Another interesting characteristic of indirect speech acts is that they are frequently conventionalized (Morgan 1978). This can be illustrated by the fact that of various, apparently synonymous linguistic expressions, only one may conventionally be used to convey an indirect speech act. Consider (4.44).

(4.44) a. Are you able to pass the salt?
        b. Do you have the ability to pass the salt?

Under Searle's analysis, both (4.44a) and (4.44b) would be expected to be able to perform the indirect speech act of requesting, because (i) they are largely synonymous with (4.40), and (ii) they, too, inquire about the satisfaction of the addressee-based preparatory condition for making a request. But this expectation is not fulfilled.

Searle's response to this puzzle is that there is also a certain degree of conventionality about indirect speech acts, and this may be accounted for in terms of convention of use/meaning. Inspired by the insight of Searle's, Morgan (1978) developed a notion of **short-circuited implicature** to cover inference involved in cases like (4.40). In these cases, while the relevant conversational implicature is in principle calculable, it is not in practice calculated (see also Horn and Bayer 1984; Horn 1988). From a linguistic point of view, then, the conventionality here is correlated with the possible occurrence of *please*. While *please* can be inserted before the verb *pass* in (4.38)–(4.40) as in (4.45a)–(4.45c), it cannot in (4.44), as shown in (4.45d) and (4.45e).

---

[15] See e.g. Vanderveken (2002) for an attempt to reformulate Grice's maxims in terms of speech acts. See Dascal (1994) for a comparison between speech act theory and the Gricean theory of conversational implicature.

(4.45) a. I request you to please pass the salt.
        b. Please pass the salt.
        c. Can you please pass the salt?
        d. ?Are you able to please pass the salt?
        e. ?Do you have the ability to please pass the salt?

Furthermore, the conventionality indicated by *please* in (4.45a) and (4.45b) is one of meaning (that is, a **convention of language**), hence the speech act of requesting is performed directly. By contrast, the conventionality signalled by *please* in (4.45c) is one of use (that is, a **convention of usage**), and thus we have an indirect speech act.[16]

A second, rather similar, approach is due to Gordon and Lakoff (1975). In their analysis, there are inference rules called 'conversational postulates' that reduce the amount of inference needed to interpret an indirect speech act. Thus, in the case of (4.40), if the question interpretation cannot be intended by the speaker, then the utterance will be read as being equivalent to his or her having said (4.38), hence resulting in the performance of the indirect speech act of requesting. Stated this way, the conversational postulates proposed by Gordon and Lakoff can be seen as another reflection of the conventionality of indirect speech acts. As to the similarities and differences between Searle's and Gordon and Lakoff's accounts, the major similarity is that both analyses assume that the interpretation of indirect speech acts involves both inference and conventionality; the major difference is concerned with the question of balance, namely, how much of the work involved in computing an indirect speech act is inferential and how much is conventional.

Finally, in contrast to the **inferential model** we have just discussed, there is the **idiom model**. According to this model, sentences like (4.40) are semantically ambiguous, and the request interpretation constitutes a **speech act idiom** that involves no inference at all. In other words, (4.40) is simply recognized as a request with no question being perceived. This is the position taken by Sadock (1974). But the idiom analysis is not without problems. One problem is that it fails to capture the fact that the meaning

---

[16] As Searle (1975b) and Green (1975) showed, the use of the *Can/Would you ...* type question to indirectly express requests and orders varies cross-linguistically (see also Wierzbicka 1991). According to Horn (1988), given that a short-circuited implicature is itself a matter of convention, this is to be expected.

of an indirect speech act can frequently be derived from the meaning of its components (cf. the Fregean principle of compositionality, see Chapter 3). In addition, these would-be idioms turn out to be quite comparable cross-linguistically. For example, like their English equivalent in (4.46), (4.47)–(4.50) in Arabic, Chinese, German, and Modern Greek can all be used to perform an indirect speech act of requesting.[17]

(4.46)   It's cold in here.

(4.47)   (Arabic)
      ?innahu   bardun   huna.
      it's-3-M-S cold   in here
      'It's cold in here.'

(4.48)   (Chinese)
      zher   zhen   leng.
      here   really   cold
      'It's really cold in here.'

(4.49)   (German)
      Es   ist   sehr   kalt   hier   drin.
      it   is   very   cold   here   in
      'It's very cold in here.'

(4.50)   (Modern Greek)
      Kani   krio edo   mesa.
      it is doing   cold here   in
      'It's cold in here.'

Furthermore, given the idiom model, an interpretation that takes into account the literal meaning or the direct illocutionary force of an indirect speech act is not allowed. This, however, leaves examples like (4.51) unexplained.

(4.51)   A: Can you pass the salt?
      B: Yes, I can. (Here it is.)

---

[17] Intuitively, the requests in (4.46)–(4.50) are more indirectly conveyed than that in (4.40). As noted by Green (1975) and Horn (1988), in contrast to the request in (4.40), the requests in (4.46)–(450) are non-short-circuited, and hence non-detachable implicatures. Consequently, they are not subject to cross-linguistic variation.

4.6.3. Why is an indirect speech act used? Some remarks on politeness and impoliteness

Why, then, do people use indirect speech acts? One answer is that the use of indirect speech acts is in general associated with politeness. Indirect speech acts are usually considered to be more polite than their direct counterparts. Furthermore, the more indirect a speech act, the more polite (e.g. Searle 1975b).[18]

There is a very extensive body of literature on politeness and impoliteness, and this is not the place for me to give a full review of it. Instead, in what follows, I shall provide a brief discussion of politeness and impoliteness with special reference to speech acts.

Politeness

What is politeness?
Politeness can be defined as any behaviour including verbal behaviour of an interlocutor to maintain his or her face and that of the individuals he or she is interacting with. As pointed out by Brown (forthcoming), different aspects of this behaviour are captured by terms such as 'manners', 'courtesy', 'tact', 'deference', 'sensibility', 'poise', 'rapport', 'urbanity', 'civility', and

---

[18] This can be illustrated by English. Consider (i)–(v).

(i)　Call Lucy a taxi, please.
(ii)　Will you call Lucy a taxi?
(iii)　Would you call Lucy a taxi?
(iv)　Would you mind calling Lucy a taxi?
(v)　I wonder if you'd mind calling Lucy a taxi?

The speech act of requesting is performed more indirectly, for example, using (iii) than using (i), and therefore the utterance in (iii) is considered more polite than that in (i). But this may not be the case with, say, Polish, as argued by, for example, Wierzbicka (1991). The same can be said of Russian, in which a high degree of unmitigated directness has been observed in the performance of a number of speech act types (Watts 2003: 15, and see also Sifianou 1992 on Greek). These were corroborated by Ogiermann (2009a, 2009b), who argued against the correlation between indirectness and politeness on the basis of a study of apologies and requests in English, German, Polish, and Russian. All this raises the question of whether or not indirect speech acts are universally more polite than their direct counterparts.

'graciousness'.[19] More recently, a distinction has been introduced by Watts, Ide, and Ehlich (2005) between first- and second-order politeness. By **first-order politeness** or **politeness 1** is meant the common-sense notion of normative politeness, that is, a judgement about whether a particular behaviour is polite or not in keeping with the norms of a socio-cultural or speech community, made by lay members of that community. In contrast, **second-order politeness** or **politeness 2** refers to a scientific concept of politeness, that is, an abstract, theoretical construct defined within a theory of politeness and impoliteness. Furthermore, it should be pointed out that there is a dynamic trade-off between the two notions of politeness. For example, second-order politeness, which is informed by first-order politeness, is a concept that is more inclusive than first-order politeness. Consequently, first- and second-order politeness should be studied hand in hand rather than in isolation. Finally, this dualistic distinction between an everyday and a technical sense of a notion can be applied to other concepts like face and impoliteness in the study of politeness and impoliteness (see also e.g. Watts 2003; Terkourafi 2012).

Brown and Levinson's 'face-saving' model of politeness
Currently, there are a variety of theoretical accounts of politeness. These include (i) the **'social norm' model**, (ii) the **'conversational maxim' model** (e.g. Lakoff 1973; Leech 1983, 2007) (see also note 11 of Chapter 2), (iii) the **'face-saving' model** (Brown and Levinson 1978, 1987), (iv) the **'conversational contract' model** (e.g. Fraser 1990), (v) the **'social practice' model** (e.g. Watts 2003), and (vi) the **'discursive'** or **'post-modern' model** (Ellen 2001; Locher and Watts 2005; Watts 2008).[20] Of these frameworks, Brown and

---

[19] The English word *polite(ness)* is derived from the Latin word *politus*, meaning 'being polished'. According to the *Oxford English Dictionary*, the first use of *polite(ness)* was recorded in 1450, with the sense of 'being polished'. The word was later redefined as 'being of refined manner' in 1762. Prescriptive etiquette writings can be traced back at least to both ancient China and Egypt. One of the earliest books on politeness in the Western tradition seems to be *Libro del cortegiano* (The book of the courtier) by Castiglioner Baldesar, which was published in 1528 (DuFon et al. 1994). Henri Bergson's (1885) *La Politesse* (Politeness) contains a philosophical discussion of three types of politeness: (i) politeness of manners, (ii) politeness of mind, and (iii) politeness of the heart (Brown, forthcoming).

[20] Cf. Brown (forthcoming) identified three analytical approaches to politeness, developed in the 1970s and 1980s, namely, (i) politeness as social rules or norms, (ii)

Levinson's classic 'face-saving' model— generally considered to have inaug-
urated the field of modern politeness and impoliteness study—remains the
most influential one.

Brown and Levinson's theory of (second-order) politeness was developed
within the framework of classical and neo-Gricean pragmatics (see
Chapter 2) and to a lesser extent that of speech act theory. At the heart of
the model lies Goffman's (1967) sociological notion of face. Simply put, **face**
is 'the public self-image that every member wants to claim for himself'
(Brown and Levinson 1987: 61). Stated in another way, face means roughly
an individual's self-esteem.[21] Furthermore, there are two aspects to face.
First, there is **positive face**, which represents an individual's desire to be
approved of, accepted, admired, liked, and validated by others. **Positive
politeness** orients to preserving the positive face of others. When one uses
positive politeness, one tends to choose the speech strategies that emphasize
one's solidarity with the addressee. These strategies include claiming 'common ground' with the addressee, conveying that the speaker and the
addressee are co-operators, and satisfying the addressee's wants (Brown
and Levinson 1987: 101–29). Secondly, we have **negative face**, which refers
to an individual's right to freedom of action and his or her need not to be
imposed on by others. **Negative politeness** orients to maintaining the negative face of others. When one employs negative politeness, one tends to opt
for the speech strategies that emphasize one's deference for the addressee.

politeness as adherence to politeness maxims, and (iii) politeness as strategic face
management.

[21] Face is originally a Chinese concept. There are a number of words in Chinese
that can be used to express the notion: *lian* (face), *mianzi* (reputation, prestige, face),
and *lianmian* (face, self-respect). According to some scholars (e.g. Ho 1976), while
lian refers to 'the confidence of a society in the integrity of the ego's moral character,
the loss of which makes it impossible for him to function properly within the
community', by *mianzi* is meant an individual's earned prestige, achieved through
accomplishment or success. It seems that this concept of (first-order) face was
introduced to the West by the Chinese anthropologist Shien Chin Hu in the 1940s
(e.g. Scollon and Scollon 1995: 34).

A number of my students at Auckland University told me that in the Pacific
cultures (such as Cook Islands, Maori, Niue, Samoan, and Tongan) face is in general
considered to be one of the most sacred parts of the body, because it is part of the
head. 'Saving face' has often saved a nation, launched a war against a tribe, and
caused thousands of people to die.

Typical linguistic realizations of the strategies of negative politeness involve, for example, the use of conventional indirectness, hedges on illocutionary force, and apologies (Brown and Levinson 1987: 130). Defined thus, face is considered to be a universal notion in any human society. As *rational* agents, conversational participants will ideally try to preserve both their own face and their interlocutor's face in a verbal interaction. (Notice that in addition to face, rationality is the other basic ingredient in this model, see e.g. Brown, forthcoming.)

Many types of speech act such as complaints, disagreements (e.g. Locher 2004; Angouri and Locher 2012), and requests intrinsically threaten face. Hence, they are called '**face-threatening acts**' (**FTAs**). In the first place, FTAs can threaten an addressee's positive face. These include expressions of disapproval, accusations, criticisms, disagreements, and insults. Secondly, they can attack an addressee's negative face. Advice, orders, requests, suggestions, and warnings are some of the examples of this variety of FTAs. Thirdly, a speaker can damage his or her own positive face by performing, for example, the speech act of apologizing. And fourthly, he or she can threaten his or her own negative face by performing the speech act of accepting apologies. Notice further that since both the speaker and the addressee are co-operating to maintain face under normal circumstances, those FTAs that attack primarily the addressee's face will also potentially damage the speaker's face, and vice versa (Brown and Levinson 1987: 65–8).

In an attempt to capture the extralinguistic context of an FTA, Brown and Levinson (1987: 74) posited three independent and culturally sensitive social variables, according to which the weightiness or seriousness of an FTA can be measured. First, there is the **social distance** (**D**) between the speaker and the addressee. Second is the **relative power** (**P**) of the addressee over the speaker. Finally, the third variable is the **absolute ranking** (**R**) of imposition in a particular language/culture. Brown and Levinson formulated their equation of calculation in (4.52).

(4.52) $W_x = D(S, H) + P(H, S) + R_x$

where W stands for weightiness, x for any particular FTA, S for speaker, and H for addressee. Given the equation in (4.52), the weightiness of a particular FTA can then be determined by the adding up of the extent of the social distance between the speaker and the addressee, the degree of power the addressee has over the speaker, and the extent to which the FTA is deemed to be an imposition in a particular language/culture. Consequently, the amount of face work needed or the degree of politeness required can be worked out to avoid or weaken the FTA.

Finally, on the Brown and Levinson model, there is a set of five linguistic and non-linguistic strategies one can choose from to redress an FTA. The set of strategies is given in (4.53) (Brown and Levinson 1987: 60).

(4.53)   Brown and Levinson's set of FTA-avoiding strategies

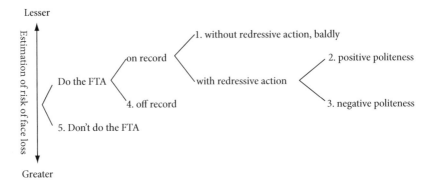

Notice that in (4.53), the set of strategies are ordered along a continuum of least-to-most remedial action or redress. More specifically, seen the other way round, the more threatening an FTA is, the more polite (i.e. the higher-numbered) the strategy a speaker must employ to mitigate its effects.

Let me now explore these strategies in somewhat greater detail. In the first place, one can perform an FTA on record, that is, directly; or off record, that is, indirectly, for example, by dropping a verbal hint. Secondly, an FTA on record can be performed either baldly, that is, without redress; or with redress. In the latter case, there are two further choices: an FTA can be performed with a **face-saving act** using either positive politeness redress (such as emphasizing solidarity with the addressee) or negative politeness redress (such as giving deference to the addressee). Positive politeness redress is ranked lower than negative politeness redress. Finally, there is also the option for one not to perform an FTA at all, for instance, by dropping a non-verbal hint. These five strategies can be illustrated in (4.54).

(4.54)   Situation: John, a student, asks Mary, another student, to lend him her lecture notes
1. *On record, without redress, baldly:*
    Lend me your lecture notes.
2. *On record, with positive politeness redress/showing solidarity:*
    How about letting me have a look at your lecture notes?

3. *On record, with negative politeness redress/showing deference:*
   Could you please lend me your lecture notes?
4. *Off record/offering verbal hints:*
   I didn't take any notes for the last lecture.
5. *Don't perform the FTA/offering non-verbal hints:*
   [John silently looks at Mary's lecture notes.]

In summary, the main aim of Brown and Levinson's 'face-saving' enterprise is to formulate a universal theory of politeness in terms of a universally applicable and testable 'etic' set of concepts such as face management, social factors, and general types of strategies of politeness, in accordance with which the universal patterns of politeness that have been observed can be accounted for in 'emic' terms for any particular speech and/or socio-cultural community. The etic–emic distinction used here is derived from that between phonetic and phonemic analyses. By an **etic** concept is meant an analytical concept that is drawn from a universal set, which is defined from outside a particular language/culture and is employed to compare behavioural or linguistic systems across different languages/cultures. In contrast, an **emic** concept comes from a within-language/within-culture set, which is utilized to describe a system in its own terms. Defined thus, the etic–emic contrast is often conflated with cross-linguistic/cross-cultural versus within-linguistic/within-cultural analysis (see especially Brown, forthcoming).

You may now be ready to tackle Exercise 10 at the end of this chapter.

Since its publication in 1978, the Brown and Levinson model has generated an enormous amount of research on politeness (and impoliteness). From an empirical point of view, while Brown and Levinson's account is based on an in-depth study of three unrelated languages/cultures, namely, Tamil, Tzeltal, and English (both British and American), politeness phenomena in a much wider array of languages/cultures ranging from Catalan through Japanese to Turkish have now been carefully studied.[22] Conceptually, many of the studies have focused on the universality of aspects of the Brown and Levinson model such as face (both positive and negative),

---

[22] But as we will see shortly, there is unevenness in politeness study geographically. For example, as observed by Brown (forthcoming), virtually no or very little research has been carried out with regard to politeness in areas or regions such as Papua New Guinea, aboriginal Australia, Oceania, South Asia, and Central and North Amerindia.

politeness (both positive and negative), the three social variables, and the set of five politeness strategies. In a cross-cultural comparison between the politeness system in England and that in Greece, Sifianou (1992) argued that whereas in British English, it is more negative face oriented, in Greek, it is more positive face oriented. (Likely, according to Watts 2003: 15, the Russian conceptualization of (first-order) politeness is also positive face oriented, emphasizing the expression of intimacy and the display of warmth and friendliness.) While arguing for the differences arising from negative versus positive face/politeness, Sifianou's study nevertheless showed that Brown and Levinson's theory provides an excellent general theoretical and descriptive framework for the study of politeness. On the other hand, a number of scholars have found it rather difficult to apply the Brown and Levinson model directly to the politeness system in the Asian, collective cultures. See, for example, Gu (1990), Mao (1994), Lee-Wong (2000), Pan and Kadar (2011), and Jiang (2012) on Chinese; Matsumoto (1988, 1989) and Ide (1989) on Japanese; Hwang (1990) and Byon (2006) on Korean; Bayraktaroglou (2001) and Zeyrek (2001) on Turkish; and Koutlaki (2002) on Persian. See Kadar and Mills (2011), which discusses politeness not only in China, Japan, and Korea but also in Vietnam and Singapore. Finally, see also Platt, Weber, and Ho (1983) on Malay English, which has a phrase *water face*, borrowed from Malay. More or less the same can be said of some African languages/cultures. Nwoye (1992), for instance, carried out a study of the notion of face in Igbo. According to this investigation, the Igbo society is more concerned with the collective self-image of a group than the individualistic self-image of any one member of the group. Put slightly differently, in such a language/culture, **group face**, defined as 'the individual's desire to behave in conformity with culturally expected forms of behaviour', is more important than **individualistic** or **self-face**. It is for 'the avoidance of behaviour capable of lowering the public self-image or self-worthiness of one's group, dictated by the fear of *imecu iru* (to darken face)'. By contrast, self-face is 'the individual's desire to attend to his/her personal needs and to place his/her public self-image above those of others' (Nwoye 1992, see also Agyekun 2004 on the concept of face in Akan). Strecker (1993) also argued that the politeness system of the Hamer in south Ethiopia presents a challenge to Brown and Levinson's theory (see also Cowell 2007 on **communal face** in Arapaho; O'Driscoll 2007 and Arundale 2010 on face in general; Ogiermann 2012 on politeness in Polish; Ogiermann and Sus-zczyńska 2011 on politeness and impoliteness in East Europe; and Haugh and

Schneider 2012 on politeness and impoliteness across Englishes). Based on these research works, it has been argued that Brown and Levinson's construal of face as individual wants needs to be rethought, especially within the non-Western languages/cultures. But more recently, this view, which has been dominating the field for around two decades, has been challenged. Leech (2007), for example, contended that face and politeness in the Western and non-Western (especially East Asian) languages/cultures are fundamentally similar, though at a deeper level (see also Chen 2010a for a survey of the debate). To this, we can add Brown and Levinson's most recent rebuttal to the non-universalist position. As already mentioned, the main goal of the Brown and Levinson model is to develop a universal theory of politeness in terms of a universally applicable and testable 'etic' set of concepts, by which face and politeness can be analysed in 'emic' terms for any particular language/culture. Consequently, in the Brown and Levinson framework, face wants and the like in 'etic' notions may sometimes not be necessarily consistent with those in 'emic' ones. While there are cross-linguistic/cross-cultural differences in face and politeness, there are also cross-linguistic/cross-cultural parallels in them. It is the universal underpinnings of face and politeness, argues Brown (forthcoming), that should be given a greater theoretical attention. In other words, a theory of politeness (and impoliteness) should be formulated in such a way as to be allowed to generalize across different linguistic/cultural systems (Brown, forthcoming; see also Schöll 2011 on the acquisition of politeness by children).

Finally, in addition to face and politeness, other theoretical issues that have been debated include (i) what is the scope of the phenomena considered under the rubric of 'politeness', (ii) politeness 1 versus politeness 2 and the individual-social relationship, (iii) whether politeness is communicated or taken for granted, and (iv) politeness should be looked at from the viewpoint of the individual, the dyad, or the social group (see Brown, forthcoming; see also Mills 2003 on politeness and gender, and Hoza 2007 on politeness in American Sign Language). But the space at my disposal precludes discussion of them.

Impoliteness

What is impoliteness?
Impoliteness may be defined as any face-aggravating behaviour including verbal behaviour relevant to a particular context. Terms like 'social gaffes/

gaucheness', 'rudeness', and 'insults' are often used to describe aspects of this behaviour. For some scholars, impoliteness has to be intentional (on the part of the speaker) and has to be perceived or constructed as intentional (on the part of the addressee) (e.g. Bousfield 2008; Locher and Bousfield 2008; Culpeper 2011).[23] For others, a speaker's intention plays no part in impoliteness (e.g. Locher and Watts 2008). If intention and recognition of it are involved, then **rudeness** rather than impoliteness occurs (e.g. Terkourafi 2008; Jobert and Jamet 2013). Like face and politeness, impoliteness can also be divided into **first-order impoliteness** or **impoliteness 1** and **second-order impoliteness** or **impoliteness 2**.

A typology of impoliteness
According to Culpeper (2011), there are three types of impoliteness: (i) affective, (ii) coercive, and (iii) entertaining. The first, **affective impoliteness** refers to the variety of impoliteness that displays a speaker's heightened emotional state, typically anger, towards the addressee or a third party for creating the negative emotional state for the speaker, as in (4.55). Secondly, by **coercive impoliteness** is meant the type of impoliteness that attempts a rebalance of values between a speaker and his or her target so that the speaker can gain, maintain, and reinforce his or her benefits. Coercive impoliteness usually involves with a conflict of interests and an imbalance of power. It is a typical means of pursuing power through language. This is exemplified in (4.56). Finally, there is **entertaining impoliteness**—the variety of impoliteness that involves a speaker's exploitative entertainment at the expense of a target. As an illustrating example, we have (4.57). Described in this way, all three types of impoliteness are second-order impoliteness.

(4.55)   You're driving me mad.
(4.56)   Shut up, or I'll zip your mouth!
(4.57)   (In response to Miss Havisham's invitation to play cards with Pip)
          Estella: With this boy! Why, he is a common labouring-boy.
          (Charles Dickens, *Great Expectations*)

[23] Interestingly enough, 2008 was named 'The Year of Impoliteness'. But it should be noted that impoliteness including conflict talk has been a research topic in sociolinguistics and anthropological linguistics since at least the 1970s. See Brown (forthcoming) for a brief survey.

Analyses

Regarding impoliteness, one of the major criticisms levelled against the Brown and Levinson model is that it marginalizes impoliteness by taking impoliteness as a phenomenon and/or concept that is related not to face itself but to the absence of it. Ellen (2001), for example, was of the view that traditional theories of politeness have three main problems with respect to impoliteness. First, they are conceptually biased toward the politeness end of the politeness–impoliteness distinction. Secondly, they conceptualize politeness and impoliteness as opposites. And thirdly, their conceptualizations of impoliteness are speaker-based, focusing largely on utterance production. In addition, while speech acts can mitigate face-threat or even boost or enhance face, they can also attack face deliberately. As a consequence, in the last decade, there has been an upsurge on work in impoliteness research that seeks to theorize impoliteness in its own right rather than treating it merely as the reverse of politeness (e.g. Garcés-Conejos Blitvich 2010).

According to Garcés-Conejos Blitvich, current theoretical approaches to impoliteness, which are broadly social constructionist in nature, can be divided into three categories: (i) the **impoliteness 1** or the **discursive/post-modern model** (e.g. Ellen 2001; Locher and Watt 2005), (ii) the **impoliteness 2** or the **universalist/context-sensitive model**, and (iii) the **blended genre model**. Notice further that within the second category, there are a number of analyses such as (i) the frame-based view (e.g. Terkourafi 2012; Haugh 2007), the Face Constituting Theory (e.g. Arundale 2010), and work by Culpeper (2011) and Bousfield (2008) (see e.g. Garcés-Conejos Blitvich 2010 for a review of these analyses).

Whereas much progress has been made, research on impoliteness is still in its infancy. There are still many fundamental questions that need an answer. These include: (i) what is the relationship between impoliteness and politeness, for example, Austin (1990) called impoliteness the 'dark side' of politeness, and (ii) what is the role played by a speaker's intention in impoliteness. In order to provide an answer to these and other (related) questions and to attain a better understanding of impoliteness, I believe that the next decade will continue to see a florescence of studies of this important topic in sociopragmatics (see also, e.g., the articles collected in Bax and Kadar 2012 for historical politeness and impoliteness, and chapter 7 of Jucker and Taavitsainen 2013 for politeness and impoliteness in Old, Middle, and Early Modern English).

4.7. Speech acts and culture[24]

4.7.1. Cross-cultural variation

Many speech acts are culture-specific. This is particularly so in the case of **institutionalized** or **ritualized speech acts**, which typically use standardized and stereotyped formulae and are performed in public ceremonies. A good example is provided by the speech act of divorcing. In some Muslim cultures, under the appropriate circumstances, the uttering of a sentence with the import of (4.58) three times consecutively by a husband to his wife (who is also a Muslim) will *ipso facto* constitute a divorce. By contrast, in the Western cultures, no one (no matter what his or her religion is) can felicitously use (4.58) to obtain a divorce.[25]

(4.58) 'I hereby divorce you.'

But how about non-institutionalized speech acts? First of all, as said already, any given speech act may be culture-specific. For example, a given speech act may be absent in a particular culture. Rosaldo (1982)

---

[24] Needless to say, the observations to be offered in this section are collective. Given that any language is spoken by, and any culture/society consists of, diverse individuals, there may be different manners of performing a certain speech act by a particular individual in a certain language/culture.

[25] In some Muslim cultures, even an unintentional use of (4.58) can effect a divorce, as can be shown by the following incident taken place in Pakistan, cited from Thomas (1995: 43).

(i) A terrible tangle has arisen in Pakistan over a local soap opera. Soap star Usman Pirzada divorced his television wife in traditional Muslim style, pronouncing *Talaq*—I divorce thee—three times. The trouble was that his TV spouse was played by his real wife, Samina. Now the ulemas are saying that the divorce is binding, even though the formula was spoken in the interest of art. Their decree maintains that the Prophet ordained that in three matters (marriage, divorce, and the freeing of slaves) words uttered unintentionally or even in jest cannot be withdrawn. Divorced they are and divorced they must remain.

This shows that Austin's notion of etiolation may need to be relaxed. By **etiolation** is meant the non-performance or void of a performative that is uttered or a speech act that is performed in a playful use of language such as on stage, in a poem or in a soliloquy.

It has recently been reported in the media that in some Muslim cultures, husbands now can even use e-mails and/or text messages to divorce their wives.

observed that the speech act of promising has no place among the Ilongots—a tribal group of hunters and horticulturalists in the Philippines. She attributed the absence of this speech act in the conceptual repertoire of the Ilongots to a lack of interest in sincerity and truth in that community. The Ilongots, argued Rosaldo, are more concerned with social relationships than with personal intentions. On the basis of anthropological evidence such as this, Rosaldo claimed that the universality of Searle's typology of speech acts cannot be maintained. Another example of this kind has been reported for the Australian aboriginal language Yolngu. According to Harris (1984: 134–5), there does not seem to be any speech act of thanking in the Yolngu speaker's repertoire.

Conversely, a given speech act may be present only in a certain culture. For example, in the Australian aboriginal language Walmajarri, one finds a speech act of requesting that is based on kinship rights and obligations. The verb in question is *japirlyung* (Hudson 1986), and the speech act may be called 'kinship-based requesting', because it conveys a message meaning roughly 'I ask/request you to do X for me, and I expect you to do it simply because of how you are related to me'. Thus, for a speaker of Walmajarri, it would be very difficult to refuse a kinship-based speech act of requesting like that (see also Wierzbicka 1991: 159–60, and see Headland 1986 on requests in Tunebo). Another example involves such kinship-based speech act verbs as *walkuni* in Yankunytjatjara and *anperneme* in Arrernte. Speech act verbs of this type are used in the two Australian aboriginal languages to perform the speech act of calling someone by a kinship form, either addressing or referring to him or her (Goddard 2011: 430). 'Exotic' speech acts like those described in the Australian aboriginal languages above do not seem to be present either in the Chinese-type East Asian or in the European-type Western cultures.

Secondly, given a particular speech situation, pertinent speech acts are carried out differently in different languages/cultures. For instance, in some East Asian and Western cultures, if one steps on another person's toes, one normally performs the speech act of apologizing. But apparently this is not the case among the Akans, a West African culture. As reported by Mey (2001: 287 crediting Felix Ameka), in that culture, such a situation does not call for an apology but calls for an expression of sympathy. 'The focus is on the person to whom the bad thing has happened rather than the person who has caused the bad thing' (Mey 2001: 287). A second example: upon an invitation to enter, for example, a house, while English and Rumanian speakers would offer thanks, French and Spanish ones would offer apologies (Dumitrescu 2006: 14). Similarly, whereas in English, thanks and compliments are usually offered to the hosts when leaving a dinner party (see also, e.g., Pedersen 2010 on thanking in Swedish and Zeyrek 2012 on thanking in Turkish), in Japanese, apologies such as *o-jama itashimashita* 'I have intruded on you' are more likely to be offered by the guests. A similar speech act of apologizing is performed in Japanese upon receiving a present, when a Japanese speaker is likely to say something like *sumima-sen*—the most common Japanese 'apology' formula or one of its variants (Coulmas 1981). Putting the matter the other way round, as pointed out by many Japanese scholars, apologies can be used in a much broader range of speech situations in Japanese than in English (see also, e.g., Hatfield and Jee-Won 2011 on apologies in Korean and Shariati and Chamani 2010 on apologies in Persian, but see Ohasi 2008 on thanking in Japanese).

Thirdly, in different languages/cultures, the same speech act may meet with different typical responses. A good example is compliments and compliment responses. Whereas there are some cross-linguistic/cross-cultural parallel patterns regarding the topic and functions of compliments, the gender difference, and the social status of compliment givers and receivers,[26] compliment responses vary from language to language and culture to culture. For instance, a compliment normally generates acceptance/

---

[26] I am not saying that there are no cross-linguistic/cross-cultural differences in these areas. Take compliment topics as an example. In many languages/cultures, appearance, possession, and ability are common topics of what is complimented. In the case of material possession, for instance, while in communist Poland, one would deliver a compliment on it more than any other categories, in communist Romania, this was avoided. The explanation for the former: it is due to scarcity of material goods speakers of Polish faced at the time (Herbert 1991); the explanation for the latter: it is because individual wealth would have been frowned upon in what was supposed to be an egalitarian society (Dumitrescu 2006). Another illustration: children and especially their academic achievement and potential career success are a frequent topic of compliments in Chinese (e.g. Yuen 2002 and Lee 2009) and perhaps Japanese and Korean, but they do not seem to be a significant compliment topic in any other languages/cultures (Chen 2010b). The same can also be said of what linguistic expressions one can use to make a compliment. For example, highly sexualized expressions like *piropos* can be used in Spanish as a compliment to certain people in certain contexts, the use of them is not acceptable in English. As observed by Dumitrescu (2006: 17): 'if English has "piropos" they would fall into the category of sexual harassment'.

thanking in (different varieties of) English, but rejection and/or self-denigration in Chinese, Japanese, Korean, and to a lesser extent Turkish, Polish, and Spanish. According to Chen (2010b), Chinese is the best studied non-European language in complimenting and compliment responding, with a wide variety of Chinese-speaking populations being covered. These include mainland, Taiwanese (see e.g. Lin et al. 2012 for a comparison of these two varieties), Hong Kong and Singaporean Chinese, and Chinese residing overseas in countries such as the USA, UK, and Australia. While there are geographical and other differences, a typical compliment response formula in Chinese would be something like (4.59).

(4.59)   A: ni cai zuode zhen hao!
          B: nali, nali, wo bu hui zuocai.
          A: bie keqi, ni cai zhende zuode hen hao!
          B: ni tai keqi le.
          A: 'You cook really well!'
          B: 'No, no, I don't really know how to cook properly.'
          A: 'Please don't be too modest. You really cook very well.'
          B: 'You're too kind.'

The same is true of Japanese. According to Mizutani and Mizutani (1987: 43), 'the Japanese will never accept a compliment without saying *iie* [no]'. This is vividly illustrated by the following conversation conducted between two women in so-called 'women's speech' (Miller 1967: 289–90).

(4.60)   A: Ma, go-rippa na o-niwa de gozamasu wa ne. Shibafu ga hiro biro to shite ite, kekko de gozamasu wa ne.

          B: Iie, nan desu ka, chitto mo teire ga yukitodokimasen mono de gazaimasu kara, mo, nakanaka itsumo kirei ni shite oku wake ni wa mairimasen no de gozamasu yo.

          A: A, sai de gozaimasho ne. Kore dake o-hiroin de gazamasu kara, hito tori o-teire asobasu no ni datte taihen de gozaimasho ne, Demo ma, sore de mo, itsumo yoku o-teire ga yukitodoite irasshaimasu wa. Itsumo honto ni o-kirei de kekko de gozamasu wa

          B: Iie, chitto mo sonna koto gozamasen wa.

          A: 'My, what a splendid garden you have there—the lawn is so nice and big, it's certainly wonderful, isn't it!'

          B: 'Oh, no, not at all, we don't take care of it at all any more, so it simply doesn't always look as nice as we would like it to.'

          A: 'Oh, I don't think so at all—but since it's a big garden, of course it must be quite a tremendous task to take care of it all by yourself; but even so, you certainly do manage to make it look nice all the time; it certainly is nice and pretty any time one sees it.'

B: 'No, I'm afraid not, not at all.'

Given the general Japanese reluctance to say 'no' under almost any other circumstances (see e.g. Ueda 1974, which listed sixteen ways to avoid saying 'no' in Japanese, and Chang 2008 on how to say 'no'), this compliment response pattern, though considered as rather traditional by the younger generation in present-day Japan, is quite striking.

Finally, similar remarks can go for Korean, as shown by (4.61), which is a vernacular version of the language.

(4.61)   A: wa ney say cakheys nemwu yeypputa. wancen mescye.
         B: aniya neyka ipko issnun cakheys. i hwelssin yeyppe.
         A: 'Wow! Your new jacket is very pretty. It is totally cool!'
         B: 'No, the jacket you are wearing is much prettier.'

According to Brown and Levinson (1978, 1987), the Chinese, Japanese, and Korean cultures are 'debt-sensitive culture[s]', under which a speaker normally feels that he or she has a heavy debt to repay when he or she is complimented. See also Sharifian (2005) on Persian, where the relevant schema is *shekasteh-nafsi* 'doing self-breaking', meaning roughly 'modesty' or 'humility'.

What is of more interest is that in some languages/cultures such as Arabic, Greek, and Samoan, upon a compliment on an object (of value), the compliment receiver may feel that he or she has to offer that object to the compliment giver (e.g. Sifianou 2001). But this 'offering' strategy is largely a 'lip service'—neither the compliment receiver nor the compliment giver intends to give or take the complimented object, at least as far as Arabic is concerned (e.g. Farghal and Haggan 2006). See also Mursy and Wilson (2001) on complimenting in Egyptian Arabic and Ruhi (2006) on compliment responses in Turkish.

In fact, regarding compliment responses, some cross-linguistic/cross-cultural variations can be indicated along a three-point continuum put forward by Holmes (1986), namely, acceptance–deflection/evasion–rejection. Given this cline, Arabic speakers are most likely to accept a compliment, followed by speakers of South African, American, and New Zealand English. Next come Irish English and Thai. (I may add Malay here.) On the other hand, speakers of Chinese, Japanese, Korean, and Turkish are most likely to reject a compliment, while speakers of certain non-English European languages like German and Spanish (I may add Rumanian here), with the possible exception of French, may be positioned at the mid-point, deflection/evasion, of this three-pronged continuum (e.g. Chen 2010b). See also, e.g., Nelson et al. (1996) for a comparison of compliment responses between Syrian Arabic and American English, Lorenzo-Dus (2001) for a comparison between British and Spanish university students, Yu (2003) for a comparison between Chinese and American English, Sharifian (2005) for a comparison between Persian and Anglo-Australian speakers, and Tang and Zhang (2009) for a comparison between Chinese and Australian English.

Finally, of particular interest is that recent studies carried out in two Chinese metropolises, Xi'an (Chen and Yang 2010) and Shanghai (Gao et al. 2012), seem to indicate that there have been some changes in the way in which (younger generations of) Chinese speakers respond to compliments, the most striking of which is that they now tend to reject compliments much less and accept them much more, to the extent that 'there is virtually no difference between them and American English speakers' (Chen 2010b: 88; see also Othman 2011 on the observation that there is a similar shift in compliment and compliment responses in Malaysian-Malay). One possible explanation for this change is perhaps the influence of the Western culture. Needless to say, contact with the Western culture is more widespread among younger generations and/or in large cities in China. Whether the change revealed in the above two investigations can be corroborated among older generations and/or in rural areas in China remains to be seen.

Leech (2007) regarded (4.59)–(4.61) as cases of what he dubbed '**pragmatic paradoxes**' of politeness. Pragmatic paradoxes are contradictions arising from the asymmetry of politeness: what is polite for a speaker (e.g. a speaker pays a compliment to an addressee) may be impolite for an addressee (e.g. the addressee makes ritual denials of the speaker's compliment) (cf. Brown and Levinson 1987). If both the speaker and the addressee were equally determined to be polite and not to give way, then this asymmetry would never be resolved, hence the paradox of, or the 'battles for', politeness.

However, in an actual speech event, the pragmatic paradoxes of this kind are often resolved by means of implicit negotiations between the speaker and the addressee. Thus, after a few rounds of, say, compliment and ritual denial, the addressee will 'reluctantly' accept the compliment, as in (4.59), or he or she will continue to deny the compliment, as in (4.60). Another example: after a few rounds of exchanges of offer and ritual refusal, the addressee will 'reluctantly' accept the gift offered by the speaker in certain cultures/languages (see e.g. Zhu, Li, and Qian 2000 and Jiang 2012 on food-plying at the dinner table, leftover food-offering, and gift-offering in Chinese, and Barron 2003 on Irish English, about which in the next subsection). This pragmatic paradoxical mechanism of offer and refusal can be schematized in (4.62).

(4.62)   A: offer 1
         B: ritual refusal 1
         A: offer 2
         B: ritual refusal 2
         A: offer 3
         B: acceptance

As our final example in this subsection, there is the following exchange of insisting on repaying a debt and ritually refusing to accept the repayment between two male speakers in Persian (Koulaki 2002).

(4.63)   A: bezær mæn ... [takes out money] ta færamuš nækærdæm
         B: aqa vel kon tora xoda
         A: næ næ xaheš mikonæm
         B: be vallahe nemixam
         A: xaheš mikonæm
         B: nemixam
         A: pænjai hæm bærat gereftæm æz bank
         B: næ nemixam axe

         A: 'Let me ... er ... [takes out money] before I forget.'
         B: 'Leave it, really.'
         A: 'Please.'
         B: 'I don't need it now, really.'
         A: 'Please.'
         B: 'I don't need it.'
         A: 'I even got it in fifty pound notes for you.'
         B: 'But I don't need it I say!'[27]

---

[27] In terms of **conversation analysis**, (4.59)–(4.63) are instantiations of what is called '**adjacency pairs**'—a sequence of two structurally adjacent utterances, produced by two different speakers and ordered as a **first pair part** and a **second pair part**. Taking the compliment response pattern as an example, the first pair part is compliment, and the second pair part is acceptance or rejection. From a cultural perspective, the main difference here is that while acceptance is the **preferred second pair part** in some languages/cultures (e.g. English or Western), ritual denial is the

Fourthly, the same speech act may differ in its **directness/indirectness** in different languages/cultures. Since the late 1970s, a great deal of research has been conducted on how particular kinds of speech acts, especially such FTAs as apologies, complaints, and requests, are realized across different languages/cultures. Of these investigations, the most influential is the large-scale Cross-Cultural Speech Act Realization Patterns Project (CCSARP) (e.g. Blum-Kulka, House, and Kasper 1989, see also Blum-Kulka and Olshtain 1984). In this project, the realization patterns of apologizing and requesting in German, Hebrew, Danish, Canadian French, Argentinean Spanish, and British, American, and Australian English were compared and contrasted. In the case of requests, the findings were that from among the languages/cultures examined, if we start from the directness end, Argentinean Spanish speakers are the most direct, which is followed by the speakers of Hebrew. In the middle are speakers of Canadian French and German. Australian English speakers cluster towards the indirectness end.

Building on the research carried out in the CCSARP, strategies for the performing of certain types of FTAs in a much wider range of languages have since been examined. These languages include different varieties of Arabic, Catalan, Chinese, Danish, Dutch, Finnish, German, Greek, Hebrew, Hungarian, Indonesian, Japanese, Javanese, Persian, Polish, Russian, Setswana, Thai, Turkish, Vietnamese, four varieties of English (British, American, Australian, and New Zealand), two varieties of French (Canadian and French), and nine varieties of Spanish (Argentinean, Chilean, Ecuadorian, Mexican, Peninsular, Peruvian, Puerto Rican, Uruguayan, and Venezuelan). Recently, there have been a number of new comparative studies. In House (2005), for example, different cultural values along five dimensions between German and English speakers are identified. They are (with German versus English): (i) directness versus indirectness, (ii) orientation towards self versus towards other, (iii) orientation towards content versus towards addressee, (iv) explicitness versus implicitness, and (v) *ad hoc* formulation versus verbal routines. Furthermore, House noticed that the five cultural differences recognized above have frequently led to cross-cultural/cross-linguistic misunderstandings between German and English speakers. Cordella (1990) examined the performance of the speech act of apologizing in Chilean Spanish and Australian English. Suszczyńska (1999)

preferred second pair part in other languages/cultures (e.g. Chinese or East Asian) (Huang 1987).

compared the different strategies used to make apologies in English, Polish, and Hungarian. In Kasanga and Lwanga-Lumu (2007), apologizing in English and Setswana is compared and contrasted. Sifianou (1992) studied the performance of the speech act of requesting between British English and Greek. Van Mulken (1996) compared the use of the politeness strategies in Dutch and French requests. Hong (1998) explored requests between Chinese and German speakers. Fukushima (2002) presented a comparative investigation of requests between speakers of British English and speakers of Japanese. Rue and Zhang (2008) examined requests in Chinese and Korean (see also Peterson 2010 on requests in Finnish, and Nguyen and Ho 2013 on requests in Vietnamese). Márquez-Reiter (2000) investigated apologies and requests between British English and Uruguayan Spanish. Bayraktaroglu and Sifianou (2001) collected a number of comparative studies of speech act realization patterns in Greek and Turkish including advice-giving, correcting, and complimenting. In Chen, Chen, and Chang (2011), American and Chinese complaint strategies are compared. Nelson et al. (2002) examined the strategies employed to make refusals in Egyptian Arabic and American English. Lorenzo-Dus (2001) was a comparison of how British and Spanish university students respond to compliments. Siebold (2012) explored explicit and implicit thanking made by Spanish and German speakers. The main finding of this contrastive study is that the norms of politeness differ markedly between the two languages/cultures. While Spanish thanking behaviour displays a strong tendency towards positive politeness, the expression of thanking in German is characterized by a strong tendency towards negative politeness. Most of the investigations surveyed here have adopted a methodology which is at least partially comparable and compatible with that used in the CCSARP.

As a result of these studies, it has now been established that there is indeed an extensive cross-linguistic/cross-cultural variation in directness/indirectness in the expression of speech acts, especially in that of FTAs such as apologies, complaints, and requests,[28] and that these differences are

---

[28] The cultural differences in directness versus indirectness in the expression of a speech act frequently lead speakers from one culture to misinterpret speakers from another culture, as the following incident, reported in Takahashi and Beebe (1987) shows.

(i) In 1974, President Nixon asked Prime Minister Sato if Japan would agree to self-imposed restrictions on the export of fabrics to the United States. Prime

generally associated with the different means that different languages utilize to realize speech acts. These findings have undoubtedly contributed to our greater understanding of cross-linguistic/cross-cultural similarities and differences in face-redressive strategies for FTAs.

4.7.2. Interlanguage variation

In the previous subsection, I have taken a look at the cross-cultural variation in speech acts. In this subsection, let me briefly examine their interlanguage variation.

Simply put, an **interlanguage** is a stage on a continuum within a rule-governed language system that is developed by second or foreign language (L2) learners on their path to acquiring the target language. For example, when a native speaker of Chinese is learning German as a second language, the German used by him or her is an interlanguage. An interlanguage is intermediate between a learner's native language and his or her target language. It gives rise to the phenomenon of what Slobin (1996: 89) called 'first language thinking in second language speaking'.

A number of studies have recently appeared that explored speech acts in interlanguage pragmatics. These include Blum-Kulke, House, and Kasper (1989), Kasper and Blum-Kulke (1993), Ellis (1994), Trosborg (1995, 2010), le Pair (1996), Baba (1999), Gass and Houck (2000), Achiba (2003), Barron (2003), Hassall (2003), Cheng (2011), Salgado (2011), Felix-Brasdefer and Hasler-Barker (2012), and Beckwith and Dewaele (2012). Some of these researches have investigated how a particular type of speech act is performed by non-native speakers in a given interlanguage; others have compared and contrasted the similarities and differences in the realization patterns of given speech acts between native and non-native speakers in a particular (inter)language. The best studied interlanguage is that developed by speakers of English as a second language. Other interlanguages that have

Minister Sato replied: 'Zensho shimasu', which literally means 'I'll take care of it'. However, when it is used by a politician, the uttering of this expression actually performs the speech act of a polite refusal in Japanese. President Nixon failed to understand it as a polite refusal and became very angry later on, when the Japanese simply took no action at all.

been examined include Chinese, German, Hebrew, Indonesian, Japanese, and Spanish.

Kasper and Blum-Kulke (1993) contained five studies of interlanguage expression of FTAs, namely, apologizing, correcting, complaining, requesting, and thanking. Of these studies, Bergman and Kasper's (1993) research showed that in performing apologies, Thai learners of English in general 'do too much of a good thing'—a phenomenon dubbed as 'gushing' by House (1988) and less benevolently as 'waffling' by Edmondson and House (1991). Takahashi and Beebe (1993) observed that American English speakers are most likely, and Japanese speakers of Japanese are least likely, to use a positive remark before making a correction, with Japanese speakers of English falling in between. Olshtain and Weinbach (1993) found that non-native speakers' complaints in Hebrew are less offensive and less face-threatening. Eisentein and Bodman (1993) pointed out that while expressing gratitude is a universal speech act, it is carried out differently in different languages/cultures. More or less the same is true of interlanguage hints in requests (Weizman 1993). One of the common findings of the studies collected in Kasper and Blum-Kulke (1993) was that the expression of interlanguage speech acts tends to be more verbose. Next, Ellis (1994) focused on the interlanguage FTAs of requesting, apologizing, and refusing. Trosborg (1995) studied requests, complaints, and apologies by Danish learners of English. Ebsworth, Bodman, and Carpenter (1996) investigated how non-native speakers of American English perform the speech act of greeting in the language. Their subject pool contains fifty native speakers and one hundred non-native speakers. The group of non-native speakers of American English represents a wide array of native languages including Hispanics, Arabs, Iranians and Afghans, and Russian, Ukrainian, and Georgian informants. Le Pair (1996) observed that Dutch learners of Spanish use fewer direct request strategies than native speakers of Spanish. Baba (1999) made a comparative study of compliment responses by Japanese learners of English and American English learners of Japanese. Cheng (2011) investigated the difference between native American English speakers and Chinese learners when they respond to compliments and found that some Chinese learners have more difficulty taking such response strategies as credit-shifting than native American English speakers. Houck and Gass (1996) explored the non-native performance of the speech act of refusals, and Gass and Houck (2000) studied refusal as performed in English by native speakers of Japanese. Hassall (2001) focused on the performance of the speech act of thanking by Australian learners of Indonesian, asking the question whether they thank too much in the interlanguage (see also Wong 2010 on the expression of thanks by Hong Kong learners of English). In Hassall (2003), the performance of the speech act of requesting by this group of learners of Indonesian as an interlanguage was investigated. Barron (2003) took a detailed look at Irish learners' acquisition of German, especially of the pragmatics of requests, offers, and refusals. Many of her findings are of interest. For example, in Irish English, the ritual refusal of an offer is typically followed by re-offers and acceptances, but this discourse sequence is not characteristic of German. However, Irish learners attempt to implement this pattern in German, although this pragmatic transfer tends to decrease over time. Walkinshaw (2009) is an investigation of disagreement in a second/interlanguage. How the speech acts of request and apology are performed by Mexican Spanish learners of English is the subject of study in Salgado (2011). Felix-Brasdefer and Hasler-Barker (2012) explored the interlanguage patterns of compliment-giving and compliment-responding by American English learners of Spanish. Beckwith and Dewaele (2012) examined the development of apologies of English learners of Japanese, comparing and contrasting a group who have spent an extended period of time in Japan with a group who have studied Japanese solely in the UK. Finally, Savic (2014) presents an interesting study of advanced Serbian Learners' performance of the speech acts of apologies, requests, and refusals in English as an interlanguage. All these studies have made an important contribution to speech act theory, second/interlanguage acquisition, and second/interlanguage teaching and learning.

> Finally, try Exercise 11 at the end of this chapter.

4.8. Summary

In this chapter, I have considered speech acts and speech act theory. Section 4.1 looked at Austin's performative/constative dichotomy. In Section 4.2, I examined Austin's felicity conditions on performatives. The focus of Section 4.3 was on the three dimensions of speech acts, namely, locutionary, illocutionary, and perlocutionary acts. Section 4.4 discussed Searle's felicity conditions on speech acts. In Section 4.5, I presented Searle's fivefold typology of speech acts. Section 4.6 was concerned with indirect speech acts including a discussion of politeness and impoliteness. Finally, in

Section 4.7, I discussed cultural and interlanguage variations in speech acts. A few recent formal and computational approaches to speech acts and speech act theory are worthy of note. One important theoretical development is the integration of speech acts with intentional logic, resulting in what is called **illocutionary logic** (Searle and Vanderveken 1985; Vanderveken 1990, 1991, 1994, 2002). Finally, recent formalizations of various aspects of speech act theory in artificial intelligence and computational linguistics can be found in Perrault (1990), Bunt and Black (2000), and Jurafsky (2004).

Key concepts

speech act theory
speech act
performative
constative
explicit performative
implicit performative
performative verb
properties of explicit performative
performative hypothesis
locutionary act
illocutionary act/force
perlocutionary act/effect
felicity condition (Austin's)
felicity condition (Searle's)
representative
directive
commissive
expressive
declaration
direct speech act
indirect speech act
literal force hypothesis
politeness
first-order politeness
second-order politeness

face
first-order face
second-order face
positive face
negative face
face-threatening act (FTA)
impoliteness
first-order impoliteness
second-order impoliteness

Exercises and essay topics

1. Of the following utterances, which are performatives, and which are constatives?
     (i) The couple live in a house on the corner of Henry Street.
     (ii) I object, your honour.
     (iii) John's future is full of hope.
     (iv) I declare this bridge open.
     (v) I second the motion.
     (vi) John is growing a beard.
     (vii) *As a call in bridge*
           Three clubs.
     (viii) The mountain range goes from Afghanistan to Pakistan.
2. Of the following performatives, which are explicit and which are implicit?
     (i) All applications must be submitted to the Dean by 31st March.
     (ii) Who do you tip for the post?
     (iii) You are hereby forbidden to leave this room.
     (iv) How about going to the British Museum this afternoon?
     (v) Keep all medicines out of reach of children.
     (vi) *One British MP to another in Parliament*
           I apologize for calling my honourable friend a liar.
3. Which of the following are performative verbs?
     (i) resign
     (ii) deny
     (iii) nominate
     (iv) threaten
     (v) punish
     (vi) ask

4. In the following, which performative verbs are used performatively and which are used non-performatively?
  (i) We thanked them for their hospitality.
  (ii) I hereby declare Tony Benn the duly elected member for this constituency.
  (iii) I'm warning you not to spend too much on alcohol.
  (iv) John withdraws his application.
  (v) All passengers on flight number thirty-six to Paris are requested to proceed to gate number nine.
  (vi) The managing director congratulated everyone in the room.

5. At the wedding of Prince Charles and Lady Diana, Diana stumbled over Charles's many names, getting one of his names out of order. Which of Austin's felicity conditions do you think Diana violated? Is it a misfire or an abuse in Austin's term?

6. What are the locutionary, illocutionary, and perlocutionary acts of the following?
  (i) Mother to son: Give me that *Playboy* magazine.
  (ii) Dean's secretary to professor: Coffee?

7. Can you work out the Searlean felicity conditions for (i) questioning, (ii) thanking, and (iii) warning?

8. Using Searle's typology, classify the following speech acts:
  (i) pleading
  (ii) welcoming
  (iii) recommending
  (iv) undertaking
  (v) baptizing a child into the Christian faith
  (vi) appointing a minister
  (vii) stating
  (viii) apologizing

9. Of the following utterances, which are direct and which are indirect speech acts?
  (i) Would all drivers please proceed to the car deck and return to their vehicles, as we will be docking shortly?
  (ii) (At a fitness club in Oxford)
      Please shower before entering the pool. Please observe pool rules located at poolside. You are advised against swimming alone.
  (iii) Who cares!
  (iv) Have a nice weekend!
  (v) Why don't we go to the new Italian restaurant near the museum?
  (vi) (The following example is taken from a letter which I received from *Marquis Who's Who in the World* in May 2003.)
      Once again, because our publication cycle operates within a firm timetable, we respectfully request that you return your verified sketch by June 27.

10. John and Mary are watching TV. John has accidentally blocked the TV screen. In (i)–(v), there are five possible ways that Mary could get John to stop blocking the screen (adapted from Peccei 1999: 90). Can you analyse them in terms of

Brown and Levinson's set of FTA-avoiding strategies? Can you also rank them in order of politeness, starting with the most polite?

(i) [Mary keeps shifting on the sofa or craning her neck.]

(ii) Would you mind moving just a bit?

(iii) What an interesting programme!

(iv) Move out of the way.

(v) How about moving over just a teensy bit?

11. The following is a typical interlanguage compliment response by Chinese L2 learners of English (Huang 1987).

(i) Foreign visitor to China: Your English is excellent.

    Chinese student: No, no. My English is very poor. There's much room for improvement. I still have a long way to go in my study ...

What is the main pragmatic error here? To what extent do you think that the Chinese L2 learner's native language has influenced his or her inappropriate realization of the speech act of compliment-responding in English?

12. Analyse the following passage from *Seinfeld*, using what you have learned of speech act theory and the Gricean/neo-Gricean pragmatic theory of conversational implicature.

(i) G: Excuse me, sir, do you have the time?

    M: There's a clock over there.

    G: Where?

    M: (pointing) There.

    G: But you have a watch on.

    M: It's right by the escalator.

    G: Why don't you just look at your watch?

    M: I told you, it's right over there.

    G: Let me see the watch.

    M: Hey! What are you, some kind of nut?!

    G: You know we're living in a society!

13. What is a performative, and what is a constative? Can a performative be distinguished from a constative? If yes, how; if no, why not?

14. What are locutionary, illocutionary, and perlocutionary acts? Illustrate with examples.

15. Which of the three approaches to illocutionary acts do you prefer, and why?

16. What are the main types of speech acts?

17. Critically assess the notion of indirect speech acts.

18. To what extent is Brown and Levinson's theory of politeness universal?

19. Impoliteness should be studied hand in hand with politeness. Do you agree?

20. Compare and contrast the realization pattern of any one FTA in any two languages/cultures you are familiar with. An example might be to compare and contrast the realization pattern of refusals in English and Spanish.

21. What are the similarities and differences between speech act theory and the Gricean/neo-Gricean pragmatic theory of conversational implicature?

Further readings

Austin (1975).
Searle (1969).
Sadock (2004).
Brown and Levinson (1987). Especially Introduction to the reissue: a review of recent work, and chapters 1, 2, and 3.
Brown (forthcoming).

5

Deixis

The term 'deixis' is derived from the Greek verb meaning 'pointing', 'indicating', or 'showing'. **Deixis** is directly concerned with the relationship between the structure of a language and the context in which the language is used. It can be defined as the phenomenon whereby features of context of utterance or speech event are encoded by lexical and/or grammatical means in a language. Linguistic expressions that are employed typically as deictic expressions or deictics for short[1] include (i) demonstratives (e.g. *this*), (ii) first- and second-person pronouns (e.g. *you*), (iii) tense markers (e.g. *-ed*), (iv) adverbs of time and space (e.g. *now, there*), and (v) motion verbs (e.g. *go*).

Deixis is a universal linguistic phenomenon, that is, all human languages contain deictic terms. Why is this the case? The reason is rather straightforward: a language without deictics cannot serve the communicative needs of

---

[1] Deictic expressions or deictics are commonly called **indexical expressions** or **indexicals** in the philosophy of language literature. For further discussion of deixis and **indexicality**, see e.g. Lyons (1982: 106), Kaplan (1989), Nunberg (1993), Manning (2001), Levinson (2004), and Hanks (2011).

its users as effectively and efficiently as a language which does have them. Example (5.1), adapted from Fillmore (1997: 60), illustrates what would happen in the absence of deictic information.

(5.1)   (Found in a bottle in the sea)
         Meet me here a month from now with a magic wand about this long.

Without the relevant deictic information, one would not be able to know who to meet, where or when to meet the writer of the message, or how long a magic wand to bring.

From a theoretical point of view, two main approaches to deixis can be identified: (i) spatialist and (ii) accessibility. Within the latter, we have (i) interactionist and (ii) ethnographic or social.

The central tenet of the **spatialist view** or **spatialism** is that space is basic and spatial deictic expressions are more fundamental than non-spatial deictic ones. As such, they tend to extend into other categories of deixis such as time, discourse, and emotional (e.g. Hanks 2011). Alternatively, this position is called **localism** (e.g. Lyons 1977: 718ff). By contrast, according to the **accessibility approach**, the *a priori* primacy of space should be rejected. Instead, what plays a vital role in the study of deixis is how the participants of a speech event have or gain access to the object referred to in a deictic act, hence the term. Within the accessibility framework, situational relevance and variation, the identity of the participants, the interactive moves made by deictic utterances, the mutual orientation of the participants, the sequential organization of conversations, the social field in which the deictic field is embedded, the non-perceptual modes of access such as real-world knowledge, and the micro-ethnography of everyday usage are examined. Thus, we have the **interactionist position** or **interactionism** and the **ethnographic** or **social position** within the accessibility approach (e.g. Hanks 2011; Sidnell 2009).

It should be mentioned at this point that, as suggested by Hanks (2011), the spatialist and interactionist models can be considered to be complementary to each other. The former is an account of the relational features of deixis, and the latter, a claim about the deictic centre. By combining both grammar and interaction, we can attain a blended account of deixis that will present a better account of this important pragmatic phenomenon.

In this chapter, however, I shall adopt the more traditional, spatialist approach to deixis, combining it with some insights from the interactionist one (see e.g. Sidnell 2009 and Sidnell and Enfield (forthcoming) for an interactionist account). More specifically, I shall provide a linguistic typologically oriented descriptive analysis of deixis. Section 5.1 presents preliminaries of deixis including deictic versus non-deictic expressions (5.1.1), gestural versus symbolic use of deictic expressions (5.1.2), and deictic centre and deictic projection (5.1.3). In Section 5.2, I shall discuss the three basic categories of deixis, namely, person (5.2.1), time (5.2.2), and space (5.2.3). Next in Section 5.3, the other three, minor categories of deixis, namely, social, discourse, and emotional deixis will be examined. Finally, I shall summarize this chapter in Section 5.4. Data will be drawn from a wide variety of genetically unrelated and structurally distinct languages to show the diversity and richness of the deictic systems in the world's languages.

5.1. Preliminaries

5.1.1. Deictic versus non-deictic expression

Deictic expressions or **deictics** are expressions that have a deictic usage as basic or central; **non-deictic expressions** or **non-deictics** are expressions that do not have such a usage as basic or central. For example, while second-person pronouns are deictic expressions, as in (5.2), third-person pronouns are not, as in (5.3).[2]

(5.2)   *You* and *you*, but not *you*, go back to *your* dorms!
(5.3)   Mary wishes that *she* could visit the land of Lilliput.

It should be pointed out, however, that a deictic expression can be used non-deictically, as in (5.4), and conversely, a non-deictic expression can be used deictically, as in (5.5).

(5.4)   If *you* travel on a train without a valid ticket, *you* will be liable to pay a penalty fare.
(5.5)   *She*'s not the principal; *she* is. *She*'s the secretary.

In (5.4), *you* is used as impersonal, similar in function to lexical items such as *on* in French or *man* in German,[3] therefore, it is used non-deictically. On the

---

[2] But this is not the case for Diyari, Kwakwa'la, and many South Asian languages. See Section 5.2.3.

[3] There are languages in which the impersonal function is distinctively marked via verbal inflection. One such language is Breton (Anderson and Keenan 1985: 260).

other hand, in (5.5), the interpretation of each of the three instances of *she* depends crucially on a direct, moment-by-moment monitoring of the physical context in which the sentence is uttered. Hence the third-person pronoun here serves as a deictic expression.

5.1.2. Gestural versus symbolic use of a deictic expression

Within deictic use, a further distinction can be drawn between **gestural** and **symbolic** use (Fillmore 1971, 1997: 62–3). Gestural use can be properly interpreted only by a direct, moment-by-moment monitoring of some physical aspects of the speech event. For example, in (5.2) and (5.5), the deictic expressions can be interpreted only if they are accompanied by physical demonstration (such as a selecting gesture or eye contact) of some sort.[4] In contrast, the interpretation of the symbolic use of deictic expressions merely involves knowledge of the basic spatio-temporal parameter of the speech event. If you hear someone uttering (5.6), you do not expect it to be accompanied by any physical indication of the referent. Provided that you know the general location of the speaker, you can understand it without any problem.

(5.6)   *This* town is famous for its small antiques shops.

Clearly, gestural use is the basic use, and symbolic use is the extended use. It seems that in general if a deictic expression can be used in a symbolic way, it can also be used in a gestural way; but not vice versa. Thus, there are deictic expressions in the world's languages that can only be used gesturally. The presentatives *voici*/*voilà* in French, *ecce* in Latin, and *vot*/*von* in Russian, for example, belong to this category.

---

[4] Needless to say, the use of a deictic expression as a linguistic phenomenon and that of certain types of gesture, in particular various kinds of pointing, are intimately connected. But both the term 'gesture' and the term 'pointing' need to be interpreted in their broad sense here, since there are cultures (such as the Gunha one) in which people point primarily with their lips and eyes rather than the hands (Levinson 2004). A particular type of pointing, frequently labelled as 'lip-pointing', involves not only lips but also the actions of chin-raise and/or head-lift, gaze direction, eyebrow raise, etc. (see e.g. Sidnell and Enfield (forthcoming)). For an interesting discussion of pointing, see e.g. Kita (2003).

We can summarize the uses of deictic expressions as follows.

(5.7)   Uses of a deictic expression

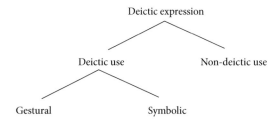

Start work in this chapter by doing Exercise 1 at the end of this chapter.

5.1.3. Deictic centre and deictic projection

Generally speaking, deixis is organized in an **egocentric** way (e.g. Lyons 1977: 646; Anderson and Keenan 1985). The default **deictic centre** or **deictic origo** (in the terminology of Bühler 1934), that is, the zero-point, of the three major categories of deixis, namely, person, time, and space, is (i) the person who is speaking, (ii) the time at which the speaker produces an utterance, and (iii) the place where the speaker produces an utterance, respectively (see also Levinson 1983: 63–4). Put informally, we may say that deixis is a 'self-centred' phenomenon, its centre being typically 'I-here-now'.

However, this 'egocentric' organization of deixis is not always adhered to, which gives rise to what Lyons (1977: 579) called a '**deictic projection**' or what Hanks (2011) termed a '**deictic transposition**'. As an illustration, consider (5.8).

(5.8)   a. Can I go to your office tomorrow afternoon at 2:00?
         b. Can I come to your office tomorrow afternoon at 2:00?

Go and *come* are both motion verbs. In (5.8a), the use of *go* encodes movement away from the deictic centre, namely the speaker, therefore we do not have a deictic projection. By contrast, in (5.8b), the use of *come* marks movement toward the deictic centre, namely the addressee, therefore we have a deictic projection. In other words, the deictic centre in (5.8b) has been projected from the speaker onto the addressee.[5] I shall have more to say about motion verbs in Section 5.2.3.

Now see whether you can tackle Exercises 2 and 3 at the end of this chapter.

5.2. Basic categories of deixis

Traditionally, three basic categories of deixis are discussed in the linguistics and the philosophy of language literature, namely, person, time, and space. The *raison d'être* behind this tripartition is that all 'pointing' is done by human beings, and therefore all 'pointing' expressions have to be related to the uttering person, the time of utterance, and the place of utterance (e.g. Mey 2001: 54).

5.2.1. Person deixis

Person deixis is concerned with the identification of the interlocutors or participant-roles[6] in a speech event. It is commonly expressed by (i) the traditional grammatical category of person, as reflected in personal pronouns and, if relevant, their associated predicate agreements, and (ii) vocatives, which can be encoded in, for example, kinship terms, titles and proper names, and their combinations.

Personal pronouns
Let me begin with personal pronouns. **Personal pronouns** usually express person, number, and gender, so-called φ-features in the generative syntax literature. They sometimes also encode distance and social relations. In this subsection, I shall concentrate on person, number, and gender. I shall

---

[5] There are languages in which deictic projection is formally marked. One such language is Inukitut. In this language, when the deictic centre is shifted from the speaker to another person in a speech event, the 'field shifting prefix' *ta-* is used (Denny 1982; Diessel 1999: 47).

[6] Following Goffman (1979) and Fillmore (1971, 1997: 62), Levinson (1983: 68, 72, 1988) argued that participant-roles or interlocutors can be further discriminated on a more accurate basis. Thus, the speaker can be differentiated as between source and transmitter of the message/utterance, and the addressee as between recipient and overhearer.

discuss distance in relation to space deixis in Section 5.2.3, and social relations in relation to social deixis in Section 5.3.1.

Person

Personal pronouns generally exhibit a three-way distinction of first, second, and third person. The category **first-person** is the grammaticalization of the speaker's reference to him- or herself, that is, the participant-role with speaker inclusion [+S]. **Second-person** is the encoding of the speaker's reference to one or more addressees, that is, the participant-role with addressee inclusion [+A]. **Third-person** is the grammaticalization of reference to persons or entities which are neither speakers nor addressees in the situation of utterance, that is, the 'participant-role' with speaker and addressee exclusion [−S, −A] (Ingram 1978; Levinson 1983: 69). Notice that third-person is unlike first- or second-person in that it does not necessarily refer to any specific partici-pant-role in the speech event (Lyons 1977: 638; Levinson 1983: 69). There-fore, it can be regarded as the grammatical form of a residual non-deictic category, given that it is closer to non-person than either first- or second-person (e.g. Huang 2000a: 178). This is why all of the world's languages seem to have first- and second-person pronouns, but some have no third-person personal pronouns. Dyirbal (Dixon 1972: 51), Hopi (Malotki 1982), Yélî Dnye (Levinson 2004), Yidiɲ (Dixon 2003), and the Ngaanyatjara dialect of the Western Desert of Australia (Dixon 1980: 357) are, for instance, examples of such languages. Lack of third-person personal pronouns is also common in the Caucasian languages (Corbett 1991: 132).[7]

---

[7] At this point, mention should be made of what is referred to as **obviation** in the literature. As pointed out in Huang (2000a: 10–11), within obviation, **proximate** and **obviative** (also often misleadingly termed third- and **fourth-person**, respectively) are assigned to different third-person NPs on the basis of their relative salience in a discourse. In general, NPs which are contextually and/or rhetorically more promin-ent are encoded by means of proximate morphology; contextually and/or rhetoric-ally less central NPs are put in obviative form. This proximate–obviative opposition is indicated not only on NPs but, if relevant, on verbs as well. Consequently, only proximates can be interpreted as coreferential with proximates; and obviatives, as coreferential with obviatives. Obviation can thus be seen as representing a natural extension of the gender or class system to the category of person, with proximates indicating the unmarked third-person category and obviates marking a subsidiary 'fourth-person', or in the case of Potawatomi, even another further-obviative 'fifth-person' category (Anderson and Keenan 1985). Obviation is found in many Ameri-can Indian languages including Algonquian (such as Blackfoot, Cree, and Fox), Apachean (such as Navajo), Eskimo, Keresan, and Kutenai (e.g. Comrie 1989).

Number

Languages vary greatly here, ranging from those like Pirahã, Kawi, and perhaps Classical Chinese that have no number category, through those like Yimas, Murik, and Meryam Mir that have a singular–dual (signalling 'two')–paucal (signalling 'a few')–plural distinction, to those like Lihir that have a singular–dual–trial (signalling 'three')–paucal–plural system (see Corbett 2000: 9–53 for detailed discussion of the full range of number categories). Examples of the two most common number systems are given in (5.9) and (5.10).

(5.9)   Singular-plural

   a. (Chinese)

Person	Singular	Plural
1	wo	women
2	ni	nimen
3	ta	tamen

   b. (West Dani, Voorhoeve 1975: 403)

Person	Singular	Plural
1	an	nit
2	kat	kit
3	at	it

   c. (Mizo, Lalitha Murthy and Subbarao 2000)

Person	Singular	Plural
1	kei	keni
2	nang	nangni
3	ani	anni

(5.10)   Singular-dual-plural

   a. (Arabic)

Person	Singular	Dual	Plural
1	'anaa		naHnu
2	'anta	'antumaa	'antum
3	huwa	humaa	hum

   b. (Tok Pisin, Mühlhäusler and Harré 1990: 51)

Person	Singular	Dual	Plural
1	mi	mitupela	mipela
2	yu	yutupela	yupela

   c. (Yankunytjatjara, Goddard 2011: 339)

Person	Singular	Dual	Plural
1	ngayulu	ngali	nganana
2	nyuntu	nyupali	nyura

Two points are worth mentioning regarding non-singular of first-person. In the first place, plural of first-person does not mean the same as that of third-person. For example, in English, *we* does not mean plural speakers in the same way that *they* means more than one third-person entity (Levinson 1983: 69). Secondly, many of the world's languages have two non-singular first-person personal pronouns, one meaning 'we-inclusive-of-addressee' and the other meaning 'we-exclusive-of-addressee'.[8] The languages in (5.11) exemplify the **inclusive–exclusive** distinction with regard to plural first-person personal pronouns, those in (5.12) illustrate the opposition with relation to dual and plural first-person personal pronouns, and finally those in (5.13) exemplify the distinction with regard to personal pronouns with more 'exotic' number systems. (See Harley and Ritter 2002, Cysouw 2003, Bhat 2004, and Siewierska 2004 for further discussion of person and number in personal pronouns.)

(5.11)   Plural 'we'

	Inclusive	*Exclusive*
Gujarati	aapNe	ame
Malay	kita	kami
Zayse	nuy	nii

(5.12)   Dual-plural 'we'

    a. (Diyari, Austin 1982: 274)

Singular	*Dual*	*Plural*	
	Ngalda	ngayani	Inclusive
nganhi			
	ngali	ngayana	Exclusive

    b. (Palaung, cited in Goddard 1998: 299)

Singular	*Dual*	*Plural*	
ɔ	ar	ɛ	Inclusive
	yar	yɛ	Exclusive

[8] In some languages, the inclusive–exclusive distinction is marked on the verb. This is the case of Oriya (Ray 2000: 576).

(i) aame   jibaa
    we   will go-INC

(ii) aame   jibũ
    we   will go-EXC

c. (Tongan, adapted from Mühlhäusler and Harré 1990: 66)

Singular	Dual	Plural	
kita (e)	kitaua (ta)	kiautolu (tau)	Inclusive
au	kimaua (ma)	kimautolu (mau)	Exclusive
(ou~ku~u~kau)			

(5.13) 'Exotic' number systems

a. (Singular-dual-trial-paucal-plural, Lihir, cited in Corbett 2000: 25)

Person	Singular	Dual	Trial	Paucal	Plural
1 exclusive	yo	gel	getol	gehet	ge
1 inclusive	–	kito	kitol	kitahet	giet
2	wa	gol	gotol	gohet	go
3	e	dul	dietol	diehet	die

b. (Singular-dual-plural-greater plural, Mokilese, Harrison 1976: 88)

Person	Singular	Dual	Plural	Greater plural
1 exclusive	ngoah(i)	kama	kamai	kimi
1 inclusive	–	kisa	kisai	kihs
2	koah	kamwa	kamwai	kimwi
	koawoa			
3	ih	ara/ira	arai/irai	ihr

> Try to complete Exercises 4 and 5 at the end of this chapter.

Gender

Personal pronouns may also mark **semantic** (or **natural)** and **grammatical** (or **conventional gender**). Cross-linguistically, the general pattern for pronominal gender marking may be captured in the following implicational universal. In all languages with pronominal gender marking, gender can be distinguished on third-person, where commonly two (that is, **masculine** and **feminine**) or three (that is, masculine, feminine, and **neuter**) genders may be identified; in some, gender assignment can also be for second-person; in a few, gender can be marked on first-person as well (e.g. Greenberg 1963: 96; Anderson and Keenan 1985: 269). For example, a gender distinction in Catalan, English, Marathi, and Russian can be indicated on third-person only. By contrast, in Arabic, Modern Hebrew (Anderson and Keenan 1985: 269), Tunica, and Shilha (Corbett 1991: 129), gender marking is for third- and second- but not for first-person (and not for first-person singular in the case of Shilha). Finally, Nagla is a language in which gender can be distinguished on first-person as well (Trudgill 2000: 63). But there are exceptions to this implicational universal. As reported in Burquest (1986),

Angas, an Afro-Asiatic language, has a gender distinction in the second-person only, except in reported speech.

Also worth mentioning is that gender can be marked in verbal morphology, especially when the personal pronoun itself fails to make such a distinction. This is illustrated in (5.14)–(5.16).

(5.14)   Modern Hebrew (Anderson and Keenan 1985: 270)
    a. Ani   medaber.
       I   speak-M-SG
       'I speak.' (male speaker)

    b. Ani   medaberet.
       I   speak-F-SG
       'I speak.' (female speaker)

(5.15)   Punjabi
    a. mai   aura.
       I   come-M
       'I'm coming.' (male speaker)

    b. mai   auri.
       I   come-F
       'I'm coming.' (female speaker)

(5.16)   Russian (Corbett 1991: 128)
    a. ja   čital- Ø.
       I   read-PAST-M
       'I was reading.' (male speaker)

    b. ja   čital-a.
       I   read-PAST-F
       'I was reading.' (female speaker)

Finally, gender can also be indicated on adjectives and nouns. The following examples are from French.

(5.17)   a. Je   suis   heureux.
       I   am   happy-M
       'I'm happy.' (male speaker)

    b. Je   suis   heureuse.
       I   am   happy-F
       'I'm happy.' (female speaker)

(5.18) a. Je   suis   le   président.
       I   am   the-M   president-M
       'I'm the president.' (male speaker)

     b. Je   suis   la   présidente.
       I   am   the-F   president
       'I'm the president.' (female speaker)

Next, while in most languages the unmarked gender is masculine, there are languages in which the unmarked gender is feminine. These include a group of Australian languages (such as Kala Lagaw Ya) (Alpher 1987), a few North American Indian languages (such as Iroquois) (Brown 1975), and perhaps Arakul, a Caucasian dialect (see also Mühlhäusler and Harré 1990: 242–5).

A further point of interest is that with regard to person-gender marking, languages tend to encode more gender distinctions in the singular than the plural. This is because less marked categories are likely to be more differentiated internally than more marked ones (e.g. Greenberg 1966; Anderson and Keenan 1985). A familiar language that confirms this principle is English (third-person singular: M: *he*, F: *she*, N: *it*; third-person plural: *they*). Another, less familiar one is Moni (third-person singular: M: *ogo*, F: *oa*, third-person dual: *uiya*, third-person plural: *ui*) (Voorhoeve 1975: 409). Counterexamples, however, are afforded by, say, Spanish, in which gender is distinguished in all persons in the plural but only in third-person in the singular.

Finally, in some of the world's languages, personal pronouns may not need to be realized phonetically at all. In other words, they can be encoded in terms of an empty category or a zero anaphor. Languages which allow the dropping of a personal pronoun in the subject position of a finite clause have come to be known as '**null subject**' or '**pro-drop**' languages in the generative syntax literature. Generally speaking, pronouns can be omitted in a language if their content can be recovered either morphologically (e.g. via rich verbal agreement), as in (5.19), or from the discourse in one way or another, as in (5.20) (see e.g. Huang 1992a, 1992b, 1995, 2000a for further discussion).

(5.19) (Pashto, cited in Huang 2000a: 55)
       Ø   mana   xwr-əm.
        apple   eat-1-M-SG
     '(I) ate the apple.'

(5.20) (Chinese)

     Ø   qu   guo   Beijing   ma?

     go   EXP   Beijing   Q

     'Have (e.g. you) been to Beijing?'

Vocatives

Person deixis can also be accomplished by **vocatives**. Vocatives are NPs that refer to the addressee, but form no part of the arguments of a predicate. Prosodically, they are separated from the body of an utterance that may accompany them. Vocatives in general are grouped into two types, **calls** or **summonses**, as in (5.21), and **addresses**, as in (5.22).

(5.21) a. Hey *Daddy*, look, a spider in the corner!

     b. *John*, if we don't leave now, we'll be late for our next appointment.

     c. *Doctor Williams*, do you think I need a blood test?

(5.22) a. I'm afraid, *Sir*, we are closing.

     b. Do you fancy going to a concert of African music, *Lucy*?

     c. My view, *Dean*, is that we should set up a new department of linguistics.

Three points may be briefly mentioned here. First of all, calls/summonses, being gestural in nature, are utterance-initial; addresses, on the other hand, being symbolic in character, are parenthetical, and can occur wherever other parentheticals can occur. The second point to note is that while all addresses can be used as calls/summonses, only some calls/summonses can be used as addresses (Zwicky 1974; Levinson 1983: 70–1; Brown and Levinson 1987: 292; Marmaridou 2000: 78–80). Finally, as (5.21) and (5.22) show, vocatives are in general socially marked. I shall return to this issue in Section 5.3.1 where I shall discuss social deixis.[9]

---

[9] According to Fillmore (1997: 119), in English, *Miss* can be used in polite attention-calling, *Mr* can be used in impolite attention-calling, but *Mrs* cannot be used in attention-calling at all. We can offer a partial neo-Gricean pragmatic analysis here. The use of *Madam* as a vocative pre-empts *Mrs* used in that way. The use of *Sir* as a polite vocative has the priority over that of *Mr* as a polite vocative, thus relegating it to an impolite vocative. Finally, since there is nothing to pre-empt it, *Miss* is free to be used as a polite vocative.

5.2.2. Time deixis

We move next to time deixis. **Time deixis** is concerned with the encoding of temporal points and spans relative to the time at which an utterance is produced in a speech event.

Time
Before considering how time deixis is grammaticalized in language, let us first take a look at the concept of time. As pointed out by Fillmore (1997: 45–6), time is one-dimensional and unidirectional. Generally speaking, the passage of time is represented in two distinct ways: (i) to regard time as constant and the 'world' as moving through time from the past into the future, and (ii) to think of the 'world' as stable and of time as flowing through the 'world' from the future to the past. Thus, in terms of the 'moving world' metaphor (i), we can talk about 'the years ahead'; on the other hand, in terms of the 'moving time' metaphor (ii), we can talk about 'the coming years'.

A distinction can be made between time points such as 'eight o'clock' and time periods such as 'tomorrow evening'. Time periods can be uniquely defined in terms of their beginning and ending points. They are most commonly encoded in the world's languages on the basis of the natural and prominent recurring cycles of days and nights, weeks, months, seasons, and years. Such time units can be calendrical or non-calendrical. In the **calendrical** usage, time measure periods designate a fixed-length sequence of naturally given time units. 'July', for example, is such a calendrical unit. On the other hand, in the **non-calendrical** usage, time measure periods are used only as units of measure relative to some fixed points of interest. 'Fortnight', for instance, is an example of a non-calendrical unit (Fillmore 1997: 48–50, see also Levinson 1983 and Anderson and Keenan 1985: 296). Calendrical units can further be divided into **positional** ones like 'Monday', 'January', and 'morning', and **non-positional** ones like 'week', 'month', and 'year' (Fillmore 1997: 50, 52, 69).

Another distinction we need to make is between the moment of utterance, to be called '**coding time**' (**CT**) and the moment of reception, to be called '**receiving time**' (**RT**). Under normal circumstances, assuming the default deictic centre, RT can be taken to be identical to CT, in which case, we have what Lyons (1977: 685) called **deictic simultaneity**. But there are situations of utterance, such as the writing of a letter and the pre-recording of a media programme, where messages are not sent and received at the same time. In these cases, the speaker has to decide whether the deictic centre will remain on the speaker and CT, as in (5.23) or will be shifted to the addressee and RT, as in (5.24) (Filmore 1997: 67–8; Levinson 1983: 73–4).

(5.23)   This interview is being recorded today, Wednesday 3 July, to be relayed on Sunday 7 July.

(5.24)   This interview was recorded last Wednesday 3 July, to be relayed today, Sunday 7 July.

Encoding of time deixis
Time deixis is commonly grammaticalized in (i) deictic adverbs of time, and (ii) tense.

Deictic adverbs of time
Let me start with **deictic adverbs of time**. Consider first *now* and *then* in English, the two pure time deictics which Anderson and Keenan (1985: 297) called '**temporal demonstratives**'. *Now* designates '**proximal**' time and following Levinson (1983: 74), it can be defined as the 'pragmatically given (time) span including CT'. By contrast, *then* refers to '**distal**' time, and can be reduced to meaning 'not now' (see also Section 5.2.3). It can indicate time either in the past or in the future.

   Look next at calendrical unit terms such as *today*, *tomorrow*, and *yesterday*. These deictic names of days divide time into diurnal spans. Thus *today* can be glossed as 'the diurnal span including CT', *tomorrow* as 'the diurnal span following today', and *yesterday* as 'the diurnal span preceding today' (see also Levinson 1983: 74). Note further that both *now/then* and *today/tomorrow/yesterday* can relate to either a time point, as in (5.25), or an interminable time period within the relevant span, as in (5.26), or the whole span itself, as in (5.27).

(5.25)   Start the engine *now*!
(5.26)   John is *now* working as a government's spin-doctor.
(5.27)   *Yesterday* was a public holiday.

Another interesting point is that the use of *today/tomorrow/yesterday* pre-empts, that is, it has priority over, the use of the calendrical terms for the relevant days. Thus, speakers of English would normally avoid saying (5.28) if either today or tomorrow is Saturday. This is because on a Saturday they would have used *today*, and on a Friday they would have used *tomorrow* (Fillmore 1997: 72; Levinson 1983: 75).

(5.28)   I'll test-drive a BMW on Saturday.

Finally, languages differ in precisely how many deictically anchored terms of days they lexicalize. For example, while English names only one day in either direction from today, Arabic, Chinese, and German go two days in each direction. There are languages which display a richer system. Greek, Hausa (Anderson and Keenan 1985: 300), and Japanese (Fillmore 1997: 71), for instance, have three lexicalized deictic names of days on either side of the present day. Chinantec is reported by Fillmore (1997: 71) to go even four days both ahead and back.

Also of interest is that some languages use the same word for tomorrow and yesterday, thus reducing the number of lexicalized names of days. The major dialects of Igbo, for example, belong to this type of language. The relevant word employed in the language is *eci* (Anderson and Keenan 1985: 300). More interestingly, Punjabi has a single word *kall* for tomorrow and yesterday, and another single word *parso* for the day after tomorrow and the day before yesterday. The same, according to Fillmore (1997: 73), is true of Hindi. Put slightly differently, in these languages, the same words are utilized to indicate times both one day and two days from today in either direction. The potential interpretative difficulties caused by these lexically ambiguous day names can normally be avoided either grammatically (e.g. via tense) or pragmatically (e.g. by shared knowledge).

Furthermore, the distribution of lexicalized deictic names of days in a language can be asymmetric. Spanish seems to be such a case. It names one day ahead from the present day but two days back. Persian is said to go two days ahead but four days back, and Vietnamese, three days ahead but four days back (Fillmore 1997: 71). The following are some of the examples I have collected.

(5.29) Lexicalized deictic names of days

Language	0–3	0–2	0–1	0	0+1	0+2	0+3
English			yesterday	today	tomorrow		
Diyari			waldawirti	karrari	thangku-parna		
Arabic		al-baariHata	al-baariHa	al-yawma	ghadan	badaghuden	ba'da-ghadin
Chinese		qiantian	zuotian	jintian	mingtian	houtian	
German		vorgestern	gestern	heute	morgen	übermorgen	
Greek	antiproch-thes	prochthes	chthes	sinera	avrio	methavrio	antimen-tha
Punjabi		parso	kall	ajj	kall	parso	
Spanish		anteayer	ayer	hoy	mañana		

Finally, there are complex deictic adverbs of time such as *this month*, *next Monday*, and *last year*. These deictic adverbs of time contain two components: a deictic component like *this*, *next*, and *last* and a non-deictic component like *month*, *Monday*, and *year*. As pointed out by Fillmore (1997: 69–71) and Levinson (1983: 75–6), the interpretation of such adverbs is systematically determined by two distinctions: (i) the distinction between calendrical and non-calendrical modes of reckoning of time, and (ii) the distinction between positional and non-positional calendrical units.

This X, where *X* is a non-positional calendrical unit such as week, month, and year, normally refers to the unit including CT. Furthermore, the adverb of time is ambiguous between a calendrical and a non-calendrical interpretation. Thus, *this year* refers to the same year as the moment of utterance, and is ambiguous between the calendrical unit that runs from 1 January to 31 December,[10] and the non-calendrical measure of 365 days that starts on the day including CT. More or less the same can be said of *this week* and *this month*, and perhaps *this decade* and *this century*. By contrast, *this Y*, where *Y* is a positional calendrical unit such as Thursday, July, or evening, which is included in a larger calendrical unit *Z*, usually means the unit which is included in the larger unit, which includes CT. Thus, *this July* does not necessarily make reference to the month the speaker is now in. Instead, it

---

[10] There are, of course, other culturally specific calendrical units such as the academic year, the tax year, and the Chinese (lunar) year.

refs to the July of the same calendar year as the moment of utterance. Moreover, the July in question is by preference taken to be the future rather than the past July. In the similar vein, we can say *this morning* either during the morning or during the rest of the day (Fillmore 1997: 69–73; Levinson 1983: 75–6).[11]

Tense

I turn next to a brief discussion of **tense**. Following Lyons (1977: 682) and Levinson (1983: 77), one can distinguish between **metalinguistic tense (M-tense)** and **linguistic tense (L-tense)**. Whereas by M-tense is meant the theoretical category of tense, L-tense refers to the linguistic realization of M-tense typically through verbal inflection but also in the form of other periphrastic constructions in a particular language. Generally speaking, all languages have M-tense, but some lack L-tense. In the latter case, M-tense may be lexically realized by means of adverbs of time or the like—lexical expressions equivalent to *yesterday*, *this week*, and *next year* in English. This contrast can be illustrated by a consideration of (5.30).

(5.30)   a. The giant panda lives on bamboo shoots.
         b. (Chinese)
            Xiaoming   qunian   jie-le-hun.
            Xiaoming   last year   get married
            'Xiaoming got married last year.'

Note that the English example (5.30a) is M-tenseless but L-tensed, in that its verb form is morphologically marked for simple present tense. By contrast, the Chinese example (5.30b) is M-tensed but L-tenseless, in that no L-tense is morphologically marked on its verb form.

   M-tense can be given a purely deictic interpretation. In such a system, one can easily distinguish past tense (i.e. time earlier than CT) from present tense (time coinciding with or including CT) and from future tense (time later than CT). Furthermore, one can also distinguish time points from time spans (Lyons 1977: 683).

---

[11] There are languages that use different lexical items to refer to 'this morning' in the morning and in the afternoon or evening. One such language is Chinantec (Fillmore 1997: 71). There are also languages that utilize different words to refer to 'evening'. Punjabi, for example, has two expressions for 'evening': *numasha* and *shami*. The former can only be used in the evening and the latter can be used outside the evening.

But it is unclear to what extent L-tense can be marked in a purely deictic way. In the first place, L-tense may include aspectual and modal elements. For example, future tense nearly always has modal overtones. Secondly, L-tense may not distinguish past from future. A typical example is the Shiriana languages of South America (Fillmore 1997: 73–4). Thirdly, L-tense may make use of calendrical units. In the Peruvian language Ama-haucan, for instance, there is an L-tense form which means 'yesterday' if it is used in the morning but which means 'this morning' if it is used later on in the day (Fillmore 1997: 73). Another interesting case can be found in the Australian language Tiwi, in which verbs are inflected to indicate whether the action denoted took/is taking/will take place in the morning or in the evening (Anderson and Keenan 1985: 300). All this adds complexity to the deictic marking of L-tense in individual languages. (See Comrie 1985 and Dahl 1985 for discussion of tense. See also Fritz 2003 for a Q_{scalar} implica-ture analysis of future tense.)

5.2.3. Space deixis

The third and final basic category of deixis I am going to discuss is that of space deixis.[12] **Space deixis** is concerned with the specification of location in space relative to that of the participants at CT in a speech event.

Three universal linguistic frames of spatial reference
Recently, there has been a renewed interest in the anthropology, linguistics, and psychology of the concept of space (e.g. Levinson 1996). One of the central topics of enquiry is concerned with linguistic frames of spatial reference.
    Linguistic frames of spatial reference or linguistic systems of spatial reckoning are coordinate systems used to compute the location of objects with respect to other objects in space. Cross-linguistically, there are three universal linguistic frames of reference to express spatial relationships between an entity to be located (referent or **figure**) and its landmark (rela-tum or **ground**): (i) intrinsic, (ii) relative, and (iii) absolute.[13] An **intrinsic**

---

[12] Other terms include 'place', 'spatial', 'local', and 'locational deixis'.

[13] The three terms are derived from those that are used in a number of different disciplines such as brain science, linguistics, philosophy, developmental and behav-ioural psychology, and vision theory. Other terms for 'relative' and 'absolute' are

frame of reference is based on object-centred coordinates, which are determined by the 'inherent features' such as the sideness or facets of an object to be used as ground. The binary spatial relationship represented by this frame of reference can be illustrated by (5.31), where the notion of 'behind' expresses a binary spatial relation between 'the girl', which is the figure, and 'the car', which is the ground.

(5.31)   The girl is behind the car.

The second, **relative frame of reference** is roughly an egocentric system. It represents a ternary spatial relationship between a **viewpoint**, a figure, and a ground that are distinct from the viewpoint. It utilizes the coordinates fixed on the viewpoint to assign directions to the figure and the ground. This can be exemplified by (5.32), where the viewpoint is given by the location of a viewer or perceiver, in this case the speaker. The deictic use of this frame of reference is prototypical.

(5.32)   The girl is to the left of the car.

Finally, the **absolute frame of reference** also involves a coordinate system, but one that is based on absolute coordinates like 'north/south/ease/west'. The binary spatial relationship represented by this system can be shown by (5.33), where the fixed bearing 'east' is used to specify the relationship between the figure and the ground (e.g. Levinson 1996, 2003, 2004; Majid et al. 2004).

(5.33)   The girl is (to the) east of the car.

In one respect, what the intrinsic and absolute frames of reference have in common is that both express a binary spatial relationship and both are allocentric. This is in contrast to the relative system, which represents a ternary spatial relationship, and which is egocentric in nature. On another dimension, the relative and absolute frames of reference can be placed in the

'deictic' and 'extrinsic' in linguistics. The intrinsic, relative, and absolute frames of reference correspond to object-centred, viewer-centred, and environment-centred frames of reference, respectively, in psycholinguistics. The intrinsic–relative–absolute distinction can also be somewhat related to some other oppositions proposed in other disciplines like the allocentric–egocentric contrast in brain science, the $3\frac{1}{2}$-D model–$2\frac{1}{2}$-D sketch distinction in vision theory, and the orientation-bound–orientation-free opposition in imagery debates in psychology. For a detailed discussion, see e.g. Levinson (1996).

same group together because both are orientation-bound and presuppose a Newtonian or Kantian spatial envelope. By contrast, the intrinsic frame of reference is orientation-free and is essentially Leibnizian (e.g. Levinson 1996: 150–1).

Note next that (5.31) can also be put in the relative frame of reference, in which case the notion 'behind' expresses a ternary spatial relation between the viewpoint 'the speaker', the figure 'the girl', and the ground 'the car'. In a similar vein, (5.32) can also be placed in the intrinsic frame of reference. In this case, its logical structure is that 'to the left of' represents a binary spatial relation between the figure and the ground. In other words, both (5.31) and (5.32) are ambiguous or vague between the intrinsic and relative frame of reference readings. Put slightly differently, in terms of the deictic versus non-deictic distinction, *behind* in (5.31) and *to the left of* in (5.32) can have both a deictic and a non-deictic function. *Behind* in (5.31) is deictic if the car intervenes between the girl and the speaker's location, and it is non-deictic if the girl is at the intrinsic rear-end of the car. As for *to the left of* in (5.32), under the deictic interpretation, the girl is to the left of the car from the speaker's point of view, and under the non-deictic reading, the girl is to the car's own left (e.g. Levinson 1983: 82–3; Fillmore 1997).

Languages vary greatly in the use of the three universal spatial coordinate systems. Some rely predominantly on one frame of reference only (intrinsic or absolute[14]). Guugu Yimidhirr, for example, is a language that employs the absolute frame of reference almost exclusively. Other languages—good examples are Arrernte, Mopan, Tzeltal, and Warwa—utilize two of the three systems (intrinsic and relative or intrinsic and absolute). Still others use all three frames of reference. This is the case of Balinese, Belhare, English, Ewe, French, Kgalagadi, Samoan, and Yukatek, among many others. Furthermore, languages also differ in which frame of reference is the dominant one. For example, while in English and other European

---

[14] According to Levinson (1996: 148), the presence of the relative frame of reference requires that of the intrinsic frame of reference. Levinson (1996: 144) further pointed out that, contrary to the claim of certain psycholinguists, the relative system is not fundamental from a linguistic perspective, though it is from a perceptual point of view. This can be evidenced by the fact that (i) linguistically, the frame of reference is not universal, that is, many languages in the world simply do not have such an coordinate system; and (ii) it is acquired very late by Western children, who do not master, for example, 'projected' left/right until the age of 11 or 12.

languages, the relative frame of reference is the dominant one, in other languages like Tzeltal, the absolute frame of reference dominates. In other words, Tzeltal employs an absolute system where English and other European languages would use a relative one (Levinson 1996: 134, 2003, 2004; Majid et al. 2004).

Why is this the case? In the first place, this is partially due to the fact that familiar spatial notions such as 'up/down', 'front/back', and 'left/right' are absent from many—perhaps a third—of the world's languages. Secondly, there are languages like many of those spoken in Australia which adopt an (absolute) frame of reference to replace topological terms such as *in, on,* or *above/below/over/under* (Levinson 1996: 134). Of further interest is the fact that cross-linguistic variations have been observed in how the same spatial coordinate system is instantiated in a particular language. Both Hause and English, for instance, use the relative frame of reference. But in constructing such a system, the two languages enter into different spatial configurations: while Hausa enters into a 'tandem' configuration, English enters into a 'mirror' configuration. Another way of putting it is that in Hausa, translation (movement without rotation or reflection) is involved; in English, rotation is involved. This difference has the interesting consequence that in Hause, the front of, say, a calabash is not facing the speaker, but is away from him or her. Thus, the Hausa sentence in (5.34) is semantically equivalent to the English sentence in (5.35).

(5.34)   Ga   cokali   can   baya   da   k'warya.
         look   spoon   there   back   with   calabash
         Literally: 'There's a spoon *behind* the calabash.'

(5.35)   There's a spoon *in front of* the calabash.

In other words, there is a reversed relation between Hausa and English here: 'behind' in Hausa means what would be meant by *in front of* in English (Hill 1982).

Another interesting case in point is concerned with a comparison between Tamil and English. While both Tamil and English rotate coordinates, what differentiates them is whether the rotation is complete or incomplete. In Tamil, the rotation is complete, that is, not only 'front/back' but 'left/right' are reversed as well; in English, 'left/right' is not rotated. Consequently, a sentence with the gloss in (5.36) would (on the relevant reading) mean (5.37) in Tamil but (5.38) in English (Levinson 1996: 143).

(5.36)   The girl is on the left side of the car.
(5.37)   The girl is on the viewpoint's *right* of the car.
(5.38)   The girl is on the viewpoint's *left* of the car.

Grammaticalization of space deixis

Spatial deictic notions are commonly expressed by the use of (i) demonstratives, including both demonstrative pronouns (such as *this* in *This is an iPod*) and demonstrative adjectives (such as *this* in *this iPod*), (ii) deictic adverbs of space (such as *here*),[15] (iii) deictically marked third-person pronouns (such as *eh* in Punjabi), and (iv) deictic directionals including both motion

---

[15] Two other typologies of demonstratives are worth mentioning here. Diessel (1999: 57–92) classified demonstratives into four types: (i) demonstrative pronouns, (ii) demonstrative determiners (i.e. our 'demonstrative adjectives'), (iii) demonstrative adverbs (i.e. our 'deictic adverbs of space'), and (iv) demonstrative identifiers. Demonstrative identifiers are demonstratives used in copular and non-verbal clauses, as in this Ambulas example (cited in Diessel 1999: 80).

(i)   kén   bakna   walkaum   taalé.
      this   just   little   place
      'This is just a little place.'

Some languages (e.g. Acehnese) do not distinguish any of the four types of demonstratives. Others (e.g. Korean) have only two categories. Others (e.g. Nung-gubuyu) have three. Still others (e.g. Pangasinan) distinguish all the four types (Diessel 1999: 89–92).

Another typology is presented by Dixon (2003), who posited three types of demonstratives: (i) nominal demonstratives including both demonstrative pronouns and adjectives, (ii) local adverbial demonstratives, and (iii) verbal demonstratives. Dixon claimed that the first two types of demonstrative occur in every language, except in Jul'hoan. But this claim may not stand (see e.g. Diessel 1999: 89). Only two languages (i.e. Boumaa Fijian and Dyirbal) have been reported as containing verbal demonstratives. However, in each case there is just one such verbal demonstrative meaning 'do it like this' (Dixon 2003).

See also Diessel (1999: 115–55) for discussion of the diachrony of demonstrative pronouns and deictic adverbs of space in a range of languages. The discussion covers both sides of the diachrony coin: on the one hand, how demonstratives and deictic adverbs of space develop into a wide variety of grammatical markers such as definite articles, third-person pronouns, and complementizers; on the other, what is the historical source of demonstratives and deictic adverbs of space.

affixes, morphemes and particles (such as -*dé* in Kiowa) and motion verbs (such as *come*).[16]

Demonstratives and deictic adverbs of space
Let me begin with demonstratives and deictic adverbs of space. I shall examine them in terms of five deictic parameters: (i) distance or spatial immediacy, (ii) visibility and audibility, (iii) elevation and geography, (iv) side or interiority, and (v) stance and movement, which Hanks (1992, 2001), Agha (1996), and Manning (2001) considered to belong to the relational type of the indexical category of deixis.

Frei (1944) was perhaps the first linguist to classify deictic systems according to the number of opposed terms, demonstratives, and deictic adverbs of space in the world's languages display. This approach was followed by Anderson and Keenan (1985), Fillmore (1997), and more recently, typological work carried out by, for example, Sidnell (2009), Hanks (2011), and Sidnell and Enfield (forthcoming).

Distance or spatial immediacy
The first and perhaps most common dimension of deictic contrast is relative **distance** or **spatial immediacy** from the speaker and/or addressee.[17]

One-term systems. A number of the world's languages have only one demonstrative pronoun or demonstrative adjective, unmarked for distance. A possible candidate is *der* (and its variants *dies* and *das,* depending on the gender of the head noun) in (Colloquial) German (Himmelmann 1997; Sidnell and Enfield forthcoming).[18] Other deictic markers may include *ten* in Czech and *ce-cet/cette* in French (Anderson and Keenan 1985: 280). But as pointed out by Diessel (1999: 36) and Levinson (2004), most and perhaps all such one-term systems of demonstratives are supplemented by a two-

---

[16] There are, of course, other means to express space deixis. One such way, as already noted in Section 5.1.2, is to use deictic presentatives such as *voici/voilà* in French, *ecce* in Latin, *vot/von* in Russian, and *he'ela, he'elo, he'ebe* in Maya. See also note 25 in this chapter.

[17] It should be made clear that the assumption that these deictic expressions encode the basic semantic distinction of relative distance is widely, but not universally, accepted. For example, Enfield (2003) claimed that the demonstratives *nii* and *nan* in Lao do not mark distance.

[18] Though a grammar of German states that there are two other demonstrative adjectives, *dieser* and *jener*, neither of them is commonly used.

term system of deictic adverbs of space. As a consequence, unlike English (nominal: *this*/*that*; spatial: *here*/*there*; temporal: *now*/*then*) or French (nominal: *ceci*/*cela*; spatial: *ici*/*la*; presentative: *voici*/*voilà*), many languages have different numbers of terms with regard to demonstratives and deictic adverbs of space. German, for example, has one demonstrative but two deictic adverbs of space. Indonesian possesses two demonstratives but its deictic adverbs of space specify three degrees of distance. Yagua has two demonstratives but four deictic adverbs of space (Dixon 2003). Ewondo has three demonstratives but expresses a four-way contrast in deictic adverbs of space (Diessel 1999: 19). Other such languages include the Tuscan dialect of Italian, with three demonstratives but five adverbs of space (G. Vognoli, personal communication), and Malagasy, which has six demonstratives but seven adverbs of space (Anderson and Keenan 1985). Dixon (2003) and Levinson (2004) hypothesized that, in general, deictic adverbs of space make more distinctions than do demonstratives. But two counterexamples have been noted in the literature. In Tariana, there are four spatially distinguished terms in demonstratives but only two for deictic adverbs of space (Dixon 2003). Lillooet has three demonstratives but only two deictic adverbs of space (van Eijk 1997).[19]

Two-term systems. Many languages in the world display a bipartite system of demonstratives and deictic adverbs of space. In such a language, a fundamental distinction between **proximal** (or relatively close to the speaker) or **immediate** and **distal** (or non-proximal, sometimes relatively close to the addressee) is grammaticalized and/or lexicalized. This two-term system (of deictic adverbs of space) seems to be the most typical and perhaps the universal system of space deixis in the world's languages (e.g. Diessel 1999: 38; Levinson 2004). Catalan, Chinese, Diyari, English, French, Guugu Yimidhirr, Modern Hebrew, Hopi, Hungarian, Nama Hottentot,

---

[19] Dixon (2003) also noted an interesting inverse correlation between the size of demonstratives and deictic adverbs of space and that of the language community: the smaller the number of speakers of a language, the more complex the system of demonstratives and deictic adverbs of space in that language. Consequently, languages that are spoken by a large number of speakers tend to have just a two-term system. Supporting evidence can be drawn from Dravidian languages. Within this language family, systems with three or four terms are found in small tribal languages. By contrast, in each of the four major languages with tens of millions of speakers (i.e. Kannada, Malayalam, Tamil, and Telugu), there are only two-term spatially deictic systems.

Italian, Kannada, Kayardild, Lao, Malayalam, Spoken Portuguese, Punjabi, the Paasaal variety of Sisaala, Tamil, Telugu, Russian, and Vietnamese, for example, belong to this type of language. Some examples are given in (5.39).

(5.39)		*Proximal*	*Distal*
	Chinese	zheli	nali
	Diyari	nhingki	nhaka
	English	here	there
	French	ceci	cela
	Hungarian	itt	ott
	Kayardild	dan-	dathin-[20]
	Sisaala	nyɛ	ɛɛ

In a two-term system, one of the terms is unmarked and the other is marked. For example, in English, the distal *that* is unmarked but the proximal *this* is marked (Levinson 2004, but see Dixon 2003 for a dissenting view). By contrast, in Russian, the proximal *éto* is unmarked but the distal *tot* is marked. A neo-Gricean pragmatic analysis, as hinted by Levinson (2004), may be elaborated as follows. The two terms of demonstratives or deictic adverbs of space here form a privative opposition, more specifically, a Q- or Horn scale of some sort (see also Huang 2000a, 2007b), where the marked term is semantically stronger than the unmarked term. Consequently, if the semantically weaker, unmarked term is used, then a $Q_{-scalar}$ implicature will arise, namely, the speaker cannot use the semantically stronger, marked term truth-conditionally. Thus, if the English *that* is used, the conversational implicature is that *this* cannot be employed. Since *this* is marked as [+proximal], we obtain *that* as [–proximal], that is, [+distal]. On the other hand, in Russian, if *éto* is employed, then *tot* is not appropriate. Given that *tot* is marked as [+distal], *éto* will be Q-implicated as [–distal], that is, [+proximal] (see also Sidnell and Enfield (forthcoming) for a similar analysis of Lao). Alternatively, the two terms can form an M-scale, and we will obtain the same result via the operation of the M-principle (Chapter 2).

Another point to note is that two-term systems are usually speaker-centric, that is, the speaker is typically the deictic centre. Finally, regarding the diachrony of the two-term system, Diessel (1999: 167) was of the view

---

[20] Though the language has a third, rarely used form *nganikin-* 'that, beyond the field of vision' (Sidnell and Enfield (forthcoming)).

that such a system is in general derived from a system with three terms by dropping the middle term. This is, for instance, the case of the Zagreb dialect of Croatian. However, present-day Turkish seems to present a counterexample to this claim. It employs three terms: *bu/su/o* for demonstratives, and *bura/sura/ora* for deictic adverbs of space, but historically, the language had only two terms *bu* and *ol* (Anderson and Keenan 1985: 285).[21]

Go to the end of this chapter and try Exercise 6.

Three-term systems. There are many languages in the world which possess a basic tripartite system. These include Classic Arabic, Breton, certain dialects of Chinese (e.g. Danyang), Lower Chinook, Czech, certain dialects of English (e.g. Scottish), Georgian, Greek, Guyanese Creole, Japanese, Latin, Old Church Slavonic, Palauan, Portuguese, Southern Sotho, Spanish, Tagalog, Turkish, Warwa, and Welsh. Of these languages, two types can further be classified. In languages like Ambulas, Classic Arabic, Scottish English, Hopi, Southern Sotho, Tiriyo, Lango, Ponapean, Hixkaryana, Yimas, and perhaps Boumaa Fijian, we have a three-way contrast between proximal, **medial**, and distal (extremely far from the speaker and/or the addressee).[22] Of crucial importance here is the fact that in a three-term system of this sort, the middle term specifies a location also relative to the deictic centre, typically the speaker. Following Anderson and Keenan (1985: 282) and Diessel (1999: 39), we call this three-term system '**distance-oriented**'. In other words, it is a **speaker-anchored** (Levinson 2004) or **distance-centric system** (Hanks 2011). Generally speaking, if a language has a distance-oriented series of demonstratives, it will also have a distance-oriented series of deictic adverbs of space (Levinson 2004). The distance-oriented three-term system is illustrated in (5.40).

---

[21] See also Diessel (1999: 115–55) for discussion of the diachrony of demonstrative pronouns and deictic adverbs of space in a range of languages. The discussion covers both sides of the diachrony coin: on the one side, how demonstratives and deictic adverbs of space develop into a wide variety of grammatical markers such as definite articles, third-person pronouns, and complementizers, as is the case of English, where the demonstrative *that* develops into the complementizer *that* and relativizer *that*; on the other, what is the historical source of demonstratives and deictic adverbs of space.

[22] Alternatively, the three-way contrast is termed 'proximal', 'distal' (or 'mid-distance'), and 'extreme-distal' (e.g. Malotki 1982: 234).

(5.40)		*Proximal*	*Medial*	*Distal*
	Classic Arabic	huna	hunaak	hunaalik
	Scottish English	this	that	yon
	Hopi	i	pam	mi
	Southern Sotho	see	seo	sane
	Yimas	p-k	m-n	p-n

On the other hand, in languages like Basque, Ewondo, Georgian, Japanese, Korean, Quechua, Swahili, Thai, Old Church Slavonic, Palauan, Pangasinan, Ponapean, Samoan, and Tagalog, the three terms can be identified as proximal to the speaker (Sp), proximal or **identifiable** to the addressee (Adr), and distal from both the speaker and the addressee. In this paradigm, the middle term points to a location that is close to the addressee. Following Anderson and Keenan (1985) and Diessel (1999: 39) again, we label this three-term system '**person-oriented**'. In essence, a person-oriented system is a **speaker-and/or-addressee-centred** (Levinson 2004) or **speaker-centric one** (Hanks 2011). By way of illustration, take (5.41).

(5.41)		*Proximal (Sp)*	*Proximal (Adr)*	*Distal (Sp + Adr)*
	Ewondo	ɲɔ	ɲɔlo	ɲɔli
	Georgian	es	eg	is/igi
	Japanese	kore	sore	are
	Manambu	k-	wa-	a-
	Palauan	tia	tilechaa	se
	Pangasinan	(i)yá	(i)tán	(i)mán
	Ponapean	me(t)	men	mwo
	OC Slavonic	sy	ty	ony

In addition, there are languages whose three-term system is not easily assigned as distance- or person-oriented. Latin, Spanish, and Turkish seem to belong to this category (see e.g. the debate between Frei 1944, Lyons 1977, and Anderson and Keenan 1985).

It has been claimed that a distance-oriented system tends to have fewer members than a person-oriented one. The former is normally confined to three deictic terms, but there is no such restriction on the latter (Fillmore 1982: 48–9; Diessel 1999: 40). But such a view is challenged by Anderson and Keenan (1985: 286–95). A second claim is that distance- and person-oriented systems cannot co-exist in the same language. Daga appears to be a counterexample to this claim. According to Anderson and Keenan (1985: 291), in this language, the demonstratives *uta/utu/use* and *ita/ita/ise* present a distance-oriented three-term system, while the demonstratives *ma* and *ame* contrast on a person-oriented system. Another counterexample is Yélî Dnye.

(5.42)   Demonstrative adjectives in Yéli Dnye (Levinson 2004)

	Distance-oriented	*Person-oriented*
Proximal	ala	ye
Medial	kî	
Distal	mu	

As can be seen in (5.42), Yélî Dnye combines a distance-oriented and a person-oriented system: while *ala/kî/mu* is speaker-based, *ye* is clearly addressee-based[23] (Levinson 2004). See also Jungbluth's (2003) rejection of a pure distance- versus person-oriented distinction based on the analysis of Spanish, Meira's (2003) arguments against it based on the study of Brazilian Portuguese and Tiriyo, and Leonard's (1985) discussion of demonstratives in Swahili.

Finally, it should be pointed out that, firstly, the distance- versus person-oriented distinction can in principle be applied to any systems with more than three terms as well. Secondly, the distance-oriented system seems to be the dominant one in the three- and more-than-three-term systems of demonstratives and deictic adverbs of space. For example, two-thirds of the one hundred and forty-nine languages surveyed in Hyslop (1993) are found to be distance-oriented.

Four-term systems. Some of the world's languages present a quadripartite system of space deixis. Hausa, Kusaiean, Marshallese, Samal, Sre, Tlingit, and Waray are languages of this type. Of these, Kusaiean and Tlingit represent distance-oriented systems. This can be shown in the four-way contrast in the Kusaiean demonstratives *nge* 'this', *ngacn* 'that', *ngoh* 'that over there', and *ngi* 'that way over there' (Goddard 2011: 344). Clearly, the fourth term points to some entity that is more remote from the speech situation. The same can be said of Tlingit (Anderson and Keenan 1985: 286). By contrast, Hausa, Marshallese, Quileute, Samal, Sre, and Waray are examples of a person-oriented system. In Hausa, the terms are *nân* 'close to the speaker', *nan* 'close to the addressee', *cân* 'away from both, but still

---

[23] In a person-oriented system, internal distinctions may be made concerning the degrees of distance from the addressee. Satawal is a language of this type. As reported in Imai (2003: 72), this language uses different terms to mean 'in the addressee's hand' and 'close to the addressee'.

visible', and *can* 'further away from both, less visible' (Jaggar and Buba 1994; Saeed 2003: 183). The four demonstratives in Sre are *dɔ* 'close to the speaker', *dɛn* 'close to the addressee', *nɛ* 'not close to the speaker, not close to the addressee', and *həʔ* 'remote, out of sight' (Anderson and Keenan 1985: 287). In Quileute, we find *yü′x:o′* 'close to the speaker', *yi′tca′* 'close to the addressee', *sa″a* 'close to the speaker and the addressee', and *ha* 'away from the speaker and the addressee' (Diessel 1999: 41). The same is true of Waray: *adi* 'close to the speaker', *itu* 'close to the addressee', *ini* 'close to the speaker and the addressee', and *itu* 'distal or far away' (Imai 2003). In Marshallese, there are *y&y/yih&h* 'close to the speaker', *yin* 'close to the speaker, close to the addressee', *ney/neyney* 'not close to the speaker, close to the addressee', and *yen/yiyen* 'not close to the speaker, not close to the addressee' (& represents a vowel in the Marshallese orthography) (Goddard 2011: 344). Finally, Samal is a language whose four-way distinction can be glossed as 'close to the speaker', 'close to the addressee', 'close to the audience, i.e. the other participants in the conversation', and 'away from all of the above' (Fillmore: 1997: 65–6, but see Levinson 1983: 81 for a different gloss).

See whether you are ready to do Exercise 7 at the end of this chapter.

More than four-term systems. There are also languages in the world with more than four terms. These include Kwakiutl (with six terms), Malagasy (with six or seven terms), Koasati (with seven terms), Yucatec Maya, and Yup'ik. There are even languages which have several hundred terms/forms. One such language is Santali, in which there are well over 200 distinct forms of demonstratives and deictic adverbs of space. Another is Inuktitut, whose demonstrative and deictic adverb of space system comprises 686 different forms (Hanks 1992; Diessel 1999: 13). While some of the languages with more than four terms like CiBemba are defined along the basic, single deictic dimension of distance, as in (5.43), most are involved with more than one dimension of deictic organization, to which I shall now turn.

(5.43) Spatial deictic terms in CiBemba (cited in Sidnell 2009)

        ù-nó   this (immediately adjacent to or on speaker)

        ù-yú   this (nearer speaker than addressee)

        ù-yóò   this (equally near or relevant to both)

        ù-yó   that (immediately adjacent to or on addressee)

        ù-lyà   that (away from both)

Visibility and audibility

One additional dimension of deictic contrast that is deployed by many of the world's languages is that of **visibility**, which is in general concerned with whether or not the entity to be pointed to is within sight of the speaker from the place of speaking. Demonstratives in Kwakwa'la, for example, show a basic person-oriented three-way contrast along the deictic dimension of distance. But in addition, each of the three persons is marked for visibility.[24] In Yup'ik, the set of 'restricted' demonstratives is employed to point to visible entities, and the set of 'obscured' demonstratives is used for entities that are not in sight. Daga utilizes the suffix *-t/-m* for visibility marking and the suffix *-pa/-pe* for invisibility marking (Anderson and Keenan 1985). The Kashmiri distal demonstrative pronoun has two variants: *hu* for an entity within sight and *su* for an entity out of sight. Coastal Yidiɲ utilizes a demonstrative stem *yu-* to refer to entities that are both distant and visible (Dixon 1977: 180–1). Finally, Mayan is also a family of languages which contains a visibility–invisibility contrast in its deictic system. For example, in Mopan Maya, while *tilo'* is the third-person locative for something visible, *te'* is the third-person locative for something that is invisible (Danziger 1994). By contrast, the category of invisibility in Kabardian is marked by *a* (Colarusso 1989: 269). According to Becker and Mary (1997: 156), Moroccan Arabic has three markers for simple/compound locatives: *hna(yalhafayn)* for proximate, *temma(-yalk/rah)* for distal, and *lheh/dikjih* for invisible entities. Invisibility in Ute is indicated by *'ú/'úru/'úmu*. Other American Indian languages which have particular demonstratives for invisible entities include Epena Pedee, West Greenlandic, Halkomelem, Passamaquoddy-Maliseet, Tümpisa Shoshone, and Quileute. Quileute is particularly interesting in that (while most languages have a single deictic term to refer to invisible objects) it has a set of three deictic adverbs of space to indicate invisibility: *xa'x:e* for entities nearby (which may be partially visible), *tci"tc'* for entities whose location is known, and *xu'xwa'* for entities whose location is unknown (Diessel 1999: 42). Locationals in Khasi (Diessel 1999: 43) and Malagasy (Anderson and Keenan 1985: 288, 293) can also be

---

[24] Note that in Kwakwa'la, the marking of visibility is not restricted to demonstratives. Every noun phrase in the language is overtly indicated for visibility (Anderson and Keenan 1985)—a feature that is considered by Levinson (2004) to be characteristic of many American Indian languages.

marked for invisibility. Furthermore, Imai (2003) distinguished three types of invisibility: (i) invisible-remote, (ii) invisible-occlusion, and (iii) invisible-periphery. The first type of the invisibility parameter, **invisible-remote** is used to mark entities that are out of sight and far from the speaker. Most languages which encode invisibility belong to this category. Secondly, **invisible-occlusion** is employed to point to entities that are behind an obstacle or inside a container. Finally, there is **invisible-periphery**, which is utilized to encode entities that are not visible but **audible** and/or **olfactory**, that is to say, things that the speaker cannot see but can identify by their noise and/or smell. The deictic term *anagha* in Muna is said to be used to make reference to some entity that is invisible but audible (Imai 2003). Another, perhaps better example is provided by *he?eb'e* in Yucatec Maya, which encodes its referent as audible (Hanks 1992). Thus, we have another dimension of contrast within the relational component of spatial deictic expressions here, namely **audibility**. Other languages that mark visibility/invisibility include Bengali, Crow, Jarawara, Kwakiutl, Lillooet, Palikur, Shoshore, and West Greenlandic (Dixon 2003; Fortescue 1984; Hanks 1992; see also Danziger 1994 on Mopan Maya). Note further that in any language that presents a privative contrast between visibility and invisibility, it is invisibility that is normally marked specially. In other words, no language has a special form encoding what is visible, unless it also has a form to indicate what is invisible (Hanks 2011).

In addition to languages that encode a deictic referent as being visible, audible, or olfactory, as mentioned above, occasionally there are also languages that mark other types of perceptual (such as tactile and gustatory) access to deictic referents. For example, Yucatec Maya deictic presentatives have a tripartite contrast between tactual (for entities within the touch of speaker), visual (for entities visible to both speaker and addressee), and peripheral sensory (for entities perceived by hearing, smell, or taste).[25] Of these various perceptual parameters, the parameter of vision is clearly the

---

[25] Again, of particular interest is the use of gestures for expressing spatially deictic information such as distance and visibility. As an illustrating example, Dixon (2003) cited the Tucano and Arawak languages of the Vaupes river basin. In these languages, different deictic gestures are used for varying distances and visibility. For example, pointing with the lips is for 'visible and near'; pointing with the lips plus a backwards tilt of the head signifies 'visible and not near'; and pointing with the index finger is for 'not visible' (if the direction in which the object lies is known).

most important one. This is because vision plays the most vital role in locating an object in space (Hanks 2011).

Elevation and geography

Another additional kind of spatial specification is that of what Hyslop (1993) and Diessel (1999) called **elevation**, that is, the physical dimension of height of the entity relative to the deictic centre, typically the speaker. In languages that use this **geometric parameter**, to borrow the term from Imai (2003), the deictic centre, typically the speaker sets a horizontal line as the zero point. When the entity is above the line, 'up' or 'upwards' is used; when it is below the line, 'down' or 'downwards' is employed. Nine languages in Diessel's (1999) sample, for example, mark this landscape feature. They are Byanisi, Khasi, Lahu, Hua, Usan, Tauya, Dyirbal, Ngiyambaa, and Lezgian. Of those languages which signify elevation, most make a basic distinction between 'up' or 'upwards' and 'down' or 'downwards'. Abkhaz, Lahu, and Paamese are such languages. Khasi uses *u-tey* for 'up' and *u-thie* for 'down'. In Lahu, *nô* signifies 'up (there)', and *mô* 'down (there)' (Diessel 1999: 43; Dixon 2003). West Greenlandic has four separate deictic roots that combine distance with **verticality**, namely, 'medial-up', 'medial-down', 'distal-up', and 'distal-down' (Fortescue 1984: 259–62). Tauya utilizes the prefix *pise-* to mark a location above the deictic centre and *tofe-* to indicate a location below the deictic centre (MacDonald 1990). In Tuscan, the deictic adverb of space *quassù* is employed to point to an entity which is in a higher position than the speaker, *quaggiù* ('close to the speaker but far from the addressee') and *laggiù* (far from both the speaker and addressee') are used to refer to an entity which is in a lower position than the speaker (G. Vognoli, personal communication). Other languages distinguish three degrees of height: 'above the speaker', 'below the speaker', and 'level with the speaker'. These include Angguruk, Epo, Daga, Yale, and the Arakul dialect of Lak. Of these languages, the Arakul dialect of Lak uses *ho* to encode 'higher or lower than the speaker' and *hara* to indicate 'farther away from but on the same level with the speaker' (Dixon 2003). Daga also marks more than one degree of elevation above and below the speaker.

One variant of elevation is where height is marked in terms of 'uphill' versus 'downhill' and/or 'upriver' versus 'downriver', depending partially on the geographic environments in which a particular language is spoken. The former is usually found in languages that are spoken in mountainous regions—for example, those of Australia, Papua New Guinea, and the

Himalayas; and the latter, in languages that are used in areas where there are rivers. This Diessel (1999) called **geography** and Imai (2003) termed the **geographic parameter**. From the perspective of the frame of spatial reference, the information contained in the geographic parameter is in the absolute system. Lahu is a language which marks the geographic feature 'uphill/downhill' (Hanks 2011: 329), and so is Tzeltal (Brown and Levinson 1993). Dyirbal encodes both 'uphill/downhill' and 'upriver/downriver'. In this language, there are two sets of deictic markers which are employed to suffix a noun marker. One set indicates a contrast of height relative to the speaker, but the other set marks both uphill/downhill (*-day/-baydi*) and upriver/downriver/across river (*-dawala/-balbala/-guya*) (Dixon 1972: 48, 2003).

(5.44) dayi   short distance uphill
        daya   medium distance uphill
        dayu   long distance uphill
        baydi   short distance downhill
        bayda   medium distance downhill
        baydu   long distance downhill

Another language is Yup'ik whose large series of demonstratives contain the 'upstream/downstream/across river' opposition (Levinson 2004). In Kri, the geographic features 'up/down riverine' and 'up/down environment' are signified. Finally, other languages that mark the geographic features of elevation include Eskimo, Hua, Muna, Tepehuan, West Greenlandic, and Zayse (Dixon 2003; Diessel 1999: 44–5; Imai 2003).

Side/interiority
A further deictic dimension of contrast is involved with the concept of **side** or **interiority**. It is concerned with whether the entity referred to is **inside, outside**, or **lateral** to the deictic centre. In Aleut, *ukán* is used to indicate a referent that is 'inside the house', and *sadán* is employed to mark a referent that is 'outside the house'. West Greenlandic utilizes *qam-* for 'in/out' and *kig-* for 'outside', and *av-* for 'in the north' and *qav-* for 'in the south'. It is also a language in which there is a set of deictic terms which encodes on which side of a settlement an entity is located: seaward or west side, inland or east side, north side, and south side. This is given in (5.45) (Fortescue 1984: 259–63, see also Goddard 2011: 345).

(5.45)   sanna   far down on the seaward/west side
         kanna   not far down on the seaward/west side
         panna   far up on the inland/east side
         pinnga   not far up on the inland/east side
         anna   on the north side
         quanna   on the south side

Inuktitut is a language that encodes a five-way spatial distinction for the distal locative 'there', namely, 'up-there', 'down-there', 'in-there', 'out-there', and 'over-there (horizontal)' (Denny 1982: 361). In Yucatec Maya, the regional forms of spatial deictics distinguish between 'inside (inclusive of the *origo*)' and 'outside (exclusive of the *origo*)'. Santali marks lateral to *origo* (Hanks 2011). There are also languages that differentiate side-proximal from side-distal.

Stance and movement or directionality
Finally, there is the deictic dimension of **stance**. According to Ceria and Sandalo (1995), in languages of the Waikurúan family, the demonstratives must indicate the stance or **movement** or **directionality** of the referent—whether it is 'standing', 'sitting', 'lying', 'coming', or 'going' (see also Dixon 2003 on languages in the Siouan family). Nunggubuyu has what Heath (1980: 152) called 'kinetics', which indicate a three-way distinction between *-ala-* ('approaching'), *-ali-* ('going away'), and *-waj-* ('across'). Other languages that mark an entity in motion include Crow, Inuititut, Kiowa, and Santali (Hanks 2011). I shall return to motion later.

Deictically marked third-person pronouns
The next category on our list is **deictically marked third-person pronouns**. These pronouns specify the location of the intended referent with respect to the deictic centre, typically the speaker.[26] In some of the languages employing deictically marked third-person pronouns, the encoding of distance is optional; in others, it is obligatory. Diyari, for example, is a language in which third-person pronouns may be optionally suffixed by *-rda* (indicating that the referent is in the immediate vicinity, usually up to a few metres

---

[26] By contrast, third-person pronouns in languages like Chinese, English, and Russian are not marked deictically, and as such, they are not considered as deictic expressions. This is because they do not have a deictic usage as their basic or central usage.

away), *-ya* (indicating that the referent is close by and visible), or *-wa* (indicating that the referent is distant including distant and visible) (Austin 1982). By contrast, in Kwakwa'la, there are no third-person pronouns which are unmarked for deixis (Anderson and Keenan 1985: 290).

Specially marked deictic third-person pronouns are found in many South Asian languages. These include Dravidian languages like Kannada, Malayalam, Tamil, and Telugu, Indo-Aryan languages like Bangala, Hindi/Urdu, Kashmiri, Oriya, Punjabi, and Sinhala, and Austro-Asiatic languages like Juang (Lust et al. 2000). A few examples from the South Asian languages are given in (5.46).

(5.46)		*Proximal*	*Distal*
	Bangala	e	o
	Kannada	ivanu	avanu
	Oriya	ye	se
	Punjabi	eh	oh
	Tamil	ivan	avan

The same is true of some Australian aboriginal languages. For example, the Thargari third-person singular pronoun distinguishes 'near', 'far', and 'remote'. In Pittapitta, there are also three third-person forms, marking (i) proximity to the speaker's front or side, (ii) proximity to the speaker's back, and (iii) remoteness anywhere from the speaker. Finally, for the Western Desert language, the third-person pronoun displays a quadripartite system, namely 'near', 'mid-distant', 'distant', and 'non-visible' (Dixon 1972: 8).

There are also languages in which the third-person pronoun encodes visibility. One such language is the Western Desert language, just mentioned. Another is Mantauran (Rukai) spoken in Taiwan. In this language, visibility is marked by *ana* for third-person singular and *ana-lo* for third-person plural, and invisibility, by *ona* for third-person singular and *ona-lo* for third-person plural (Zeitoun 1997).

Deictic directionals
Finally, we come to deictic directionals. Deictic directionals can be grouped into two categories: (i) motion affixes, morphemes, and particles, also called '**kinetics**', which usually mean 'hither/thither', and (ii) motion verbs—verbs such as 'come' and 'go' that encode motion towards or away from the deictic centre, typically the speaker. Many languages in the world do not have motion verbs, and make do instead with motion affixes, morphemes,

and particles. In Yélî Dnye, the 'hither' particle can be used with the unmarked 'go' verb *lê* to express 'come here'. The interesting point is that this language does not have a 'thither' particle (Levinson 2004). By contrast, in Abaza, there are two directional verbal prefixes: *ʕa* indicates that the movement denoted by the verb is directed towards the speaker's location at CT, and *na* indicates that it is directed away from the speaker's location at CT (Anderson and Keenan 1985: 277; Manning 2001: 79). Ngandi utilizes *-ni-* for proximity and *-na-* for non-proximity (Hanks 1992). Diyari is a language which uses *yarra* (venitive or towards the speaker's location) and *yada* (andative or away from the speaker's location) to express the direction of (induced) motion (Austin 1982). In Somali, one combines *soo* and *sii* with a verb to indicate that the motion proceeds towards or away from the speaker, respectively. This is shown in (5.47) (Saeed 2003).

(5.47) a. Soo   soco.
          hither   walk
          'Come this way.' or
          'Come here.'
    b. Sii   soco.
          thither   walk
          'Go away.'

Kiowa has a set of three directional markers: *-dé* indicates movement towards the deictic centre, *-p*, movement away from the deictic centre, and *-pé*, movement across the visual field of the speaker (Watkins 1984). As already mentioned above, a similar set of three directional suffixes can be found in Nunggubuyu (Heath 1980, see also Diessel 1999: 45–6). In Ponapean, there is a set of three verbal suffixes that mark directionality: *-do* (toward me), *-wei* (toward you), and *-la* (away from you and me) (e.g. Sidnell 2009). Among the set of post-verbal particles reconstructed for Proto-Polynesian, and widely found in its daughter languages, are five which are considered to be directional: *mai* (towards the speaker), *atu* (away from the speaker), *hake* (upwards), *hifo* (downwards), and *aŋe* (alongside, obliquely) (Hopper 2002). Finally, many North American Indian languages have rich sets of verbal motion affixes, morphemes, and particles, which express both deictic and absolute coordinate information (Mithun 1999; Levinson 2004).

We turn next to motion verbs such as 'come' and 'go'. Of these two verbs, 'go' is the unmarked one, whose condition of use can be roughly stated as movement away from the speaker's location at the CT.[27] However, when we consider 'come', we find that its use is more complicated. Following the seminal work of Fillmore (1971, 1997), the conditions for the use of 'come' in English can be summed up as follows: (i) movement towards the speaker's location at CT, (ii) movement towards the speaker's location at **arrival time**, (iii) movement towards the addressee's location at CT, (iv) movement towards the addressee's location at arrival time, and (v) movement towards the **home-base** maintained at CT by either the speaker or the addressee. These conditions can be illustrated by a consideration of (5.48).

(5.48)   Sophia will come to the library next week.

(5.48) is five-way ambiguous or vague. In the first place, the sentence can be used when the speaker is in the library at the time of speaking. A second possible situation is when the speaker is in the library at arrival time, namely, the time when Sophia will arrive in the library. Thirdly, the sentence can be uttered when the addressee is in the library at speech time. Fourthly, the sentence can be used when the addressee is in the library at arrival time. Suppose that you work in the library but I don't. I can use (5.48) to tell you that Sophia will come to your library next week, either if you are there at the time of speaking or if you will be there when Sophia arrives (see also Marmaridou 2000: 91–3). Finally, the sentence can also be said in a situation where the destination is not the participants' *actual* location, but their *nominative* location such as their home, workplace, or school at the time of speaking. This nominative location Fillmore (1971) called home-base. Suppose that you and I both work in the library. One of us can say (5.48) or even better (5.49) when neither you are nor I am in the library (see also Levinson 1983: 83–5).

(5.49)   Sophia will come to the library next week, but both of us will be on holiday then.

There are even languages which utilize different deictic expressions to express movement towards or away from the home-base and non-home-base. One such language is Diuxi Mixtec. In this language, distinct verbal categories are employed to encode the distinction between home-base and

---

[27] There are languages that do not have a semantic equivalent to the English motion verb *go*. These include German, Polish (Goddard 2011), and Longgu, a language spoken on the Solomon Islands (Wilkins and Hill 1995).

non–home-base: *ndisi* for motion towards, and *nuʔu* for motion away from, the home-base, and *vásí* for motion towards, and *hiʔi* for motion away from, the non-home-base (Manning 2001: 75).

> At this point, see whether you can tackle Exercise 8 at the end of this chapter.

The use of 'come' in Catalan, Chinese, French, German, and Punjabi seems to behave like their equivalent in English, though the relevant details of each individual language need to be worked out. On the other hand, in languages like Hungarian (Batori 1982), Japanese (Coulmas 1982), and Spanish (Hottenroth 1982), 'go' has to be used if movement is towards the addressee (see also Sinha 1972 on Hindi; Gandour 1978 on Thai; Gathercole 1977 on Turkish; Fillmore 1997 and Levinson 1983: 84 on Chinantec; Wilkins and Hill 1995 and Goddard 2011: 258–63 on Arrernte; and Botne 2005 on Chindali).

Recently, Levinson (2004) has suggested that another parameter—specifying whether 'come' is marked for **telicity** or not—be added to the parameter of whether it requires the destination to be the place of speaking, as discussed above. The suggestion is based on the following observation. Suppose that Sophia comes towards me but stops short before she arrives at the tree over there, I can say 'Sophia came to the tree' in English but not in Longgu or Italian, where I must say 'Sophia went to the tree'. Using the two parameters, one arrives at the following classification of the 'come'-type motion verbs in the world's languages (Levinson 2004).

(5.50) Levinson's (2004) classification of 'come'-type motion verbs

	+Telic	−Telic (unmarked)
Destination is place of speaking	Longgu	Italian
Destination need not be place of speaking	Ewe	Tamil

Furthermore, Levinson (2000) put forward a neo-Gricean pragmatic analysis of 'come' and 'go' by arguing that they form a privative Q_{scalar} opposition <come, go>. As such, the use of the semantically weaker, unmarked 'go' where the semantically stronger, more informative 'come' might have been used will Q-implicate that the speaker is not in a position to use 'come'. The reason is because at least one of the conditions specified for 'come' in (5.50) is not met.

5.3. Other categories of deixis

In the last section, I discussed the three main types of deixis, namely, person, time, and space. In this section, I shall take a look at three other types of deixis, namely, social, discourse, and emotional.

5.3.1. Social deixis

Social deixis is concerned with the codification of the social status of the speaker, the addressee, or a third person or entity referred to as well as the social relationships holding between them (e.g. Fillmore 1997: 111–12; Levinson 1983: 63; Anderson and Keenan 1985; Manning 2001). The information encoded in social deixis may include social class, kin relationship, age, sex, profession, and ethnic group. Defined thus, social deixis is particularly closely associated with person deixis. In fact, there are scholars (e.g. Marmaridou, 2000: 79, 81) who argue that person deixis cannot be studied independently of social deixis, hence the term '**socio-person deixis**'.[28]

Absolute versus relational social deixis
Following Comrie (1976), Levinson (1983: 90–1), and Brown and Levinson (1987), two main types of socially deictic information can be identified: (i) **absolute**, and (ii) **relational**. Absolute information in social deixis can be illustrated by forms that are reserved for authorized speakers or authorized recipients. For example, in imperial China, there was a form *zhen* that was specially reserved for the emperor to refer to himself. The same situation is

---

[28] As pointed out by Mühlhäusler and Harré (1990: 264–5), the presence of social deixis implies that of person deixis, but not vice versa. This can be supported by the fact that in the historical reduction of pronoun systems, those pronouns that mark social deixis tend to be lost. Furthermore, the V form is typically replaced by the T form. For example, pidgin German spoken in various parts of the world employs *du* rather than *Sie* as its second-person singular pronoun. The French-derived pidgins of New Caledonia and West Africa use *tu* rather than *vous*. On the other hand, given that pidgins usually develop in contexts where power plays an important role, pronouns encoding differential social status can be introduced relatively early in their developments, as is the case of Tay Boi, the Pidgin French of French Indochina, the Portuguese-derived Kriol of Guiné-Bissau, and Zambuangueño, the Spanish Creole spoken in the Philippines.

reported by Fillmore (1997) to be true of Japanese. Going next to forms that are reserved for authorized recipients, restrictions are placed on most titles of addresses such as *Your Majesty*, *Mr President*, and *Professor* in English.

Four axes of relational social deixis

Relational information in social deixis can be represented between (i) speaker and referent (e.g. referent honorifics), (ii) speaker and addressee (e.g. addressee honorifics), (iii) speaker and bystander (e.g. bystander honorifics), and (iv) speaker and setting (e.g. levels of formality). **Referent honorifics** are forms that are employed by the speaker to show respect towards the referent; **addressee honorifics** are forms that are used by the speaker to show deference towards the addressee. Defined thus, the main difference between the speaker-referent axis and the speaker-addressee axis, according to Comrie (1976), is that while in the former, respect or honour can only be conveyed by referring to the target of the respect, in the latter, it can be conveyed without such a direct reference being necessary. Respectful pronouns such as the French *vous* used to address a singular addressee (to be elaborated below) are not addressee honorifics (as has been commonly mistakenly believed) but referent honorifics, which happen to refer to the addressee. By contrast, the Tamil particle *-nka* is an addressee honorific, which can be adjoined freely to any constituent of a sentence, and which conveys respect to addressees only, but not to any referents in the sentence honorifics (e.g. Levinson 1983, 2004; Brown and Levinson 1987: 180). Referent honorifics are more common than addressee honorifics.

Next, **bystander honorifics** are forms that are used by the speaker to signify respect to a bystander, including participants in the role of audience and non-participant overhearers. A classic example is the use of so-called '**mother-in-law**' and '**brother-in-law**' languages in Australian aboriginal languages such as Dyirbal, Guugu Yimidhirr, and Umpila. This special 'avoidance' language, style, or register is used in the presence of someone, especially a relative, prototypically a mother-in-law, with whom close social contact is taboo. One of the interesting characteristics of such a language is that a part or nearly all of its vocabulary has to be replaced by special 'avoidance' lexical items. Dyirbal, for example, has a *guwal*, or everyday language, and a *dyalŋuy*, or 'mother-in-law' language. While these varieties are identical in phonology and largely identical in grammar, they are entirely different in vocabulary (Dixon 1972: 32–3). More or less the same can be said of Guugu Yimidhirr. In this language, a brother-in-law would typically be the tabooed kin whose presence would trigger the use of alternative lexical items. Contrast (5.51a) in Guugu Yimidhirr everyday language and (5.51b) in its 'brother-in-law' variety.

(5.51) a. Ngayu   mayi   buda-nhu.
           1SG-NOM   food-ABS   eat-PURP
           'I want to eat food'.

        b. Ngayu   gudhubay   bambanga-nhu.
           1SG-NOM   food-ABS   eat-PURP
           'I want to eat food'.

In (5.51b), while the grammatical word *ngayu* is retained, the lexical words *mayi* and *buda-* are replaced by the respectful words *gudhubay* and *bambanga-*, respectively (Haviland 1979: 368–9). This kind of grammaticalization of bystander honorifics and/or other bystander social deictic information has also been cited by Levinson (1988: 191, 204) for other, non-Australian languages such as Abipon, Ponapean, and Tojolabal (see also Keating 1998 on Pohnpei and Levinson 2004 on Yélî Dnye).

Finally, the **speaker–setting axis** has to do with the relation between the speaker (and perhaps other participants) and the speech setting or event. Although the formal–informal style can be said to be characteristic of perhaps all languages to a certain extent (for example, many European languages have distinct registers used on formal and informal occasions), the distinction is more firmly grammaticalized and/or lexicalized in a number of East, Southeast, and South Asian languages including Balinese, Japanese, Javanese, Korean, Thai, and Tibetan. Social deictic information is encoded in Japanese across all levels of grammar including morphology, syntax, and lexicon (e.g. Shibatani 1990). The same is true of Tamil, which has diglossic variants, with distinct morphology for formal and literary styles (Levinson 1983: 91, 93, 2004). Thai has what Diller (1993) called diglossic grammaticality, which differs markedly in its 'high' and 'low' syntax. Javanese is reported to have ten different speech levels. An example is given here.

(5.52) (Javanese, Anderson and Keenan 1985: 275)
        a. *Krama/Keromo* 'Formal'
           Kulo   saweg   maos   buku   Djawi.
           I   be-PROG   read   book   Javanese
           'I'm reading a Javanese book.'

b. *Ngoko* 'Informal'

Aku	lagi		motjo	buku	Djowo.
I	be-PROG	read		book	Javanese

'I'm reading a Javanese book.'

More or less the same is also true of two Austronesian languages, Madurese (Levinson 1983; Brown and Levinson 1987: 180) and Samoan (Haviland 1979). In addition, many languages in the world have replacement vocabularies. For example, in English, on formal occasions, one may use *dine* to replace *eat*, *residence* to replace *home*, and *bestow* to replace *give* (Brown and Levinson 1987: 181). Many Australian aboriginal languages have replacement vocabularies that are employed only during special initiation rites (Dixon 1980: 65–8, see also Haviland 1979 on Gudadja). Finally, Yélî Dnye is a language where there is a replacement vocabulary that is used only when on the sacred islet of Lów:a (Levinson 2004).

The expression of social deixis

Social deixis can be accomplished by a wide range of linguistic devices including personal pronouns, forms of address, affixes, clitics, and particles, and the choice of vocabulary.

Personal pronouns

Personal pronouns can be used to achieve a number of socially deictic effects.

Marking of respect. It is well known that a number of European languages have the familiar *tu/vous* type of distinction in second-person singular pronouns. The distinction has been known as the **T/V distinction** since Brown and Gilman (1960).

In a T/V system, there are two second-person singular pronouns: one familiar or T, and the other polite or V. The following is a list of T/V pronouns in the European languages I have collected.

(5.53) T/V pronouns in European languages

	T	V
French	tu	vous
German	du	Sie
Italian	tu	lei
Spanish	tu'	usted
Romansh	ti	vus
Russian	ty	vy
Slovenian	ti	vi

Danish	du/I	De
Swedish	du	Ni
Dutch	jij	u
Norwegian	du	De
Greek	esi	esis
Welsh	ti	chwi

In fact, the T/V distinction is not restricted to European languages. Based on a study of one hundred of the world's languages, Helmbrecht (2003) divided languages into four types with respect to second-person singular pronouns. First of all, there are languages which do not show the T/V distinction in their personal pronoun systems. Out of his one hundred language sample, seventy-six languages belong to this type. They include English, Manipuri, Mongolian, Burushaski, Hmong Njua, Rama, Imonda, Goonyiandi, Luvukaleve, Acoma, Mapuche, and Zulu. Second is the type of language which displays the European-type binary T/V distinction. In addition to the European languages listed in (5.53), Helmbrecht singled out Basque, Finnish, Persian, Georgian, Turkish, Chinese, Mixtec, Fijian, Quechua, Luvale, Nama, Sango, and Yoruba. To Helmbrecht's list we can add Ainu, Punjabi, Bangala, Kashmir, Marathi, Oriya, Telugu, Mparntwe Arrernte, Djaru, Khasi, Usan, Dullay, Tigak, Guarijio, Guugu Yimidhirr, Tamil, and Ponapean (see e.g. Brown and Levinson 1987: 198–203; Corbett 2000: 220–1; Lust et al. 2000). Note that in Bangala and Oriya, in addition to the T and V forms, there is also a third, **neutral form (N)**. Thirdly, there are languages which show two or more *degrees* in the T/V distinction. Three South Asian languages—Hindi/Urdu, Kannada, and Tagalog—are considered to be such languages. Finally, there are languages in which second-person pronouns are in general avoided in polite address. Instead, professional titles or kinship terms are used as a mark of respect. Helmbrecht mentioned six East and Southeast Asian languages, namely, Burmese, Indonesian, Japanese, Korean, Thai, and Vietnamese. To this list we can add Dzongkha, and to a lesser extent Chinese (see also Shibatani 1999).

The V form is most commonly derived from the second-person plural pronoun. This is the case of, for example, French, Persian, Yoruba, Nama, and Fijian. The next most common way is for the V pronoun to be developed out of the third-person plural pronoun, as is exemplified by German, Lurale, and Tagalog. There are other sources. In some languages, the V form is borrowed from the third-person singular pronoun. Italian and Indonesian belong to this category of languages. In others, it comes from the first-person plural pronoun, as in Ainu and Nahuatl; or it is derived from the second-person demonstrative pronoun, as in Sinhalese; or it is developed out of the reflexive pronoun, as in Hungarian and Imbabura Quechua. The V form can come from status terms. *Usted* in Spanish, for instance, is derived from *vuestra merced* meaning 'your grace'. Other languages which belong to this category include Burmese, Dutch, Rumanian, Vietnamese, and Thai. Finally, there are also languages whose V forms are derived from more than one source. The V form in Hindi comes from both the reflexive and the third-person plural pronoun, and that in Kannada, from both the second- and third-person plural pronouns (Helmbrecht 2003). See also the papers collected in Taavitsainen and Jucker (2003) for discussion of the diachronic development of the T/V system covering English, Anglo-Norman, German (both Middle High and Modern Standard), Swedish, Czech, French, Spanish, and Finnish.

In addition to languages with second-person polite pronouns, there are languages which have third-person honorific pronouns. This is the case of many Southeast Asian languages like Kashmiri, Malayalam, and Oriya. In Bangala, for example, the T form is *se* for singular and *ta-ra* for plural, and the V form is *tini* for singular and *tã-ra* for plural. Another Southeast Asian language which imposes the social restrictions on the use of third-person pronouns is Punjabi. In this language, the spatially deictic contrast in the third-person singular pronoun carries over into the socially deictic domain. While the proximal form *eh* 'he/she' is used to refer to intimates and inferiors, its distal counterpart *oh* is employed to refer to non-intimates and superiors. In other words, whereas the former acts as T, the latter serves the function of V, to signify the social relationship between the speaker and the referent. Next in Tamil, another Southeast Asian language, the plurality of the T/V distinction is extended to third-person pronouns. *Avaanka* 'they' is used to refer respectfully to a male or (especially) a female. Furthermore, this plurality also carries over into the first-person, with the use of the royal 'we' (Brown and Levinson 1987: 180), which brings us to first-person pronouns. Javanese is a language that is well known in this respect. It has three distinct first-person pronouns: *aku* is the form used to talk to equals, *kulo* is employed when talking to intimate superiors, and *kawulo* is used to talk to non-intimate superiors.

Marking of kinship relations. Personal pronouns are used to mark kinship relations. The Australian aboriginal language Parnkalla, for example, has three forms in the first-person dual pronoun: *nadli* is used for general first-person dual; *nadlaga*, for mother and child, and uncle and nephew; and *narrine*, for father and one of his children. But more systematic is the use of different sets of pronouns in some other Australian aboriginal languages to distinguish between harmonic and disharmonic kinship relations. Put rather crudely, two people are considered to be generationally **harmonic** if they are both members of the same generation (e.g. ego and brother), or of generations that differ by an even number (e.g. grandparent and grandchild). By contrast, two people are **disharmonic** if they belong to the alternate generations (e.g. ego and parent or child), or they are three generation levels apart (e.g. great grandparent and great grandchild). This is the case of Lardil, where there are two sets of pronouns in dual and plural (Dixon 1980). Finally, even more complicated systems can be found in still some other Australian aboriginal languages. Adnyamadhanha is one such language; Aranda is another. In addition to its harmonic–disharmonic sets, this language has a third set of personal pronouns, which are marked for reference to a group of people non-agnatic to the speaker (e.g. Mühlhäusler and Harré 1990: 165).

Other socially deictic information such as age and sex can also be indicated through the use of personal pronouns. For example, in the Oceanic language Dehu, there are four first-person dual pronouns: *n~iho* is used for two young people exclusive, *eaho* for one young and one old person exclusive, *niso* for two young people inclusive, and *easo* for one young and one old person inclusive (Mühlhäusler and Harré 1990: 170). Turning next to sex, there are languages whose personal pronouns differ with the sex of the addressee. An example is provided by Malagasy. In this language, the second-person singular pronoun has two variants that are used according to the sex of the addressee: *ialahy* for males and *indriaku* for females (Anderson and Keenan 1985).

Forms of address

Forms of address are another common way of realizing social deixis. They include different types of names such as first name (e.g. *John*), last name (e.g. *Matthews*), and a combination of first and last names (e.g. *John Matthews*), kinship terms (e.g. *uncle*), titles borrowed from names of occupations (e.g. *doctor*), ranks in certain social/professional groups (e.g. *colonel*), and other sources (e.g. *madam*), and a combination of titles and names (e.g. *Professor Sir John Lyons*). Terms of address can be used to perform a variety of socially deictic functions. First, in English and many other languages, the use of address forms which include a title and the last name but not the first name such as *Mr Lakoff*, *Dr Cram*, and *Lady Huxley* marks the higher social status of the addressee, and signals the social distance between the speaker and the addressee. For example, when I was a visiting professor at the Zentrum für Allgemeine Sprachwissenschaft Typologie und Universalienforschung (ZAS) in Berlin, I was always addressed as 'Sehr geehrter Herr Prof. Dr. Yan Huang' in writing. Secondly, many languages in the world utilize generalized forms of address such as *ayi* 'aunt' in Chinese, *sir* in English, and *bankilal* 'elder brother' in Tzeltal to show respect to strangers. Thirdly, certain modes of address are used in many languages to claim in-group solidarity. Typical examples are *huoji* 'mate' in Chinese, *pal* in English, and *tampi* 'younger brother' in Tamil (see e.g. Brown and Levinson 1987: 107–11, 182–5 for further discussion). In conclusion, it is not unreasonable to say that in human languages there is no such thing as a socially neutral form of address.

Affixes, clitics, and particles

Socially deictic information can also be encoded by **affixes**, **clitics**, and **particles**. Verb forms in Korean, for example, may select one of the following suffixes attached to them: *-na* marking intimate, *-e* familiar, *-ta* plain, *-eyo* polite, *-supnita* deferential, and finally *-so* authoritative (Trudgill 2000: 93). Another language which signals social relations by means of verbal affixes is Nahuatl. In this language, different affixes may be attached to verbs to indicate such social relations as (i) intimacy, (ii) neutral or somewhat formal, (iii) respect, and (iv) *'compadrazgo'*[29] between the speaker and the addressee. An unusual variant of this socially deictic mechanism has also been reported for the Basque 'familiar voice' forms of non-second-person verbs (Anderson and Keenan 1985).

Choice of vocabulary

Finally, socially deictic information can also be reflected in the choice of the vocabulary used. We have already seen the use of the so-called 'avoidance' language and 'replacement' vocabulary in certain Australian aboriginal languages. Another case in point involves the use of **'triangular kin terms'**. These terms encode the kinship relations not only between the speaker and the referent, the propositus (typically the addressee) and the referent, but also between the speaker and the propositus. Mayali, for example, has a set

---

[29] *Compadrazgo* is a social relation which exists between persons standing in a ritual relation of kinship by virtue of being parent/godparent or godparent/godparent of the same child (Anderson and Keenan 1985).

of terms for referring to the 'father' of one participant in the speech event, depending on the kinship relations between the speaker and the addressee. *Kornkumo* is employed by a mother to her child, referring to the child's father (that is, her husband); *na-ngarrkkang* is used by a woman to her son's child to refer to the child's father (that is, her son); the child in this situation will use *na-rroyngu* back to his or her grandmother to refer to his or her father (that is, her son). Spouses will employ *na-bolo* to refer to the father of either one of them (and father-in-law to the other). And there are even more elaborate terms (Evans 1993).

But more commonly, there are languages which have a whole series of '**deferential**' and '**humiliative**' pairs of lexical items in their vocabularies. Thus, in Chinese, we have *lingzun* '(your) honourable (father)'/*jiafu* '(my) humble father', *guifu* '(your) honourable residence'/*hanshe* '(my) humble hut', and *guixing* 'What's (your) honourable surname?'/*bixing* '(my) humble surname'. The same holds for Japanese, which contains a large number of honorific–humbling sets of lexical items adopted from Chinese such as *rei-situ* '(your) honourable wife'/*gu-sai* '(my) stupid wife', and *gyoku-koo* '(your) splendid article'/*sek-koo* '(my) humble article'. Similar humble forms are also used in the Urdu of Delhi Muslims and in Ponape. As pointed out by Brown and Levinson (1987: 178–9, 185), the use of the honorific–dishonorific terms has a two-sided nature: the lowering of the self on the one hand, and the raising of the addressee on the other (see Duranti 1992 on the Samoan respect vocabulary, see also Traugott and Dasher 2001 for discussion of diachronic development of social deixis).

5.3.2. Discourse deixis

We come next to discourse deixis.[30] **Discourse deixis** is concerned with the use of a linguistic expression within some utterance to point to the current, preceding, or following utterances in the same spoken or written discourse.[31] Alternatively, discourse deixis can be said to refer to propositions (e.g. Lyons

---

[30] Other terms are 'text' and 'textual deixis'.

[31] Defined thus, discourse deixis is essentially endophoric. The **endophoric** use of a deictic expression is secondary in that it is derived from the **exophoric** one. First, from the point of view of ontogeny, children acquire exophoric functions first. Secondly, endophoric uses are frequently developed out of exophoric ones (Sidnell and Enfield (forthcoming)).

1977; Fillmore 1997: 103–6; Diessel 1999: 101). A few illustrative examples from English are given in (5.54).

(5.54)   a. This is how birds evolved from predatory dinosaurs.
   b. That is tonight's evening news.
   c. Here goes the main argument.
   d. In the last section, we discussed conversational implicature, in this section, we consider conventional implicature, and in the next section, we shall compare and contrast them.
   e. As already mentioned, the three main branches of the legal profession in England are solicitors, barristers, and legal executives.

The use of the proximal demonstrative *this* in (5.54a) anticipates upcoming information to be conveyed in a subsequent stretch of the discourse. The same is true of the use of the proximal adverb of space *here* in (5.54c). By contrast, the use of the distal demonstrative *that* in (5.54b) refers back to a preceding segment of the discourse. This is also the case with the use of *already* in (5.54e). The terms *last*, *this*, and *next* used in (5.54d) make reference to a preceding, current, and following portion of the discourse, respectively. The use of discourse deictics such as those in (5.54) can be found in most, if not all, languages in the world. For example, Ambulas uses the proximal manner demonstrative *kéga* and the medial manner demonstrative *aga* to point to a forthcoming segment of the discourse, and the distal manner demonstrative *waga* to refer back to a preceding stretch of the discourse (Diessel 1999: 17). In Usan, one finds *ende* and *ete*, which are used only as discourse deictics. The former is the backward- and the latter the forward-referring discourse deictic (Reesink 1987: 81). Ainu is another language in which manner demonstratives function as discourse deictics (Diessel 1999: 105). I shall provide more data when we come to the marking of the feature 'previously mentioned in the discourse'.

 Next, some of the lexical expressions in English that are claimed to trigger a conventional implicature, discussed in Chapter 2, can also take a discourse deictic function when they occur at the initial position of an utterance. These may include *actually*, *anyway*, *after all*, *besides*, *but*, *even*, *however*, *in conclusion*, *moreover*, *so*, *therefore*, and *well*. As pointed out by Levinson (1983: 87–8), a major function of the utterance-initial usage of these words is to indicate that there is a relation between the utterance that contains them and some portion of the prior discourse.

 Finally, a number of East and Southeast Asian languages have a special mechanism to mark the **topic** in a **topic construction**. A topic construction usually contains two parts: a topic, which typically occurs first, and a **comment**—a clause which follows the topic and says something about it (e.g. Huang 2000a: 266). This can be illustrated by (5.55).

(5.55)   (Korean, cited in Huang 2000a: 267)
         Kkoch-un   kwukhwa-ka   olaykan-ta.
         flower-TOP   chrysanthemum-NOM   last long
         'Flowers, chrysanthemums last long.'

In (5.55), *kkoch* is the topic, *kwukhwa-ka olaykan-ta* is the comment and *un* is the topic marker. In a similar vein, topics are marked in Japanese by *wa*, in Lahu by ɔ, and in Lisu by *nya* (Li and Thompson 1976; Huang 2000a 266–76). In terms of information structure, topics are often associated with **given**, and comments with **new**, information. Clearly one of the main functions of topic marking in these East and Southeast Asian languages is 'precisely to relate the marked utterance to some specific topic raised in the prior discourse, i.e. to perform a discourse-deictic function' (Levinson 1983: 88).

   In fact, marking of previous mention of an entity or given information in the discourse is not restricted to such East and Southeast Asian languages as Chinese, Japanese, and Lisu, which are considered to be **topic-prominent**. Such marking is found in a range of languages around the world. In Daga, for example, *me(pe)* can be suffixed to any of the fourteen demonstratives to yield a further set of discourse deictics to indicate the feature 'previously mentioned in the discourse' (Anderson and Keenan 1985: 291). Lezgian has a deictic marker *ha* to refer to what is aforementioned (Sidnell and Enfield (forthcoming)). Epio is a language which employs *-tebuk* to mark something that has been previously mentioned in the discourse. Yale behaves in a similar fashion (Heeschen 1982: 85, 88, 95). In Hausa, one finds *wànnán* 'the one previously mentioned' as opposed to *wánnàn* 'this (new)', and *wàncán* 'that other (mentioned) one' as opposed to *wáncàn* 'that (new)' (Anderson and Keenan 1985: 289). In Aina, *tan* is used to mark the new topic of a conversation (Dixon 2003).[32]

> Now look at Exercise 9 at the end of this chapter.

---

[32] Recall our discussion of obviation in note 7. As pointed out by Bloomfield (1962: 38), '[t]he proximate third person represents the topic of discourse, the person nearest the speaker's point of view, or the person earlier spoken of and already known'. Therefore obviation may be seen as performing the function of discourse deixis of some sort.

5.3.3. Emotional deixis

One of the extended uses of deixis is to encode **emotional proximity** or **distance** between the deictic centre, typically the speaker and the entity referred to. The employment of a proximate or immediate deictic expression such as *this* in English usually shows empathy from the speaker. By contrast, the use of a distal deictic term such as *that* in English normally conveys emotional distance. This is illustrated by the use of *that woman* by President Bill Clinton in (5.56) and the use of *that one* by the 2008 presidential candidate Senator John McCain in (5.57).

(5.56)   (At the White House press conference held on the 21 January 1998)
Now, I have to go back to work on my State of the Union speech. And I worked on it until pretty late last night. But I want to say one thing to the American people. I want you to listen to me. I am going to say this again: I did not have sexual relations with *that woman*, Miss Lewinsky. I never told anybody to lie, not a single time; never. These allegations are false. And I need to go back to work for the American people. Thank you!

(5.57)   (At the 2008 Second Presidential Debate between John McCain and Barack Obama, quoted from Sidnell and Enfield (forthcoming))
1   By the way my friends: I-I know you grow a little wea:ry
2   with this back-and-forth.
3   (.)
4   It was an energy bill on the floor of the Senate loaded down
5   with goodies. billions for the oil companies. An' it was
6   sponsored by- Bush and Cheney.
7   (0.2)
8   You know who voted for it, might never know, *That one*.
9   You know who voted against it? Me. I have fought time
10   after time against these pork barrel – these-these bills
11   that come to the floor and they have all kinds of goodies
12   an' all kinds of things in them for everybody and they
13   buy off the votes,

I do not think that I need to say anything about (5.56). As for the passage in (5.57), it was produced by McCain in response to a question about energy raised by the debate moderator. Instead of using *Senator Obama* or even *Obama*, McCain selected the deictic expression *that one* to refer to Obama, who was sitting close by at the time. This marked usage by McCain was widely picked up in the American media. Some commentators were of the view that the usage was disrespectful, rude, or even racist, accusing McCain of 'improperly trying to capitalize on Obama's "otherness"' (see also Sidnell and Enfield (forthcoming) for further discussion).

5.4. Summary

In this chapter, I have provided a typologically oriented descriptive analysis of deixis, utilizing a wide range of genetically unrelated and structurally diverse languages around the world. Section 5.1 discussed deictic versus non-deictic expressions, gestural versus symbolic use of deictic expressions, and deictic centre and deictic projection. In Section 5.2, I examined first person, then time, and finally space, deixis. Next, in Section 5.3, I considered social, discourse, and emotional deixis. Although what I have described is at best the tip of the deictic iceberg, whatever little we know about this important linguistic category seems to indicate that despite the universality of deixis, its manifestation in the grammar and/or lexis of natural languages is anything but universal. In other words, different languages may use different linguistic forms to encode deictic information.

Key concepts

deixis
spatialism (of deixis)
interactionism (of deixis)
deictic versus non-deictic expression
indexicality
indexical versus non-indexical expression
gestural versus symbolic use (of a deictic expression)
deictic centre
deictic origo
deictic projection
person deixis
inclusive versus exclusive 'we'
vocative

call
address
time deixis
calendrical versus non-calendrical usage
coding time (CT) versus receiving time (RT)
space deixis
linguistic frames of spatial reference (intrinsic, relative, absolute)
distance (proximal, medial, distant)
distance- versus person-oriented system
visibility
audibility
elevation
geography
side
stance
social deixis
absolute versus relational social deixis
referent, addressee, bystander honorifics
T/V pronoun
deferential versus humiliative form
discourse deixis
emotional deixis

Exercises and essay questions

1. Of the following italicized expressions, which are used deictically, and which are used non-deictically? For those used deictically, which are used in a gestural way, and which in a symbolic way?
    (i) Hi, is Mary *there*?
    (ii) Press the button *now*.
    (iii) *You* will never fail until *you* give up.
    (iv) Does *that* shirt become *you*?
    (v) John said that *he* was thoroughly exhausted.
    (vi) In 1888, Ivanov moved to Moscow and lived *there* for the rest of *his* life.
2. The following is a Yiddish joke cited in Levinson (1983: 68, see also Mey 2001: 55). What is the 'mistake' made by the Hebrew teacher?

A melamed (Hebrew teacher), discovering that he had left his comfortable slippers back in the house, sent a student after them with a note for his wife. The note read: 'Send me your slippers with this boy.' When the student asked why he had written 'your' slippers, the melamed answered: 'Yold (Fool)! If I wrote "my" slippers, she would read "my" slippers and would send her slippers. What could I do with her slippers? So I wrote "your slippers", she'll read "your" slippers and send me mine.'

3. Of the following utterances, which involve a deictic projection?

   (i) *We* may lose customers if *our* prices are very high.

   (ii) (London underground train announcement)
        The *next* station is Piccadilly Circus. Please change *here* for the Piccadilly line.

   (iii) Can you prepare a list of hints and tips for safe camping *now*?

   (iv) (My letter to a colleague in New Zealand from England)
        I shall be delighted to lecture in your department *next* (*New Zealand*) summer.

   (v) *Take this there; bring that here*!

   (vi) I'll *bring* the DVD to you tomorrow.

   (vii) Crisis? What crisis? Judging by the flood of super-rich foreign tourists into France *this northern summer*, the recession is over—at least for some. (*New Zealand Herald* Wednesday 18 August 2010)

   (viii) May I *go* to your flat at the weekend?

4. Compare (i) and (ii) below, and explain why (ii) is anomalous.

   (i) Let's go to the airport to collect him next Monday.

   (ii) ?Let's go to the airport to collect you next Monday

5. In many languages, 'we' can be used to indicate 'I' or 'you'. Can you explain why 'we' is used in the following sentences?

   (i) (Doctor to patient)
       How are we feeling today? (we = you)

   (ii) (Director of personnel services to job applicant)
        We regret to inform you that your application was not successful. (we = I)

6. Consider the use of *here* in (i)–(iv) (adapted from Hanks 1992). What are the differences?

   (i) (Shouted to companion through the woods)
       I'm over here!

   (ii) (With sweeping arm gesture to countryside)
        Oh, it's just beautiful here!

   (iii) (With hand on abdomen)
         Doctor, it hurts here.

   (iv) (Pointing to a small map)
        They live over here, but we live here.

7. In the following pairs of sentences, which expressions are used deictically and which are not?
   - (i) a. Let's go to a *nearby* café.
     - b. John took Mary to a *nearby* café.
   - (ii) a. There was a fatal car accident in Oxford yesterday. A *local* driver was arrested.
     - b. Why not employ a *local* tour guide?
8. As already noted, *we* is ambiguous between an inclusive and an exclusive interpretation. This ambiguity is retained for the *we* in (i) but not for the *we* in (ii). *We* in (ii) can only have an exclusive reading. Can you explain this contrast in terms of the conditions for the use of *go* and *come*?
   - (i) We'll go there this afternoon.
   - (ii) We'll come there this afternoon
9. Ignoring the tense markers, point out all the deictic expressions in the following sentences and indicate in each case which type of deixis is involved.
   - (i) I live here in New York and Lucy lives there in California.
   - (ii) Good morning, ladies and gentlemen. This is the 10:15 Thames Express service to London Paddington, calling at Reading, Slough, and London Paddington.
   - (iii) We may get a pay cut if sales go down this year. That's what I've been told.
   - (iv) I came over several times to visit you last week, but you were never there.
   - (v) Good afternoon, Sir, how can I help you?
   - (vi) I'll never talk to that person again!
10. Deixis shows that meaning cannot be studied without reference to context. Do you agree?
11. What are the main categories of deixis? Discuss with examples.
12. What are the main semantic parameters of space deixis? Of these parameters, which is the most important one?
13. Give a brief description of the deictic system of a language other than English.
14. What is the main tenet of spatialism of deixis? Can you find any evidence in this chapter for or against it?

Further readings

Fillmore (1997).
Anderson and Keenan (1985).
Levinson (2004).
Hanks (2011).
Sidnell and Enfield (forthcoming).

6

Reference

In the last chapter, I discussed deixis. In this chapter, I turn to reference.[1]

Reference is a relation that involves speakers, linguistic expressions, and the object, or the set of objects,[2] that these linguistic expressions stand for, or that is picked out by a speaker in using these linguistic expressions. For

---

[1] From an ontogenetic point of view, deixis is in general considered to be primary to anaphora and reference (see e.g. Lyons 1977). But recently this view has been questioned by, for example, Levinson (2004) on the basis of some acquisitional facts.

[2] I use the term 'object' to cover an individual, entity, activity, property, relationship, event, situation, or the like, and the term 'a set of objects' to cover a clearly delimited collection of individuals, entities, activities, properties, relationships, events, situations, or the like.

example, if John said (6.1), he used the **referring expressions** *Peter*, *the original manuscript*, and *the safe* to **refer to** or pick out, or enable his addressee to refer to or pick out, a particular person, a particular manuscript, and a particular safe in the outside world. What is picked out or referred to is called a **referent**. The individual named 'Peter', for example, is the referent of the linguistic expression *Peter*.

(6.1)   Peter found the original manuscript inside the safe.

On the one hand, the same referring expression can be used to pick out different referents, depending on context, as in (6.2). On the other hand, different referring expressions can be employed to refer to the same referent, also depending on context, as in (6.3).

(6.2)   The President of the United States of America has visited the Great Wall in China.
(6.3)   a. Barack Obama is a wise man.
       b. The President of the United States of America is a wise man.

If (6.2) was uttered in 2006, the referring expression *the President of the United States of America* was used to refer to George W. Bush; if it is used in 2012, the same expression was deployed to stand for Barack Obama. On the other hand, the two different referring expressions *Barack Obama* and *the President of the United States of America* in (6.3) were used to refer to the same individual, namely, Barack Obama, in 2012. This shows that there is little referential constancy in human language considered in isolation from context. In other words, referential indeterminacy pervades in human language. In daily communication, much, if not all, of reference is determined with the help of the context in which a referring expression is situated. When so construed, reference is essentially a context-dependent aspect of utterance meaning and therefore the study of it falls largely under the domain of pragmatics (e.g. Lyons 1977; Bach 2006b).[3]

Lying 'at the very heart and soul of human language' (Abbott 2010: 1), reference represents one of the most complex phenomena in natural language, and is a source of fascinating problems in its own right. As a natural consequence, it has long been a central topic of inquiry in both philosophy of language and linguistics, and it has often engaged the passionate attention from both philosophers and linguists.

---

[3] But Barbara Abbott (personal communication) reminded me that the referential indeterminacy or indexicality described above applies also to the semantic definition of reference, to be discussed shortly.

The organization of this chapter is as follows. In Section 6.1, I consider the question of what reference is, providing first a semantic and then a pragmatic definition. Section 6.2 presents a typology of referring expressions. In Section 6.3, I examine some anaphoric uses of pronouns from a truth-conditional, semantic perspective. Next, Section 6.4 says more about proper names and definite descriptions, discussing a number of classical philosophical distinctions and analyses of reference. Finally, Section 6.5 takes a look at deferred or transferred reference. Given that, since the nineteenth century, the nature of reference has been taken largely as a philosophical issue, the focus of this chapter except Section 6.5 is more on philosophical than linguistic theories of reference.

6.1. What is reference?

Reference can be defined in two distinct ways. First, it is definable as a two-place relation between a linguistic expression and an object or a clearly delimited set of objects in the external world,[4] to which the linguistic expression applies, independent of the context in which the linguistic expression is used. Furthermore, it is intimately connected with truth. In other words, as summarized nicely by McGinn (1981), 'reference is what relates words to the world of objects on whose condition truth hinges'. This is the **semantic definition**, also known as the **naïve theory**, of reference. The semantic tradition can be traced to Mill (1843) and especially Frege (1892). According to the semantic definition, we can say that, at the time of writing (2012), the linguistic expression *the President of the United States of America* refers to the individual who is called 'Barack Obama'.

Secondly, reference or referring can be defined as an act of a speaker using a linguistic expression to pick out a particular object or a particular set of objects, **denoted** by that linguistic expression, in the outside world, which he or she wants to say something about. In other words, an act of referring is performed through a speaker's utterance of a linguistic expression on a particular occasion of use to identify a particular object or a particular collection of objects in the external world, hence it is a three-place relation

---

[4] Or in some mental representations, given that there are linguists (Chomsky included) and linguistic theories (especially cognitively oriented ones) that regard language in general as relating to mental representations rather than the external world.

among speakers, linguistic expressions, and objects. This is the **pragmatic definition** of reference. The pragmatic approach was initiated by Strawson (1950) (see also Searle's 1969 analysis of referring as a speech act, and Bach 2006b). Under the pragmatic definition, it is wrong to say that the linguistic expression *the President of the United States of America* refers to Barack Obama. Rather we say that a speaker uses the linguistic expression *the President of the United States of America* to pick out a particular individual named 'Barack Obama' in the course of a particular utterance on a particular occasion of use (see also Abbott 2010: 2–3).

6.2. Referring expressions

A **referring** or **referential expression** is a linguistic expression that can refer (given the semantic definition above) or can be used in an utterance to refer (given the pragmatic definition above). The major types of referring expression include (i) proper names (e.g. *Nelson Mandela*), (ii) definite descriptions (e.g. *the British Prime Minister*) including definite genitive NPs (e.g. *the President's office*) and definite pronouns (e.g. *he*), (iii) demonstrative NPs (e.g. *this city*) including demonstrative pronouns (e.g. *that*), and arguably (iv) indefinite NPs (e.g. *a beautiful girl*) including indefinite genitive NPs (e.g. *a dictionary's cover*) and indefinite pronouns (e.g. *someone*). In addition, common nouns referring to natural kinds, called '**natural kind terms**' (e.g. *water*) are also considered to be referring expressions by some philosophers. Syntactically, a referring expression usually belongs to the category of NP (but see Section 6.2.9).[5]

6.2.1. Proper names

A **proper name** is an NP which is used as the name for individual people, places, dates and periods of time, works of literature, music, art, etc., distinguished only by it having that name, e.g. *John, London,* and *Pride and Prejudice.*

---

[5] For some scholars, a distinction is made between **directly referring expressions** and **contextually referring expressions**—ones whose referential function is accomplished by the context of utterance in which they are used. The former is called '**type-referential**' and the latter '**token-referential**' (e.g. Recanati 1993). I shall not make such a distinction here.

(6.4)   *Gorbachev* has been remembered as the architect of perestroika.

Proper names can be partially descriptive. *Dr Smith* in (6.5) is a **partially descriptive proper name**, because in addition to its referent, its semantic value contains some descriptive content—in this case being a medical doctor (Soames 2002; Abbott 2010: 126).

(6.5)   *Dr Smith* gave the patient a prescription for antibiotics.

At this point, let me introduce the **rigid–non-rigid designator distinction**. A **rigid designator** is a referring expression that designates the same object with respect to all possible worlds[6] in which that object exists. According to this definition, a proper name is in general taken to be a rigid designator because it refers to the same object, no matter what world is being talked about. By contrast, **a non-rigid designator** is a referring expression that picks out different objects in different worlds without change of meaning. This distinction was introduced by the American philosopher Saul Kripke (1972).

6.2.2. Definite descriptions

A **definite description** is a subtype of a definite NP, which contains two parts: a descriptive part and a referential part, e.g. *the city*, *the author of Pride and Prejudice*, and *the girl over there*. A definite description is used to refer to and identify a definite object or a set of definite objects within the relevant universe of discourse in part by means of its descriptive content. In other words, we use a definite description to stand for something that is partially described by its descriptive part, the meaning of which establishes a link between the linguistic expression and the object denoted. Another point to note is that the use of a definite description frequently presupposes that there

---

[6] A term that is frequently encountered in logic and formal semantics, '**possible world**' does not refer to a place, but to a possible way the world could be or could have been. According to this notion, our actual world—the world as it is—is only one of an infinite number of possible worlds, that is, conceivable alternative worlds. Some possible worlds may be similar to our real world; others may be very different. **Possible world(s) semantics** is then a formal approach to semantics based on the concept of a possible world. It recognizes that things could be other than they actually are, with sentences typically being true in some possible worlds but false in others. A prominent example of a formal approach to the semantics of natural language based on the concept of a possible world is Montague Grammar.

is a unique and most salient object in the relevant context that is to be referred to (see Abbott 2010: 214–18 for her distinction between semantic and referential uniqueness).

(6.6)   *The British Prime Minister* has announced plans to create one million new jobs.

Definite descriptions can be further divided into **complete definite descriptions** and **incomplete definite descriptions**.[7] By the former is meant those definite descriptions whose descriptive content applies uniquely to the intended object, as *the author of Lady Chatterley's Lover* in (6.7). Other examples include *the present President of the Philological Society*, *the largest city in Africa*, and *the most beautiful girl in John's class*. By contrast, incomplete definite descriptions are ones whose descriptive content does not apply uniquely, as in (6.8). Put slightly differently, the descriptive component of an incomplete definite description is true of more than one entity. The semantics of an incomplete definite description does not pick out some unique object. The computation of its referent is usually pragmatic in nature, determined by a speaker's intention. Other examples of incomplete definite descriptions include *the pillow on the bed*, *the woman drinking a whisky*, and *the man you danced with*.

(6.7)   Rosemary met *the author of Lady Chatterley's Lover* in 1922.

(6.8)   (Strawson 1950)
  The table is covered with books.

Notice that unlike a proper name, a definite description is in general held to be a non-rigid designator, because what they refer to is dependent on what world is being discussed. In other words, it designates different objects with regard to different ways the world might be, relying on which object meets the descriptive part expressed by the description.[8]

---

[7] Other pairs of terms for 'complete' and 'incomplete definite descriptions' are 'semantic' and 'pragmatic definite descriptions' (Löbner 1985) and 'role-type' and 'particularized definite descriptions' (Rothschild 2007). Alternative terms for 'incomplete definite descriptions' are 'indefinite definite descriptions', 'improper definite descriptions', 'imperfect definite descriptions, 'ambiguous definite descriptions', and 'pragmatic definites'.

[8] But there are definite descriptions that are rigid designators. For example, *the successor of nine* designates the number ten with respect to all possible worlds. Kripke called definite descriptions like these '*de facto* **rigid**', in contrast to the *de jure* rigidity of proper names.

Both proper names and definite descriptions are used to encode **definite reference**, that is, reference to a specific object or a set of specific objects.

As mentioned already, different referring expressions can be used to refer to the same referent, depending on circumstance of use. Consequently, utterances with different referring expressions standing for the same object are expected to have the same meaning. This is usually the case, as in (6.3). However, there is a class of exceptions to this generalization. This class of exceptions normally occurs in a referentially opaque context. A **referentially opaque context** is one in which **Leibniz's law**—a law of intersubstitutability *salva veritate* (Latin for 'with the truth unchanged') does not hold. In other words, it is a context in which truth and hence meaning may not be preserved when the co-referential expressions are substituted for each other. Thus (6.9a) and (6.9b) will have different truth-conditions or meanings. This is because the referring expression *the first African-American President of the United States of America* in (6.9b) may be given an intensional reading, namely, the interpretation that the speaker wanted to dine with whoever happened to be the first African-American President of the United States of America, and did not care and might not have known who that was.

(6.9)   a. I wanted to dine with *Barack Obama*.
        b. I wanted to dine with *the first African-American President of the United States of America*.

A referentially opaque context is typically created by a particular type of verb, namely, what are called '**propositional attitude verbs**'. A **propositional attitude** is a mental state or attitude such as belief, knowledge, desire, hope, doubt, expectation, fear, and so on and so forth which a person has with respect to a content that can be expressed in a particular proposition. This is exemplified in (6.10), which is said to express or report John's belief that the Berlin Wall came down on 9 November 1989 is the case.

(6.10)   John believes that the Berlin Wall collapsed on 9 November 1989.

A propositional attitude verb is, then, one that is used to report a mental state or attitude of some person to a particular proposition. This class of verbs includes *believe, think, know, doubt, help, want, hope, fear*, and *wonder about* in English.

6.2.3. Indefinite descriptions

An **indefinite description** is a subtype of an indefinite NP that is marked by an indefinite article or its equivalent of a kind in a language like English, e.g. *a (certain) musician*.

(6.11)   *A young lady* was here looking for you a few minutes ago.

An indefinite description is used to establish **indefinite reference**, that is, reference to an object or a set of objects, the identification of which may not be known to the addressee.

It has been argued that only when an object is the current focus of attention of both the speaker and the addressee can reference be made to it with an indefinite expression (e.g. Bach 2006b). But as (6.12) shows, this constraint seems a bit too strong.

(6.12)   A young lady was here looking for you a few minutes ago—do you know who she is?

Note that an indefinite description like *a top American university* in (6.13) is considered to be ambiguous by some linguists: on a particular occasion of use, if the speaker has a particular top American university in mind, the indefinite description is used as a referring expression; otherwise it is not. On the other hand, if the word *certain* is added, the indefinite description is usually used as a referring expression, as in (6.14).

(6.13)   Hans wants to attend a top American university.
(6.14)   Hans wants to attend a certain top American university.

Often an indefinite description is used to introduce a new object into a discourse, and a definite expression will then be deployed to refer to it. This is illustrated in (6.15).

(6.15)   A spy hid in the bush. The spy/He kept watch on the house.

In other words, an indefinite description frequently initiates what Chastain (1975) called a '**chain of reference**'. This contrast of use between indefinite and definite referring expressions was captured by the **novelty–familiarity condition** proposed by Heim (1982).

The object referred to by *a spy* in (6.15) is called a 'discourse referent' by Karttunen (1969), who introduced the important concept of **discourse reference**. A **discourse referent** is a representation of an object presented as existing by a linguistic expression, which may or may not actually match up to a real-world referent. By comparison, a **real-world referent** is one that must actually exist in the external world. Karttunen's notion of discourse reference was somewhat incorporated into Kamp's (1981) Discourse Representation Theory (DRT) and Heim's (1982) file change semantics—two different but related dynamic semantico-pragmatic frameworks (see also Portner 2005).

6.2.4. Quantificational NPs

A **quantificational NP** is one that is modified by a quantifier which indicates a relative or indefinite quantity, e.g. *each person*, *some iPads*, and *every teacher who is working in my school*. Traditionally, a quantificational NP is not considered to be referential, because it does not pick out a fixed object in the external world, as can be shown by both (6.16) and especially (6.17).

(6.16)   *Every faculty member* at the meeting hoped that the coffee break was soon.

(6.17)   *Nobody* on the committee followed the proper procedures.

However, in an example like (6.18), the quantificational NP *all the players of the football team* seems to function in a referential way (Abbott (forthcoming)).

(6.18)   All the players of the football team have gone out on strike.

6.2.5. Possessive NPs

A **possessive NP** is one in which the possessor, which is marked in the genitive case, determines the possessed, e.g. *my daughter*, *the Professor's workload*, and *a newspaper's publishing company*. In *my daughter*, for example, *my* is the possessor, and *daughter* is the possessed.

(6.19)   *Mao's 'Cultural Revolution'* has inflicted much suffering on the Chinese people.

6.2.6. Generic NPs

A **generic NP** is one that can be used to make a **generic reference,** that is, reference to an entire class of entities rather than to a specific or non-specific member of that class.[9] *Giant pandas* in (6.20a), *the giant panda* in (6.20b), or *a giant panda* in (6.20c) has a generic reference. The sentences in (6.20) are said to constitute a generic statement or express a generic proposition.

(6.20)   a. Giant pandas live on bamboo shoots.
        b. The giant panda lives on bamboo shoots.
        c. A giant panda lives on bamboo shoots.

6.2.7. Demonstratives

A **demonstrative** is an NP that is basically used to locate a referent in relation to a speech event participant, especially a speaker or an addressee. Demonstrative NPs can be divided into (i) **demonstrative descriptions** or **complex demonstratives** (e.g. *these new machines*) and (ii) **demonstrative pronouns** (e.g. *that*).

(6.21)   *This tree* was struck by the lightning last night.
(6.22)   *That* is a ravenous dog.

   Demonstrative reference is a category of **deictic** or **indexical reference** (see Chapter 5).

---

[9] From a linguistic point of view, generic reference in its broad sense may also be expressed by (i) what is called 'arbitrary reference' in Chomsky's generative syntax and (ii) the so-called '**impersonal construction**'. By **arbitrary reference** is meant reference of, for instance, the phonetically unrealized subject of a finite clause in a language like Spanish, represented by *pro*, and of a non-finite clause in a language like English, represented by PRO.

(i) (Spanish)
    pro llaman a la puerta
    'People are knocking at the door.'
(ii) PRO smoking is bad.

   For the impersonal use of *one* and *you* in English, which is similar in function to linguistic expressions like *on* in French and *man* in German, see Chapter 5.

6.2.8. Pronouns

(6.23)   (Referent in the physical environment, and with speaker's selecting gesture)
He's the robber!

6.2.9. Common nouns/bare NPs

Common nouns referring to natural kinds, called '**natural kind terms**', when they function as bare NPs, are added to the list of referring expressions by some philosophers (e.g. Kripke 1972; Putnam 1975; Carlson 1977). Natural kind terms are usually names of species of animals and plants, and of substances and natural phenomena (Abbott 2010: 107). In fact, this is not restricted to common nouns or bare NPs. On the semantic view of reference, it has been extended to linguistic expressions of almost any kind including adjectives, adverbs, and verbs (Green 1996). Examples include *water, gold, heat, red*, and *extrapolate*.

(6.24)   *Water* is essential for life.

In (6.24), the bare NP *water* refers to the commonest molecular compound on the Earth that happens to be a liquid. This compound covers about 75% of the Earth's surface. Chemically analysable as containing two parts hydrogen and one part oxygen, it normally freezes to ice at 0°C and boils to steam at 100°C, and so on and so forth. In other words, we can say that *water* denotes the totality of water, which is the totality of H_2O molecules. In a similar way, we can say that *gold* refers to the totality of gold, *red* to the totality of red objects, and *extrapolate* to the totality of instances of extrapolation.[10] I shall have nothing more to say about common nouns or bare NPs in what follows, and the interested reader is referred to Portner (2005) for further textbook discussion.

Now try to tackle Exercises 1 and 2 at the end of this chapter.

[10]   As pointed out by Green (1996), one should not confuse the semantic analysis of common nouns or bare NPs referring to natural kind(s), discussed here, (which belongs to linguistics, especially semantics or pragmatics), with that of the kind itself (which is part of chemistry, biology, etc.) or with people's beliefs, knowledge, and/or understandings about the kind(s), (which fall in the domain of, say, anthropology or cognitive psychology).

6.3. Anaphoric uses of pronouns

In this section, let me digress into anaphoric uses of pronouns.

Anaphora is defined as a relation between two or more linguistic expressions, wherein the interpretation of one (called an **anaphoric expression**) is in some way determined by the interpretation of the other (called an **antecedent**) (e.g. Huang 1994, 2000a: 1). From a truth-conditional, semantic point of view, anaphoric uses of pronouns (and sometimes other categories of referring expressions) can be divided into five types.

6.3.1. Referential pronouns

An anaphoric pronoun can be used to refer to some object (in the external world) via its **co-reference** with its antecedent in the same sentence or discourse. In its referential use, a pronoun refers to what its antecedent refers to; the pronoun is thus said to be **co-referential** with its antecedent. Defined in this way, the anaphoric use of a referential pronoun constitutes a case of '**identity of reference' anaphora**—anaphora in which the anaphoric expression and its antecedent are related in reference.[11]

(6.25)   *The farmer* said that *he* has aerated the soil this morning.

In (6.25), *the farmer* is the antecedent for *he*. *He* refers to what *the farmer* refers to. We shall discuss the syntax and pragmatics of the distribution and interpretation of pronouns and other types of referring expressions in Chapter 9.

6.3.2. Bound-variable pronouns

A **bound-variable pronoun** is one that is interpretable by virtue of its dependency on some quantificational expression as its antecedent in the same

---

[11] This contrasts with '**identity of sense' anaphora**—anaphora in which the anaphoric expression and its antecedent is related in sense. This is illustrated by the use of *one* in (i).

(i)   John brought a new iPad, but Bill brought a second-hand one.

sentence or discourse, thus seeming to be the natural language counterpart of a bound variable in first-order logic.

(6.26)   *Every little girl* wishes that *she* could visit the land of Lilliput.

As observed in Huang (2000a: 88–9, 232–6, 2006), an interesting character-istic of bound-variable anaphora is that different languages may afford their speakers different types of anaphoric expressions to encode such a depend-ency. For example, while English normally does not allow either a zero anaphor or a reflexive,[12] Catalan, Serbo-Croatian, and Tarifit allow a zero anaphor (see 6.27), Marathi permits a reflexive (see 6.28), and Chinese, Japanese, and Korean allow both (see 6.29) to express the bound-variable relationship (CL = classifier).

(6.27)   Zero anaphors (Serbo-Croatian)
       svaki   sudent   misli   da   ce   Ø   dobiti   desetku.
       every   student   thinks   that   will   get   A
       'Every student thinks that he will get an A.'

(6.28)   Reflexives (Marathi)
       sarvaanaa   vaatta   ki   aapan   libral   aahot.
       everybody   believes   that   self   liberal   is
       'Everybody believes that he is liberal.'

(6.29)   Both zero anaphors and reflexives (Chinese)
       mei   ge   ren   dou   shou   Ø/ziji   xihua   zhongguocai
       every   CL   person   all   say   self   like   Chinese food
       'Everybody says that he likes Chinese cuisine.'

6.3.3. E-type pronouns

An **E-type pronoun** is one which, for technical reasons, is neither a pure referential pronoun nor a pure bound-variable pronoun, but which never-theless seems to constitute a unified semantic type of its own (Geach 1962; Evans 1977). The term 'E-type pronoun' was given by the British philoso-pher Gareth Evans. Classic examples are given in (6.30) and (6.31).

---

[12] Cf. (i) Each side proceeds on the assumption that itself loves peace, but the other side consists of warmongers (Bertrand Russell).

(6.30)   Every man who owns a donkey beats *it*.

(6.31)   If a man owns a donkey, he beats *it*.

Given the use of the word *donkey* in the classic examples in (6.30) and (6.31), E-type pronouns are also commonly called '**donkey pronouns**' or '**donkey anaphora**'. Sentences containing E-type pronouns are called '**donkey sentences**'. There is still no consensus on exactly what the donkey pronoun *it* means in the donkey sentences (6.30) and (6.31). The phenomenon of donkey pronouns/sentences was brought to the attention of modern linguistics by the British philosopher Peter Geach.

6.3.4. Pronouns of 'laziness'

A **pronoun of 'laziness'** is so-called because it is neither a referential pronoun nor a bound-variable pronoun, but functions as a shorthand for a repetition of its antecedent. In other words, it is a device for a repeated occurrence of a linguistic form (that is, the antecedent of the pronoun) rather than the truth-conditional, semantic content of that linguistic form. The phenomenon was first pointed out by Karttunen (1969). The term was introduced by Geach (1962). A famous example, due to Karttunen, is given in (6.32).

(6.32)   The man who gave his paycheck to his wife was wiser than the man who gave *it* to his mistress.

Sentences of the type given in (6.32) are called '**paycheck sentences**'.

6.3.5. Bridging-cross reference anaphora

A **bridging-cross reference anaphora** is one that is used to establish a link of association with some preceding linguistic expression (that is, its 'antecedent') in the same sentence or discourse via the addition of background assumptions. What is tacitly 'bridged' is typically the information that is not structurally retrievable from either the sentence or discourse that triggers the inferential process. A typical example of bridging-cross reference is presented in (6.33).

(6.33)   John walked into a library. The music reading room had just been refurbished.

In (6.33), the anaphoric expression is the definite description *the music reading room*, and its 'antecedent' is the indefinite description *a library*. The pragmatically enriched background assumption is that the library John walked into has a music reading room (cf. the notion of accommodation in Chapter 3).

As pointed out in Huang (2000a: 249, 2006c), bridging-cross reference has three characteristic properties. In the first place, the anaphoric expression, which is usually a definite NP, must occur in the appropriate context of its 'antecedent', which is usually an indefinite NP. Secondly, there is some semantic or pragmatic relation between the anaphoric expression and its 'antecedent'. Thirdly and finally, the anaphoric expression and its 'antecedent' do not stand in a strictly co-referential relation. Rather, they are linked to each other via the addition of some pragmatic inference or enrichment (see Huang 2000a for further discussion).

At this point, have a go at Exercise 3 at the end of this chapter.

6.4. More on proper names and definite descriptions: some classical philosophical distinctions and analyses of reference

Having diverged into anaphoric uses of pronouns in the last section, I return to proper names and definite descriptions, discussing some classical analyses of them in the philosophy of language in this section.

6.4.1. Proper names

Proper names have long been a central concern in the philosophy of language. Roughly, there are two major views. The first is that proper names are (concealed) definite descriptions. This is known as the '**description/ descriptional/descriptivist theory**' (of proper names) or '**descriptivism**' for short. The description theory is represented by the German philosopher Gottlob Frege and the British philosopher Bertrand Russell. The second view of proper names holds that they are not definite descriptions, but they are directly referential. This is referred to as the '**direct reference theory**' (of proper names). The representative of this approach is the American philosopher Saul Kripke.

The description/descriptional/descriptivist theory

In Frege's (1892) theory, a distinction is made between **sense** and **reference** of a linguistic expression. But this distinction is somewhat anticipated by Mill's (1843) distinction between **denotation** and **connotation**. Denotation is a relation that holds primarily between word and world, that is, between linguistic expressions and objects in the external world. In short, a linguistic expression can be said to denote a class of various sorts of extralinguistic objects in the outside world. For example, the word *cat* may be taken as denoting the set of all cats in the external world. In contrast, by **connotation** is meant the attributes or properties the object denoted by the linguistic expression has. For example, the connotation of *cat* is the property of being a cat.[13]

Returning now to Frege's sense–reference distinction, it is quite similar to Mill's connotation–denotation one. On Frege's view, there are three basic types of meaningful linguistic expressions in a language: (i) sentences, (ii) concept words, and (iii) proper names. Linguistic expressions of each type have a sense (*Sinn*) and, if not empty, a referent (*Bedeutung*). While by reference is meant 'that to which the sign refers', by sense is meant the meaning as distinct from reference. As Frege explained, the sense of a linguistic expression gives a **mode of presentation** of its referent. To illustrate this distinction, let me take a famous pair of phrases from Frege.

(6.34)   the Morning Star
(6.35)   the Evening Star

---

[13] Notice that 'connotation' in Mill's sense is different from the term that is used today. In today's usage, 'connotation' refers to aspects of communicative value of a linguistic expression that cannot be reduced to its core, descriptive meaning. One such aspect is concerned with the expressive, affective, or emotive component of meaning, especially the use of linguistic expressions which have 'favourable' or 'unfavourable' overtone. For example, in Bertrand Russell's example *I am firm, you are obstinate, he is pig-headed*, while *firm* rates high on the 'good/bad' scale, *obstinate* and *pig-headed* rate low on that scale. Another aspect involves the social and situational circumstances of use. Finally, 'connotation' can also reflect the cultural association of a linguistic expression. For example, *dragon* in English and its broad equivalent *long* in Chinese have quite different cultural connotations.

Whereas both (6.34) and (6.35) have the same referent, that is, the planet Venus (as discovered by the Babylonians), they have different senses. The sense of the former is paraphrasable roughly as 'the brightest star that is seen in the morning'; that of the latter as 'the brightest star that is seen in the evening'. Furthermore, Frege argued that the reference of a complex expression is the compositional function (that is, the combination) of the reference of its parts and their syntactic mode of combination. For instance, the reference of 'the wife of Barack Obama' is determined by applying the concept THE WIFE OF (a function from objects to truth values) to the individual denoted by the proper name *Barack Obama*. This process applies from the level of the words through the level of the phrases composed of the words to the level of the sentences, which refer to their truth value. This is the Fregean principle of compositionality (see Chapter 3). It provides an explanation of why we can produce and comprehend novel expressions without limit.

On Frege's view, a proper name has a sense, namely, the description of its referent (though the sense of a proper name varies from speaker to speaker). For example, the proper name *Aristotle* can be described as 'the pupil of Plato and the teacher of Alexander the Great', *Barack Obama* as 'the first African-American President of the United States of America', and *Jane Austen* as 'the author of *Pride and Prejudice*'. Furthermore, the sense of a proper name is similar to that of a definite description. Consequently, a proper name is semantically very much like or equivalent to a definite description in how it refers. That is, it is semantically tied to a definite description and the referent of the name is the object which satisfies the descriptive part of the description. This description theory of proper names was more or less shared by the British philosopher Bertrand Russell. Essentially, Russell (1905) treated an ordinary proper name such as *John, Mary,* and *Margaret Thatcher* as a simple symbol and considered it as an abbreviation of a definite description. Later, in the 1950s and 1960s, in order to tackle certain philosophical problems, the view that a proper name is associated with a single description was rejected in favour of the view that it is associated with a cluster of different descriptions. Consequently, according to this account, the referent of a proper name is the object that fits a sufficient number of the definite descriptions in a cluster associated with that name. This position, known as the **cluster view** (of proper names), was represented by both the later Wittgenstein (1953) and Searle (1958) (see also Abbott 2010: 102–3). For a long period of time, the description theory dominated the study of proper names in the philosophy of language (see Marti 2012 for further arguments in favour of the description theory).

The direct reference theory

Contrary to the descriptional view, discussed above, the direct reference theory holds that a proper name has direct reference[14] but no sense. It is directly referential but entirely devoid of its descriptive content. Or, put more accurately, a proper name refers in a way that is not mediated by descriptive content.[15] This view of proper names, initiated by Mill (1843), has become prominent since the 1970s. One of its most influential modern proponents is Kripke (see also Donnellan 1970). According to Kripke (1972), unlike definite descriptions, proper names do not have any sense and therefore are non-descriptive in nature. Rather, they refer directly. The reference of a proper name works via a reference-preserving chain of communication. It is fixed through an initial act of veridical naming or 'dubbing'. After that original act, the proper name is passed on from link to link in the community. In other words, on Kripke's view, it is the causal or historical connection of a proper name that is responsible for the reference of that name to be fixed. Thus, William Shakespeare is called *William Shakespeare* because there is a continuous causal or historical chain of cultural transmission. Another way of putting it is that William Shakespeare is named *William Shakespeare* because he was so called initially by some-one, somewhere, sometime and the proper name has since been passed on.[16]

---

[14] Barbara Abbott (personal communication) pointed out to me that the term 'direct reference' was introduced by the American philosopher David Kaplan for his particular view of rigid designation. Kaplan's view is not shared by Kripke (see Abbott 2010: 110–12 for further discussion).

[15] Whether or not, and to what extent, a proper name has sense (on a particular notion of sense or meaning) seems to vary cross-culturally. In the Chinese culture, for example, there are many proper names that do have meaning. One such first name is *jianhua*, meaning 'build China', which is especially adopted for men in mainland China. Another, more traditional, one is *yuexian* with the meaning of 'fairly maiden in the moon'. This first name is usually for women.

Of more interest is the pen name of the Chinese writer who won the 2012 Nobel Prize in Literature. It is *Mo Yan*, which means 'don't speak'. The Nobel laureate said that he had adopted the pen name as a warning to himself not to be too outspoken. See also note 18.

[16] Essentially, the same analysis has been proposed for common nouns or bare NPs denoting natural kind since Putnam (1965) and Kripke (1972).

Therefore, on this view, the use of different proper names in different utterances, at different times, and on different occasions for the same object will decide different causal or historical chains. This has the consequence that what appear to be different senses attached to different proper names, like *the Falkland Islands* and *the Malvinas Islands*, are causally or historically determined chains of use rather than senses.[17] This theory is called the **causal (chain) theory** (of proper names). See also Green (1996), Carlson (2004), and Portner (2005). In addition, see Dummett (1973) for a descriptivist response to Kripke, Kripke (1980) for a reply to Dummett, and Dummett (1981) for a further response.[18]

Aspects of Kripke's causal (chain) theory were subsequently challenged by the British philosopher Gareth Evans (1973, 1982). While agreeing largely with Kripke that, unlike definite descriptions, proper names refer directly, on Evans' view, Kripke failed to appreciate the essential role played by social context and community knowledge of the use of a proper name in ascertaining its referent. First, as remarked above, a proper name is sometimes used for reference even if the speaker and/or the addressee have no knowledge of what its referent is. This is illustrated in (6.36) and (6.37).

(6.36)   I was asked to make an appointment with Tom Matthews, but I don't know who he is.

(6.37)   Mum just rang, I assumed to wish me luck for the new job. 'Guess what, darling?' she began. 'What?' 'Elaine has invited you to their ruby wedding!' she said, pausing breathlessly and expectantly. My mind went blank. Elaine? Brian-and-Elaine? Collin-and-Elaine? Elaine-married-to-Gordon-who-used-to-be-head-of-Tarmacadam-in-Kettering-Elaine? 'She thought it might be nice to have one or two young 'uns there to keep Mark company.' Ah.

---

[17] But the selection of one name and not the other sometimes does carry a conventional implicature (cf. Chapter 2). For example, the use of *the Falkland Islands* conventionally implicates that the speaker takes the British perspective; that of *the Malvinas Islands* or its Spanish name *Islas Malvinas* carries the conventional implicature that the speaker sides with the Argentine position.

[18] Recently, there has been some experimental work comparing and contrasting the two positions on proper names. The experiment carried out by Machery et al. (2004) seems to indicate that there is cultural variation: while English-speaking students in the USA tend to lean toward Kripke's causal–historical stance, Cantonese-speaking students in Hong Kong tend to display descriptivist leanings. But the significance of the experiment is challenged by Lam (2010). Machery et al. (2009) showed that there is a high level of intra- rather than cross-cultural variation.

> Malcolm and Elaine. Begetters of the over-perfect Mark Darcy. (Helen
> Fielding, *Bridget Jones's Diary,* pp. 207–8, original italics)

In (6.36), although the speaker does not know its intended referent, he still
uses the proper name *Tom Matthews.* On the other hand, in (6.37), even if
the addressee, Bridget, cannot figure out its intended referent initially, (both
she and) her mother still employ the proper name *Elaine.*

Next, there is the case where upon hearing a non-recognizable proper
name, the addressee will make efforts to achieve recognition. Consider the
conversational exchange in (6.38).

(6.38)   (There used to be two Pauls at the Department of Linguistic Science at the
         University of Reading, UK: Paul Fletcher and Paul Kerswill.)
         I: Paul wants to have a word with you.
         H: Which Paul?
         I: Paul Kerswill, sorry.
         H: OK.

Here, the speaker introduces the intended referent into the conversation by
using his first name, *Paul,* anticipating that the addressee will be able to
identify it. But the addressee cannot. Consequently, the addressee launches
an other-initiated recognition search sequence *Which Paul* to achieve recognition. The crucial point to note here is that other-initiated recognition
search sequences of this type usually generate a step-by-step escalation on
the part of the speaker in his or her efforts to secure recognition until
recognition is achieved or abandoned. Thus, in (6.38), upon the recognition
search sequence other-initiated by the addressee, a one-step escalation from
the use of the intended referent's first name *Paul* to the use of his full name
Paul Kerswill is launched on the part of the speaker to help the addressee
secure recognition. This step-by-step escalation stops as soon as recognition
is achieved, which is signalled by the addressee saying *OK.* Notice further
the use of *sorry* by the speaker in his repair turn, which indicates that he has
realized his error in over estimating the addressee's ability to work out the
intended reference. The other function of *OK* uttered by the addressee is,
therefore, to accept the speaker's apology.

The type of other-initiated self-repair of referring expressions as exemplified in (6.38) can be accounted for in terms of the interaction between
Levinson's Q- and I-principles (see Chapter 2): the other-initiation of the
recognition search sequence by the addressee is due to the addressee-based
Q-principle, whose effect is that a speaker should say as much as he or she

can to help the addressee achieve recognition; on the other hand, the gradual, step-by-step relaxation of the use of minimal referential forms by the speaker is due to the speaker-based I-principle, whose effect is that a speaker should say as little as he or she can to achieve minimization.

Finally, we have the case where a speaker, upon using a minimal proper name, will ensure that its intended referent is to be identified by the addressee. This is shown in (6.39).

(6.39)   (Sacks and Schegloff 1979)
      A: ... well I was the only one other than than the uhm tch *Fords*?,
          uh Mrs. Holmes Ford?
      B: (pause)
      A: You know uh//the the cellist?
      B: Oh yes. She's she's the cellist.
      A: Yes
      B: Ye//s
      A: Well she and her husband were there.

Of some interest here is the observation I made in Huang (1994) in connection with reference in Chinese conversation that in this type of self-initiated, self-repair of referring expressions, there is often an explicitly or implicitly self-initiated check sequence preceded or followed by a pause between it and the speaker's repair. Furthermore, as can be seen in (6.39), the standard formula for the self-initiated recognition check sequence is '(Do) you know X?', where X is the problematic referential form. By being introduced typically in a prefatory sequence, this format, as Auer (1984) pointed out for a similar pattern in German conversation, often serves as a 'pre' for some more substantive talks. Note next that the failure to acknowledge recognition in the pause by the addressee is typically interpreted as pragmatically implicating that he or she does not recognize the intended referent. Again, this will be followed by a step-by-step escalation on the part of the speaker in his or her efforts to secure recognition until recognition is achieved or abandoned. Thus, in (6.39), the speaker is uncertain about the recognition of the intended referent from the addressee. So he uses a minimal recognitional referential form, namely the referent's last name *Fords* first, which is marked by an upward intonation contour. This, Sacks and Schegloff (1979) and Schegloff (1996) called a 'try-marker', that is, a minimal recognitional form, but one which is marked as a 'try'. This try-marker is followed by a very brief pause, which is treated by the speaker as displaying the addressee's failure to identify the referent. Consequently, the speaker steps up his efforts to achieve recognition by making use of the referent's full name *Mrs. Holmes Ford* in the next turn. Again, the sequence is followed by another pause—but a longer one this time, which prompts the speaker to launch a self-initiated recognition check sequence with more information, that is, with the definite description *the the cellist,* being provided. The step-by-step escalation on the part of the speaker stops as soon as the addressee explicitly acknowledges the recognition of the referent. Once again, on the one hand, the operation of the Q-principle is evidenced by the fact that the kind of check sequence self-initiated by the speaker we have just witnessed is essentially oriented to achieving recognition, and on the other, the operation of the I-principle is seen by the fact that more information, that is, from the use of *Fords* through *Mrs. Holmes Ford* to *the the cellist,* is provided in a gradual way only after the initial, minimal referring form fails to secure recognition (see Huang 2000a: 318–28 for discussion about other types of referential repair in conversation).[19]

Secondly, Evans pointed out that the fact that a proper name can change its referent goes against Kripke's theory. *Madagascar,* for example, used to be the place name for part of the African mainland, but now it is the name for the world's fourth largest island in the Indian Ocean due initially to a mistake by Marco Polo—the Venice-born Italian merchant and traveller. In other words, the referent of *Madagascar* has gradually changed over centuries. Arguably, there does not seem to be a causal or historical reference-preserving chain that links our use of *Madagascar* to the use of the name by its initial speakers. As an alternative, Evans provided an account of the use of a proper name in terms of social context, community knowledge, and a

---

[19] As pointed out in Huang (2000a: 320), cross-linguistically, there is clear evidence that the use of proper names generally takes precedence over that of definite descriptions. Consequently, proper names have become the predominant referential form for introducing (known) human referents into conversation. Schegloff (1996), for example, proposed a '**name first' principle**, namely, if you think your addressee knows the referent by personal name, use a name; indeed use *that* name. If your addressee knows the referent in some other way, use *that* way as the referential form. Why is this the case? Currently, one view is that the predominant use of proper names is attributable to a preference to communicate via a concrete image of an individual rather than via the abstract and impersonal image a definite description by role creates.

speaker's intention to use that name in accordance with his or her community knowledge, and argued that reference is secured via the mechanism of social practice.[20]

6.4.2. Definite descriptions

Another equally, if not more important topic of referential inquiry in the philosophy of language is definite descriptions. Since the publication of Russell's (1905) classic essay, the debate over the proper analysis of definite descriptions has been going on for more than a century, but despite much progress, the semantics and pragmatics of definite descriptions has yet to be worked out.

Russell's analysis
Unlike Mill and Frege, both of whom treated a definite description as a referring expression, in which its denotation (Mill) or reference (Frege) is determined by its connotation (Mill) or sense (Frege) (see e.g. Elbourne 2013 for the latest defence of the Fregean view), Russell was of the view that a definite description (and a proper name,[21] which was taken as a variety of a definite description in Russell's analysis) is not a referring expression, and so does not refer at all. Instead, Russell analysed a definite description on a par with a quantificational NP. More specifically, he treated the definite article *the* in a definite description as if it is a quantificational determiner such as *each*, and considered a sentence that contains a definite description as expressing a (disguised) existential statement. A famous example of Russell's is given in Chapter 3, repeated here in (6.40).

(6.40)   The (present) king of France is bald.

---

[20] On Portner's (2005) view, Kripke's analysis may be seen as a specific case within Evans' more general account. Another, somewhat different approach is taken by so-called '**causal descriptivists**', including the American philosopher David Lewis. Causal descriptivists maintain that the causal theory itself provides the relevant associated descriptions (see e.g. Kroon 1987). See also Garcia-Carpintero (2000) for a similar view.

[21] More accurately, by 'proper name' is meant '**ordinary proper name**' in Russell's parlance. In contrast, there are '**logical proper names**' in his theory, which are entirely non-descriptive. I am grateful to Fred Kroon for pointing this out to me.

On Russell's view, (6.40) is equivalent to (6.41a) (setting aside the analysis of the country name *France*).

(6.41)   a. ∃x [(present) king of France (x) & ∀y [(present) king of France (y) → y=x]
            & bald (x)]
         b. There is one and only one (present) king of France, and he is bald.

The logical formula in (6.41a) has three clauses. The first says that there is an individual *x* who is the (present) king of France. In other words, it requires the existence of such an individual. The second clause states that there is at most one such individual, that is, the individual is unique. Finally, according to the third clause, it is predicated that the unique individual is bald. All this is informally expressed in English in (6.41b). Notice that (6.41b) is a general existential statement rather than a referential one. In other words, the meaning of (6.41b) does not refer to a (present) king of France. Rather, it just says that one and only one (relevant, present) king of France exists and he is bald. That is to say that *the (present) king of France* has a clear sense but no reference. If there is no (present) king of France, what is the truth status of (6.40)? Russell's answer is that since (6.40) asserts both that there is a (present) king of France and that he is bald, if the (present) king of France does not exist, (6.40) is false,[22] as we have already seen in Chapter 3.

Strawson's analysis

Russell's analysis seemed to provide a satisfactory solution to a number of difficult problems of reference in the philosophy of language. One such problem is concerned with non-existent objects, as just mentioned. Another has to do with language users' beliefs about reference (Abbott (forthcoming)). Hailed as 'that paradigm of philosophy' by the British philosopher Frank Ramsay, the Russell theory remained unchallenged for almost half a century. As mentioned in Chapter 3, in 1950, the British philosopher Peter Strawson published an article to show that Russell's analysis, and indeed his whole narrow view, of reference 'embodies some

---

[22] The issue of the non-existence of a referent has been a particularly complex one in the philosophy of language. This includes fictional reference and failure of reference in cases such as dreams and hallucinations. Carlson (2004) argued that fictional reference and reference failure should be distinguished. Some scholars are of the view that, just as reference success is a pragmatic achievement, the non-existence of a referent will ultimately be a pragmatic failure.

fundamental mistakes'. On Strawson's view, Russell failed to make a distinction between a sentence and the use of a sentence (via an utterance) on a particular occasion. In using (6.40), a speaker does not assert but merely presupposes that there exists a unique (present) king of France and employs the definite description *the (present) king of France* to refer to that individual and predicate the baldness of him. In other words, according to Strawson, when a speaker uses a definite description to refer to an object, he or she does refer to it (assuming that the presupposition is satisfied). That is, a definite expression is a referring expression. Returning to (6.40), if there is no (present) king of France, there is a presupposition failure. Consequently, (6.40) is neither true nor false: there is simply a truth gap.[23]

Furthermore, Strawson argued that the existence and widespread use of so-called incomplete definite descriptions in natural language, as in (6.8) and (6.42), supports his analysis that language users use definite descriptions as referring expressions.

(6.42)   *The road* disappeared towards *the border*.

In many cases, the semantics of the sentence in which an incomplete definite description is used is not sufficient to determine the unique referent of the description given that there is a multitude of objects fitting the description used in the world at large. In these cases, it is usually the context of utterance in which the incomplete definite expression is uttered that plays a crucial role. According to Bach (2000), for example, the determination of the referent in such cases is usually pragmatic in nature (but see Stanley and Szabó 2000b for a dissenting view). This cannot be explained by Russell's theory, because given a Russellian analysis, a definite description denotes only if its descriptive component is true of exactly one entity. However, contrary to what Russell's account has predicted, a sentence containing an incomplete definite description can, relative to some relevant context, express truth (see also Löbner 2000 for the argument that definite descriptions are decidedly not quantificational).

---

[23] Frege also held the view that a sentence containing a non-referring expression lacks a truth value. But apparently, Strawson did not seem to be aware of this at the time when he published his article (Abbott 2010).

Donnellan's analysis: the referential–attributive use distinction

Another important contribution to the debate was made by the American philosopher Keith Donnellan. On Donnellan's (1966) view, neither Russell nor Strawson was correct about definite descriptions, because neither of them was aware that definite descriptions are ambiguous in having two distinct functions or uses. In addition to the **attributive use**, which reflects Russell's view, definite descriptions also have a **referential use**. On the referential use, a speaker uses a definite description to enable his or her addressee to determine whom or what he or she is talking about. By contrast, used attributively, the definite description is employed to attribute the predicated property to whomever or whatever satisfies the description. In other words, the referring aspect of a definite description treats the descriptive content merely as a route to the referent, and therefore the descriptive content is not central to the utterance. On the other hand, the describing function requires that whoever or whatever meets the descriptive content has the predicated properties, and consequently the descriptive content is central. To illustrate this distinction, let us consider Donnellan's account of his famous example in (6.43).

(6.43)   Smith's murderer is insane.

[S]uppose that Jones has been charged with Smith's murder and has been placed on trial. Imagine that there is a discussion of Jones's odd behaviour at his trial. We might sum up our impression of his behaviour by saying, 'Smith's murderer is insane'. If someone asks to whom we are referring, by using this description, the answer here is 'Jones'. This, I shall say, is a referential use of the definite description (Donnellan 1966: 285–6).

On the other hand,

[W]e come upon poor Smith folly murdered. From the brutal manner of the killing and the fact Smith was the most loveable person in the world, we might exclaim, 'Smith's murderer is insane'. I will assume, . . . that . . . we do not know who murdered Smith (though this is not in the end essential to the case). This, I shall say, is an attributive use of the definite description (Donnellan 1966: 285).

The referential use and the attributive use can be paraphrased in (6.44a) and (6.44b), respectively.

(6.44)   a. That person, who murdered Smith, is insane.
         b. Whoever murdered Smith is insane.

Regarding next the question of whether the **referential–attributive use distinction** is semantic or pragmatic in nature, Donnellan (1966) was ambivalent and Donnellan (1978) was of the view that it was semantic (see also Kaplan 1978). Two recent defences of Donnellan's semantic position are Davitt (2004) and Abbott (2010).

Kripke's analysis: semantic reference versus speaker's reference
On Kripke's (1972, 1977) view, while Donnellan's referential-attributive use distinction 'is of fundamental importance', it has a methodological weakness, namely, it has to claim that a definite description is ambiguous (cf. Occam's razor in Chapter 1).

Kripke held the view that a definite description has a single semantic meaning. However, the ability of a definite description to refer should be taken not as part of its semantics but as part of its pragmatics, that is, as part of speaker-meaning (cf. Grice 1989). A speaker may use a definite description to refer to an object in the external world, but this does not mean that the definite description itself refers to that entity by virtue of its semantics. Thus, according to Kripke, Donnellan's distinction is not a semantic one, but a pragmatic one. In other words, the distinction should be accounted for in pragmatic terms.

Following the footsteps of Grice (1989), Kripke distinguished between semantic reference, as part of what is linguistically encoded, and speaker's reference, as part of what a speaker intends to convey by means of uttering the linguistic expression.

By **semantic reference** is meant reference to what is denoted by a referring expression. That is to say, a **semantic referent** of a referring expression is the referent the referring expression has in a particular language and is determined by the conventions of that language. By contrast, **speaker's reference** is reference to an entity which a speaker wishes to talk about in the use of a particular referring expression on a particular occasion. In other words, a **speaker's referent** of a referring expression is fixed by what the speaker intends to refer to in a given situation.

In addition, Kripke argued that the distinction can also be generalized to other types of definite NPs including proper names. He used the following example involving proper names to illustrate the distinction.

Two people see Smith in the distance and mistake him for Jones. They have a brief colloquy: 'What is Jones doing?' 'Raking the leaves.' 'Jones', in the common language of both, is a name for Jones; it *never* names Smith. Yet, in some sense, on this occasion, clearly both participants in the dialogue have referred to Smith, and the second participant has said something true about the man he referred to if and only if Smith was raking the leaves (whether or not Jones was) (Kripke 1977: 263).

In this case of misidentification, although both participants used the proper name *Jones*, what they have clearly referred to is Smith. Therefore, Jones, the man named by *Jones*, is the semantic referent, and Smith is the speaker's referent (see Exercise 4 for an example involving definite descriptions and Exercise 5 for one involving demonstratives).[24]

> See whether you can do Exercises 4 and 5 at the end of this chapter.

Thus, as pointed out by Levinson (2000: 226), Kripke's **semantic– speaker's reference distinction** 'is one between semantic correctness on the one hand and pragmatic success with semantic error on the other—more precisely, that it's a distinction between a proper semantic use and an improper but occasionally successful use of referring expressions'.[25]

Furthermore, Kripke argued that a speaker's general intention gives rise to semantic reference, and his or her specific intention on a given occasion to speaker's reference. In what Kripke called the 'simple' case, which is similar to Donnellan's attributive use, specialized to definite descriptions, a speaker's specific referential or semantic intention is simply to refer to the semantic referent, his or her specific intention is simply his or her general intention, and therefore his or her semantic referent and speaker's referent converge to one and the same referent. By contrast, in the 'complex' scenario, which is correspondent to Donnellan's referential function, the speaker has a specific intention that is distinct from his or her general intention, and therefore his or her speaker's referent need not be the same as his or her semantic referent. Construed thus, speaker's reference is

---

[24] As pointed out by Wilson (1991), there are important differences between the case where a proper name is used and the case where a definite description is employed. In the former, the speaker mistakes one individual for a different one; in the latter, he or she makes a mistake in the description of somebody.

[25] This quote from Levinson is originally about Donnellan's referential–attributive use distinction. In my view, it suits Kripke's semantic–speaker's reference distinction better.

somewhat parasitic on semantic reference (see Salmon 2004 for a survey, and Bach 2004 for a pragmatic approach. See also Bianchi 2011).[26]

6.5. Deferred or transferred reference

Having discussed some classical theories of reference from the philosophy of language in the last section, let me now embark on a discussion of deferred or transferred reference in this section. In what follows, I shall summarize the phenomenon in Section 6.5.1. Section 6.5.2 provides a survey of a few analyses. At the end of the overview, I shall outline an alternative analysis in terms of Kripke's semantic–speaker's reference distinction and neo-Gricean pragmatics.

6.5.1. The phenomenon

By **deferred** or **transferred reference**[27] is meant the phenomenon whereby a referring expression can be **metonymically** used to stand for an object that is related to but not denoted by the conventional meaning of that expression (Nunberg 2004; Ward 2004). In other words, deferred or transferred reference can be considered to be a case in which (under certain circumstance) one can point or refer to *a* to mean *b*. Consider first (6.45).

(6.45)   a. (Pointing to a picture of a roasted chicken)
              That's delicious!
         b. (Pointing to a copy of *The Times*)
              Murdoch has just bought *that* for millions of pounds.
         c. (Elbourne 2005) (Pointing at the Pope)
              He is usually an Italian.

(6.45a) is a case of **deferred ostension** *à la* Quine (1953) or **deferred indexical reference**, in which case the speaker uses *that* to refer to the roasted chicken

---

[26] Work done by Donnellan, Kripke, Putnam, and Kaplan on proper names, definite descriptions, and indexical expressions has in general been referred to as 'the **new theory of reference**' in the philosophy of language.

[27] Alternative terms include 'metonymic reference', 'shifted reference', 'referential transfer', 'referential shift', 'reference transfer', and 'reference shift'.

in the picture rather than the picture itself. In (6.45b), *that* does not stand for the copy of *The Times*, but to the newspaper's publishing company. Finally, *he* in (6.45c) is used to mean 'the Popes'. In other words, (6.45c) is not about a particular individual but about a class of individuals who share a property, namely, the property of being the Pope.

Next, the same results of deferred ostension can be obtained without ostension proper (Montalbetti 2003). A few classic examples of referential transfer, due originally to Nunberg (1979, 1995, 2004), Fauconnier (1985), and others, are given in (6.46).[28]

(6.46)   a. (A customer hands his key to an attendant at a parking lot)
             I am parked out back.
         b. Plato is on the top shelf.
         c. (A waiter says to another waiter in a restaurant)
             The ham sandwich left without paying.
         d. The trams are on strike.
         e. The table is made of oak.

In (6.46a), the predicate *parked out back* denotes literally a property of a car when it is parked out back. As a result of what Nunberg (1995, 2004) called 'predicate transfer', it carries a different sense, which comes to denote a property of a person, for example, the owner or the driver whose car is parked out back. In (6.46b), the proper name *Plato*, which literally denotes a certain individual, is used to refer, through reference shift, to one or more books written by him. Next, the use of *the ham sandwich* in (6.46c) is a result of certain ways of referring to customers in the exchange between waiters in a restaurant that have become largely conventionalized. The NP *the ham sandwich* is employed to stand for, via referential shift, 'the customer who

---

[28] According to Nunberg (1995, 2004), in English, while we can use the (French) names of grapes to refer to the wines derived from them (for instance, a glass of Sauvignon Blanc), we cannot do it using, for example, the names of fruits for their liquids (for instance, ?a glass of pineapple). Furthermore, he claimed that whereas we can use the names of painters to stand for their paintings (for example, a Picasso), of designers to refer to their clothes, and of film-makers to stand for their films (only when the films they have produced are genre films), it does not apply to names of composers. However, the following sentence constitutes a counter example to this claim.

(i)   If you give me a free Beethoven, I'll buy five Mozarts.

ordered the ham sandwich', 'the customer who ate the ham sandwich', 'the customer who said that he loved the ham sandwich', etc. depending on context. In (6.46d), *the trams* is used to refer to their drivers. Finally, as a consequence of the process known as 'grinding', the common noun *oak* that denotes a kind of tree (that is, a tree name) is deployed for its wood (that is, a wood name).[29]

More interestingly, a sentence can sometimes be ambiguous between a literal and a transferred referential reading.

(6.47)   The ham sandwich smells.

(6.48)   (Nunberg 1995)

Yeats is still widely read.

(6.49)   The village woke up.

On one interpretation, *the ham sandwich* in (6.47) is used to refer to the order (the literal referent), and on the other, it is employed to stand for the customer who has, for instance, ordered the ham sandwich (the transferred referent). This can be seen more clearly by (6.50), where the ambiguity is resolved.

(6.50)   a. The ham sandwich smells. It has to be thrown away.
         b. The ham sandwich smells. He needs to have a shower.

In the same vein, (6.48) is also ambiguous. It can be understood either in the manner of literal reference, as in (6.51a), or in the manner of transferred reference, as in (6.51b).

(6.51)   a. Yeats is still widely read, though he has been dead for more than fifty years.
         b. Yeats is still widely read, even though most of it is out of print.

Finally, the same goes for (6.49). In one reading, *the village* is interpreted literally as 'waking up' in the sense that it is full of noise made by, for example, its inhabitants, animals, and farming machines. In this case, a pragmatic modulation has to apply to the VP *woke up* to engender its

---

[29] Cross-linguistically, the extent to which deferred or transferred reference can take place varies widely. For example, Chinese allows a much narrower range of metonymic reference than English does. It normally does not permit the use of *the ham sandwich* type even in a restaurant context. See Nunberg (1995, 2004) and Ward (2004) for comments on the differences between English and Greenlandic Eskimo, French, Italian, and Japanese.

metaphorical usage. By contrast, in the other reading, *the village* is computed in a metonymical way, being pragmatically modulated as 'the inhabitants of the village'.

(6.52)   a.   The village woke up. It was full of life.
        b.   The village woke up. They were having breakfast.

Green (1996) claimed that when the literal referent could be the intended referent, it must be. But as (6.47)–(6.49) show, this constraint is too strong. The preference for the literal reference reading is at best a tendency, due perhaps to Grice's first sub-maxim of Manner ('Avoid ambiguity') (cf. Chapter 2). According to this pragmatic sub-principle, an addressee tends to prefer a less effortful, literal reference reading than a more effortful, transferred reference one.[30]

Furthermore, both the literal and transferred referents can be subsequently referred back to either intra-sententially or in the same discourse, provided that it is normally not ruled out by the restrictions on sortal crossing or grammatical coercions in the sense of Pustejovsky (1995). This is illustrated in (6.53) and (6.54).

(6.53)   The ham sandwich left without paying his bill because it was inedible.
(6.54)   a.   Plato is on the top shelf. It is in paperback.
        b.   Plato is on the top shelf. He's a very important philosopher.

In (6.53), *his* is used to refer back to its shifted antecedent and *it* is used to refer back to its non-shifted antecedent. Given that neither use violates the restrictions on sortal crossing or grammatical coercion, the sentence is grammatical. The same story can be told of (6.54). By contrast, in (6.55), both the second sentences are excluded by restrictions on sortal crossing or grammatical coercion, hence they are not grammatical.

(6.55)   a.   Plato is on the top shelf. *He is in paperback.
        b.   Plato is on the top shelf. *It's a very important philosopher.

However, when reflexivization is involved, grammatical coercion can be relaxed, as in (6.56).

---

[30] Note also that the processing of deferred reference is also dependent on whether a metonym is a familiar or a novel one. Frisson and Pickering's (2007) experimental work showed that it takes longer reading time for people to process novel metonymies such as 'read Needham' than familiar ones such as 'read Dickens'.

(6.56)   a. (Jackendoff, 1992, 1997)
                 Ringo squeezed himself into a narrow space.
           b. (Nunberg 1995)
                 Yeats did not like to hear himself read in an English accent.
           c. John couldn't find himself in the phone book.

In (6.56a), *himself* is interpreted as referring to Ringo's car rather than Ringo, in (6.56b), *himself* is used to stand for Yeats' books but not Yeats, and finally in (6.56c), *himself* refers to John's telephone number rather than John the person.[31]

Now try Exercise 6 at the end of this chapter.

6.5.2. Analyses

It is widely accepted by both linguists and philosophers, and both pragmaticists and semanticists, that deferred or transferred reference is pragmatic rather than semantic in nature (e.g. Bach 1994; Recanati 2004a; Stanley 2005). As Stanley (2005: 229) put it, deferred or transferred reference 'ha[s] to do with the *use* of a term, rather than the semantics of a particular expression', and 'it involves how we can use constructions that have a certain semantics to communicate something different than such constructions semantically express'. This is because (i) virtually every linguistic expression can potentially be used to make a deferred or transferred reference in a language, given an appropriate context, and (ii) the relation between the literal and the transferred reference is highly context-sensitive; it can be different from case to case, context to context, and situation to situation.

Fauconnier
On Fauconnier's (1985) view, in deferred or transferred reference, there is a pragmatic function that appropriately connects two or more objects or a trigger and its corresponding target. Such a link is set up for 'psychological, cultural, or locally pragmatic reasons'. Once created, the connection allows a speaker of a language to use a linguistic expression denoting object *a* to refer to object *b*,

---

[31] Since *himself* in (6.56a)–(6.56c) is not co-referential with its antecedent, sentences such as (6.56a)–(6.56c) allow sortal crossings.

which is related to object *a*. In (6.46a), the link between the possessed and the possessor is the pragmatic function. The possessed, namely, the speaker's car is the trigger, which is then connected pragmatically to its corresponding target, namely, the speaker. The pragmatic function in (6.46b) is 'from an author to his or her works'. This allows the author Plato to be linked to the works by him. The culturally salient link between restaurant customers and their orders constitutes a third type of pragmatic function. This is the case of (6.46c), in which the name of the food ordered functions as the trigger and the customer who, for example, ordered the food becomes the corresponding target. Essentially the same analysis can be applied to (6.46d) and (6.46e).

Nunberg

Contrary to his earlier work (Nunberg 1979), Nunberg (1995, 2004) has recently been of the view that in deferred or transferred reference, the transfer machinery applies to the senses rather than referents of linguistic expressions. More specifically, he isolated two linguistic mechanisms for what he called '**meaning transfer**': (i) predicate transfer and (ii) common noun transfer. In the former, the VP carries a transferred sense. This is the case of (6.46a), in which the predicate *be parked out back* provides a property of 'being parked out back', the meaning of which undergoes a process of transfer and contributes to the derived property of 'being a person whose car is parked out back'. Next, in the case of nominal transfer, meaning shift operates on common nouns. In (6.46c), for example, the property is furnished by the noun *ham sandwich*, whose transferred meaning contributes to the derived property of 'being a person who has, for example, ordered the ham sandwich'. Furthermore, Nunberg pointed out that the notion of related **noteworthiness**—a pragmatic condition on use— also plays a decisive role in deferred or transferred reference. In other words, deferred or transferred reference is possible only when the link between the properties contributed by the new and the old predicates is noteworthy or salient.

Ward

Based mainly on an analysis of what he called '**deferred equatives**', as in (6.57),[32] Ward (2004) held the view that an adequate and comprehensive

---

[32] An **equative sentence** is one that is used to assert the identity of the referents of two referring expressions, and is therefore also known as an **identity statement**. For example, in (i) below, the two referring expressions have the same referent.

account of deferred or transferred reference requires both transfer of sense (as argued by Nunberg 1995, 2004) and of reference.

(6.57)   I am the ham sandwich.

In the case of deferred equatives, Ward claimed that the felicitous use of them requires a process of **pragmatic mapping**—a contextually salient correspondence. This pragmatic process operates between (sets of) relevant entities in a discourse. These (sets of) entities must remain accessible in the discourse model. Since the pragmatically mapped entities are explicitly evoked in the equative, they involve no transfer of either sense or reference. In other words, their meanings remain intact, namely, they are non-deferred or non-transferred. In (6.57), for example, the relevant pragmatic mapping is between the set of restaurant customers and that of their orders. Both sets (that is, 'I' and 'ham sandwich') are explicitly evoked in the equative, and neither of them undergoes any transfer. Furthermore, on Ward's view, there must also be a contextually licensed open proposition—whose instantiation encodes the particular mapping between entities.

Recanati

Next, in Recanati's (2004a) analysis, deferred or transferred reference (or **semantic transfer** in Recanati's 2004a: 26–7 terminology) constitutes a primary pragmatic process (cf. Chapter 2). In this type of primary pragmatic process, the output proposition is neither an enriched nor an impoverished version of the concept literally expressed by the input proposition. Rather, it represents a different concept, provided that there is a salient functional relation between the new concept and the old one encoded by the original input proposition. Within Recanati's (2010) framework of truth-conditional pragmatics, meanings of a sentence uttered that go through semantic composition are treated as meanings that are (optionally) pragmatically modulated out of the constituents of the sentence. There is a

---

(i)   Barack Obama is the President of the United States of America.

   In fact, it was the informative nature of an equative/identity sentence like (i), compared with an uninformative one like (ii) that first led Frege to argue for a distinction between sense and reference.

(ii)   Barack Obama is Barack Obama.

pragmatic modulation function that takes a linguistic expression and a context as an argument. When the contextually salient modulation function is applied to the character of the linguistic expression in that context, it gives rise to the pragmatically modulated meaning of the linguistic expression in that context, For example, in (6.46c), the contextually salient metonymic function is applied to the character of the linguistic expression *the ham sandwich* in the context. As a consequence, it engenders the pragmatically modulated content 'the customer who has, for example, ordered the ham sandwich'. This pragmatically modulated meaning is then composed with the meaning of *left without paying* to generate the truth-conditional, propositional content of the whole sentence, thus the transfer of reference.

Finally, I think that it is not unreasonable to suggest that deferred or transferred reference be re-analysed in terms of Kripke's semantic versus speaker's reference distinction, incorporating insights from the analyses discussed above. In such an analysis, the trigger is the semantic referent and the target, namely, the intended, transferred referent is the speaker's referent. The pragmatic process involved is pragmatic modulation along the lines of Recanati (2010) via a neo-Gricean GCI. Thus, in (6.46a), the speaker is the semantic referent and the speaker's car is the speaker's referent. In (6.46b), Plato is the semantic referent and one of the books written by Plato is the speaker's referent. In (6.46c), the ham sandwich is the semantic referent and the customer who has, for example, ordered the ham sandwich is the speaker's referent. Next in (6.46d), the trams are the semantic referent and the drivers and conductors of the trams are the speaker's referent. Finally, in (6.46e), the type of tree called 'oak' is the semantic referent and its wood is the speaker's referent. Tuning next to the cases where ambiguity is involved such as (6.47)–(6.49), under the literal interpretation, the semantic and the speaker's referent converge on one and the same object, as in (6.50a)–(6.52a). Thus, the ham sandwich in (6.50a), Yeats in (6.51a), and the village in (6.52a) are the semantic and the speaker's referent. On the other hand, in the case of the transferred reference, the literal referent is the semantic referent and the intended, deferred referent is the speaker's referent. For example, in (6.51b), the poet Yeats is the semantic referent and his work is the speaker's referent.

6.6. Summary

In this chapter, I have discussed reference. Section 6.1 defined reference first from a semantic point of view and then from a pragmatic perspective. In Section 6.2, I presented a typology of referring expressions. This was followed by a discussion of various anaphoric uses of pronouns in Section 6.3. Section 6.4 then examined proper names and definite descriptions in more detail. Finally, in Section 6.5, I considered deferred or transferred reference.

Key concepts

reference
semantic definition (of reference)
pragmatic definition (of reference)
referring expression
directly referring expression
contextually referring expression
type-referential
token-referential
referent
proper name
partially descriptive proper name
rigid–non-rigid designator distinction
referentially opaque context
Leibniz's law
propositional attitude
propositional attitude verb
definite description
complete definite description
incomplete definite description
definite reference
indefinite description
indefinite reference
specific indefinite reference
non-specific indefinite reference

novelty–familiar distinction
discourse reference
real-world reference
generic reference
demonstrative reference
natural kind term
anaphora
anaphoric expression
referential pronoun
bound-variable pronoun
E-type pronoun
donkey sentence
pronoun of 'laziness'
bridging-cross reference anaphora
sense
denotation
connotation
description theory (of proper names)
direct reference theory (of proper names)
causal (chain) theory (of proper names)
referential–attributive use distinction
semantic reference–speaker's reference distinction
deferred or transferred reference
equative/identity sentence/statement

Exercises and essay questions

1. Can the following possibly be used to refer?
 (i) Confucius
 (ii) the director of the institute
 (iii) but
 (iv) a dentist
 (v) light
 (vi) now
 (vii) my pets
 (viii) those briefcases
 (ix) she
 (x) this

2. What is the type of referring expression used in the following sentences? To which category of reference does it belong?
    (i) *The United Nations* is a talking shop.
    (ii) *That* is a volcanic cone.
    (iii) If *Chomsky* had only written about politics, linguistics wouldn't flourish this day.
    (iv) *A tiger* is a dangerous animal.
    (v) *A tiger* is sleeping in the cage.
    (vi) During the last election, *his party* had suffered severe losses.
    (vii) *Professor Matthews* likes Venetian glass.
    (viii) *A Dr Ellis* wants to speak to you.
    (ix) *The carpet* is rather old-fashioned.
    (x) *Silver* is used for making coins.
    (xi) *The average German voter* has 2.7 cars.
    (xii) *The sun* is shining into the cave.
3. What is the anaphoric use of the pronouns and other types of referring expressions in the following sentences, that is, referential, bound-variable, E-type, 'laziness', or bridging-cross reference?
    (i) The hut collapsed. *The wood* was rotten.
    (ii) Most people who bought a donkey have treated *it* well.
    (iii) Mary said that *she* was not a gifted girl.
    (iv) Every PhD student in the department worried that *the supervisor* was inadequate.
    (v) John's grandmother normally puts her cash under her pillow, but his aunt, like everyone with any sense, always puts *it* in her bank.
    (vi) In the last five years, the Dean was a philosopher; in the next five years, *he* will be a historian.
    (vii) Of every ritual bronze that was found in the tomb, it was subsequently discovered that *the bronze* belonged to the Shang elite in ancient China.
    (viii) Barack Obama said that *the President* will not yield to the pressure from the Congress.
4. What are the semantic referent and the speaker's referent in the following?

    In a park, a man sees a woman in the distance and says 'The woman reading a newspaper is smiling'. While a salient woman is indeed smiling, she is not reading a newspaper but browsing a magazine. One the other hand, there is another woman in the vicinity, obscured partly by a fountain, who is indeed reading a newspaper but is not smiling.
5. What are the semantic referent and the speaker's referent in the following (*à la* Kaplan 1978, Carlson 2004)?

    A man points above his head to the wall behind him where a portrait of President Barack Obama normally hangs and says: 'That man is still popular', not realizing that someone has replaced the portrait in the night with one of former President George W. Bush.

6. What are the intended transferred referents in the following?
   - (i) (A hotel chambermaid to another chambermaid)
     Room 336 wants another blanket.
   - (ii) The White House said that it had thwarted an attempt to infiltrate its computer system.
   - (iii) That pretty face has a brain.
   - (iv) John washed his car yesterday afternoon.
   - (v) New Zealand beat France.
   - (vi) I'm in the phone book.
   - (vii) (A waitress to another waitress in a restaurant)
     The roast beef at table three needs a drink of water.
   - (viii) (A flight attendant to another flight attendant)
     16A wants a decaf.
   - (ix) Botley voted for the Conservative Party.
   - (x) Pearl Harbor remembers Pearl Harbor.
   - (xi) John took himself off the email list.
   - (xii) I began, but then her handbag started ringing. (Helen Fielding, *Bridget Jones's Diary*, p. 192)
7. What is reference? What is the main difference between the semantic and pragmatic definitions of reference?
8. What are the most common types of referring expressions in natural language?
9. From a truth-conditional, semantic point of view, what are the main uses of an anaphoric expression, including an anaphoric pronoun?
10. A proper name expresses a sense, which in turn determines its reference. Do you agree?
11. Compare and contrast proper names and definite descriptions. For example, do proper names fundamentally describe? Do definite descriptions fundamentally refer?
12. Critically discuss Donnellan's referential–attributive distinction.
13. What do you think of Kripke's concepts of semantic and speaker's reference?
14. Compare and contrast any two of the analyses of deferred or transferred reference discussed in this chapter.

Further readings

Frege (1892).
Russell (1905).
Strawson (1950).
Donnellan (1966).
Kripke (1972).
Lyons (1977). Chapter 7.
Lepore and Smith (2006).
Abbott (2010). Chapters 1, 2, 5, and 6.

Part II

Pragmatics and its interfaces

This part deals with those topics which represent new ground in pragmatics, but which are under-represented in any of the existing pragmatics course-books. In particular, it focuses on various interfaces between pragmatics and other (core) areas of inquiry. Chapter 7 discusses the pragmatics-cognition interface, concentrating on Sperber and Wilson's relevance theory. The interface between pragmatics and semantics is the topic of Chapter 8. Finally, Chapter 9 examines the interaction and division of labour between pragmatics and syntax, focusing on anaphora and binding.

7

Pragmatics and cognition: relevance theory

Relevance theory was originated by the French scholar Dan Sperber and the British scholar Deirdre Wilson. It can best be regarded as both a reaction against, and a development of, the classical Gricean pragmatic theory (see Chapter 2). The main ideas of relevance theory are presented in Sperber and Wilson (1986, 1995), and more recently updated in Wilson and Sperber (2004) and Wilson (2010) (see also Clark 2013 for a textbook introduction to the theory). Grounded in a general view of human cognition, the central thesis of the theory is that the human cognitive system works in such a way as to tend to maximize relevance with respect to communication. Thus, the communicative principle of relevance is responsible for the recovery of both the explicit and implicit content of an utterance. Furthermore, it is hypothesized that pragmatics, which incorporates the relevance-theoretic comprehension procedure, is a submodule of the 'theory of mind', that is, a variety of mind-reading (Sperber and Wilson 2002; Wilson and Sperber 2004; Wilson 2010).[1]

This chapter begins, in Section 7.1, with a discussion of the two principles of relevance. Section 7.2 then examines the concepts of explicature, r-implicature, and conceptual versus procedural meaning in relevance theory. Next, in Section 7.3, I shall discuss the recent relevant-theoretic shift from treating pragmatics as a Fodorian central, inferential process to the view that it is a submodule of the 'theory of mind'. Finally, in Section 7.4, I shall briefly compare and contrast relevance theory and the classical/neo-Gricean pragmatic theory of conversational implicature.

7.1. Relevance

7.1.1. The cognitive principle of relevance

At the heart of Sperber and Wilson's (1986, 1995) relevance theory lies the notion of **relevance**. This is embodied in the two principles of relevance put forward by Sperber and Wilson (1995): a **first**, or **cognitive principle of**

---

[1] There are, of course, a number of other cognitive pragmatic theories. One such theory is **cognitive pragmatics theory** developed by the Italian cognitive scientist Bruno Bara. Cognitive pragmatics theory offers an explanation of the cognitive processes that are involved in intentional verbal and non-verbal communication. The practitioners of the theory contend that a 'partner' (addressee) in communication establishes the communicative intention of an 'actor' (speaker) by identifying the behaviour game that the actor intends him or her to play. Pragmatic phenomena are accounted for in terms of the complexity of the inferential steps (the 'inferential load') that are needed to refer an utterance to a particular behaviour game and the complexity of the underlying mental representations. Cognitive pragmatics theory has been applied to studies of developmental pragmatics in children, the comprehension of pragmatic phenomena in head-injured subjects, and pragmatic decay in subjects with Alzheimer's disease (e.g. Bara 2010). In these cases, cognitive pragmatics theory overlaps with clinical and neuropragmatics (e.g. Huang 2013a). Finally, there are also cognitive pragmatic accounts of abductive reasoning, which have been recently developed out of research in artificial intelligence and computational pragmatics (e.g. Hobbs 2004).

relevance, and a **second**, or **communicative principle of relevance**.[2] Let us consider the cognitive principle of relevance first.

(7.1) Sperber and Wilson's (1995) cognitive principle of relevance
   Human cognition tends to be geared to the maximization of relevance.

What, then, is relevance? According to Sperber and Wilson, relevance is a function (or measure) of two factors: (i) **cognitive** or **contextual effects** and (ii) **processing effort**. The first factor is the outcome of an interaction between a newly impinging stimulus and a subset of the assumptions that are already established in a cognitive system. The second factor is the effort a cognitive system must expend in order to yield a satisfactory interpretation of any incoming information processed.[3] Defined thus, relevance is a matter of degree. The degree of relevance of an input to an individual is a balance struck between cognitive effects (i.e. reward) and processing effort (i.e. cost). This is given in (7.2) (Sperber and Wilson 1995).

(7.2) Relevance of an input to an individual
   a. Other things being equal, the greater the positive cognitive effects achieved by processing an input, the greater the relevance of the input to the individual at that time.
   b. Other things being equal, the greater the processing effort expended, the lower the relevance of the input to the individual at that time.

Furthermore, Sperber and Wilson isolated three main types of cognitive effects which the processing of new information in a context may give rise to: (i) generating a conclusion derivable from new and old information together, but from neither new nor old information separately, which is called a **contextual implication**, (ii) a warranted strengthening of an existing

---

[2] Notice that in Sperber and Wilson (1986), there was only one principle of relevance, namely, the communicative principle of relevance, which goes thus: every ostensive stimulus conveys a presumption of its own optimal relevance. On Sperber and Wilson's (2005: 261) view, '[t]he change is, of course, expository and not substantive'.

[3] In fact, a somewhat similar concept of relevance can be traced back to the work of the logicians Noel Belnap and A. R. Anderson, and the social phenomenologist Alfred Schutz. Belnap (1969) and Anderson and Belnap (1975, 1992) developed a logic of relevance to account for inferences that are relevant but not quite valid. Schutz (1970) argued that relevance is a principle according to which an individual organizes his or her cognitive structures into 'provinces of meaning'. See also Allwood (2000).

assumption, and (iii) a warranted revision (including contradicting and cancelling) of an existing assumption. As an illustration, consider the following scenario, taken from Blakemore (2002: 60–1). Suppose that a bus driver is to leave from a bus stop. He sees in his rear mirror the reflection of an anxious-looking woman carrying a bus pass, trying to cross the road behind him. In this situation, the bus driver's overall representation of the world can be improved in the following three ways corresponding to the three types of cognitive effects mentioned above. In the first place, given the assumption that if a person is holding a bus pass, then he or she intends to travel on a bus, the bus driver will derive the new assumption or the contextual implication that the woman in question has the intention of travelling on his bus. Secondly, the bus driver's existing assumption that the woman is trying to cross the road to catch his bus may be supported and strengthened by the assumption that she is carrying a bus pass. Thirdly and finally, the bus driver's existing assumption that the woman intends to take his bus is contradicted and eliminated when he sees the woman walk off in the opposite direction after handing the bus pass to someone who is standing by the bus stop.

Next, I move to processing effort. Consider another scenario. Suppose that Xiaoming, a Chinese student who has just arrived in England, wants to rent a room from the Smiths, his potential landlords. He wants to know whether the Smiths keep any cats. His question in (7.3) could receive any of the replies in (7.4).

(7.3)   Do the Smiths have any cats?
(7.4)   a. They have three cats.
       b. They have three pets.
       c. Either they have three cats or the capital of China is not Beijing.

Given (7.1), all the three replies in (7.4) are relevant to Xiaoming's question in (7.3). However, according to the notion of relevance in (7.2), (7.4a) is more relevant than either (7.4b) or (7.4c). (7.4a) is more relevant than (7.4b) because the former requires less processing effort than the latter. The reason is because (7.4a) entails (7.4b), and hence generates all the conclusions, among other things, deducible from (7.4b), together with the context. On the other hand, (7.4a) is also more relevant than (7.4c). This is because, although (7.4a) and (7.4c), being logically equivalent, yield exactly the same amount of cognitive effect, the effect is much more easily obtained from (7.4a) than (7.4c), since the latter has a second, false disjunct to be computed. In other words, the processing effect required to compute (7.4a) is smaller than that required to compute (7.4c). Given that relevance stated in this way is a trade-off of effect and effort, it is comparative rather than quantitative. One feature of such a comparative notion is that, as Sperber and Wilson were aware, it provides clear comparisons only in some but not all cases. This gives rise to one of the most common criticisms levelled against relevance theory, namely that it fails to provide an explanation of how to measure contextual effects and processing effort in an objective way, how to make them commensurate with each other, or why there is always a unique way to meet the cognitive principle of relevance (e.g. Levinson 1989, Bach 1997, but see Wilson and Sperber 2004 for a spirited defence).

By way of summary, what the cognitive principle of relevance basically says is this: 'as a result of constant selection pressures, the human cognitive system has developed a variety of dedicated (innate or acquired) mental mechanisms or biases which tend to allocate attention to inputs with the greatest expected relevance, and process them in the most relevance-enhancing way' (Wilson 2010: 394). In other words, in human cognition, there is a tendency for communicators to achieve as many cognitive effects as possible for as little processing effort as possible. This means that relevance plays an essential role not only for utterance interpretation, but for all external stimuli or internal mental representations like sights, smell, and thoughts as well (Wilson 2010).

7.1.2. The communicative principle of relevance

I turn next to the **communicative principle of relevance**. Before proceeding, let me first take a look at two general approaches to communication.

Code versus inferential models of communication
On Sperber and Wilson's (1986, 1995) view, theories of communication can be roughly divided into two models: (i) the **code model** and (ii) the **inferential model**. According to the classical code model, communication is accomplished by encoding and decoding messages, that is, a communicator encodes his or her intended message into a signal, which is then decoded by the audience utilizing an identical copy of the code. With respect to human verbal communication, there are two main assumptions underlying

this model: (i) human languages are codes; and (ii) these codes associate thoughts to sounds.[4]

But the code model is descriptively inadequate. This is because comprehension involves much more than the decoding of a linguistic signal. As already established in Chapter 1, there is a huge gap between the semantic representation of a sentence and the messages that are actually conveyed by the speaker in uttering that sentence on a particular occasion of use. In other words, linguistically encoded meaning radically underdetermines the proposition expressed by an utterance. This is known as the linguistic underdeterminacy thesis. Furthermore, the gap is filled not by more coding but by inference. To illustrate the thesis, I have already given a few examples, (1.2)–(1.5) in Chapter 1.

Directly opposed to the code model is the **inferential model**, whose foundation was laid largely by Grice's original theory of meaning$_{nn}$. As pointed out in Chapter 2, the essence of meaning$_{nn}$ is that it is communication which is intended to be recognized as having been intended. In other words, on Grice's view, meaning$_{nn}$ or speaker-meaning is a matter of intention. According to the inferential model, communication is achieved by expressing and recognizing intentions. That is to say, a communicator provides evidence of his or her intention to convey a certain meaning, which is then inferred by the audience on the basis of the evidence presented. Both the classical/neo-Gricean pragmatic theory of conversational implicature I discussed in Chapter 2 and relevance theory I am discussing here fall under this model. A further point to note is that while inferential communication can be used on its own, coded communication can be employed only as a means to strengthen inferential communication (Sperber and Wilson 1986, 1995).

Ostensive-inferential communication

In relevance theory, inferential communication is called **ostensive-inferential communication**. Why? This is because inferential communication involves, in addition to a **first-order informative intention**, a higher-order intention, which Sperber and Wilson (1986, 1995) called **communicative intention**. Furthermore, they called the behaviour which yields the attribution of

---

[4] On Sperber and Wilson's (2002) view, much animal communication uses the code model. This, for example, is the case for the bee dance employed to indicate the direction and distance of nectar.

such an intention '**ostensive communication**', '**ostensive behaviour**', or simply
'**ostension**'.

(7.5) Ostensive-inferential communication
   a. The informative intention
      An intention to inform an audience of something.
   b. The communicative intention
      An intention to inform the audience of one's informative intention.

In ostensive-inferential communication, there is generally an ostensive
stimulus, the use of which gives rise to an expectation of a particular level
of relevance which Sperber and Wilson called **optimal relevance**.

(7.6) Presumption of optimal relevance
   a. The ostensive stimulus is relevant enough to be worth the audience's
      processing effort;
   b. It is the most relevant one compatible with communicator's abilities and
      preferences.

Stated in this way, ostension and inference are the two sides of the same
communication coin: the former is from the perspective of the communicator, and the latter is from the point of view of the audience.

   With (7.5) and (7.6) in place, we can now present Sperber and Wilson's
(1995) communicative principle of relevance as follows.

(7.7) Sperber and Wilson's (1995) communicative principle of relevance
   Every ostensive stimulus (e.g. every utterance) conveys a presumption of its
   own optimal relevance.

   The specific relevance-theoretic procedure employed by the comprehension system is then given in (7.8).

(7.8) Wilson's (2010) relevance-guided comprehension heuristic
   a. Follow a path of least effort in constructing an interpretation of the
      utterance (and in particular in resolving ambiguities and referential inde-
      terminacies, adjusting lexical meaning, supplying contextual assumptions,
      deriving implicatures, etc.).
   b. Stop when your expectations of relevance are satisfied.

In other words, given (7.8), an addressee will presume not only that the
utterance is relevant enough to be worth his or her processing effort, but also
that it is the most relevant utterance compatible with the speaker's abilities
and preferences.

7.2. Explicature, r-implicature, and conceptual versus procedural meaning

In the previous section, I discussed Sperber and Wilson's cognitive and communicative principles of relevance. In this section, let me take a look at the notions of explicature, implicature, and conceptual versus procedural meaning in relevance theory.

7.2.1. Grice: what is said versus what is conversationally implicated

Recall that in Chapter 2, I pointed out that on a classical Gricean account, meaning$_{nn}$/speaker-meaning or the total signification of an utterance is divided into what is said and what is conversationally implicated. Simply put, what is said is generally taken to be (i) the conventional meaning of a sentence uttered with the exclusion of any conventional implicature, and (ii) the truth-conditional propositional content of the sentence uttered (e.g. Grice 1989: 25; Levinson 1983: 97, 2000: 170; Neale 1992: 520–1; Clark 1996: 141; Carston 2002: 114–15; Huang 2010i). What is conversationally implicated is then defined in contrast to, and calculated on the basis of, what is said (and in the case of M-implicatures, together with *how* what is said is said). Stated thus, what is said is supposed to provide the input to deriving what is conversationally implicated. But to work out what is said, according to Grice (1989: 25), one has to (i) resolve reference, as in (7.9); (ii) fix deixis, as in (7.10); and (iii) disambiguate expressions, as in (7.11), (7.12), and (7.13).[5]

(7.9)   a. John told Bill that he wanted to date his sister.
             Preferred interpretation: he = John, his = Bill's
         b. John told Bill that he couldn't date his sister.
             Preferred interpretation: he = Bill, his = John's
(7.10) Mary: How do *I* look?
         John: *You* look really cool!

[5] To these, Levinson (2000, 172–86) added (i) unpacking ellipsis and (ii) narrowing generalities. I shall talk about these in the next chapter.

(7.11)   (Structural ambiguity)
Flying planes can be dangerous.
a. The act of flying planes can be dangerous.
b. Planes that are flying can be dangerous.

(7.12)   (Lexical ambiguity, Levinson 2000: 174)
a. The view could be improved by the addition of a plant out there.
    Preferred interpretation: plant = living organism such as a flower, tree,
    and vegetable
b. The view would be destroyed by the addition of a plant out there.
    Preferred interpretation: plant = factory

(7.13)   (Structural-lexical ambiguity)
John saw her duck.
a. John saw her lower her head.
b. John saw the duck belonging to her.

I shall return to the Gricean dichotomy between what is said and what is
conversationally implicated in the next chapter.

7.2.2. Explicature

On Sperber and Wilson's (1986, 1995) view, Grice failed to recognize that
pragmatics contributes to what is said, or using the relevance-theoretic
term, to explicit content or explicature. Consequently, according to Sperber and Wilson, in the classical Gricean framework, too much attention
has been given to the pragmatic contribution to implicit content or
implicature.

In an attempt to account for the crucial role played by pragmatic inference in **explicit content**, Sperber and Wilson put forward a notion of
explicature, parallel to the classical Gricean notion of implicature. An
explicature is an inferential development of one of the linguistically given
incomplete **conceptual representations** or **logical forms** of a sentence uttered
(but see Burton-Roberts 2007a for the comment that 'development' in this
definition is not defined in relevance theory). In other words, it consists of
the explicit assumptions communicated by an utterance. That is, it functions
to inferentially **explicate** or flesh out the linguistically given incomplete
conceptual representation or logical form encoded by the utterance, yielding
its fully propositional content (but see Bach's 2004 comments on the term
'explicature'). Defined thus, an explicature is a partially pragmatically

inferred component of what is said (though what is said is largely abandoned in relevance theory).

In the current version of relevance theory, explicatures typically serve to complete and enrich conceptual representations or logical forms into propositional forms in the following five areas: (i) disambiguation, (ii) reference resolution, (iii) saturation, (iv) free enrichment, and (v) *ad hoc* concept construction (e.g. Carston 2004). Let me take them one by one.

Disambiguation

Disambiguation usually involves the selection of one sense out of two or more potential senses provided by the linguistic system. Explicatures will complete the incomplete logical form by selecting a particular interpretation, depending on context. Notice that all the examples of disambiguation discussed in relevance theory literature are cases of lexical ambiguity.

(7.14)   John and Bill passed the port in the evening.
      a. port = harbour
      b. port = wine
      Explicature: e.g. John and Bill passed the harbour in the evening

Reference resolution

Reference resolution is not determined by the linguistic system but is achieved by assigning an appropriate contextual value to the relevant referential or anaphoric expression on the explicit side. In addition to (7.9), we have (7.15).

(7.15)   John narrowly defeated Peter in the local election, and he immediately demanded a recount.
      Explicature: Peter immediately demanded a recount

Saturation

Saturation is a pragmatic process whereby a given slot, position, or variable in the linguistically decoded logical form is saturated or filled (e.g. Recanati 1989, 2004a, 2004b, 2010). A few examples are given in (7.16).

(7.16)   a. Yan works too hard. [for what?]
      b. Chomsky's minimalist program is less promising. [than what?]
      c. Sperber and Wilson's notion of explicature is different. [from what?]

Here, the bracketed questions are taken to be the slots or the like in the incomplete logical forms of the sentences in (7.16). These slots need to be explicitly completed so that the full propositional forms of the sentences containing them can be obtained. Saturation may yield such explicatures as those in (7.17) for (7.16), depending on context.

(7.17) a. Yan works too hard [for a not terribly well-paid British university professor]
    b. Chomsky's minimalist program is less promising [than his principles-and-parameters predecessor]
    c. Sperber and Wilson's notion of explicature is different [from Grice's notion of implicature]

Free enrichment

I mentioned free enrichment in Chapter 2. Like saturation, the notion of free enrichment is also borrowed from Recanati (2004a, 2004b). In **free enrichment**, although there does not seem to be either an overt indexical or a covert slot in the linguistically decoded logical form of a sentence uttered, the logical form nevertheless still needs to be conceptually enriched in the explicature. The process of free enrichment is 'free' because it is pragmatically rather than linguistically based. In the relevance theory literature, two types of free enrichment are identified. In the first place, we have the type in which the enrichment focuses on a particular lexical item in the utterance and narrows the concept it encodes. Compare (7.18) and (7.19).

(7.18) a. John has a brain.
    b. The university campus is some distance from the rail station.
    c. I haven't washed my face yet.
    d. It's snowing.
    e. The police moved in and the hostages were released.
(7.19) a. John has a [scientific] brain
    b. The university campus is a [considerable] distance from the rail station
    c. I haven't washed my face yet [this morning][6]
    d. It's snowing [in Boston]
    e. The police moved in and [then, as a result, etc.] the hostages were released[7]

---

[6] The enrichment of (7.19c) is dependent on our shared beliefs about the world, in particular about our shared face-washing practices. This would explain, for example, why *I haven't had sex* would be enriched in a different way, as pointed out by Taylor (2001). See Taylor (2001) for a 'roughly but still deeply Gricean' explanation.

[7] Note that (7.19e) is treated as carrying a generalized conversational (I-) implicature in the Gricean and neo-Gricean framework.

Here, (7.18a) and (7.18b) are truisms, that is, they express a trivial truth. It goes without saying that every human being has a brain and that there is distance between any two places. Next (7.18c) and (7.18d) are so vague that the minimal propositions recovered from both utterances by decoding and reference assignment fall short of what the speakers must have meant. Consequently, the vagueness in both utterances needs to be resolved. Finally, the use of *and* in (7.18e) requires the strengthening of the conjunct relation. On this basis, we will obtain explicatures such as those shown in the brackets in (7.19).

Secondly, there is the type of free enrichment in which a contextually provided conceptual constituent needs to be added in the explicature. Consider (7.20).

(7.20)   a. Everyone wore a new wool cardigan.
       b. There's nothing to watch on TV tonight.
       c. They eat everything.

The process involved here is again that of narrowing or specifying. In the case of (7.20a), the domain of the quantifier *everyone* needs to be narrowed down, hence specified, resulting in an explicature such as (7.21a), depending on context. In the case of (7.20b), the incomplete logical form has to be enriched by something like '(nothing) the speaker considers worth (watching)'. In the case of (7.20c), 'everything' needs to be enriched to 'everything that is edible for human beings'.

(7.21)   a. Everyone [at Mary's party] wore a new cardigan
       b. There's nothing [the speaker considers worth] watching on TV tonight
       c. They eat everything [that is edible for human beings][8]

Ad hoc concept construction
Finally, we come to *ad hoc* concept construction. The notion is introduced by Barsalou (1983). By ***ad hoc* concept construction** is meant the pragmatic adjustment of a lexical concept in the linguistically decoded logical form, the

---

[8] It should be pointed out that in Recanati's (1989, 1993, 2004b) original analysis, (7.19a)–(7.19c) are taken to be cases of strengthening or logical enrichment, whereas (7.21b) is considered as a case of expansion, *à la* Bach (1987). The main difference between strengthening and expansion is whether the output proposition needs to entail the original input proposition. I shall have more to say about Recanati's work in the next chapter.

adjustment being a narrowing or strengthening, a broadening or weakening, or a combination of both. As an illustration, take (7.22) first.

(7.22)   John is happy/angry/depressed ...

The general concepts expressed by the lexical items *happy*, *angry*, and *depressed* can access a large, if not an indefinite, number of more specific subconcepts indicating different kinds, degrees, and qualities of the emotions. For example, *John is depressed* can be used to mean that John feels a bit low, John feels very low, or John feels suicidal, depending on context. Explicatures here serve to recover the narrower, more specific concepts in the logical form. Next, consider (7.23), some of which are taken or adapted from Carston (2002, 2004).

(7.23)   a. There is a rectangle of lawn at the back.
       b. The fridge is empty.
       c. Holland is flat.
       d. Classic FM plays continuous classics.
       e. John is a bulldozer.

All the sentences in (7.23) are used in a broad, 'loose' way. Recall that in Chapter 4, I mentioned Austin's notion of 'loose' use and his example *France is hexagonal*. This is exactly what is happening in (7.23). In (7.23a), the rectangle is likely to be approximately rectangular, hence what is expressed is not the encoded concept RECTANGLE, but a broadened or loosened concept RECTANGLE. More or less the same can be said of the 'loose' use of many other geometrical terms such as *round*, *triangular*, and *oval*. In (7.23b), there could still be some odd groceries left in the fridge. In (7.23c), Holland is not, strictly speaking, flat. In (7.23d), Classic FM also broadcasts, say, news, commercials, and listeners' call-ins. Finally, loosening is applicable to cases of metaphor as well, as in (7.23e). In all these cases, the lexical concepts will undergo an *ad hoc* pragmatic adjustment or weakening (see also Carston 2004).

> See what you make of Exercise 1 at the end of this chapter.

At this point, mention should be made of a subtype of explicature—what is called **higher-level** or **higher-order explicature** in the relevance theory literature. These are explicatures which involve embedding the propositional form of an utterance under a higher-level description. Higher-level descriptions include propositional attitude descriptions, speech act descriptions, and certain other comments such as evidentiality markers on the embedded propositions. By contrast, non-higher-level explicatures are called **basic explicatures** by Wilson and Sperber (2004). As an illustration of higher-level explicature, consider the explicatures of (7.24) in (7.25).

(7.24)   Susan: My husband is a womanizing alcoholic.

(7.25)   a. Susan believes that her husband is a womanizing alcoholic
         b. Susan is angry that her husband is a womanizing alcoholic

Here, (7.25a) and (7.25b) may be the higher-level explicatures for (7.24). The propositional form of (7.24) is embedded under a propositional attitude description. Next, witness the explicatures of (7.26) in (7.27).

(7.26)   John to Bill: Bring me a glass of water, please.

(7.27)   a. John is telling Bill to bring him a glass of water
         b. It is moderately desirable to John (and achievable) that Bill bring him a glass of water
         c. John is requesting Bill to bring him a glass of water

The uttering of (7.26) by John performs the speech act of requesting (see Chapter 4). It gives rise to the higher-level explicatures in (7.27). Finally, consider the explicatures of (7.28) in (7.29).

(7.28)   Evidently, Frederick the Great entertained Voltaire at Sanssouci.

(7.29)   a. It is evident that Frederick the Great entertained Voltaire at Sanssouci
         b. The speaker strongly believes that Frederick the Great entertained Voltaire at Sanssouci

Evidentials make clear the source or reliability of the evidence on which a statement is based, as shown by the use of *evidently* in (7.28). (7.29a) and (7.29b) may be the higher-level explicatures for (7.28).

Now see whether you can do Exercise 2 at the end of this chapter.

7.2.3. R-implicature

I turn next to what is taken as implicit content or implicature in relevance theory. An implicature is defined as a communicated assumption derivable solely via pragmatic inference. Thus, the recovery of it differs from that of an explicature in that while the latter involves both decoding and inference, the former involves only inference (Sperber and Wilson 1986, 1995). Let me call implicatures in the relevance-theoretic sense **r-implicatures**, in the hope that no confusion will arise with Grice's notion of (conversational) implicatures.

Two kinds of r-implicature can then be identified in relevance theory: (i) **r-implicated premises** and (ii) **r-implicated conclusions**. The former is a contextual assumption intended by the speaker and supplied by the addressee, and the latter is a contextual implication communicated by the speaker. By way of illustration, take (7.30).

(7.30)   Car salesman: Are you interested in test-driving a Rolls-Royce?
         John: I'm afraid I'm not interested in test-driving any expensive car.

John's reply may yield the following two r-implicatures:

(7.31)   a. A Rolls-Royce is an expensive car
         b. John isn't interested in test-driving a Rolls-Royce

Here, (7.31a) is an implicated premise, and (7.31b) is an implicated conclusion, of John's reply. (7.31b) follows deductively from (7.31a) combined with (7.30). However, this analysis is not unequivocally accepted. In the first place, in Recanati's (2004: 48) view, an implicated premise is not an implicature, because it is not part of what the speaker means. Rather, it is part of what he or she takes for granted or presupposes and expects the addressee to take for granted. Secondly, as pointed out in Huang (2012b), the treatment of (7.31a) as an implicated premise is limited to the class of examples like (7.30) in the relevance theory literature, and more generally, is applicable only to what is treated as a PCI in the Gricean and neo-Gricean framework (see Chapter 2). How it can be applied to a GCI in the Gricean sense is, to say the least, unclear. For example, it is not clear what the r-implicated premise is in (7.32) (but see Sperber and Wilson 1995: 276–8 and Carston 1998 for a relevance-theoretic analysis of generalized conversational implicatures in the Gricean sense).

(7.32)   John and Mary watched the Berlin Wall crumble in 1989.
(7.33)   a. R-implicated premise: ?
         b. R-implicated conclusion: John and Mary watched the Berlin Wall crumble in 1989 together

To sum up, in relevance theory, the recovery of both explicatures and r-implicatures is guided by the communicative principle of relevance. More specifically, in an overall, relevance-theoretic comprehension process, three sub-tasks are involved, as listed in (7.34) (Wilson and Sperber 2004).

(7.34)   Sub-tasks in the overall comprehension process
   a. Constructing an appropriate hypothesis about explicit content (explica-tures) via decoding, disambiguation, reference resolution, and other pragmatic enrichment processes.
   b. Constructing an appropriate hypothesis about the intended contextual assumptions (implicated premises).
   c. Constructing an appropriate hypothesis about the intended contextual implications (implicated conclusions).

In other words, in relevance theory, utterance interpretation involves (i) the completion or expansion of incomplete logical forms, and the derivation of explicatures via the completion or expansion of the logical forms, and (ii) the generation of r-implicatures including the recovery of r-implicated premises and r-implicated conclusions. Furthermore, the first satisfactory interpretation discovered by the use of the relevance-theoretic comprehension procedure is the only satisfactory reading. This interpretation is the one that the addressee should select. Put in a different way, the relevance-guided comprehension mechanism has a clear stopping point. Once the addressee discovers a reading that crosses the threshold set up by the relevance-theoretic comprehension heuristic, he or she will take it to be what the speaker intends to communicate (Wilson 2010).

This relevance-theoretic analysis is, however, not without problems. For instance, it is incapable of accounting for examples of the following type, discussed in Horn (2006).

(7.35)   If it's warm, we'll lie out in the sun. But if it's hot, we'll go inside and sit in front of the air-conditioner.

As pointed out by Horn (2006), in (7.35), the recovery of the stronger, pragmatically enriched reading of what is said, namely, the explicature 'warm but not hot' arising from the use of *warm* in the first clause, can be obtained only when the stronger scalar expression *hot* in the third clause is reached. In other words, the explicature under consideration is not the first satisfactory interpretation picked up by the addressee. Rather, it is the outcome of a retroactive adjustment of the earlier, weaker reading 'at least warm'. Clearly, in order to derive the correct explicature of (7.35), the addressee cannot stop where he or she is predicated to stop by the relevance-theoretic comprehension procedure (see also Borg's 2009 discussion of various relevance-theoretic possible but untenable manoeuvres to tackle counterexamples of this kind).

> By now you should be able to do Exercise 3 at the end of this chapter.

A second dichotomy relating to r-implicatures is that between strong and weak r-implicatures. Following Grice's idea that conversational implicatures may sometimes be indeterminate (see Chapter 2), Sperber and Wilson (1986, 1995) posited that r-implicatures may be more or less strong. In other words, the strength of an r-implicature may vary along a continuum. Simply put, **strong r-implicatures** are those r-implicatures whose recovery is essential to understand the speaker's intended meaning. By contrast, **weak r-implicatures** are those r-implicatures whose recovery is not essential, because the r-implicatures may be one of a wide array of equally possible r-implicatures engendered by an utterance. As an illustrating example, consider (7.36), taken from Wilson and Sperber (2004).

(7.36) Peter:Did John pay back the money he owed you?
　　　　Mary:No. He forgot to go to the bank.
(7.37) a. John was unable to repay Mary the money he owes because
　　　　　　he forgot to go to the financial institution
　　　　b. John may repay Mary the money he owes when he next goes
　　　　　　to the financial institution
　　　　c. ...

Mary's reply in (7.36) may give rise to a range of r-implicatures, as in (7.37). Of these r-implicatures, (7.37a) is a strong r-implicature. Otherwise, Mary's reply would not be relevant. On the other hand, Mary's reply may encourage the addressee to derive further r-implicatures such as (7.37b). But (7.37b) is a weak r-implicature because it is indeterminate and its recovery is not essential (Wilson and Sperber 2004).

> Try your hand at Exercise 4 at the end of this chapter.

7.2.4. Conceptual versus procedural meaning

We come finally to the dichotomy between conceptual and procedural meaning in relevance theory, a dichotomy developed largely by Blakemore (1987, 2002, 2004). On Blakemore's view, **conceptual meaning** contributes concepts to the logical form of a sentence, that is, it enters into the semantic representation. In other words, in conceptual encoding, linguistic forms encode conceptual information. For example, *lion*, *eat*, and *happy* are lexical items which encode conceptual information. By contrast, **procedural meaning** does not contribute any concept but rather provides a constraint on, or indication of, the way in which certain aspects of pragmatic inference should proceed, that is to say, it indicates particular computational processes. Another way of putting it is that in procedural encoding, linguistic forms encode procedural information (but see Bach 1999 for a dissenting view). Discourse markers or connectives like *after all*, *but*, and *so* (which are treated as triggers of conventional implicatures in the Gricean framework) are examples of linguistic expressions which encode procedural meaning. Consider, for instance, (7.38).

(7.38)   Mary promised to make a donation to Oxfam but she didn't.

Here, the discourse marker *but* functions as a pointer to the pragmatic inference the addressee is to work out. More specifically, it instructs the addressee to interpret the clause that follows it as contradicting and eliminating a proposition which is most likely derived from the preceding clause, thus the generation of a denial of the expected interpretation. Stated thus, *but* encodes only procedural information (Blakemore 2002, see also Blass 1990 on Sisaala).

In Blakemore (1987), it was suggested that whereas conceptual encodings contribute to explicatures, procedural encodings constrain only pragmatic inferences which yield r-implicatures. This position, however, was called into question by Sperber and Wilson (1993). On Sperber and Wilson's view, procedural encodings play an important role not only on the implicit but also on the explicit side of communication. More specifically, Sperber and Wilson proposed that pronouns, demonstratives, and even mood, tense, and inverted word order encode information about the inferential computations in which basic and higher-level explicatures are derived (see also Blakemore 2004).

7.3. From Fodorian 'central process' to submodule of 'theory of mind'

7.3.1. Fodorian theory of cognitive modularity

Let me start with the question of whether or not there is a **pragmatics module** in the mind. Or, put in a more precise way, whether utterance comprehension is a specialized cognitive domain with its own innately specified principles and mechanisms. In order to provide an answer to this question, we need first to take a look at the Fodorian theory of cognitive modularity.

One of the current, most influential theories of mind is the one put forward by the American cognitive scientist Jerry Fodor (1983), inspired in part by Chomsky's view on language and linguistics.[9] The central thesis of the classical Fodorian theory of **cognitive modularity** is the claim that the mental architecture of *homo sapiens* is divided roughly into a basic dichotomy between a **central processor** and a number of distinct **cognitive systems**. These specialized cognitive systems, called **modules**, have a number of relatively well-defined characteristics: they are **domain-specific** (they are specialized for particular domains), **primary** (they are not 'assembled', that is, they are not composed of other more elementary mechanisms), **computationally autonomous** (they do not share mental resources, such as memory, with other cognitive systems), **fast** and **mandatory** (for example, we have no choice but to hear sound we are exposed to), **innately specified** (their structure and function are not determined by some learning process only), and **informationally encapsulated** (they have no access to information of a certain kind, and operate without interference from central control). The five senses—sight, hearing, smell, taste, and touch—are such cognitive systems, each of which constitutes one or a cluster of modules. Language is

---

[9] Another is **connectionism**—also frequently called **parallel distributed models** or **neural networks**. The main thesis of connectionist models is that human cognition operates through the interactions of numerous simple units. The processing is highly distributed throughout the entire system. There are, for example, no specialized modules in the Fodorian sense. See Bechtel and Abrahamsen (1991) and Horgan and Tienson (1996) for an introduction to connectionism. In the late 1980s and early 1990s, there was an intense debate about the architecture of cognition between connectionists and symbolists in cognitive science and cognitive linguistics. See, for example, the exchanges between Fodor and Pylyshyn (1988) and Chalmers (2003).

taken to be another module or a cluster of modules. These modules feed into the central system, which is neither domain-specific nor informationally encapsulated. The central system is responsible for general mental capacities such as rational thought formation, problem solving, and belief fixation.[10] Furthermore, whereas not restricted exclusively to this role, one of the major functions of a module is to provide 'input' to the central system. Hence Fodor considered language as a dedicated input system, analogous to those devoted to the five senses[11] (see Fodor 1983, see also Smith 2004).[12]

[10] A particular version of Fodor's modularity of mind thesis is the **massive modularity of mind** thesis. The term 'massive modularity' was introduced by the French scholar Dan Sperber. According to this view, the human mind is largely, if not entirely, composed of modules. Two forms of the massive modularity of mind thesis can then be identified: strong and weak. On the authority of the strong massive modularity of mind thesis, the human mind does not contain any overarching general-purpose mechanism. In other words, every central process is modular. By contrast, the weak massive modularity of mind thesis maintains that while central processes are largely modular, there are also non-modular, general-purpose processes. The massive modularity of mind thesis is not, however, espoused by Fodor (e.g. Meini 2010). Furthermore, in the opinion of the British philosopher Gabriel Segal, modularity can be divided into **diachronic** and **synchronic modularity**. The former is a cognitive module that follows a genetically and developmentally determined pattern of growth. By comparison, synchronic modularity refers to a module that is static. Finally, there are competence and performance modules. A **competence module**, also referred to as a 'Chomskyan' or 'information module', is one that constitutes a system of mental representation. It is said to contain linguistic, biological, psychological, physical, and mathematical knowledge. It runs in contrast with a performance module, also termed a 'computational module'. A **performance module** is one that functions as a computational mechanism. In other words, it is a device that processes mental representations (e.g. Carston 2010a).

[11] The characterization of language as an input system was, however, challenged by Chomsky (1986: 18). On Chomsky's view, the language faculty is a cognitive system of knowledge rather than an input or output system. See Smith (2004) for discussion of further differences between Fodor and Chomsky.

[12] See also Atlas' (1997) comments from a philosophical perspective. On Atlas' view, speech is both modular and hermeneutic. It is modular in the sense that sounds are first translated algorithmically into semantic information; it is hermeneutic in the sense that the speaker's intention behind the propositional content is then interpreted.

Also one of the anonymous referees pointed out that modularity, as espoused by Fodor, plays no role in processing accounts of how language is produced and

7.3.2. Sperber and Wilson's earlier position: pragmatics as Fodorian 'central process'

Given the distinctive properties of modules, mentioned above, the question that presents itself is whether or not pragmatics or utterance comprehension is a module in the classical Fodorian sense. The answer provided by the earlier Sperber and Wilson is that it is not (e.g. Sperber and Wilson 1986). As an alternative, Sperber and Wilson argued that like scientific theorizing—a paradigmatic case of a non-modular process in the Fodorian sense—pragmatics is part of the Fodorian central, inferential process, albeit a spontaneous, intuitive rather than a conscious, reflective one. Furthermore, they hypothesized that the Fodorian central system is a non-demonstrative inference process which works in such a way as to tend to maximize relevance. The main difference is that while Fodor conceded that the central processor operates in a mysterious way along non-deductive lines, and is therefore essentially unstructured and putatively uninvestigatable, Sperber and Wilson took the central processor as an inference-generating system with a strong deductive component.

7.3.3. Sperber and Wilson's current position: pragmatics as submodule of 'theory of mind'

On Sperber and Wilson's view, in recent years, there has been a general tendency in cognitive science to shift away from Fodor's basic dichotomy between the relatively undifferentiated central system and the specialized modules towards an increasingly modular concept of the human mind.[13] Against this background, Sperber and Wilson have abandoned their earlier position of treating pragmatics or utterance comprehension as a Fodorian central, inferential process (Sperber and Wilson 2002; Wilson and Sperber

understood. In fact, much of the recent research in neuroscience has shown that linguistic, for example, lexical and syntactic, information is processed in parallel.

[13] This is strongly disputed by the same anonymous referee, who said that contrary to Sperber and Wilson's claim, in cognitive science, there is in fact increasingly compelling evidence for immense plasticity and connectivity during development, and for parallel processing in dealing with language. For recent accounts of the acquisition process, see e.g. Clark (2004) and Tomasello (2004).

2004). Instead, they are now of the view that utterance comprehension involves a more modular ability for **mind-reading**, or '**theory of mind (ToM)**', which involves the more general metapsychological ability to inferentially attribute mental states or intentions to others on the basis of their behaviour (e.g. Davies and Stone 1995; Carruthers and Smith 1996).[14] Furthermore, Sperber and Wilson argued that, contrary to the popular assumption that a submodule is not needed to handle pragmatic abilities in mind-reading (e.g. Bloom 2000, 2002), utterance comprehension is subject to a distinct interpretation submodule of the 'theory of mind', that is, a specialized, automatic computational device, with its own special principles and mechanisms. The workings of this comprehension submodule of the 'theory of mind' are underpinned by the communicative principle of relevance, and contain the relevance-theoretic comprehension procedure as a basic component. Given the relevance-theoretic comprehension procedure, which is a dedicated domain-specific inferential apparatus, the addressee will be able to infer what the speaker means on the basis of the evidence provided (Sperber and Wilson 2002; Wilson and Sperber 2004).

7.4. Relevance theory and the classical/neo-Gricean pragmatic theory compared

What, then, are the main similarities and differences between relevance theory and classical/neo-Gricean pragmatics? As pointed out in Huang (2012b), there are at least three main similarities. In the first place, both relevance and neo-Gricean pragmatic theories share the Gricean assumption that sentence-meaning is a vehicle for conveying meaning$_{nn}$ or speaker-meaning, and the essence of meaning$_{nn}$ is communication which is intended to be recognized as having been intended. In other words, speaker-meaning is a matter of expressing and recognizing intention. A second similarity is that both theories maintain with Grice that speaker-meaning cannot be simply decoded, but has to be pragmatically enriched. This indicates that

---

[14] Currently, there seem to be three contenders to a theoretical account of ToM: (i) to treat ToM as a cognitive module, (ii) to regard ToM as a theory construction, and (iii) to take ToM as an imaginative projection. The first approach is called 'the modular theory of ToM', the second, 'the theory theory account of ToM', and the third, 'the simulation theory of ToM'. See Cummings (2013) for further discussion.

both theories belong to the camp of 'contextualism' in the current divide between contextualism and semantic minimalism or literalism in the philosophy of language (to be discussed in the next chapter). Thirdly and finally, both theories assume that in computing speaker-meaning, an addressee is guided by the expectation that an utterance should meet certain standards (see also Wilson 2010).

On the other hand, there are major differences between relevance theory and neo-Gricean pragmatics. The first difference is concerned with whether a pragmatic theory of human communication should be based on the study of usage principles or cognitive principles. One of the central issues of any pragmatic theory is to explain how the addressee works out the speaker's intended meaning on the basis of the evidence available (but see notes 5 and 6 of Chapter 2).[15] As already remarked in Chapter 2, the answer provided by Grice is that utterances automatically raise certain expectations, and these expectations guide the addressee towards what the speaker intends. More specifically, Grice put forward an account of these expectations in terms of his co-operative principle and set of attendant conversational maxims. The Gricean co-operative principle and its associated maxims of conversation are essentially usage principles based on the rational nature of human communication, and indeed of any goal-oriented (human) activity (Grice 1989: 28). In other words, they are general communicative norms recognized jointly, though tacitly, by the speaker and the addressee in order to communicate effectively and efficiently.

Where do the co-operative principle and its attendant conversational maxims come from, and how do the speaker and the addressee come to

---

[15] Also according to Saul (2002), while Grice's main goal is to develop a theory of speaker-meaning or utterance production, Sperber and Wilson (1986/1995) are primarily concerned with the construction of a cognitive psychological theory of utterance comprehension. Their theory does not attend to the question of how and why the speaker, given what he or she wants to convey, utters what he or she utters (see also Horn 2006). Put slightly differently, in Mate and Tirassa's (2010: 240) words, 'however satisfactory as theory of language comprehension, relevance theory has never been able to become a theory of language generation or of dialogue, nor has it ever even tried to'. This view was also held by Bach (1999), who argued that utterance comprehension is not a problem for pragmatics, but for cognitive and social psychology. Both Saul and Bach thought that relevance theory has misunderstood the main goal of Grice's thinking.

know them? Whereas Grice was non-committed on the source of these pragmatic principles and their place in our overall cognitive architecture, one possible answer provided by him is that they are likely to be learned. To quote him: 'it is just a well-recognized empirical fact that people do behave in these ways; they learned to do so in childhood and have not lost the habit of doing so; and, indeed, it would involve a good deal of effort to make a radical departure from the habit' (Grice 1989: 29). Relevance theory, on the other hand, is an attempt 'to shift the whole centre of gravity of pragmatic theorizing away from the study of usage principles to the study of cognitive principles' (Levinson 1989). In the relevance-theoretic framework, pragmatics is reduced to a single notion of relevance, which is realized in two principles of relevance. But unlike Grice's co-operative principle and its attendant maxims of conversation, the principles of relevance are not a maxim addressed to the speaker, known by the addressee, and obeyed or exploited in communication. Rather, grounded in a general view of human cognition, they are an automatic reflex of the human mental capacity that works without the communicators having any overt knowledge of it. How do the speaker and the addressee follow the principles of relevance? They do not. According to Sperber and Wilson (1995: 162), '[c]ommunicators and audience need no more know the principle of relevance to communicate than they need to know the principles of genetics to reproduce. Communicators do not "follow" the principle of relevance; and they could not violate it even if they wanted to. The principle of relevance applies without exception: every act of ostensive communication communicates a presumption of relevance'. Relevance is thus a form of unconscious inference. In other words, the principles of relevance are governing cognitive principles that are not themselves an object of processing.[16] This raises the larger issue of whether relevance theory can be falsified or not. Given that relevance is an exceptionless generalization, it is likely to be immune from any possible

[16] See also Cummings (2005) for a philosophical critique of the three critical features of relevance theory, namely (i) the elimination rules of the logical entries of concepts, (ii) the role of deduction in utterance interpretation, and (iii) the functional concept of confirmation. In fact, Cummings' criticism is in part based on Putnam's (1981) similar charge of self-refutation against logical positivism. On Cummings' view, the relevance-theoretic claims display a striking similarity with those of logical positivism.

counterexamples (see e.g. Levinson 1989; Huang 1994, 2000a, 2007a; but see Wilson and Sperber 2004 and Wilson 2010 for counterarguments).[17]

In the second place, relevance theory and the classical/neo-Gricean pragmatic theory differ in whether or not separate notions of explicature and implicature are needed in the recovery of so-called explicit and implicit content, respectively. As is well known, on Grice's view, the propositional content of what is said is not fully worked out until reference is identified, deixis is interpreted, and ambiguity is resolved. How can all this be done? Grice (1989: 25) seemed to take the recovery of the explicit truth-conditional, propositional content as largely the outcome of linguistic and contextual decoding. This led Sperber and Wilson to their criticism that in the Gricean paradigm, only the recovery of implicit context (r-implicature) is taken to be properly pragmatic, and that as a result, the key part pragmatics plays in computing explicit content is overlooked. Consequently, Sperber and Wilson posited their notion of explicature. Explicature plays an extremely important role in relevance theory, and as a consequence, many types of implicature in the Gricean and neo-Gricean sense are reduced to explicature. This, for example, is the case for 'scalar implicature', 'conjunction buttressing', and many others. By contrast, in the neo-Gricean pragmatic framework, the relevance-theoretic explicature–implicature distinction is rejected. On Levinson's (2000: 195–6) view, pragmatic intrusion into what is said, that is, into determining the truth-conditional, propositional content is not an explicature. Rather, it is the same beast as a neo-Gricean conversational implicature. If neo-Gricean conversational implicature can intrude onto truth-conditional content of an utterance, then a problem known as **Grice's circle** arises, namely, how what is conversationally implicated can be defined in contrast to, and calculated on the basis of, what is said, given that what is said seems to both determine and to be determined by what is conversationally implicated (e.g. Levinson 2000; Huang 2003). Levinson's proposal was that one should reject the 'received' view of the pragmatics–semantics interface, namely, the view that the output of semantics is the input to pragmatics, and allow conversational implicatures to play a systematic role in 'pre'-semantics, that is, to help determine the truth-conditional, propositional content of an utterance.

---

[17] One of the minimal Popperian criteria for a scientific theory is falsifiability, which dictates that empirically based scientific theories (under which linguistics falls) can only be refuted, but not proven true (e.g. Popper 1973).

Putting it slightly differently, in order to avoid Grice's circle, one needs both 'pre'-semantic pragmatics and 'post'-semantic pragmatics. I shall have more to say about the debate in the next chapter.

Thirdly, as already discussed in Chapter 2, a heated debate has been going on for the last decade or so, focusing on the nature of Gricean and neo-Gricean GCIs in general and Q_{scalar} implicatures in particular. The neo-Gricean view is that GCIs in general and Q_{scalar} implicatures in particular convey default meaning, that is, their intended meaning is automatically expressed and computed on encountering a scalar implicature trigger like *some* (the default inference theory). By contrast, the relevance-theoretic position, known as the contextual inference theory, maintains that the derivation of scalar implicatures depends heavily on contextual factors.

In the fourth place, there is the debate relating to whether a pragmatic theory of human communication should contain two levels or three levels. Building on the Gricean GCI–PCI dichotomy, Levinson (2000) developed a theory of presumptive meaning. On a traditional, standard view, there are only two levels of meaning to a theory of communication: a level of sentence-meaning versus a level of speaker-meaning, or, to make use of the type–token distinction by Lyons (1977), a level of sentence-type-meaning versus a level of utterance-token-meaning. But Levinson (2000: 23) argued that such a view 'is surely inadequate, indeed potentially pernicious, because it under-estimates the regularity, recurrence, and systematicity of many kinds of pragmatic inferences'. He proposed to add a third level—utterance-type-meaning—to the two generally accepted levels of sentence-type-meaning and utterance-token-meaning. This third layer is the level of generalized, pre-ferred, or default interpretation, which is not dependent upon direct compu-tations about speaker-intentions but rather upon expectations about how language is characteristically used. GCIs, Levinson argued, should be included on this layer, as these pragmatic enrichments have an expectable, stable, and even standardized or conventionalized interpretation (see also experimental pragmatic works such as Noveck 2001; Hamblin and Gibbs 2003; Papafragou and Musolino 2003; Bezuidenhout and Morris 2004; Breheny et al. 2006). Stated in this way, a neo-Gricean pragmatic theory of conversational implicature, which is largely concerned with GCIs rather than PCIs, is essentially a theory of utterance-type-meaning on a level intermediate between sentence-type-meaning on the one hand and utter-ance-token-meaning on the other. In other words, it is ultimately a theory of presumptive meaning—pragmatic enrichment that is generalized, default, and presumed. However, as pointed out by Levinson (2000), this middle layer of utterance-type-meaning has been constantly subject to attempts to reduce it on the one hand to the upper layer of sentence-type-meaning, as in, for instance, Chierchia's (2004, 2013) structural inference theory, and on the other to the lower layer of utterance-token-meaning, as in, for example, relevance theory. In my view, such reductionist efforts, though highly desirable given 'Occam's razor', cannot be successful. The reason they will fail is this: on the one hand, GCIs are defeasible, thus not code-like, as claimed by Sperber and Wilson. This will make it difficult for them to be semanticized. On the other hand, other things being equal, a theory about types is in principle better than a theory about tokens in that the former enjoys more predictive and explanatory power. Therefore, any attempts to reduce GCIs to kinds of context-induced 'nonce' inferences should be resisted. If these arguments are correct, a three-tiered theory of communication with a layer of default but defeasible interpretation sitting midway is in principle to be preferred over a two-levelled one without such an intermediate layer (Huang 2003, 2007a, 2012b).

Finally, somewhat related to the difference concerning communication theory levels above is the difference with respect to the distinction in conversational implicature type or context type. In the Gricean framework, there are two types of conversational implicature, that is, GCIs and PCIs. Alternatively, one can argue that there is only one type of conversational implicature but two types of context, that is, default and specific. In relevance theory, by contrast, there is neither any distinction in conversational implicature type nor any distinction in context type. As noted already, all conversational implicatures are reduced to a kind of context-induced, 'nonce' inference, namely, what I have called r-implicatures.

7.5. Summary

In this chapter, I have considered the interface between pragmatics and cognition, focusing on Sperber and Wilson's relevance theory. Section 7.1 looked first at the cognitive, and then at the communicative, principles of relevance. Section 7.2 considered the concepts of explicature, implicature, and conceptual versus procedural distinction in relevance theory. The topic of Section 7.3 was the recent relevance-theoretic shift from treating pragmatics, and in particular utterance comprehension, as a Fodorian central, inferential process to the view that it is a submodule of the 'theory of mind'. Finally, in Section 7.4, relevance theory was compared and contrasted with the classical and neo-Gricean pragmatic theory.

Key concepts

relevance theory
relevance
cognitive principle of relevance
communicative principle of relevance
cognitive/contextual effect
processing effort
code model versus inferential model (of communication)
ostensive-inferential communication
explicature
saturation
free enrichment
ad hoc concept construction
loose use
higher-level/order versus basic explicature
r-implicature
r-implicated premise versus r-implicated conclusion
strong versus weak r-implicature
conceptual versus procedural meaning
Fodor's theory of cognitive modularity
module
central processor
theory of mind-reading (ToM)
Grice's circle
two versus three levels in a theory of communication
sentence-type-meaning
utterance-type-meaning
utterance-token-meaning

Exercises and essay questions

1. What are the explicatures of the following?
     (i) I've visited the Great Wall in China.
    (ii) The thieves have stolen everything.
   (iii) 'Much of the Walled Garden at the Botanic Garden is made up of rectangular botanical family borders.' *The University of Oxford, Botanic Garden Living Library*
    (iv) The oven is hot enough.
     (v) Jane has found a mole.
    (vi) Nobody understood the professor's talk on genetic engineering.
   (vii) The building collapsed some time after the bomb went off.
  (viii) Little Johnny ate the chocolate heart on the cake.
    (ix) John told Steve that he had won the prize.
     (x) I haven't shaved.
    (xi) They went to a pizza restaurant. The Italian waiter was handsome.
   (xii) The children are coming.
2. What are the higher-order explicatures of the following?
     (i) Frankly, I don't fancy him.
    (ii) Father to son: Please pick up the books scattered on the floor.
   (iii) Their European patent has been granted.
    (iv) John to wife: I shan't drink heavily any more.
3. In the following exchanges, what are the r-implicated premises and the r-implicated conclusions?
     (i) John: Let's go and watch *The Last Emperor* directed by Bernardo Bertolucci.
         Mary: Period epics are tedious.
    (ii) Guest: I'm afraid I'm late. Am I still in time for dinner?
         Receptionist: I'm afraid, Sir, the kitchen has already closed.
   (iii) John: Has Steve's paper been accepted for presentation at the conference?
         Mary: His was one of the best papers submitted.
    (iv) John: Lucy does not seem to have a boyfriend these days.
         Mary: She has been paying a lot of visits to London lately.
     (v) John: How about going out to play football?
         Mary: It's snowing heavily.
    (vi) John: I've run out of soy sauce.
         Mary: There's a small Chinese supermarket just around the corner. I think it's still open.
4. What are the strong r-implicatures, and what are the possible week r-implicatures, of the following?
     (i) John: Would you like any beef, or pork perhaps?
         Mary: I'm a vegetarian.

5. What is cognitive effect, and what is processing effort? How can they be measured?
6. What is the cognitive principle of relevance? What is the communicative principle of relevance? What is the relationship between them?
7. In which main areas does pragmatics play an important role in enriching the incomplete logical form of an utterance into an explicature?
8. What are the essential properties of the Fodorian modules?
9. What is the recent relevance-theoretic shift regarding the place of utterance comprehension in the overall architecture of the human mind?
10. What are the main differences between relevance theory and the classical/neo-Gricean pragmatic theory?

Further readings

Sperber and Wilson (1995).
Wilson and Sperber (2004).
Wilson (2010).
Carston (2002). Chapters 1 and 2.

8

Pragmatics and semantics

In the previous chapter, I looked at the interface between pragmatics and cognition with special reference to relevance theory. In this chapter, I shall turn my attention to pragmatics and semantics.

Semantics and pragmatics are the two major branches of linguistics devoted to the study of meaning in language. This much is largely agreed upon. However, what constitutes the domain of semantics, and that of pragmatics? Can semantics and pragmatics be distinguished in a principal way? Are they autonomous or do they overlap with each other? How and to what extent do they interact with each other? These are some of the questions that have puzzled, and are still puzzling, linguists and philosophers of language. In this chapter, I shall present a critical survey of some recent attempts at providing more satisfactory answers to these questions by both linguists and philosophers of language.

The structure of this chapter is as follows. In Section 8.1, I shall identify two main theoretical positions with regard to the relationship between semantics and pragmatics. The focus of Section 8.2 is on a number of influential ways in which the semantics–pragmatics distinction has been drawn. Then, in Section 8.3, I shall concentrate on the issue of pragmatic intrusion into the classical Gricean concept of what is said, which has recently become the centre of intense debate among both linguists and philosophers of language, and among both semanticists and pragmaticists. The discussion in this section will be concerned with Grice's characterization of what is said versus what is conversationally implicated (8.3.1), the current debate between contextualism and semantic minimalism in the philosophy of language (8.3.2), and the relevance theorists' notion of explicature, Recanati's idea of the pragmatically enriched said, Bach's concept of conversational impliciture, and Levinson's argument that the pragmatic inference under consideration is nothing but a neo-Gricean conversational implicature (8.3.3). Next, the question of whether explicature, pragmatically enriched said, and impliciture on the one hand, and conversational implicature on the other, can be distinguished will be commented on in Section 8.4. Finally, this chapter will end with a brief comparison of Grice's, and of the above four, analyses in Section 8.5.

8.1. Reductionism versus complementarism

Regarding the relationship between semantics and pragmatics, two main theoretical positions can be isolated: (i) **reductionism** and (ii) complementarism[1] (e.g. Huang 2001a). According to the first view, the putative distinction between semantics and pragmatics should be abolished (e.g. Lakoff 1987; Jackendoff 1992: 32; Langacker 1987: 154; see also Matthews 1995)—a position Levinson (2000) dubbed '**pragmantics**'. This reductionist camp can further be divided into two subcamps: (i) those taking the view that pragmatics should be entirely reduced to semantics, to be called **semantic reductionism**; and (ii) those holding the position that semantics is wholly included in pragmatics, as represented, for example, by what Recanati (2004b) called the **speech act theoretical view**. This can be labelled **pragmatic**

---

[1] The term 'complementarism' is borrowed from Leech (1983: 6).

reductionism (Huang 2001a).[2] This reductionist approach, however, runs counter to the fact that there are linguistic phenomena such as entailment (see Chapter 1) which are relatively uncontroversially semantic, and there are also linguistic phenomena such as conversational implicature (see Chapter 2) which are relatively uncontroversially pragmatic.

In contrast to the reductionist position, on a complementarist view, the division between semantics and pragmatics—a distinction that was first introduced by philosophers in the ideal language tradition (e.g. Frege 1897; Morris 1938; Carnap 1942) (see Chapter 1)—can in principle be retained. Within complementarism, a further distinction can be made between what may be called **radical semantics** and **radical pragmatics**. Whilst radical semanticists (such as those philosophers in the ideal language tradition, semantic minimalists, and formal linguistic semanticists) have argued that much of the study of meaning should be attributed to semantics, radical pragmaticists (such as those philosophers in the ordinary language tradition, contextualists, and linguistic pragmaticists) have attempted to assimilate as much of the study of meaning as possible to pragmatics.[3] The complementarist viewpoint, which sees semantics and pragmatics as complementary though distinct branches of linguistics, shedding light on different aspects of meaning, is more widely accepted.

8.2. Drawing the semantics–pragmatics distinction

The distinction between semantics and pragmatics has been formulated in a variety of different ways. Lyons (1987), for example, attempted to explain it in terms of the following dichotomies: (i) meaning versus use,

---

[2] Leech (1983: 6) called the two extreme positions '**semanticism**' and '**pragmaticism**'. Posner's (1980) terms were '**monism of meaning**' and '**monism of use**', and Dascal (1981) labelled them '**radical literalism**' and '**radical contextualism**'.

[3] In Posner's (1980) terminology, these two intermediate positions are occupied by his '**meaning-maximalist**' and '**meaning-minimalist**' categories, respectively. Dascal (1981) dubbed the two intermediate positions '**moderate literalism**' and '**moderate contextualism**'. More recently, Recanati (2004a: 83–6) has called the various extreme and intermediate positions '**literalism**', '**indexicalism**', the '**syncretic view**' (or '**syncretism**'), '**quasi-contextualism**', and '**contextualism**'. He has also put them on the above ordered scale, with the first three lying on the literalist side, and the last two on the contextualist side. See also Section 8.3.2.

(ii) conventional versus non-conventional meaning, (iii) truth-conditional versus non-truth-conditional meaning, (iv) context independence versus context dependence, (v) literal versus non-literal meaning, (vi) sentence (or proposition) versus utterance, (vii) rule versus principle, and (viii) competence versus performance. To these, one may add: (i) type versus token, (ii) content versus force, (iii) linguistic meaning versus speaker's meaning, (iv) saying versus implicating, (v) linguistically encoded versus non-linguistically encoded meaning, (vi) compositionality versus non-compositionality, and (vii) intention dependence versus intention independence (see e.g. Bach 1997; Nemo 1999; Szabó 2005a).[4] Of these formulations, three, according to Bach (1997, 2004), are particularly influential. They are (i) truth-conditional versus non-truth-conditional meaning, (ii) conventional versus non-conventional meaning, and (iii) context independence versus context dependence. Let me take a look at them in turn.

8.2.1. Truth-conditional versus non-truth-conditional meaning

In the first place, the semantics–pragmatics distinction has been characterized in terms of truth-conditional versus non-truth-conditional meaning. According to this formulation, semantics deals with truth-conditional meaning, or in Recanati's (2004b) terminology, words–world relations; pragmatics has to do with non-truth-conditional meaning. This characterization of pragmatics is captured in a well-known Gazdarian formula: pragmatics = meaning – truth conditions (Gazdar 1979: 2).

There are, however, a number of problems at the very core of this Carnapian approach to the semantics–pragmatics division, as Recanati (2004b) called it. First of all, there are linguistic forms that do not denote anything and therefore do not make any contribution to truth-conditional content. Paradigmatic cases include greetings like *Good morning!*, conventional implicature triggers like *but*, and syntactic constructions like imperatives. Secondly, as already noted in Chapters 1 and 7, and as will be discussed in detail in Section 8.3, the linguistically coded meaning of a sentence does not always fully determine its truth conditions (cf. the

---

[4] See also Nemo and Cadiot (1997), which listed more than thirty ways in which the boundary between semantics and pragmatics can be drawn, and the papers collected in Turner (1999), Bianchi (2004a), and Szabó (2005b), respectively.

linguistic underdeterminacy thesis discussed in Chapter 1). Furthermore, there is often pragmatic intrusion into the truth-conditional content of a sentence uttered. Following the lead from earlier work by Cohen (1971), Wilson (1975), Atlas (1977), and Gazdar (1979), Levinson (2000), for example, showed that neo-Gricean conversational implicatures can intrude onto, that is, contribute to, the truth conditions of a sentence uttered. All this has led Recanati (1993, 2004b) to dub part of pragmatics 'truth-conditional pragmatics'. If this is correct, one has to conclude that the truth-condition constraint cannot itself distinguish semantics from pragmatics in a principled way. I shall return to the issue of pragmatic intrusion into truth-conditional content in Section 8.3.

8.2.2. *Conventional versus non-conventional meaning*

Secondly, the demarcation line between semantics and pragmatics has been defined in terms of conventional (linguistic expression) versus non-conventional meaning. On this view, which has remained influential since Katz (1977), semantics studies the conventional aspects of meaning; pragmatics is concerned with the non-conventional aspects of meaning. Consequently, while a semantic interpretation, being conventional in nature, cannot be cancelled, a pragmatic inference, which is non-conventional in character, can.

But, as pointed out by Bach (1997, 2004) among others, this way of invoking the semantics–pragmatics division runs into trouble with the fact that there are linguistic expressions whose conventional meanings are closely associated with their uses. A case in point is discourse deictic expressions. As we saw in Chapter 5, a major function of discourse deictic expressions such as *anyway, after all, besides, by the way*, and *in conclusion* is to indicate that there is a relation between the utterance that contains them and some portion of the prior discourse. In other words, 'the only way to specify their semantic contribution (when they occur initially or are otherwise set off) is to specify how they are to be used' (Bach 1997). A further point to note is that the conventionality of a linguistic phenomenon may be a matter of more or less rather than a matter of yes or no. For example, as observed by Levinson (2000), of the three types of implicature identified by Grice (1989) (see Chapter 2), conventional implicature is the most conventional, hence the most 'semantic' and the least 'pragmatic' (but see below); PCI is the least conventional, hence the least 'semantic' and the most 'pragmatic', with GCI lying somewhere in between (but see Bach 1995, who was of the view that GCIs are not conventional but standardized). In other words, the three types of implicature form a semantics–pragmatics continuum whose borderline is difficult to mark. From facts like these, one can arrive at the conclusion that there is not a neat correlation between the semantics–pragmatics distinction and the conventional–non-conventional meaning distinction, either, (if in the meantime, the semantics–pragmatics distinction is also grounded in the meaning–use distinction).

Notice next that a particular linguistic phenomenon can sometimes be categorized as part of the domain of either semantics or pragmatics, depending on how the semantics–pragmatics distinction is defined. This is the case with conventional implicature. If semantics is taken to be concerned with those aspects of meaning that affect truth conditions, then the investigation of conventional implicature falls on the pragmatic side of the divide rather than on the semantic side, since, as noted in Chapter 2, conventional implicature does not make any contribution to truth conditions (but see Bach 1997). On the other hand, if pragmatics is conceived of as dealing with those inferences that are non-conventional, hence cancellable, then conventional implicature falls within the province of semantics but outside that of pragmatics, since it cannot be defeated (Horn 1988; Huang 2001a).

8.2.3. Context independence versus context dependence

Finally, the semantics–pragmatics distinction has been equated with context independence versus context dependence. According to this formulation, if a linguistic phenomenon is invariant with respect to context, then it is the concern of semantics. By contrast, if it is sensitive to context, then it is a topic of pragmatics.

This characterization of the semantics–pragmatics distinction, however, rests on a mistaken assumption that context has no role to play in semantics. Contrary to this assumption, context does have a role to play in semantics, too. According to Bach (1997), in the case of deictics and demonstratives, especially in the case of pure indexicals like *I, here*, and *now*, as philosophers of language prefer to call them (e.g. Kaplan 1989), it is on the semantic side of the ledger that content varies with context. Consequently, Bach postulated two types of context: (i) narrow and (ii) broad. By **narrow context** is meant any contextual information that is relevant to the determination of the content of, or the assignment of the semantic values to, variables such as those concerning who speaks to whom, when, and where. Narrow context thus defined is semantic in nature. In contrast, **broad context** is taken to be any contextual information that is relevant to the working out of what the speaker overtly intends to mean. It is also relevant to the successful and felicitous performance of speech acts (see Chapter 4). Hence, it is pragmatic in nature. Needless to say, narrow context is much more restricted in scope and much more limited in role than broad context (see also Recanati 2004b). Given that context plays a role in both semantics and pragmatics, the semantics–pragmatics distinction cannot correspond to the context independence–dependence distinction, either.

To sum up, the semantics–pragmatics distinction does not *systematically* coincide with any of the distinctions between truth-conditional versus non-truth-conditional meaning, conventional versus non-conventional meaning, and context independence versus context dependence. But this does not necessarily mean that semantics and pragmatics do not have their own characteristics. Recanati (2004b) isolated three essential features of a pragmatic interpretation. The first is charity. By **charity** is meant that a pragmatic interpretation is possible only if we presuppose that the interlocutors are rational. Secondly, there is **non-monotonicity**. This amounts to saying that a pragmatic interpretation is defeasible or cancellable. The third and final property identified by Recanati is **holism**. Given the feature of defeasibility or cancellability of a pragmatic interpretation, there is virtually no limit to the amount of contextual information that can in principle affect such an interpretation. Combined together, the three properties form what Recanati called the **hermeneutic** character of a pragmatic interpretation. This hermeneutic character of a pragmatic interpretation presents a striking contrast with the algorithmic, mechanical character of a semantic interpretation.

8.3. Pragmatic intrusion into what is said and the semantics–pragmatics interface

In recent years, there has been an intense debate about the division of labour between, and interaction of, semantics and pragmatics among both linguists and philosophers of language and among both semanticists and pragmaticists. Much of this debate has centred round pragmatic intrusion into the classical Gricean notion of what is said. In what follows, I shall first revisit the Gricean dichotomy between what is said and what is conversationally implicated (8.3.1). I shall then discuss the current debate between semantic minimalism and contextualism in the philosophy of language (8.3.2). Finally, I shall examine the four most influential pragmatic proposals, made by the relevance theorists, Recanati, Bach, and Levinson (8.3.3).

8.3.1. Grice: what is said versus what is conversationally implicated revisited

As already mentioned in Chapters 2 and 7, on a classical Gricean account, a distinction is made between what is said and what is conversationally implicated. However, as pointed out by Levinson (2000: 170), Grice's characterization of what is said is rather complex and by no means straight-forward, though it may roughly be presented as follows:

(8.1)   Grice's concept of what is said
     U said that p by uttering x if and only if:
     a. x conventionally means p
     b. U speaker-meant p
     c. p is the conventional meaning of x minus any conventional implicature

where U stands for the utterer, p for a proposition, and x for a linguistic expression. Given this definition, what is said is generally taken to be (i) the conventional meaning of the sentence uttered with the exclusion of any conventional implicature, and (ii) the truth-conditional propositional content of the sentence uttered (e.g. Grice 1989: 25; Levinson 1983: 97, 2000: 170; Neale 1992: 520–1; Clark 1996: 141; Carston 2002: 114–15; Huang 2010i).[5] However, according to Grice (1989: 25), before one works out

---

[5] Notice that the term 'what is said' is ambiguous in at least three distinct ways. In the first, 'what is said' is understood in 'a technical and artificially strict sense' (Salmon 1991). In the second, it is interpreted in an ordinary, everyday sense of 'what is stated' (Levinson 2000: 194). Finally, in the third, 'what is said' is ambiguous between 'general content' in one, technical sense and 'contextually enriched content' in another, everyday sense (Berg 2002 crediting François Recanati, see also Recanati 1989, 1993, 2004a, 2005; Barker 2003). Other ambiguities of 'what is said' involve it in the 'locuationary' versus 'illocutionary sense' (e.g. Bach 1994, 2001, 2004a, 2004b, 2005; Szabó 2005a).

what is said, one has (i) reference to identify, (ii) deixis to fix, and (iii) ambiguity and ambivalences to resolve. These are illustrated in (7.9), (7.10), and (7.12) in Chapter 7, which are repeated here as (8.2), (8.3), and (8.4), respectively.

(8.2) a. John told Bill that he wanted to date his sister.
           Preferred interpretation: he = John, his = Bill's
       b. John told Bill that he couldn't date his sister.
           Preferred interpretation: he = Bill, his = John's
(8.3) Mary: How do *I* look?
       John: *You* look really cool!
(8.4) (Lexical ambiguity, Levinson 2000: 174)
       a. The view could be improved by the addition of a plant out there.
           Preferred interpretation: plant = living organism such as a flower, tree and vegetable
       b. The view would be destroyed by the addition of a plant out there.
           Preferred interpretation: plant = factory.

To (i)–(iii) above, Levinson (2000: 172–86) added (iv) unpacking ellipsis, as in (8.5) and (v) narrowing generality, as in (8.6).

(8.5) A: The couple won't visit their parents.
       B: Old grudge.
(8.6) I don't drink.

According to Bach (2004), the Gricean notion of what is said is needed in order to describe three kinds of cases. In the first, the speaker means what he or she says and something else as well, as in conversational implicatures and indirect speech acts. The second of these cases is where the speaker says one thing and means something else instead, as in non-literal utterances such as metaphor, irony, and hyperbole. Thirdly and finally, there is the case where the speaker says something and does not mean anything by it. A case in point may be where the speaker reads someone else's poems out loud. On the basis of the existence of this case, Bach (personal communication) argued that (8.1b) should be dropped.[6]

---

[6] Bach's third case apart, what is said can be contrasted with what is communicated/conveyed/meant (see note 4 of Chapter 2). A further distinction between what is meant in the illocutionary sense and what is meant in the perlocutionary sense is made in Szabó (2005a).

What is conversationally implicated is then defined in contrast to, and calculated on the basis of, what is said (and in the case of M-implicatures, together with how what is said is said). Simply stated, what is conversationally implicated can be defined along the following lines (Levinson 2000: 171).

(8.7)   Grice's concept of what is conversationally implicated
        By saying p, U conversationally implicates q if:
        a. U is presumed to be following the conversational maxims,
        b. the supposition of q is required to maintain (a),[7] and
        c. U thinks that the recipient will realize (b).

Stated in this way, what is said is supposed to provide input to what is conversationally implicated.

It turns out, however, that the determination of (8.2)–(8.6) involves pragmatic enrichment of some kind. In the linguistic context of (8.2a), *John and Bill's* are the most likely choices for antecedent of the pronoun *he* and *his*, whereas in the linguistic context of (8.2b), *Bill and John's* become the most likely candidates for antecedent of *he* and *his*. The Gricean maxim of Relation plays a role in interpreting the deictic expressions in (8.3). The disambiguation of the lexical item *plant* in (8.4) is crucially dependent on our real-world knowledge about what would most likely be improving or destroying a view. Next, the interpretation of the elided constituent in (8.5) requires a substantial amount of inference of the Gricean sort. Finally, the predicate *drink* in (8.6) has to be pragmatically narrowed down to 'drink alcohol'. Put another way, it is now widely acknowledged that in examples like (8.2)–(8.6), there is pragmatic intrusion of some sort, namely, the pragmatically enriched content, into the conventional, truth-conditional content involved in the working out of what Grice called what is said.

Two issues are of particular interest in the analysis of pragmatic intrusion into the classical Gricean characterization of what is said and beyond. The first is concerned with the question of what the pragmatic intrusion under consideration is. Secondly, there is the question of what is the best way to delimit the respective territories of semantics and pragmatics, taking pragmatic intrusion into account. Below, I shall consider some of the answers provided by linguists and philosophers of language. But before proceeding

---

[7] Bach (personal communication) pointed out to me that 'the supposition of q' in (8.7b) should be replaced with 'the supposition that U means q'.

to do that, let me take a look at the current debate between contextualism
and semantic minimalism in the philosophy of language.

8.3.2. Contextualism versus semantic minimalism
in the philosophy of language

Currently, there is an ongoing, heated debate between contextualism and
semantic minimalism in the philosophy of language.[8] As a broad school of
thought in the contemporary philosophy of language and linguistics, **contextualism** (also known as '**contextualist semantics**' in opposition to '**minimal
(ist) semantics**') endeavours to provide an account of contextual variations
in semantic content in terms of a criterion of contextual best fit. According
to this view, pragmatically enriched entities such as speech acts are the
primary bearers of truth-conditional content. Only in the context of an
utterance does a sentence express a determinate semantic content. In other
words, semantics covers only part of the way towards the computation of
utterance meaning, and it is pragmatic enrichment that completes the
process as a whole. Two versions of contextualism can be identified: **moderate** and **radical** or **full-fledged**. Whereas the former acknowledges limited
pragmatic influence on semantic content, the latter holds the view that
pragmatic processes such as free enrichment play a central role in explaining
contextual variations in semantic content (e.g. Recanati 2005b, and see also
Bezuidenhout 2006). For some scholars, the contextualist position can be
distinguished from a 'pragmatist' position. One main, though subtle, difference between the two positions is that while the former appeals primarily to
facts about linguistic meaning, the latter involves pragmatic principles or
maxims (e.g. Carston 2010b). Closely associated with contextualism is the
position known as '**truth-conditional pragmatics**', namely, the view that
various pragmatic processes influence and determine the truth-condition
of an utterance (e.g. Recanati 2010). Contextualism is represented by

---

[8] Needless to say, this debate can be traced back at least to the differences
between philosophers in the tradition of ideal language philosophy such as Gottlob
Frege, Alfred Tarski, Bertrand Russell, the early Ludwig Wittgenstein, and Rudolf
Carnap, and philosophers in the camp of ordinary or natural language philosophy
like J. L. Austin, H. P. Grice, Peter Strawson, the later Ludwig Wittgenstein, and
John Searle (see Chapter 1).

some of the work of the American philosopher John Searle, the Canadian philosopher Charles Travis, the French philosopher François Recanati, relevance theory, and to a lesser extent neo-Gricean pragmatics.

In contradistinction to contextualism, the central thesis of **semantic minimalism** or **literalism** is that context is allowed only to have a very limited or minimal effect on the semantic content of an utterance. In addition, semantic minimalism holds that semantic content is entirely determined by syntax, that semantic context-sensitivity is grammatically triggered, and that it is not the job of semantic content to capture one's intuitive judgement of what a speaker says when he or she utters a sentence. Consequently, the object of study of semantics should be separated strictly from pragmatic intrusion (e.g. Borg 2004, 2007, 2010). Currently, there are a number of variants of semantic minimalism. These include the British philosopher Emma Borg's **minimal semantics**, the Norwegian philosopher Herman Cappelen and the American philosopher Ernest Lepore's insensitive semantics, and the American philosopher Kent Bach's radical semantic minimalism. For Borg, semantics should operate independently of, and prior to, the actual use of a linguistic expression by a speaker to communicate. The role of semantics is simply to explain formal linguistic meaning, but not to give a full account of the nature of meaning or indeed to explain communication (e.g. Borg 2004). **Insensitive semantics** takes the view that apart from a very specific and limited set of linguistic expressions such as *I*, *foreigner*, and *local*, called the 'basic set', which are context-sensitive, all other linguistic expressions have constant meanings. The semantic meaning of a sentence expresses a complete truth-conditional proposition independently of context of use. In other words, semantics is 'insensitive' in that it operates independently of, or is not sensitive to, any features of context of utterance. This 'insensitive' view of semantics is supplemented by Cappelen and Lepore's speech act pluralism. **Speech act pluralism** is of the view that what is said may express indefinitely many propositions, or a token of an utterance can carry more than one speech act. In other words, each minimal representation may correspond to a wide variety of speech acts which it is capable of conveying, hence the name. What is said depends on a wide range of factors other than the proposition semantically expressed. It depends on a potential infinitude of features of context of utterance and of the context of those who report on or think about what was said (e.g. Cappelen and Lepore 2005). Finally, Bach's **radical semantic minimalism** maintains that the semantic properties of a sentence should be taken as on a par with the sentence's syntactic and phonological properties. There is no pragmatic intrusion into what is said, because certain aspects of communicative content do not need to be recognized as either part of what is said or part of what is conversationally implicated. Rather, they constitute a middle ground between what is said and what is implicated. Bach called this middle level of speaker-meaning 'impliciture' (e.g. Bach 2004; Huang 2007a: 223, 2010e).[9]

Next, there is **indexicalism**. This is the position in the contemporary philosophy of language and linguistics that assumes that there is a role for speaker's meaning to play in the determination of the truth-conditional content of a sentence, but only when a slot is set up by a sentence itself to be pragmatically filled in its logical form. To this end, a range of '**covert**' or '**hidden**' indexicals is posited to provide syntactic triggers for the additional context sensitivity demanded by contextualists, thus also referred to as '**hidden indexicalism**'. Only bottom-up but no top-down pragmatic influence is allowed to affect the truth-conditional content of the sentence. This position is represented by the work of the American philosopher Jason Stanley and the American linguist Zoltán Szabó (e.g. Stanley 2000, Stanley and Szabó 2000). Interestingly enough, indexicalism is considered to be a version of moderate contextualism by semantic minimalists, and a form of liberal semantic minimalism by contextualists.

More recently, a number of alternatives to contextualism and semantic minimalism have emerged in the contemporary philosophy of language and linguistics. These include Predilli's (2005) revised version of semantic minimalism, Corazza and Dokic's **situationalism** (e.g. Corazza 2007), Gauker's (2003) **objective contextualism**, MacFarlane's (2007, 2009) non-indexical contextualism, sometimes also known as 'semantic relativism', and Recanati's (2008) **(strong) moderate relativism**. Of these alternatives, MacFarlane's non-indexical contextualism or semantic relativism seems to be most influential.

Non-indexical contextualism is an approach that falls largely in the semantic minimalist camp. On this view, contrary to indexicalists, context-sensitivity called for by contextualists is not caused by the semantic content or truth condition of a sentence but by a variation in its circumstances of evaluation. In other words, a sentence like (8.8) is context-sensitive not because it expresses different propositions in different contexts,

---

[9] According to Bezuidenhout (forthcoming), from the perspective of cognitive architecture, semantic minimalism can be divided into semantic minimalism$_1$ and semantic minimalism$_2$.

but because the truth or falsity of its occurrences depends on the circumstances in which it is evaluated.

(8.8)   John is tall.

A **circumstance of evaluation** has two parameters: (i) one for the possible world(s) and (ii) one for 'counts-as'. The 'counts-as' parameter is a function from properties (such as tallness) to intensions. It is so called because 'it fixes what things have to be like in order to count as having the property of tallness (or any other property) at a circumstance of evaluation' (MacFarlane 2007: 246). Thus, according to this analysis, the different utterances of (8.8) on different occasions of use may have different truth values because they have different circumstances of evaluation, even if they are situated at or reside in the same possible world, and express the same proposition (see e.g. Predelli 2005 for a similar position, see also Bianchi 2011).

As mentioned earlier, MacFarlane's approach has been relabelled '**semantic relativism**' by some philosophers (e.g. Garcia-Carpintero and Kölble 2008). This is because, in their opinions, the truth of a sentence has to be relevant, or relativized, to both a parameter of a possible world and a parameter of 'counts-as'. While acknowledging that varying standards, interests, knowledge, etc. have a semantic role to play, proponents of relativism also reject the contextualist claim that the role in question is relevant to the determination of what is said by an utterance. Rather, the role played by varying standards, etc. is relevant to determining whether what is said is true or false. Some semantic relativists distinguish a **context of use** from a **context of assessment**, and insist that epistemic standards, for example, are features of the context of assessment. For instance, on a semantic relativist view, the proposition expressed by the sentence in (8.9) does not vary across different contexts (specifically in relation to the meaning of *know*).

(8.9)   John knows that there was a network outage yesterday.

Rather, its truth value is relative to, or varies with, a standard of knowledge. Recanati (2008), for instance, claimed that his moderate relativism is similar to MacFarlane's non-indexical contextualism but this claim is refuted by MacFarlane. According to MacFarlane (2009), there is another difference between non-indexical contextualism and relativism: whereas in the former, the evaluation of truth is dependent upon the assessment of a context of use, in the latter, the evaluation of truth is dependent upon a context of assessment. I shall return to some of the works discussed here in the next section (see also Huang 2013a, 2013d).

8.3.3. Four (pragmatic) analyses: explicature, pragmatically enriched said, impliciture, and conversational implicature

Having surveyed the debate between contextualism and semantic minimalism in the contemporary philosophy of language, let me turn to four (pragmatic) accounts of pragmatic intrusion into the Gricean notion of what is said.

Relevance theorists: explicature
As discussed in detail in the last chapter, in relevance theory, pragmatic intrusion into Grice's notion of what is said is analysed as explicature—an inferential development of one of the incomplete conceptual representations or logical forms encoded by a sentence uttered. In other words, an explicature functions to flesh out the linguistically given incomplete logical form of the utterance, yielding its fully propositional content. It falls on the side of what is said rather than on the side of what is conversationally implicated (though in relevance theory, the Gricean notion of what is said is abandoned). This has the consequence that in Sperber and Wilson's framework, the explicit–implicit distinction, that is, the distinction between the explicit content and the implicit import of an utterance is recast in terms of the relevance-theoretic notions of explicature and r-implicature (Sperber and Wilson 1986, 1995).

Recanati: the pragmatically enriched said
Somewhat similar to the relevance-theoretic view is the position taken by Recanati (1989, 1993, 2001, 2002, 2004a, 2004b). According to Recanati, there are aspects of what is said that must be pragmatically enriched. In other words, on Recanati's (2002, 2007, 2010) view, what is said or the proposition associated with what is said necessarily involves unarticulated constituents (see also e.g. Searle 1983; Travis 1985; Perry 1986, 1998; Hall 2008; Bach 2012; and Huang 2013e; but see Stanley 2000, 2002; Stanley and Szabó 2000a, 2000b; Taylor 2001; King and Stanley 2005; Marti 2006 and Cappelen and Hawthorn 2007 for a dissenting view). The concept of unarticulated constituent was introduced by the American philosopher

John Perry (1986). By an **unarticulated constitute (UC)** is meant a propositional or conceptual constituent of a sentence that is not explicitly expressed linguistically. Put slightly differently, an UC is definable as an element in the proposition or concept expressed by a speaker that does not correspond to any linguistic expression in the sentence uttered (e.g. Bach 2012). Two stock examples are given in (8.10a) and (8.11a). On the other hand, the brackets in (8.10b) and (8.11b) contain the possible, pragmatically recovered propositional or conceptual material for the UCs in (8.10a) and (8.11a), respectively.

(8.10) a. John is ready.
        b. John is ready [for the interview]

(8.11) a. Some people are a bit surprised when they find out I've got a brain. (Catherine McQueen)
        b. Some people are a bit surprised when they find out I've got a [good] brain

Furthermore, Recanati postulated three types of primary pragmatic processes[10] to bridge the gap between linguistic (or sentence) meaning and what is said.[11] In the first place, there is what Recanati (1989, 1993: 243, 2002, 2004a: 23) called '**saturation**'. As already mentioned in Chapter 7, saturation is a pragmatic process whereby a given slot, position, or variable in the linguistically decoded logical form is contextually filled. In other words, in this type of pragmatic enrichment, a slot, position, or variable must be contextually saturated for the utterance to express a complete proposition. Saturation is a typical linguistically mandated, 'bottom-up' process, that is, a process which is triggered by a linguistic expression in the utterance itself.

---

[10] According to Recanati (1993: 260–1), primary pragmatic processes are ones which play a role in the very constitution of what is said. In other words, they pragmatically enrich what is said. By contrast, **secondary pragmatic processes** are ones which presuppose that something has been said or a proposition has been expressed. Implicatures in the relevance-theoretic sense (i.e. what I have called r-implicatures) fall under this category.

[11] While linguistic (or sentence) meaning in the sense of Recanati corresponds roughly to Kaplan's (1989) notion of **character** and Perry's (1993) concept of **role**, what is said is roughly equivalent to Kaplan's notion of **content** (i.e. proposition) and Perry's notion of **value**. See also Braun (1995, 1996) for his reworking of Kaplan's notions of character and content. It has been argued by some scholars (e.g. Kaplan 1989; Stalnaker 1999) that '[w]hat semantics assigns to expression-types, independent of context, is not a fully-fledged content but a linguistic meaning or character that can be formally represented as a function from contexts to contents' (Recanati 2004b: 447).

Expressions that give rise to saturation include unspecified comparison sets, as in (8.12a); possessive constructions, as in (8.12b), and expressions with free variable slots, as in (8.12c).

(8.12)   a. Elizabeth is cleverer.
         b. I enjoyed reading John's book.
         c. John was late.

(8.12) can be pragmatically saturated into, or filled in, for example, (8.13).

(8.13)   a. Elizabeth is cleverer [than Naomi]
         b. I enjoyed reading the book [written by] John
         c. John was late [for the seminar]

The second type of primary pragmatic process is what Recanati called **'free enrichment'**. We have already seen in Chapters 2 and 7 that in this case, although there does not seem to be either an overt indexical or a covert slot in the linguistically decoded logical form of the sentence uttered, the logical form nevertheless needs to be conceptually enriched. The process of free enrichment is 'free' because it is entirely pragmatically rather than linguistically based. Free enrichment is a typical optional and contextually driven 'top-down' process (Recanati 2004a: 24–6). Furthermore, Recanati identified two subtypes of free enrichment. First, there is the subtype of **strengthening** or **logical enrichment**. Strengthening takes a complete proposition resulting from saturation as input and yields as output a richer proposition which entails the original input proposition. By way of illustration, take (8.14).

(8.14)   a. Clinton made a lot of noise and had a very big impact. He has the shoulders. If he comes, the world is interested, and it brings attention to Lesotho. When I climb on the foothills of Clinton, perhaps people will notice more. (*FT Magazine* 19/20 August 2006)
         b. It took some time for Yan to write *The Oxford Dictionary of Pragmatics*.
         c. I have brushed my teeth.

The propositions expressed by the sentences in (8.14) are strengthened into the propositions expressed by the sentences in (8.15). As the reader can verify for him- or herself, the enriched propositions expressed by the sentences in (8.15) entail the original input propositions in (8.14).[12]

---

[12] But on Bach's (1994a) view, entailment does not play a role in strengthening. This is because if the sentences in (8.14) are negated, the relevant entailments will go the other way, and yet the pragmatic enrichments will be the same.

(8.15)   a. Clinton made a lot of noise and had a very big impact. He has the [strong]
             shoulders. If he comes, the world is interested, and it brings attention to
             Lesotho. When I climb on the foothills of Clinton, perhaps people will
             notice more
         b. It took [a considerable] time for Yan to write *The Oxford Dictionary of
             Pragmatics*
         c. I have brushed my teeth [this morning]

The second subtype of enrichment is **expansion**, *à la* Bach (1987). In this
subtype, a contextually provided conceptual constituent needs to be added,
but the output proposition yielded by the input one does not need to entail
the original input proposition. This can be illustrated by a consideration
of (8.16).

(8.16)   a. The windows are bullet proof.
         b. The windows [of the president's limousine] are bullet proof

Note that (8.16a) contains an incomplete definite description *the windows*
(see Chapter 6), and the proposition expressed by (8.16a) is expanded into
the proposition expressed by (8.16b). But the enriched proposition
expressed by the sentence in (8.16b) does not entail the proposition
expressed by the sentence in (8.16a).[13]

Finally, there is the third type of primary pragmatic process, namely,
what Recanati (2004a: 26–7) termed **semantic transfer**, following Nunberg
(1979, 1995, 2004) and Fauconnier (1985), or what I called deferred/trans-
ferred reference in Chapter 6. As already discussed in that chapter, in this
type of primary pragmatic process, the output proposition is neither an
enriched nor an impoverished version of the concept literally expressed by
the input proposition. Rather, it represents a different concept, provided
that there is a salient functional relation between the new concept and the
old one encoded by the original input proposition. In short, it is a case in
which one uses a linguistic expression that goes from a reference to *a* to a
reference to *b*. For the exemplification of semantic transfer, see Section 6.5.2
in Chapter 6. See also Recanati (2004a: chapter 3) for discussion of the
differences between the relevance-theoretic analysis and his account.

---

[13] Recanati (personal communication) pointed out to me that strengthening and
expansion are two ways of construing enrichment rather than two distinct phenomena. He believed that a unitary notion can account for both of them.

Bach: conversational impliciture

A third approach is due to Bach (1994a, 1994b, 1997, 2001, 2004, 2006a, 2012). On Bach's view, there is no pragmatic intrusion into what is said, because certain aspects of communicative content do not need to be recognized as either part of what is said or part of what is conversationally implicated. Rather, they constitute a middle ground between what is said and what is conversationally implicated. This middle level of speaker-meaning Bach called **conversational impliciture** or **impliciture** for short.

What, then, is an impliciture? Consider first (8.17).

(8.17)   a. John is competent.
         b. John is too tired.
         c. Steel is not strong enough.
         d. This iPad is expensive.
         e. John prefers blondes.
         f. John has finished
         g. John needs a boat.
         h. President Obama has just arrived.
         i. Even John's grandma can surf the internet.

According to Bach, each of the sentences in (8.17) expresses an incomplete proposition. In other words, it is **subpropositional**. Consequently, it cannot be evaluated truth-conditionally. Bach dubbed propositional fragments of this kind '**propositional radicals**', which need to be completed or filled in contextually to become fully propositional. The pragmatic process of **completion** will provide extra propositional or conceptual content or material to the propositional radicals in (8.17), resulting in the corresponding minimal but full propositions in (8.18). The full and determinate propositions in (8.18) can then be assigned a truth value.

(8.18)   a. John is competent [to be a divorce lawyer]
         b. John is too tired [to carry the suitcase]
         c. Steel is not strong enough [for that part of the roof]
         d. This iPad is expensive [relative to other iPads]
         e. John prefers blondes [to brunettes]
         f. John has finished [writing his MBA thesis]
         g. John needs a boat [to cross the river]
         h. President Obama has just arrived [at Buckingham Palace]
         i. Even John's grandma can surf the internet [in addition to John's grandpa]

Next, let us move to (8.19).

(8.19) a. I've eaten lunch.
        b. I've been to New Zealand.
        c. I've got absolutely nothing to wear.
        d. Everyone was touched by *Captain Corelli's Mandolin*.
        e. John and Clare are married.
        f. John has eaten a lot of oily fish recently and his blood cholesterol level has been lowered.
        g. You are not going to die.
        h. There are nine thousand students in this university town.
        i. John and Mary painted a portrait of Mandela.
        j. Yan has got two doctorates.

According to Bach, unlike in (8.17), each of the sentences in (8.19) expresses a full, though minimal, proposition. But such a proposition falls short of what the speaker intends to mean. Consequently, it needs to be expanded. The pragmatic process of **expansion** will flesh out the proposition expressed by the sentence uttered and engenders a richer proposition. The pragmatically enriched proposition will then be identical with what the speaker has intentionally meant, thus allowing the assignment of an appropriate truth condition to it. The pragmatically expanded propositions of (8.19) are given in (8.20).

(8.20) a. The speaker has eaten lunch [today]
        b. The speaker has visited New Zealand [before]
        c. The speaker has got nothing [appropriate/suitable] to wear [for tonight's party]
        d. Everyone [who went to see the film] was touched by *Captain Corelli's Mandolin*
        e. John and Clare are married [to each other]
        f. John has eaten a lot of oily fish recently and [as a result] his blood cholesterol level has been lowered
        g. You are not going to die [from the cut]
        h. There are [approximately/roughly] nine thousand students in this university town
        i. John and Mary painted a portrait of Mandela [together]
        j. Yan has [exactly/precisely] two doctorates

Clearly, in both (8.18) and (8.20), each of the bracketed elements of meaning contributes to what is communicated. The result of completion and expansion, that is, the vehicle of each of the pragmatically completed or enriched propositions, Bach called an impliciture, because it is what is implicit in what is said. More specifically, an impliciture is an implicit strengthening, weakening, or specification of what is said. Stated in this way, impliciture represents a third category of communicated content—a category that is intermediate between Grice's what is said and what is conversationally implicated. As Bach (1994b: 273) remarked: 'Implicitures go beyond what is said, but unlike [conversational] implicatures, which are additional propositions external to what is said, implicitures are built out of what is said'. Furthermore, Horn (2004) told us that impliciture cannot be constitutive of what is said, because it can be felicitously cancelled, as can be seen in (8.21); neither can it be derived as a conversational implicature, because it is truth-conditionally relevant (but see my comments below).

(8.21) a. I have had a shower, but not this morning.
        b. John and Mary are married, but not to each other. Also:
           The title of a country song
           When you are married, but not to each other.
        c. John has eaten a lot of oily fish recently and his blood cholesterol level
           has been lowered, but the latter is not necessarily the result of the former.

An impliciture will then provide input to the classical Gricean pragmatic mechanism (his co-operative principle and its component maxims of conversation) (see Chapter 2), yielding conversational implicatures as output. Thus, in Bach's theory, the traditional Gricean dichotomy between what is said and what is conversationally implicated is replaced by a trichotomy between what is said, what is implicit, and what is implicated, with what is implicit constituting the middle level of speaker-meaning.

One of the main attractions of Bach's model is that, as noted by Horn (2004), the classical Gricean semantic conception of what is said, along with a post-semantic orthodox Gricean characterization of what is conversationally implicated, is retained in a neo-classical way. But as I pointed out in Huang (2010f), this main attraction of Bach's analysis is also its main drawback in that the retaining of the classical Gricean notion of what is said and what is conversationally implicated is achieved only at the expense of postulating a further representational level (see Huang 2010f for further comments, and see also Carston 2002 and Vincente 2002 for a critique of Bach's notion of impliciture from a relevance-theoretical point of view).

Begin work in this chapter by having a go at Exercise 1 at the end of this chapter.

Levinson: conversational implicature

We finally come to Levinson's (2000) analysis of pragmatic intrusion into what is said. On Levinson's view, pragmatic intrusion into what is said is neither an explicature, nor the pragmatically enriched said, nor an impliciture. Rather, it is nothing but a neo-Gricean conversational implicature.

Following in the footsteps of Cohen (1971), Wilson (1975), Atlas (1977), and Gazdar (1979), Levinson (2000) argued that contrary to Grice, conversational implicatures can intrude upon truth-conditional content. This has already been evidenced by temporally and causally asymmetric conjunctions in (2.105) and conditionals in (2.107) and (2.108) of Chapter 2, which were used by Cohen (1971) to argue against Grice's analysis of the truth-functionality of *and* and *if*.

Levinson extended this classic Cohen–Wilson argument into the working out of what is said or how propositions are literally expressed. Firstly, he showed how neo-Gricean conversational implicatures are involved in the determination of indexicality and related phenomena.

Reference resolution
Consider (8.22).

(8.22)   (Levinson 2000: 218, 227)
(Context: Two men are clearly visible, one has two children near him and the other has three children near him. The first is the speaker's brother, the second his brother-in-law.)
The man with two children near him is my brother; the man with three children near him is my brother-in-law.

What is said by the speaker in (8.22) corresponds to (8.23).

(8.23)   The man with *at least* two children near him is my brother; the man with *at least* three children near him is my brother-in-law.

This has the consequence that the referring expression *the man with two children near him* refers equally to the speaker's brother and his brother-in law. Thus, on any purely semantic theory of definite description, (the use of) the referring expression will either render (8.22) false (Russell 1905) or truth-valueless (Strawson 1950) (see also Chapter 6). But this is intuitively wrong; (the employment of) the definite expression neither makes (8.22) false nor fails to denote. On the contrary, it denotes felicitously and refers successfully. How can this be possible? According to Levinson, it is because the individual referents are picked up by a $Q_{-scalar}$ implicature enriching *the man with two children near him* to 'the man with exactly two children near him' and *the man with three children near him* to 'the man with exactly three children near him' (see Chapters 1 and 2). This is represented in (8.24).[14]

(8.24)   The man with [exactly] two children near him is my brother; the man with [exactly] three children near him is my brother-in-law.

Next, we turn to (8.25).

(8.25)   a. John said that he won the ten metres platform diving yesterday.
        b. John said that the young man won the ten metres platform diving yesterday.

(8.25) involves anaphoric reference. Intuitively, while the pronoun *he* in (8.25a) is preferably co-referential with *John*, the definite description *the young man* in (8.25b) is disjoint in reference with *John*. As shown by Huang (1991a, 1994, 2000a, 2004a, 2006c, 2007a) and Levinson (1987, 1991, 2000), this contrast can be accounted for in terms of the interaction between the I- and M-implicatures. The preferred co-referential interpretation between *he* and *John* in (8.25a) is due to the working of the I-principle (you use a semantically general anaphoric expression *he*, I get a semantically more specific interpretation *he = John*); the disjoint reference interpretation in (8.25b) is the outcome of the operation of the M-principle (you use a marked, more prolix anaphoric expression *the young man*, I get a marked interpretation *the young man ≠ John*). All this indicates that neo-Gricean conversational implicatures do contribute to the resolution of both definite and anaphoric reference. I shall return to the discussion of the syntax and pragmatics of anaphoric reference in the next chapter.

Deixis fixing
Witness the interpretation of the time deictic expression *Sunday* in (8.26).

(8.26)   We'll go to church on Sunday.

As noted in Chapter 5, the use of time deictic expressions like *yesterday*, *today*, and *tomorrow* pre-empts the use of the calendrical terms for the relevant days. Thus, *Sunday* said on a Saturday will engender the Q-scalar

---

[14] See Levinson (2000: section 3.4.1) for the argument that implicaturally determined definite reference cannot be reduced either to Donnellan's (1966) referential versus attributive distinction or to Kripke's (1977) semantic- versus speaker-reference distinction (see also Chapter 6).

implicature to the effect that the Sunday in question is not tomorrow, as is indicated in (8.27).

(8.27)   (Said on a Saturday)
         <tomorrow, Sunday>
         We'll go to church on Sunday.
         Sunday +> ~ tomorrow

The reason is this: if the Sunday under consideration were tomorrow, the speaker would have used the semantically more informative deictic expression *tomorrow*, since there are many Sundays, but only one tomorrow given a today. There is thus evidence in support of Levinson's argument that neo-Gricean conversational implicatures play a role in fixing deictic or indexical parameters.

Disambiguation
Consider how the syntactic structures of (8.28) are disambiguated by Q_{scalar} implicatures.

(8.28)   (Levinson 2000: 175).
         John is an indiscriminate dog-lover: he likes some cats and dogs.
         a. John likes [some cats] and dogs
             John likes some cats and dogs in general
         b. John likes [some [cats and dogs]]
             John like some cats and some dogs

Notice that the second clause in (8.28) is structurally ambiguous. It can be understood in the manner of (8.28a) or in the manner of (8.28b). Now, given the syntactic structure of (8.28a), the use of the clause creates the Q_{scalar} implicature that John does not like all cats. This conversational implicature is in keeping with the semantic content of the first clause. By contrast, given the syntactic structure of (8.28b), the uttering of the clause gives rise to the Q_{scalar} implicature that John does not like all cats and all dogs. But such an interpretation is incompatible with the semantic content of the first clause. Consequently, in order for the whole sentence in (8.28) not to be contradictory, the syntactic structure of (8.28a) is allowed but that of (8.28b) is excluded. This shows that neo-Gricean conversational implicatures intrude on the disambiguation of the syntactic structures of examples like (8.28).

Ellipsis unpacking

As pointed out in Huang (2000a: 133, 147), the resolution of VP-ellipsis sometimes has to be effected pragmatically. As an illustrative example, take (8.29).

(8.29)   (Huang 2000a: 133)
         I will, if you will.

The interpretation of the elided element in (8.29) is contextually dependent. That is to say, the elided constituent will be supplied from the surrounding physical context. This can be achieved via the I-implicature, together with a PCI due to Grice's maxim of Relation. One contextually derived interpretation might be the one in (8.30).

(8.30)   (By a swimming pool)
         I will jump into the swimming pool, if you will jump into the swimming pool.

Generality narrowing

Finally, the same story can be said to hold for generality narrowing. Here, generality narrowing can be classified into two groups, (i) Q-implicature-based, as in (8.31), and (ii) I-implicature-based, as in (8.32).

(8.31)   John cut a finger.
(8.32)   Mary had two eggs for breakfast this morning.

The utterance in (8.31) is Q-narrowed to the proposition expressed in (8.33) and the utterance in (8.32) is I-narrowed to the proposition expressed in (8.34).

(8.33)   John [didn't] cut a [thumb].
(8.34)   Mary had two [hen] eggs for breakfast this morning.

There is thus the conclusion that neo-Gricean conversational implicatures are also involved in generality narrowing.

   Secondly, Levinson argued that the classic Cohen–Wilson argument can also be extended into other logical connective constructions such as comparatives, disjunctions, and *because*-clauses. This is illustrated in (8.35)–(8.37).

(8.35)   Comparatives
         Brushing your teeth and going to bed is better than going to bed and brushing your teeth.

(8.36) Disjunctions
        Miriam either suffered a heart attack and underwent quadruple by-pass
        surgery, or underwent quadruple by-pass surgery and suffered a heart
        attack; but I don't know which.

(8.37) *Because*-clauses
        Because some of her PhD students came to her talk, Professor Heim was
        unhappy.

Together with conditionals, these constructions are labelled '**intrusive constructions**' by Levinson. The reason is that, in these constructions, 'the truth
conditions of the whole depend in part on the [conversational] implicatures of
the parts' (Levinson 2000: 198). The truth-conditional content of the comparative (8.35) is dependent crucially on the I-implicature stemming from the
use of *and* to 'and then', as in (8.38). Otherwise, (8.35) would be contradictory.
The same I-implicature intrusion is found in the disjunction (8.36). Without
and being I-strengthened to 'and then', as in (8.39), the two disjuncts would
have the same semantic content. This would render the speaker's assertion of
ignorance over the two possibilities inconsistent or anomalous. Finally, the
quantifier *some* in the *because*-clause (8.37) has to be Q-implicated to 'some
but not all', as in (8.40). Otherwise, Professor Heim's unhappiness would be
left unexplained (but see Horn 2004 for a different view of the *because*-clauses,
see also King and Stanley 2005). Once again, there is no avoiding the
conclusion that the truth condition of the complex construction has to be
calculated taking into account the conversational implicature of its part.

(8.38) Brushing your teeth and [then] going to bed is better than going to bed and
        [then] brushing your teeth.

(8.39) Miriam either suffered a heart attack and [then] underwent quadruple by-
        pass surgery, or underwent quadruple by-pass surgery and [then] suffered a
        heart attack; but the speaker doesn't know which.

(8.40) Because some [but not all] of her PhD students came to her talk, Professor
        Heim was unhappy.

Notice that (8.35)–(8.37) are also cases of so-called 'embedded implicatures', discussed in Chapter 2. Given that the conversational implicatures
involved in these sentences are truth-condition contributing ones, they are
difficult, if not impossible, to be cancelled. On the other hand, there are also
cases of embedded implicatures where the conversational implicatures
involved are defeasible, as in (8.41c).

(8.41)   a. Peter believes that some of his students hate e-books.
       b. +> Peter believes that not all of his students hate e-books
       c. Peter believes that some, and perhaps all, of his students hate e-books

The same holds for the relevance-theorists' explicature, Recanati's pragmatically enriched said, and Bach's impliciture: some of them are cancellable and some of them are non-cancellable. Why this is the case is still being hotly contended both in the philosophy of language and linguistic semantics and pragmatics (see also Capone 2009 and Burton-Roberts 2010).

If neo-Gricean conversational implicatures can intrude onto truth-conditional content, argued Levinson (2000), then one has to reject the 'received' view of the semantics–pragmatics interface, according to which, the output of semantics provides input to pragmatics, which then maps literal meaning to speaker meaning. Rather, one should allow Gricean/neo-Gricean pragmatics to play a systematic role in 'pre'-semantics, that is, to help determine the truth-conditional content of the sentence uttered. As Levinson (2000: 242) told us: 'There is every reason to try and reconstrue the interaction between semantics and pragmatics as the intimate interlocking of distinct processes, rather than, as traditionally, in terms of the output of one being the input to the other'. Such a radical proposal amounts to saying that the whole architecture of the theory of meaning needs to be radically reconstructed.

> Now see whether you are ready to do Exercise 2 at the end of this chapter.

8.4. Can explicature, the pragmatically enriched said, and impliciture be distinguished from conversational implicature?

In the last four subsections, I discussed the relevance theorists', Recanati's, Bach's, and Levinson's accounts of pragmatic intrusion into the classical Gricean concept of what is said. Given the relevance theorists' analysis of the pragmatic enrichment under discussion as explicature, Recanati's account of it as the pragmatically enriched aspect of what is said, and Bach's analysis of it as impliciture on the one hand, and Levinson's treatment of it as conversational implicature on the other hand, one important question arises: can explicature/the pragmatically enriched said/impliciture be discriminated from conversational implicature in a principal way? In other words, how can a pragmatically determined aspect of an utterance be recognized as an explicature, part of what is said, or an impliciture rather than part of what is conversationally implicated? Recanati (1993) provided two answers to this question, neither of which, however, is without problems.

In the first place, Recanati claimed that the distinction between explicature/the pragmatically augmented said/impliciture and conversational implicature can be delineated on an intuitive basis. This is embodied in his **availability principle** in (8.42).

(8.42)   Recanati's (1993) availability principle
In deciding whether a pragmatically determined aspect of utterance meaning is part of what is said, that is, in making a decision concerning what is said, we should always try to preserve our pre-theoretical intuition on the matter.

What the availability principle basically says is this: the pragmatically enriched aspect of what is said is consciously available to the speaker and the addressee. As a case in point, consider (8.43).

(8.43)   a. Mary has broken a leg.
b. Mary has broken a leg, either her own leg or someone else's
c. Mary has broken her own leg

On a standard Gricean account, what is said in (8.43a) is represented in (8.43b). But this pragmatically determined interpretation seems to run contrary to our pre-theoretical intuition. Consequently, according to Recanati's availability test, (8.43b) is rejected as what is said. By contrast, given our pre-theoretical intuition, the pragmatically amplified interpretation in (8.43c) is part of what is said. It follows therefore that, by the availability principle, this pragmatically determined aspect is considered to be part of what is said rather than part of what is conversationally implicated. However, as pointed out by Richard (1990), Horn (1992), Bach (1994a: 137–9), Levinson (2000: 197), and Carston (2002), given the fact that our pre-theoretical intuition tends not to be very reliable in many cases, Recanati's availability test has to be taken with great caution.[15]

---

[15] Gibbs and Moise (1997) presented an off-line experimental investigation of the Gricean dichotomy between what is said and what is implicated. Across a range of experimental conditions, their subjects are overwhelmingly in favour of the pragmatically enriched over the non-pragmatically enriched, minimal interpretation as

The second test put forward by Recanati for drawing the division between explicature/the pragmatically enriched said/impliciture and conversational implicature is the **scope principle**, essentially following an earlier proposal by Cohen (1971).

(8.44)   The Cohen–Recanati scope principle

A pragmatically determined aspect of meaning is part of what is said (and, therefore, not a conversational implicature) if—and, perhaps, only if—it falls within the scope of logical operators.[16]

At first glance, the scope test appears to provide a workable basis for the distinction between explicature/the pragmatically enriched said and conversational implicature. As an example, take (8.45b).

(8.45)   a. The FBI agents searched John's office.
         b. The FBI agents searched the office [in which] John [works]

Here, given Recanati's analysis, the bracketed part in (8.45b) is the pragmatically enriched said of (8.45a). Next, when (8.45a) is negated, as in (8.46a), what is saturated is retained, as can be shown by (8.46b).

best reflecting what a speaker says. On the basis of this evidence, Gibbs and Moise concluded that (i) people have clear intuitions about the distinction between what is said and what is implicated, (ii) they take what is said to correspond to the pragmatically enriched, rather than the non-pragmatically enriched, minimal proposition, and (iii) the results lend support to Recanati's availability principle (see also Bezuidenhout and Cutting 2002, Gibbs 2002). However, in a later psycho-pragmatic study, by replicating some of Gibbs and Moise's experiments, Nicolle and Clark (1999) reported that some of their subjects tend to opt for a conversational implicature rather than a pragmatically enriched said or a non-pragmatically enriched, minimal interpretation. This led Nicolle and Clark to conclude that there is no experimental support either for people's intuitions about what is said versus what is implicated or for Recanati's availability principle. See Gibbs (1999) for a reply to Nicolle and Clark (1999), and see also Carston (2002: 167–8) and Huang (2004b).

[16] The Cohen–Recanati scope principle is explicitly endorsed by the relevance theorists (see e.g. Carston 2002: 191–5). I think that in principle it can also be used to allegedly differentiate implicitures from conversational implicatures with the addition indicated in italics in (i).

(i) A pragmatically determined aspect of meaning is part of what is said *or what is implicit* (and, therefore, not a conversational implicature) if—and, perhaps, only if —it falls within the scope of logical operators.

(8.46)   a. The FBI agents didn't search John's office.

　　　　b. The FBI agents didn't search the office [in which] John [works]

In other words, the pragmatically determined element of meaning in (8.45b)/(8.46b) falls within the scope of negation—a logical operator. By the Cohen–Recanati scope criterion, it is not a genuine conversational implicature but an explicature/a pragmatic constituent of what is said/an impliciture.

By contrast, let us look next at a case of PCI in the Gricean and neo-Gricean sense. Mary's reply in (8.47) has the pragmatic enrichment in (8.48). But this pragmatically enriched element of meaning does not fall within the scope of conditional, as can be seen in (8.49).

(8.47)   John: Has Steve's paper been accepted for presentation at the conference?
　　　　Mary: His is one of the best papers submitted.

(8.48)   Steve's paper has been accepted for presentation at the conference.

(8.49)   If Steve's is one of the best papers submitted, it has the chance to win a prize.

The reason is that the consequent of (8.49) is not dependent on the paper being accepted for presentation at the conference. Consequently, according to (8.44), the pragmatic enrichment under consideration is not an explicature, the pragmatically enriched part of what is said, or an impliciture. Rather, it is a genuine conversational implicature.

There is, however, a serious problem attaching to the Cohen–Recanati scope test. As pointed out by Recanati himself, the problem concerns metalinguistic negation. We have already seen in Chapter 2 that metalinguistic negation is a device for rejecting a previous utterance on any grounds whatever including its morphosyntactic form, its phonetic realization, its style or register, and/or the conversational implicatures it potentially engenders. In addition to the examples listed in Chapter 2, some further exemplification is given below.

(8.50)   a. The water isn't cold, it's downright freezing.

　　　　b. Mary won't give you a [vɑːz], she'll give you a [veiːz].

　　　　c. I don't use elevators, I use lifts.

Of these examples, (8.50a) is of particular relevance to our discussion here. But before proceeding to discuss it, let us first consider (8.51). As noted in Chapter 2, the uttering of (8.51) gives rise to the now familiar Q_{scalar} implicature in (8.52).

(8.51)   <freezing, cold, cool>
          The water is cold.
(8.52)   The water is not freezing

Notice that when (8.51) is negated descriptively, as in (8.53), the original Q-scalar implicature is preserved. In other words, the conversational implicature falls within the scope of negation. Given the Cohen–Recanati scope test, the pragmatic enrichment cannot be a conversational implicature. Rather, it is taken to be an explicature, a pragmatic constituent of what is said, or an impliciture.[17]

(8.53)   The water isn't cold, it's cool.

Returning next to (8.50a), where (8.51) is negated in a metalinguistic way. In (8.50a), the speaker does not deny that the water is cold, because that is entailed by what the speaker asserts, namely that the water is downright freezing. What is rejected here is nothing but the very same Q-scalar implicature. Put another way, in (8.50a) the conversational implicature falls outside the scope of negation. By virtue of the Cohen–Recanati scope criterion, the pragmatic enrichment here has to be considered as a genuine conversational implicature. The contrast shown by (8.51) and (8.50a) gives rise to a puzzle, namely, why the same Q-scalar implicature may or may not fall within the scope of negation, hence may or may not be a genuine conversational implicature (see also Levinson 2000). The solution proposed by Recanati to tackle the problem is to appeal to our pre-theoretical intuition to decide on when a logical operator is or is not used metalinguistically.

---

[17] This analysis has consequences for the relevance theorists, Recanati, and Bach. For example, within their respective framework, most, if not all, cases of classical/neo-Gricean GCIs will have to be restyled as explicatures, pragmatic constituents of what is said, or implicitures. There are other consequences, too. Given that both presupposition and conventional implicature fall within the scope of negation, as shown in (i) and (ii), on the authority of the relevance-theoretic, the Recanatian, and the Bachian accounts, they have also to be treated as explicatures, the pragmatically enriched said, and implicitures, respectively.

(i)   a. The boy cried wolf again.
        b. The boy didn't cry wolf again.
           >> The boy cried wolf before
(ii)   John is poor but he is honest.
        It is not the case that John is poor but he is honest.
        +>> There is a contrast between poverty and honesty

It is considerations of this kind that have led Recanati to the view that the availability principle is of a more fundamental character than the scope principle. All this indicates that explicatures, the pragmatically enriched said, or implicitures may not be distinguished from conversational implicatures on a principled theoretical basis (Huang 2005).

In summary, I share Levinson's view that the pragmatic intrusion into what is said is a neo-Gricean conversational implicature. The reason is threefold. First of all, so-called explicature, the pragmatically enriched said, or impliciture is engendered by the same Gricean pragmatic mechanism that yields a conversational implicature. Secondly, as we have just seen in the discussion in the last subsection, currently there is no reliable test that can be employed to theoretically distinguish alleged explicature, the pragmatically enriched said, or impliciture from conversational implicature (but see Bach 2010 for the differences between explicature and impliciture). This is also the case with work carried out in experimental pragmatics. I do not think that there is any experiment that can differentiate explicature, pragmatically enriched said, or impliciture from conversational implicature. Therefore currently, there is no failsafe test (both conceptual and experimental) that can be employed to distinguish alleged explicature, the pragmatically enriched said, or impliciture from conversational implicature on a principled basis. Thirdly, other things being equal, given the metatheoretical principle known as 'Occam's razor' (Chapter 1), the conversational implicature analysis is theoretically and methodologically preferable, because it postulates fewer representational levels and/or theoretical categories in the interpretation of an utterance than the explicature, pragmatically enriched said, or impliciture account.[18] As already remarked, if neo-Gricean conversational implicature can intrude on the truth-conditional content of an utterance, then a problem known as Grice's circle arises, namely, how what is conversationally implicated can be defined in contrast to, and calculated on the basis of what is said, given that what is said seems to both determine and to be determined by what is conversationally implicated. Levinson's proposal was that one should reject the 'received' view of the pragmatics–semantics interface, namely, the view that the output of semantics is the input to pragmatics, and allow conversational implicatures

---

[18] Even if the dispute were entirely of a terminological rather than a substantive nature, the force of my arguments seems to remain. This is because to have fewer technical terms is usually better than having more.

to play a systematic role in 'pre'-semantics, that is, to help determine the truth-conditional, propositional content of an utterance. Putting it slightly differently, in order to avoid Grice's circle, one needs both 'pre'-semantic and 'post'-semantic pragmatics or what Korta and Perry (2008) called 'near- and far-side pragmatics' (see also Korta and Perry 2011).

8.5. The five analyses compared

8.5.1. Grice

Grice's concept of what is said is largely semantically based. It constitutes semantic representations or linguistic meaning of a sentence, together with a set of preconditions on the determination of the proposition expressed: namely, (i) identifying reference, (ii) completing deixis, and (iii) disambiguating lexical expressions. What is said in the Gricean sense is minimally yet fully propositional. By contrast, what is conversationally implicated, as articulated by Grice, is intended to handle both enriched and additional propositions, in the terminology of Levinson (2000: 195). Consequently, within the classical Gricean paradigm, while semantic representations and minimal propositions fall under semantics, enriched and additional propositions are the concern of pragmatics. But it is unclear where the pragmatic resolution of reference, deixis, and ambiguities should fall for Grice.

8.5.2. Relevance theorists

The relevance theorists have adopted a broader, more pragmatic notion of what is said, though they do not use the term 'what is said'. What is said in the relevance-theoretic sense can be roughly divided into two parts: semantic representations and explicatures. Explicatures are responsible for the pragmatically enriched level of what Sperber and Wilson (1986, 1995) called explicit content. They cover both pragmatic resolution of indexicals and ambiguities, and minimal and enriched propositions. On the other hand, r-implicatures account for additional propositions. It follows, therefore, that semantic representations fall in the domain of semantics; both explicatures and r-implicatures belong to pragmatics.

8.5.3. Recanati

Like the relevance theorists, Recanati has also endorsed a wider, more pragmatic conception of what is said. Both the relevance theorists' and Recanati's notion of what is said, in what Levinson (2000) labelled the 'everyday sense of what is stated', constitutes what Berg (2002) called 'contextually enriched content'. On Recanati's view, what is said has a semantic part, that is, semantic representation or sentence meaning, and a pragmatic part, that is, the pragmatically enriched said (e.g. Recanati 2004a: 6). The semantic part corresponds roughly to what Recanati (2000) called **i-content (intuitive truth-conditional content of utterance)** and what Recanati (2001) dubbed '**what is said$_{min}$**' and the pragmatic part, to what Recanati (2000) labelled **c-content (compositionally articulated content of utterance)** and what Recanati (2001) called '**what is said$_{max}$**'. Reference assignment, deixis identification, disambiguation, minimal and expanded propositions all belong to pragmatically enriched what is said. Only additional propositions are the output of conversational implicatures.

8.5.4. Bach

In contrast to the relevance theorists and Recanati, Bach has opted for a notion of what is said that is even narrower than the original minimal Gricean concept. Following Grice (1989), Bach (1994a, 2001, 2004) was of the view that what is said should be 'closely related to the conventional meaning of the . . . sentence . . . uttered' and must correspond to 'the elements of [the sentence], their order and their syntactic character' (Grice 1989: 87). He called this narrower criterion for what is said the '**syntactic correlation constraint**' (but see Carston 2002: 172–3, 181 for qualification). What is said thus understood is closely linked with both the conventional, semantic content and the syntactic structure of the sentence uttered.[19] This

---

[19] Elsewhere, in an attempt to dispense with Grice's notion of conventional implicature, Bach (1999) postulated an **Indirect Quotation test** or **IQ test**, which goes: 'An element of a sentence contributes to what is said in an utterance of that sentence if and only if it can be an accurate and complete indirect quotation of the utterance (in the same language) which includes that element, or a corresponding element, in the 'that'-clause that specifies what is said'.

locutionary sense of what is said is roughly equivalent to Berg's (2002) characterization of what is said as being general content, as opposed to contextually enriched content. In addition, on Bach's account, reference resolution, deixis fixing, and disambiguation are also part of what is said. The semantic representation of what is said may be subpropositional. In other words, it can be in the form of what Bach called propositional radicals. Propositional radicals and minimal propositions undergo a process of completion and expansion, respectively, to be transformed into what is implicit, that is, implicitures. Implicitures then provide input to the classical Gricean pragmatic mechanism (the co-operative principle and its component maxims) yielding conversational implicatures as output. Thus, in Bach's theory, the traditional Gricean dichotomy between what is said and what is implicated is replaced by a trichotomy between what is said, what is implicit, and what is conversationally implicated. Whereas what is said falls within the province of semantics, both what is implicit and what is conversationally implicated are the concerns of pragmatics.

8.5.5. Levinson

Levinson has retained the classical Gricean characterization of what is said. As mentioned already, the Gricean semantic notion of what is said consists

According to this test, *but*, *still*, and *even* are part of what is said because they can be straightforwardly embedded in an indirect quotation, as in (i). By contrast, *in other words*, *frankly*, and *nevertheless* are not constitutive of what is said, because they cannot pass the IQ test. This is illustrated in (ii).

(i) a. Mary is fast asleep, but Victoria is wide awake.
    b. John said that Mary is fast asleep, but Victoria is wide awake.
(ii) a. In other words, the patent should be granted in amended form.
    b. ?John said that in other words, the patent should be granted in amended form.

There are, however, problems with this test. For example, on Bach's view, *frankly* should not contribute to what is said. But it does seem to pass the IQ test, as the following example from Carston (2002: 176) shows.

(iii) Beth said that frankly she'd had enough of John's lies.

For a recent debate between Bach and Recanati about whether what is said is constrained by syntax or pre-theoretical intuition, see e.g. Bach (2001) and Recanati (2001).

of semantic representations and a set of preconditions to determining the propositions expressed, and minimal propositions. But unlike Grice, Levinson allows conversational implicatures to intrude onto the assignment of truth-conditional content. In other words, on Levinson's view, conversational implicatures are not only needed to account for additional propositions classically 'post'-semantically, but they are also required 'pre'-semantically to explain reference determination, deictic resolution, disambiguation, ellipsis unpacking, and generality-narrowing, as well as to affect truth conditions in complex constructions such as comparatives, conditionals, and *because*-clauses. Thus, within the Levinsonian neo-Gricean framework, only semantic representations are categorized as the proper domain of semantics. All the rest is dealt with in pragmatics.

As noted in the last chapter, Levinson's argument that conversational implicature can contribute to propositional content gives rise to the problem known as Grice's circle, namely, how what is conversationally implicated can be defined in contrast to, and calculated on the basis of, what is said, given that what is said seems to both determine and to be determined by what is conversationally implicated (e.g. Levinson 2000; Huang 2001a). The suggestion put forward by Levinson to deal with the problem is that one should give up the traditional, 'received' view that semantics and pragmatics are autonomous with respect to each other, and the output of semantics is input to pragmatics. Rather, one should treat semantics and pragmatics as two overlapping and interrelated fields of study.

The semantics–pragmatics distinction as reflected in the five analyses discussed above can be listed in (8.54).

(8.54)   The semantics–pragmatics interface (adapted from Levinson 2000: 195)

Author	Semantic representation	Dectic and reference resolution	Minimal proposition	Enriched proposition	Additional proposition
Grice	What	is	said	Implicature	
Relevance theorists		Explicature			Implicature
Recanati		Pragmatically enriched said			Implicature
Bach		What is said		Impliciture	Implicature
Levinson		What is said			
		Implicature			

Semantics	Pragmatics

To sum up, as can be seen from the table in (8.54), what everyone agrees on is that there is a level of semantic representation, or the linguistic meaning of the sentence, and this level belongs to semantics. Next, what the relevance theorists, Recanati, Bach, and Levinson have in common is the viewpoint that at least part of the original Gricean notion of what is said has to be understood as involving much more of a pragmatic contribution than Grice has acknowledged. But what they cannot agree on are two points. In the first place, while the relevance theorists, Recanati, and Levinson believe that there is substantial pragmatic intrusion into what is said, Bach denies that there is such an intrusion, and posits a level intermediate between what is said and what is conversationally implicated. Secondly, the disagreement concerns the nature of the pragmatic enrichment under consideration. For the relevance theorists, Recanati, and Bach, the pragmatic enrichment in question is of a special kind, which differs from conversational implicature; for Levinson, it is the same beast as conversational implicature. This difference certainly has implications for the domain of semantics and of pragmatics, the interface between semantics and pragmatics, and indeed for the theory of meaning as a whole. Other things being equal, given the metatheoretical principle known as 'Occam's razor' ('theoretical entities are not to be multiplied beyond necessity) (see Chapter 1), Levinson's model is theoretically and methodologically preferable, because it postulates fewer theoretical categories and/or representational levels in the production and comprehension of an utterance than its competitors.

8.6. Summary

This chapter has been concerned with the interface and division of labour between pragmatics and semantics. In Section 8.1, I discussed two theoretical positions with regard to the relationship between semantics and pragmatics, namely, reductionism and complementarism. Section 8.2 examined the three influential ways in which the boundary between semantics and pragmatics has been drawn, and showed that there does not seem to be a clear-cut demarcation between these two core components of linguistics. Next, in Section 8.3, I focused my attention on pragmatic intrusion into the classical Gricean characterization of what is said—an issue that has been, and is still being, vigorously debated by both linguists and philosophers of language, and by both semanticists and pragmaticists. The discussion was conducted against the current debate between contextualism and semantic minimalism in the philosophy of language. In particular, I concentrated on the proposals put forward by the relevance theorists, Recanati, Bach, and Levinson. I then considered the question of whether so-called explicature, the pragmatically enriched said, or impliciture can be distinguished from conversational implicature in a principal way. Finally, Section 8.5 compared and contrasted Grice's, relevance-theorists', Recanati's, Bach's, and Levinson's analyses. The general conclusion of this chapter that can be reached seems to be that semantics and pragmatics constitute two distinct domains of inquiry, but they are inextricably intertwined in such a manner that their borderline is not easy to draw in a neat and systematic way.[20] Echoing a rather pessimistic remark made by Lyons (1987: 155) almost twenty years ago that 'current presentations of the distinction between semantics and pragmatics tend to be riddled with inconsistencies and unjustified assumptions', Recanati (2004b: 461) concluded:

[I]t is futile to insist on providing an answer to the twin questions: What is the principled basis for the semantics/pragmatics distinction? Where does the boundary lie? Answers to these questions can still be given, but they have to rely on stipulation.

Key concepts

pragmatics–semantics interface
reductionism
semantic reductionism
pragmatic reductionism
complementarism
radical semantics
radical pragmatics

---

[20] There are also linguistic phenomena that straddle the semantics–pragmatics boundary. One such phenomenon is presupposition. Another is deixis.

narrow context versus broad context

charity

non-monotonicity

holism

contextualism

semantic minimalism

indexicalism including hidden indexicalism

non-indexical contextualism or semantic relativism

what is said

what is communicated/conveyed/meant

pragmatic intrusion

unarticulated constituent

primary versus secondary pragmatic process

saturation

free enrichment

strengthening

expansion

semantic transfer

availability principle

scope principle

(conversational) impliciture

propositional radical

completion

intrusive construction

Indirect Quotation (IQ) test

Exercises and essay questions

1. Of the following propositions, which need saturation (Recanati) or completion (Bach), which need free enrichment (Recanati) or expansion (Bach), which need semantic transfer/deferred/transferred reference, and which need loosening? Can you saturate/complete, freely enrich/expand, loosen, or 'transfer' them accordingly?
    (i) I haven't been to Australia.
    (ii) Christmas is some time away.
    (iii) Mary is not slim enough.
    (iv) The tram is full.
    (v) In all probability John is going to marry that pretty face.
    (vi) The Tibetan Buddhist temple is some distance away.

(vii) Peter and Susan drove to LA. Their car broke down half way.

(viii) This laptop is cheaper.

(ix) Confucius is on the top shelf. It's bound in leather.

(x) She's a real beauty with brains.

(xi) The children stood in a circle around the Christmas tree.

(xii) The semantics/pragmatics conference starts at nine.

(xiii) Susan lost everything.

(xiv) People say that he owns a van Gogh.

2. Is there any pragmatic intrusion into the following constructions? Can you point out what type of conversational implicature is involved in each case?

(i) It's better to be faithful to your wife than to be not unfaithful to her.

(ii) If some of his children oppose the government's immigration policy, the minister will not resign, but if all of them do, he will.

(iii) Helen either had a baby and got married or got married and had a baby, but I don't know which.

(iv) Living in a not undemocratic country is worse than living in a democratic one.

(v) Because a mathematician and an economist wrote the monograph, it sold well.

(vi) It's better to stop your car than to cause it to stop.

(vii) John persuaded Catherine to marry the man who loves her, but not the man who likes her.

(viii) If the coffee is warm, you drink it, but if it is hot, you wait for a few minutes.

3. What are the main differences between reductionism and complementarism regarding the relationship between semantics and pragmatics?

4. Why can semantics and pragmatics not be distinguished systematically on the basis of the distinction between truth conditions versus non-truth conditions, conventional versus non-conventional meaning, or context independence versus context dependence?

5. What are the main differences between contextualism and semantic minimalism?

6. What is an intrusive construction? Illustrate with your own examples? Why is it so called?

7. Can explicature, the pragmatically enriched said, or impliciture be distinguished from conversational implicature on a principled basis? If yes, how; if no, why not?

8. Compare and contrast any two of the analyses of pragmatic intrusion into what is said discussed in this chapter. Bach's theory of impliciture may be one of them, though he denies that there is any such intrusion.

9. What is your view about the interaction and division of labour between semantics and pragmatics?

Further readings

Bach (1994a).
Bach (2012).
Levinson (2000). Chapter 3.
Recanati (2004b).
Recanati (2010). Chapter 1.
Carston (2002). Chapter 2.

9

Pragmatics and syntax

In the last chapter, I discussed the pragmatics–semantics interface. In this chapter, I shall consider the **pragmatics–syntax interface**, focusing on anaphora and binding.

As mentioned in Chapter 6, **anaphora** can in general be defined as a relation between two or more linguistic elements, in which the interpretation of one (called an **anaphoric expression**) is in some way determined by the interpretation of the other (called an **antecedent**) (e.g. Huang 2000a: 1, 2004a, 2006c, 2007a). In terms of syntactic category, anaphora falls into two main groups: (i) **NP-**, including **N-bar**, **anaphora** and (ii) **VP-anaphora**.[1] In an NP-anaphoric relation, both the anaphoric expression and its antecedent are NPs. This is illustrated in (9.1).

---

[1] I shall not discuss VP-anaphora in this chapter. The interested reader is referred to Huang (2000a: section 3.1, 2006c).

(9.1)   Mike₁ said that he₁ almost lost his₁ life to cancer.

In (9.1), *he* and *his* are anaphoric expressions, and *Mike* is their antecedent. *He, his life*, and *Mike* are all NPs. In an N-bar-anaphoric relation, by contrast, both the anaphoric expression and its antecedent are N-bars rather than NPs. An example of N-bar-anaphora is given in (9.2).

(9.2)   John's sister is a nursery teacher, and Bill's Ø is a policewoman.

In (9.2), the empty category or gap represented by Ø is the anaphoric expression, and *sister* is its antecedent. Neither the anaphoric expression nor its antecedent is a full NP. In this chapter, I shall concentrate on that type of NP-anaphora known as binding in the generative syntax literature.

As pointed out in Huang (e.g. 1991a, 1994, 2000a, 2004a, 2006c, 2007a), anaphora is at the centre of research on the interface between syntax, semantics, and pragmatics in linguistic theory. It is also a key concern of psycho- and computational linguistics, and of work in the philosophy of language and on the linguistic component of cognitive science. It has aroused this interest for a number of reasons. In the first place, like reference, anaphora is another complex and fascinating phenomenon of natural language. Secondly, anaphora has long been regarded as one of the few 'extremely good probes' (Chomsky 1982: 23) in furthering our understanding of the nature of the human mind, and thus in facilitating an answer to what Chomsky (e.g. 1981, 1995) considers to be the fundamental problem of theoretical linguistics, namely, the logical problem of language acquisition. In particular, certain aspects of anaphora have repeatedly been claimed by Chomsky (e.g. 1981) to present evidence for the argument that human beings are born equipped with some internal, unconscious knowledge of language, known as the language faculty (to be elaborated below). Thirdly, anaphora has been shown to interact with syntactic, semantic, and pragmatic factors. Consequently, it has provided a testing ground for competing hypotheses concerning the relationship between syntax, semantics, and pragmatics in linguistic theory.

This chapter is organized as follows. I shall first summarize Chomsky's views about language and linguistics in Section 9.1. Next, Section 9.2 outlines Chomsky's binding theory. I shall then proceed to discuss the problems for Chomsky's binding theory and its latest development in Section 9.3. After that, I shall present a revised neo-Gricean pragmatic theory of anaphora as developed in Huang (2000a, 2000b, 2004a, 2006c,

2007a,) (see also Levinson 1987a, 1987b, 1991, 2000, and Huang 1991a, 1994). Finally, in Section 9.5 I shall briefly discuss the theoretical implications of our pragmatic approach for the interface between pragmatics and syntax.

9.1. Chomsky's views about language and linguistics

In Chomsky's (1986, 1995) view, linguistics is essentially concerned with the nature of the human mind/brain. The central issue of linguistics is **knowledge of language**: its nature (what constitutes knowledge of language), origin (how is knowledge of language acquired), and use (how is knowledge of language put to use). The ultimate goal of **generative grammar** is to provide an answer to what Chomsky considers to be the fundamental problem of linguistics, namely, the **logical problem of language acquisition**, that is, how is it possible for the child, on the basis of insufficient evidence about, or severely limited experience of, his or her language, to rapidly acquire the abstract and complex underlying system that represents his or her knowledge of language. This problem is taken to be a special case of what is known as **Plato-Russell's problem**, namely, to explain how we know so much given that the evidence available to us is so meagre. The answer provided by Chomsky to the logical problem of language acquisition is the **innateness hypothesis**— roughly, the argument that human beings are born equipped with some internal, unconscious knowledge of language, known as the **language faculty**. The initial state of the language faculty, being a component or module of the human mind/brain, is subject to a theory of **Universal Grammar** (**UG**). Somewhat related to the innateness hypothesis is also the assumption that the underlying system of knowledge of language is much simpler than it superficially appears (e.g. Chomsky 1986, 1995, see also Chomsky 2012). The development of generative grammar in the last fifty years is largely concerned with these fundamental problems of children's learnability, innateness, and universals. One topic of inquiry that has been at the very heart of Chomsky's generative grammar is the type of NP-anaphora known as binding in the generative syntax literature.

9.2. Chomsky's binding theory

As already mentioned in Chapter 1, within the **principles-and-parameters theory** and its **minimalist descendent**,[2] Chomsky (1981, 1995) distinguished two types of abstract feature for NPs: anaphors and pronominals. An **anaphor** is a feature representation of an NP which must be referentially dependent and which must be bound within an appropriately defined minimal syntactic domain; a **pronominal** is a feature representation of an NP which may be referentially dependent but which must be free within such a domain. Interpreting anaphors and pronominals as two independent binary features, Chomsky hypothesized that one ideally expects to find four types of NP in a language—both overt and non-overt, that is, empty.

(9.3)   Chomsky's (1995: 41) typology of NPs

	Overt	Empty
a. [+anaphor, –pronominal]	lexical anaphor	NP-trace
b. [–anaphor, +pronominal]	pronoun	*pro*
c. [+anaphor, +pronominal]	–	PRO
d. [–anaphor, –pronominal]	name	*wh*-trace/variable

Putting aside the four types of empty category (see note 9 of Chapter 1 for exemplification; see e.g. Huang 1991b, 1992a, 1992b, 1994: chapters 2

---

[2] The minimalist program is the most recent orthodox version of Chomsky's generative grammar, which grew out of Chomsky's **government and binding (GB)** version of the **principles-and-parameters** approach. While there is not yet a fully-fledged theory of minimalism, the minimalist program may be presented in a nutshell as follows. In the minimalist framework, the set of four levels of representation is reduced to two interface levels: Logical Form (LF) and Phonological Form (PF). LF provides an input to the semantic-conceptual system, and PF provides an input to the articulatory-perceptual system. This reflects Chomsky's belief known as 'conceptual necessity': since language is a mapping between sound and meaning, all else being equal, language will deploy only those mechanisms needed to connect, on the one hand, to the physical world of sound, and on the other, to the mental world of cognition. In addition to a lexicon, syntax—what Chomsky now calls the **computational system**—stands between the two interfaces. There are two generalized transformations Merge and Move, and one non-transformation Spell-out, which regulate derivation. Furthermore, a number of principles of economy are postulated. Both derivation and representation are subject to these principles (Chomsky 1995; see Seuren 2004 for a critique; see also notes 14 and 15 below).

and 3, 1995, 2000a: sections 2.1 and 2.2, 2007a for comments), the three lexically realized types of overt NP can be illustrated in (9.4).

(9.4)   Overt NPs
    a. Lexical anaphors
       The anti-war campaigners congratulated *themselves/each other*.
    b. Pronouns
       He was killed by 'friendly fire' in Iraq.
    c. Proper names/definite descriptions
       John/The section head bitterly regretted last month's attack on his boss.

Of the three types of overt NP listed in (9.4), anaphors, pronominals, and **r[eferential]-expressions** are subject to **binding conditions A, B, and C**, respectively (see also Chomsky 1995: 211 for the interpretative version of these conditions within the minimalist framework).

(9.5)   Chomsky's (1995: 96) binding conditions
    A. An anaphor must be bound in a local domain.
    B. A pronominal must be free in a local domain.
    C. An r-expression must be free.

The definition of **binding** is given in (9.6) (Chomsky 1995: 93).

(9.6) α binds β if and only if
    (i) α is in an A-position,
    (ii) α c-commands β, and
    (iii) α and β are coindexed.

Note that given (i) of (9.6), the binding conditions specified in (9.5) apply to A-binding (that is, binding by a category in an argument position) but not to non-A-binding (that is, binding by a category in a non-argument position). **C-command** is commonly defined as follows:

(9.7) α c-commands β if and only if
    (i) α does not dominate β,
    (ii) β does not dominate α, and
    (iii) the first branching node dominating α also dominates β.

Finally, the notion of local binding domain is standardly defined in terms of **governing category (GC)** or **complete functional complex (CFC)**. One common version of GC is given in (9.8).

(9.8) α is a GC for β if and only if α is the minimal category
    (i.e. the smallest NP or S) containing β, a governor of β,
    and a SUBJECT accessible to β.

The paradigmatic patterns for binding are illustrated from English in (9.9).

(9.9)   a. Bach$_1$ adored himself$_1$.
        b. Bach$_1$ adored him$_2$.
        c. Bach$_1$ adored Bach$_2$.

In (9.9a), *himself* is a reflexive and therefore an anaphor in the Chomskyan sense. As such, it falls under binding condition A, according to which it must be bound to its local antecedent *Bach*. Next in (9.9b), *him*, being a pronominal, is subject to binding condition B. Given binding condition B, it cannot be bound in its local domain, and there is thus disjoint reference between it and *Bach*. Finally in (9.9c), both *Bach*s are r-repressions. By binding condition C, the second *Bach* cannot be co-indexed with the first one. From examples like these, Chomsky concluded that the syntactic distribution of anaphors, pronominals, and r-expressions is accounted for by binding conditions A, B, and C.[3]

9.3. Problems for Chomsky's binding theory

9.3.1. Binding condition A

Cross-linguistically, Chomsky's binding theory is problematic. Let me take the binding condition A pattern first. To begin with, many languages in the world systematically allow **long-distance reflexives**—reflexives that are bound outside their local syntactic domain, and even across sentence boundaries into discourse. These include most East, South, and Southeast Asian languages (e.g. Chinese, Kannada, and Malay), some mainland and insular Scandinavian languages (e.g. Norwegian, Swedish, and Icelandic), some Germanic (other than Scandinavian) and Romance languages (e.g. Dutch, Italian, and Old Provençal), some Slavonic languages (e.g. Czech,

---

[3] Chomsky's approach is essentially a syntactic or 'geometric' approach, in which binding is formulated predominantly in configurational terms, appealing to purely structural concepts like c-command, government, and locality. In contrast to this syntactically based approach is the semantic or argument structure approach, which is represented by Reinhart and Reuland's (1993) theory of reflexivity. The semantically oriented approach attempts to give an account of binding primarily in argument-structure terms. See Huang (2000a: section 3.2, 2004a) for detailed discussion of the semantic approach.

Polish, and Russian), and languages like Modern Greek, KiNande, and Northern Pomo. Following is an example from Chinese.

(9.10)   (Chinese)

Xiaoming$_1$ shuo   Xiaohua$_2$ kanbuqi   ziji$_{1/2}$.
Xiaoming   say   Xiaohua   look down upon   self

'Xiaoming$_1$ says that Xiaohua$_2$ looks down upon him$_1$/himself$_2$'.

Given (9.8), the local binding domain of the Chinese morphologically simplex reflexive/anaphor *ziji* (self) is the embedded clause. However, contrary to the prediction of binding condition A, the reflexive *ziji* can be bound by the matrix subject *Xiaoming*, which is outside its local binding domain.[4]

A second type of counterevidence to Chomsky's binding condition A is presented by the distribution of certain morphologically simplex reflexives in languages such as Dutch, Norwegian, and Swedish. It has been observed by, for example, Reinhart and Reuland (1993) that there is a contrast in the use of this type of reflexive in intrinsic (that is, self-directed) and extrinsic (that is, other-directed) reflexivization contexts. By intrinsic or self-directed is meant that the action denoted by the predicate is typically performed by a human agent on him- or herself, whereas in the case of extrinsic or other-directed, the action denoted by the predicate is typically directed against others. The contrast is that whereas a morphologically simplex reflexive can be locally bound in the former, as in the Dutch sentence (9.11a), it cannot be locally bound in the latter, as in (9.11b).

(9.11)   (Dutch)

a. Rint   schaamt   zich.
   Rint   shames   self
   'Rint is ashamed.'
b. *Rint   veracht   zich.
   Rint   despises self
   'Rint despises himself.'

In (9.11a), the predicate is self-directed, and the Dutch morphologically simplex reflexive/anaphor *zich* (self) is allowed. However in (9.11b), the predicate

---

[4] In recent years, there have been a number of generative strategies to tackle the locality problem posed by long-distance reflexivization for Chomsky's binding theory. However, as I have demonstrated in Huang (1996, 2000a: section 2.3.3), none of these proposals really works.

is other-directed, and *zich* is not permitted. Since *zich* is an anaphor in the Chomskyan sense, why is it not allowed in its local binding domain in (9.11b)?

There is thus evidence that, cross-linguistically, the distribution of reflexives/anaphors violates Chomsky's binding condition A in both directions: on the one hand, a reflexive/anaphor can be bound outside its local domain, as in Chinese, and on the other, it may not be bound within its local domain, as in Dutch.

Go to the end of the chapter and try to do Exercises 1 and 2.

9.3.2. Binding condition B

We move next to the binding condition B pattern. Once again, evidence from various languages casts serious doubts on Chomsky's binding condition B. In the first place, many languages in the world have no reflexives and consequently utilize pronouns as one of the means to encode co-reference. These include some Low West Germanic languages (e.g. Old and Middle Dutch, Old English, Old Frisian, and perhaps West Flemish and Modern Frisian), Bamako Bambara, Biblical Hebrew, Isthmus Zapotec, the majority of Australian languages (e.g. Gumbaynggir, Jiwarli, and Nyawaygi), some Austronesian languages (e.g. Chamorro, Kilivila, and Tahitian), some Papuan languages (e.g. Harway), all Oceanic languages, and many pidgin and creole languages (e.g. the Spanish-based Palenquero, and perhaps Bislama, Chinook Jargon, the French-based Guadeloupe, the Arabic-based KiNubi, Kriyol, Martinique Creole, and Negerhollands). An example from Fijian is given in (9.12).

(9.12)   (Fijian, cited in Levinson 2000)
        Sa   va'a-.dodonu-.ta'ini   'ea   o   Mika.
        ASP   correct   3SG-OBJ ART Mike
        'Mike corrected himself/him.'

Secondly, there are languages that lack first- and/or second-person reflexives. In these languages, first- and second-person personal pronouns are instead used as bound anaphors. Some Germanic (e.g. Danish, Dutch, and Icelandic) and Romance (e.g. French and Italian) languages, for instance, belong to this type.

(9.13)   (Danish, cited in Huang 2000)
        Jeg   barberede   mig.
        I   shaved   me
        'I shaved myself.'
(9.14)   (German)
        Du   denkst   immer   nur   an   dich.
        you   think   always   only   of   you
        'You always think only of yourself.'

Thirdly, the use of a locally bound third-person personal pronoun in syntactic structures where its corresponding, third-person reflexive is not available is attested in a range of languages. This can be illustrated from Piedmontese in (9.15). Similar examples can be found in, for example, Catalan, French, Galician, Portuguese, Rumanian, Russian, Sardinian, Spanish, and Tsaxur.

(9.15)   (Piedmontese, Burzio 1991)
        Giuanin   a parla   sempre   d'   chiel.
        Giuanin   CL-speak   always   of   him
        'Giuanin always talks about himself.'

All this shows that the use of a pronoun as an anaphor in the world's languages is not highly marked, as Reinhart and Reuland (1993) claimed. Consequently, Chomsky's binding condition B cannot be entirely correct. This is because given Chomsky's binding condition B, a pronominal is not allowed to be bound within its local domain. But, as we have already seen, in (9.12)–(9.15), it is.

9.3.3. Complementarity between anaphors and pronominals

Next, given the standard formulation of Chomsky's binding conditions A and B, it is predicted that anaphors and pronominals should be in strict complementary distribution, that is, anaphors can occur only where pronominals cannot, and vice versa. This is because the two binding conditions are precise mirror-images of each other.

This predicted distributional complementarity between anaphors and pronominals, however, seems to be a generative syntactician's dream world. Even in a 'syntactic' language like English, it is not difficult to find syntactic environments where the complementarity breaks down. Well-known cases include (i) 'picture' NPs (9.16a), (ii) adjunct PPs (9.16b), (iii) possessive NPs (9.16c), and (iv) emphatic NPs (9.16d).

(9.16) a. Barack Obama$_1$ saw a picture of himself$_1$/him$_1$ in *The New York Times*.
  b. Steve$_1$ looked behind himself$_1$/him$_1$.
  c. [Pavarotti and Domingo]$_1$ adore [each other's]$_1$/their$_1$ performances.
  d. Pavarotti$_1$ said that tenors like himself$_1$/him$_1$ would not sing operas like that.

Worse still, when we take a look at a wider range of languages, we find that the total distributional complementarity jointly entailed by Chomsky's binding conditions A and B stands on shakier ground. First, as I have remarked already, there are long-distance reflexivization languages— languages that systematically allow a reflexive to be bound outside its local domain. In these languages, there is a systematic syntactic distributional overlap between anaphors and pronominals, as can be exemplified in (9.17).

(9.17) (Malay)
  Fatimah$_1$ mengadu bahawa Ali$_2$ mengecam dirinya$_1$/nya$_1$.
  Fatimah complain that Ali criticize self-3SG/3SG
  'Fatimah$_1$ complains that Ali$_2$ criticizes her$_1$/himself$_2$.'

Secondly, as suggested by Burzio (1996) and Huang (2002a: 24–5), languages can be grouped into three types with respect to bound possessive anaphora: (i) those allowing anaphors but not pronominals (e.g. Basque, Chechen, Danish, Hindi/Urdu, Ingush, Kashmiri, Norwegian, Latin, and Russian), (ii) those permitting pronominals but not anaphors (e.g. Arabic, Akan, German, Guugu Yimidhirr, and Spanish), and (iii) those permitting both anaphors and pronominals (e.g. Bangala, Bengali, Chinese, Japanese, Korean, Malay, Malayalam, Marathi, Sinhala, Tamil, and Tuki) (see also Exercise 5 at the end of this chapter). In the first, 'reflexives only' type, the possessive and the antecedent are 'near' enough to allow only a reflexive but not a pronoun to encode co-referentiality, as in (9.18).

(9.18) (Gimira, cited in Huang 2002a)
  ba/yi dor gotue.
  3-REFL/his sheep sold-3-M-FIN
  'He$_1$ sold his self's$_1$ /his$_2$ sheep.'

In the second, 'pronouns only' type, because either there is no possessive reflexive in the language or the possessive reflexive cannot be used, only a pronoun is permitted, as in (9.19).

(9.19)   John₁ loves his₁/₂ wife.

Finally in the third, 'both reflexives and pronouns' type, the possessive and the antecedent are both 'close' enough to allow a reflexive and at the same time 'distant' enough to permit a pronoun as well, as in (9.20).[5]

(9.20)   (Oriya, Ray 2000)
         raama₁   nija₁/taa₁   bahi   paDhilaa.
         Rama   self's his   book   read
         'Rama₁ read self's₁/his₁ book.'

While Chomsky's binding conditions A and B make correct predications for the distribution of bound possessive anaphora in 'reflexives only' and perhaps also in 'pronouns only' languages depending on how the local binding domain is defined, they certainly make wrong predictions for 'both reflexives and pronouns' languages.

Thirdly, still another type of distributional overlap is found cross-linguistically. This involves certain emphatic contexts. Emphatic expressions can be either morphologically simplex or complex. Morphologically complex emphatic expressions are usually in the form of 'pronoun/reflexive + adjunct/modifier', with the adjunct/modifier having the meaning of 'self', 'same', 'body', 'head', 'eye', 'soul', 'marrow', 'seed', or—in the case of possessives—'own' (e.g. Levinson 1991; Baker 1995; König and Siemund 2000). These morphologically complex emphatic expressions can alternate with pronouns.

(9.21)   Pronoun versus pronoun + 'self'
         Mary thinks that her son is more musical than her/herself.

---

[5] As noted in Huang (2002a), there may be a mixture of types within a single language. For example, Mundani is a 'reflexives only' language in third-person singular, but a 'pronouns only' language in third-person plural, as can be seen from the following examples (data from Parker 1986).

(i)   ta₁   dzi   akende   a-zi1/to₂.
     3SG   eat   banana   self's/his
     'He₁ has eaten self's₁/his₂ banana.'

(ii)   bɔ₁   le   ni   eghi   bɔb₁/₂.
     they   3PL   take   things   their
     'They₁ took their₁/₂ things.'

(9.22)   Pronoun versus pronoun + 'same'
(French)

François   pense   que   Viviane   aime   Pierre   plus
François   believes   that   Viviane   loves   Pierre   more
QUE   LUI/LUI-MÊME.
THAN   HIM/HIM-SAME
'François believes that Viviane loves Pierre more
than him/himself.'

(9.23)   Pronoun versus pronoun + 'own'
The little boy is struggling with his/his own shoe laces.

We can thus conclude that the strict distributional complementarity between anaphors and pronominals dictated by Chomsky's binding conditions A and B cannot be maintained.

9.3.4. Binding condition C

We come finally to the binding condition C pattern. Following Chomsky (1981), Lasnik (1989) argued that binding condition C be split into two subconditions, to be called **binding conditions C_1 and C_2**.

(9.24)   Lasnik's binding condition C (my phrasing)
C_1 An r-expression is r-expression-free everywhere.
C_2 An r-expression is pronoun-free everywhere.

What binding condition C_1 says is that an r-expression cannot be bound by another r-expression anywhere in the sentence, and what binding condition C_2 dictates is that an r-expression cannot be bound by a pronoun anywhere in the sentence. Furthermore, Lasnik claimed that while binding condition C_1 is subject to parametric variation, binding condition C_2 is universal.

But this way of looking at binding condition C is not tenable. Take binding condition C_1 first. Counterexamples can easily be demonstrated cross-linguistically, especially in some East, South, and Southeast Asian languages such as Chinese, Bangala, Hindi/Urdu, Japanese, Malayalam, Sinhala, Vietnamese, and Thai.

(9.25)   (Thai)
Cɔɔn$_1$ chɔɔp   Cɔɔn$_1$.
John   likes   John
'John$_1$ likes John$_1$.'

Next arises the question of whether or not binding condition C_2 can be maintained universally. The answer is again negative, as the following classic example from English (Evans 1980) shows.

(9.26)   Everyone has finally realized that Oscar$_1$ is incompetent.
         Even he$_1$ has finally realized that Oscar$_1$ is incompetent.

In (9.26), the r-expression in the second sentence is preceded and c-commanded by the pronoun in the matrix clause of the same sentence, yet it is bound by the pronoun, contra binding condition C_2.[6] There is thus no avoiding the conclusion that binding condition C_2 can also be falsified.

Now have a look at Exercise 3 at the end of this chapter.

9.3.5. Elimination of binding conditions?

As already mentioned in note 10 of Chapter 1, a current development in the Chomskyan syntactic analysis of binding is to eliminate all the conditions that are postulated specifically for binding such as Chomsky's binding conditions A, B, and C, discussed above, and to reduce these specific conditions to elementary, general, and independent principles of the computational system of language within Chomsky's minimalist program. This trend is represented by Reuland (2011). Based mainly on his study of anaphora and binding in a range of Germanic and Romance languages, Reuland argued that anaphoric dependencies and their (substantial) cross-linguistic variations (in these languages) can be derived naturally by the interaction of the lexicon, syntax, semantics, and discourse components of the language system, which reflect the cognitive capacities and design of language.

---

[6] One proposal to accommodate counterexamples of this kind is to reinterpret binding theory as a theory of referential dependency, along the lines of Evans (1980). On this view, the reference of the pronoun in (9.26) has to be antecedently assigned in the previous sentence, and consequently the pronoun can be accidentally co-indexed with the relevant r-expression, thus in conformity with binding condition C_2. But, as pointed out in Huang (2000a, 2004a), such an escape mechanism both over- and under generates, which indicates that Evans's proposal is not valid in explaining away counterexamples like (9.26).

This new development constitutes an important step forward in our understanding of anaphora and binding. Firstly, from a theoretical and methodological point of view, to account for anaphora and binding in terms of some elementary, general, and independent principles of Chomsky's minimalist program is much preferable to explaining them by means of some *ad hoc*, local conditions that are stipulated specifically for them. Secondly, while their focus is still on the syntax and semantics of anaphora and binding, the latest generative analyses of the kind exemplified by Reuland (2011) allow non-grammatical or pragmatic factors to play a role.

On the other hand, however, accounts of this type are not without problems of their own. Again, take Reuland (2011) as an example. Theoretically and methodologically, Reuland's analysis still suffers from containing too many rules, conditions, and principles. In other words, the theoretical machinery is not parsimonious enough. Next, from an empirical perspective, it is unclear to what extent Reuland's analysis can extend to languages other than the Germanic and Romance ones he has examined. For example, within Reuland's framework, the syntactic binding of a morphologically simplex SE-anaphor (e.g. *zich* in Dutch, *ziji* in Chinese, and *caki* in Korean) needs to enter an A-chain that is created by movement. In order for a SE-anaphor to enter an A-chain, structural Case must be checked, which is achieved via the inflectional system of a language. While this analysis may work for a Germanic language (such as Dutch) and/or a Romance language (such as French), it does not apply to, for example, Chinese, because Chinese is a language which lacks any inflectional mechanism. Consequently, given that in Reuland's system no structural Case checking means no A-chain, binding of a SE-anaphor in a language like Chinese has to be ruled out in narrow syntax, though allowed in pragmatics, to which I turn.

9.4. A revised neo-Gricean pragmatic theory of anaphora

In the previous section, I have shown that Chomsky's binding conditions are not adequate in accounting for the cross-linguistic binding patterns. In this section, I shall present a revised neo-Gricean pragmatic theory of anaphora, based on Huang (2000a, 2000b, 2001b, 2001c, 2001d, 2002a, 2002b, 2004a, 2006b, 2007a, 2010c, 2013b, 2014; see also Levinson 1987b, 1991, 2000 and

Huang 1991a, 1991b, 1994, 1995, 1996).[7] As I have emphasized in, for instance, Huang (1991a, 1994, 2000a: 212–14, 2004a, 2007a), the pragmatic theory of anaphora I have been advancing does not deny the existence of distinct syntactic, semantic, and pragmatic levels and modes of explanation in linguistic theory. On the contrary, it presumes the independence of an irreducible grammatical stratum for pragmatically motivated constraints: calculation of pragmatic inferences of the Gricean sort has to be made over a level of independent syntactic structure and semantic representation. What I have been arguing is that pragmatics interacts with syntax to determine many of the anaphoric processes that are thought to be at the very heart of grammar. If this is the case, then a large portion of linguistic explanation concerning anaphora which is currently sought in grammatical terms may need to be shifted to pragmatics, hence the interaction and division of labour between pragmatics and syntax. This interface and division of labour between pragmatics and syntax may be summarized in a Kantian slogan: pragmatics without syntax is empty; syntax without pragmatics is blind (Huang 1994: 259, 2000a: 213).[8] What pragmatics does here is to provide a set of complementary, explanatory principles that constrains the production or interpretation of an utterance whose linguistic representation has already been antecedently cognized. But these are important and indispensable principles for linguistic explanation, for, as Horn (1988: 115) pointed out, 'a regimented account of language *use* facilitates a simpler and more elegant description of language *structure*' (original italics). Furthermore, the extent to which syntax and pragmatics interact varies *typologically*. There is a class of languages (such as Chinese, Japanese, and Korean) where pragmatics plays a central role which in familiar European languages (such as English, French, and German) has hitherto been alleged to be played by grammar. In these pragmatic languages, many of the constraints on the alleged grammatical processes are in fact primarily due to principles of language use rather than rules of grammatical structure.

The central idea underlying my revised neo-Gricean pragmatic theory is that the interpretation of certain patterns of anaphora can be made utilizing

---

[7] For a survey of some earlier neo-Gricean pragmatic analyses of anaphora, see Huang (1991a, 1994, 2004a, 2007a).

[8] Cf. Kant's original apothegm from his *Critique of pure reason*: 'Concepts without percepts are empty; percepts without concepts are blind' (75 B, the Norman Kemp Smith translation).

pragmatic inference, dependent on a language user's knowledge of the range of options available in the grammar, and of the systematic use or avoidance of particular anaphoric expressions or structures on particular occasions. Put slightly differently, anaphoricity is not a property of specific lexical items (as can be seen by the fact that the binding conditions cannot be formulated as constraints on particular lexical items), but of the systematic use or avoidance of lexical items (see also Levinson 2000: 270). But before I take a look at the theory itself, let me first take a look at the general pattern of anaphora.

9.4.1. The general pattern of anaphora

Consider the contrast pairs of the following kind.

(9.27) a. Verdi$_1$ liked his$_{1/2}$ operas.
         b. He$_1$ liked Verdi's$_2$ operas.
(9.28) a. Mary$_1$ said that she$_{1/2}$ was an animal rights activist.
         b. She$_1$ said that Mary$_2$ was an animal rights activist.
(9.29) a. The rose$_1$ on the windowsill has come into blossom.
            The flower$_1$ is beautiful.
         b. The flower$_1$ on the windowsill has come into blossom.
            The rose$_2$ is beautiful.

There is a clear pattern here: the use of a reduced, semantically general anaphoric expression tends to indicate a locally co-referential interpretation, as shown by the a sentences of (9.27)–(9.29); whereas the use of a full, semantically specific anaphoric expression tends to mark a locally non-co-referential interpretation, as indicated by the b sentences of (9.27)–(9.29).[9] Following Levinson (1987b, 1991, 2000), let me call this the **general pattern of anaphora**.

(9.30) The general pattern of anaphora
        Reduced, semantically general anaphoric expressions tend to favour locally co-referential interpretations; full, semantically specific anaphoric expressions tend to favour locally non-co-referential interpretations.

---

[9] Cf. the binding condition B pattern, as exemplified in (9.9b), where the use of a reduced, semantically specific anaphoric expression indicates a locally disjoint reference interpretation. But as we shall see shortly, this is exactly what is predicted by my revised pragmatic theory of anaphora.

9.4.2. A revised neo-Gricean pragmatic apparatus
for anaphora

Now, assuming that the general pattern of anaphora is largely an instantiation, in the realm of anaphoric reference, of the systematic interaction of
the three Levinsonian neo-Gricean pragmatic principles, discussed in
Chapter 2, the question to be raised next is how it can be given an account
in terms of the operation of these principles.

   Applying the Q-, I-, and M-principles to the domain of anaphoric reference, one can derive a **revised neo-Gricean pragmatic apparatus** for the
interpretation of various types of anaphoric expression. Assuming the **hierarchy of referentiality for different kinds of anaphoric expression** in (9.31),
along the lines of Burzio (1991, 1996), Levinson (1991, 2000), and Huang
(1991a, 1994, 2000a: 214–16, 2007a), this pragmatic apparatus for anaphora can be presented in (9.32), with a **revised disjoint reference presumption**
(**RDRP**) given in (9.33).

(9.31) A hierarchy of referentiality for deferent types of anaphoric expression
        Anaphors < pronominals < r-expressions
        (Anaphors are less referential than pronominals, and pronominals are less
        referential than r-expressions.[10])

(9.32) A revised neo-Gricean pragmatic apparatus for anaphora (Huang 2000a,
        2004a)
        a. Interpretation principles
             (i) The use of an anaphoric expression x I-implicates a locally co-
                 referential interpretation, unless (ii) or (iii).
            (ii) There is an anaphoric Q/Horn-scale $<x, y>$, where informally x is
                 semantically stronger than y, in which case the use of y Q-implicates
                 the complement of the I-implicature associated with the use of x, in
                 terms of reference.
           (iii) There is an anaphoric M-scale $\{x, y\}$, where informally x is
                 unmarked with respect to or simpler than y, in which case the use
                 of y M-implicates the complement of the I-implicature associated
                 with the use of x, in terms of either reference or expectedness.
        b. Consistency constraints
             Any interpretation implicated by a. is subject to the requirement of
             consistency with

---

[10] Regarding the referentiality of empty categories, zero anaphors, or gaps, some
can be grouped with anaphors, and others with pronominals.

(i) The RDRP (see (9.33)).

(ii) Information saliency, so that

    (a) implicatures due to matrix constructions may take precedence over implicatures due to subordinate constructions, and

    (b) implicatures to co-reference may be preferred according to the saliency of antecedent in line with the hierarchy topic > subject > object, etc.; and

(iii) General implicature constraints, namely,

    (a) background assumptions

    (b) contextual factors

    (c) meaning$_{nn}$, and

    (d) semantic entailments.

(9.33)   A revised disjoint reference presumption (RDRP) (Huang 2000a, 2004a)
The co-arguments of a predicate are intended to be disjoint, unless one of them is reflexive-marked.[11]

At this point, it is useful to draw the reader's attention to the distinction of whether or not an anaphoric expression and its antecedent are the co-arguments of a single predicate. If they are, then the predicate may be reflexive-marked, to use Reinhart and Reuland's term. As pointed out in Huang (2000a: 163–4, 216–18, 2004a), a predicate can in general be reflexive-marked in three distinct ways. In the first place, it can be reflexive-marked lexically by the use of an inherently reflexive verb, as in (9.11a), and (9.34).

(9.34)   a. On that occasion, the boys behaved (themselves) badly.
        b. *On that occasion, the boys behaved the girls badly.

Here, the English verb *behave* is an inherently reflexive verb. This can be seen by the fact that it cannot be used as a transitive verb, as shown by the ungrammaticality of (9.34b) (see Huang 2000a: 216–17 for detailed analysis of the use of inherently reflexive verbs). Secondly, a predicate can be reflexive-marked morphologically by the employment of a reflexive affix attached to the verb. This is the case of (9.35).

(9.35)   (Chinese)
Lao Xie zisha   le.
Lao Xie self-kill PAR
'Lao Xie killed himself.'

---

[11] The disjoint reference presumption (DRP) was first put forward by Farmer and Harnish (1987), and goes thus: the arguments of a predicate are intended to be disjoint, unless marked otherwise.

In (9.35), the attachment of the Chinese reflexive prefix *zi* reflexive-marks the predicate. Finally, a predicate can be reflexive-marked syntactically by the use of a reflexive pronoun, as in (9.9a) and (9.36), or by a grammatical-ized or standardized lexeme typically denoting human body parts including the body itself, as in (9.37).

(9.36)   (Lithuanian, cited in Huang 2000a)
  Jis   gerbia   save.
  he   respects   self
  'He respects himself.'

(9.37)   (Kabuverdiano, Schladt 2000)
  Manel   feri   se   cabeca.
  Manuel hurt 3SG-POSS   head
  'Manuel hurt himself.'

In (9.36), the predicate is reflexive-marked by the Lithuanian morphologic-ally simplex reflexive pronoun in the overt syntax. In (9.37), it is reflexive-marked by the Kabuverdiano grammaticalized lexeme *cabeca*. While the latter device is attested in a wide variety of languages including Abkhaz, Basque, Biblical Hebrew, Georgian, Lisu, Malagasy, Mojave, and Tama-zight, it seems to be particular popular among African languages (see Huang 2000a: 162–3, 218–19 for detailed discussion).

Furthermore, the choice of one particular reflexivizing strategy over another in a language is in part determined by the semantics and pragmatics of the predicate in question. As already remarked, the meaning of the predicate can roughly be divided into two types here: self-directed and other-directed. By self-directed is meant that the action denoted by the predicate is typically performed by a human agent on him- or herself, whereas in the case of other-directed, the action denoted by the predicate is typically directed against others. Events such as grooming, change of body posture, and some emotions such as being ashamed/frightened/proud are typical examples of self-directed action/attitude. By way of contrast, communication, violent actions, and emotions such as love, hate, and being angry with/jealous of/pleased with fall standardly under the category of other-directed action/attitude (e.g. König and Siemund 2000; see also Haiman 1985a: 120–30, 168–74).

Now, of particular interest is that if one takes a careful look at the relationship between the meaning of a predicate and the various reflexiviz-ing devices a language has, a cross-linguistic, iconic correlation emerges (adapted from König and Siemund 2000):

(9.38)   The predicate meaning–reflexivizing strategy correlation
The more 'marked' a reflexivizing situation (e.g. other-directed) is, the more 'marked' (i.e. more complex) a reflexivizing strategy will be used to encode it.

What the **predicate meaning–reflexivizing strategy correlation** in (9.38) basically states is this: if a language has more than one reflexivizing strategy or form, one would expect the simplex ones to be employed for inherently reflexive predicates and other self-directed situations and the complex ones to be utilized for other-directed situations. Different languages, of course, may afford their speakers different means to conform to this correlation. In some languages (e.g. Modern Hebrew, Russian, and Turkish), one finds a choice between verbal and nominal strategies; in others (e.g. English, Kannada, and Spanish), the opposition is between zero and non-zero anaphoric expressions; in yet others (e.g. Dutch, Norwegian, and Swedish), there is a contrast between morphologically simplex and complex reflexives, or the opposition is between the morphologically simplex pronouns and morphologically complex reflexives, as in Frisian. Finally, the choice may be between the use of a single versus a non-single emphatic expression (e.g. Lezgian, Tsakhur, and Turkish) (Huang 2000a: 219–20; König and Siemund 2000). An example in support of this correlation is given in (9.39). (See Huang 2000a, 2004a for further exemplification.)

(9.39)   (Norwegian)
a. Edward   skammer   seg.
   Edward   shames   self
   'Edward is ashamed.'

b. Edward   foraktet   seg selv.
   Edward   despises   self self
   'Edward despises himself.'

In Norwegian, the marking of reflexivity can be accomplished by either the morphologically simplex reflexive *seg* or the morphologically complex reflexive *seg selv*. When the predicate denotes a self-directed action, as in (9.39a), the morphologically simplex *seg* is used. On the other hand, when the predicate denotes an other-directed action, as in (9.39b), the morphologically complex *seg selv* is employed—precisely as is predicted by the predicate meaning–reflexivizing strategy correlation in (9.38). This correlation is explainable in terms of the interaction between our I- and M-principle: to convey an unmarked message, use an unmarked linguistic expression, and to convey a marked one, use a marked linguistic expression.

See whether you can tackle Exercise 4 at the end of this chapter.

9.4.3. The binding patterns

With all this out of the way, I can now give a revised neo-Gricean pragmatic account of intrasentential anaphora. I shall begin with cases where the anaphoric expression and its antecedent are the co-arguments of the same predicate. Consider the paradigmatic binding patterns in (9.9). In (9.9a), since reflexivity is marked by a reflexive in the overt syntax, the RDRP is not applicable. Consequently, given (9.32a (i)) the interpretation of the reflexive is subject to the I-principle ('the speaker uses a semantically general term, and the addressee gets a semantically more specific interpretation'), which induces a locally co-referential interpretation.[12] Next, the binding condition B effect of (9.9b) can be obtained by the operation of both the Q-principle and the RDRP. By the referentiality hierarchy in (9.31) and the I-principle, a reflexive will be chosen if co-reference is intended, because the reflexive is referentially the most economic anaphoric expression for encoding reflexivity. This has the consequence that if the reflexive is not employed but a pronoun is used instead, a Q-implicature will arise; namely, no co-reference is intended. In other words, we have a Q- or Horn-scale <reflexive, pronoun> here, such that the use of the semantically weaker pronoun Q-implicates that the use of the semantically stronger reflexive cannot be truthfully entertained, that is, the co-referential reading which is associated with the use of the reflexive should be avoided (see (9.32a (ii))). Reflexives are semantically stronger than pronouns in that (i) syntactically, they typically need to be bound in some domain, and (ii) semantically, they are normally referentially dependent. For example, they cannot in general be used as deictic expressions. In the meantime, since the pronoun encodes a co-argument of a predicate which is not reflexive-marked, it is also subject to the RDRP. Thus, the potential, locally co-referential interpretation between the pronoun and the local subject encouraged by the I-principle is ruled out twice, first by the rival Q-principle (Q > I) and then by the RDRP. Finally, in the case of (9.9c), for the same reasoning, the r-expression, being semantically weaker than reflexives, will again be read first by the Q-principle and then by the RDRP as preferably being disjoint in reference with the local subject.

---

[12] A pragmatically less radical alternative is to retain binding condition A as a grammatically stipulated rule, as in Levinson (1991, 2000).

Unlike Chomsky's binding condition B, my pragmatic theory can also accommodate those binding patterns where a pronoun is happily bound in its local binding domain. This is the case with (9.12)–(9.15), and (9.40).

(9.40) (French)
        Pierre$_1$ a   honte de lui$_1$.
        Pierre has shame of him
        'Pierre is ashamed of himself.'

Here, the French reflexive *soi* cannot be used. Given the referentiality hierarchy (9.31), the pronoun *lui* becomes the next most favoured choice for encoding reflexivity. Since the RDRP is not at work here, because reflexivity is marked by the pronoun in the overt syntax, by (9.32a (i)), the preference for a locally co-referential interpretation induced by the I-principle will go through unblocked. Exactly the same analysis can be applied to (9.12)–(9.15). Thus, unlike Chomsky's binding condition B, my analysis allows reflexivity to be marked by a lower ranked anaphoric expression (such as a pronoun) if its immediately higher-ranked counterpart (such as a reflexive) is not available—an account that is empirically more accurate.

9.4.4. Beyond the binding patterns

What is even more interesting, from a pragmatic point of view, is the interpretation of cases where an anaphoric expression and its antecedent are not the co-arguments of a predicate, about which Chomsky's binding theory does not say anything. Regarding the reflexive/pronoun distribution in these cases, three patterns can be identified: (i) those permitting reflexives but not pronouns for a co-referential interpretation, as in (9.41), (ii) those allowing pronouns but not reflexives, as in (9.42), and (iii) those warranting both reflexives and pronouns, as in (9.17) and (9.43).

(9.41) (Russian, cited in Burzio 1996)
        On$_1$ dal ej   umyt' sebj$_1$/ego$*_{1/2}$.
        he   let her wash self/him
        'He$_1$ let her wash him$_{1/2}$.'
(9.42) John$_1$ said that *heself$_1$/he$_1$ wanted to further his research in nanotechnology.

(9.43)   (Icelandic, Sigurðsson 1990)

Jon$_1$ segir að   Maria   elski/elskar   sig$_1$/hann$_1$.
John   says   that   Maria   loves-SUBV/INDIC   self/him
'John$_1$ says that Maria loves him$_1$.'

Notice that in all these cases, the RDRP is irrelevant, because the anaphoric expression and its antecedent are non-co-arguments of the same predicate. Now, in the case of (9.41), the interpretation of the reflexive falls under the I-principle, which gives rise to a locally co-referential reading. The interpretation of the pronoun is then due to the working of the Q-principle. The use of a semantically weaker pronoun where a semantically stronger reflexive could occur solicits a classical Q-implicature, to the effect that a locally co-referential interpretation is not available. The same can be said of the 'reflexives only' cases of possessive anaphora in (9.18). Next, in the case of (9.42), because no reflexive is available as a possible candidate to indicate co-referentiality, by the referentiality hierarchy (9.31), a pronoun is used instead. Consequently, there is no Q- or Horn-scale <reflexive, pro­noun> to prevent the pronoun going under the I-principle, which engenders a locally co-referential interpretation. The same is just as true of the 'pronouns only' cases of possessive anaphora in (9.19). Finally, of particular interest to us is (9.43), where there is a distributional overlap between the reflexive and the pronoun. Given the referentiality hierarchy (9.31), one question arises: why should there be such an overlap? One plausible view, due to Burzio (1996), is that this may be the result of a conflict between the 'anaphors first' condition (induced by the I-principle in our theory), which favours the use of a reflexive, and the locality condition, which goes against the use of a reflexive and therefore indirectly facilitates the use of a pronoun. Regardless of whether or not this explanation is on the right track, within the proposed revised neo-Gricean pragmatic framework, (9.43) can be interpreted along the following lines. For reference, both the reflexive and the pronoun are subject to the I-implicated co-reference. However, since the grammar allows the unmarked pronoun to be used to encode co-reference, the speaker will employ it if such an interpretation is intended. This gives rise to the question as to why the marked reflexive can also be used. Put another way, a question may be raised as to whether or not there is any systematic semantic and pragmatic contrast between the reflexive on the one hand and the pronoun on the other. The answer is certainly yes. Intuitively, the use of a reflexive in these locations indicates some sort of **unexpectedness**

(Edmondson and Plank 1978). Examined in a more careful way, this unexpectedness turns out to be mainly of three types: (i) emphaticness or contrastiveness, (ii) logophoricity, and (iii) *de se* attitude or belief ascription.

Now try to do Exercise 5 at the end of this chapter.

9.4.5. Unexpectedness: emphaticness or contrastiveness, logophoricity, and de se attitude or belief ascription

Emphaticness or contrastiveness
In the first place, long-distance reflexives are used for emphatic or contrast marking. Needless to say, the use of an emphatic expression is subject to certain semantico-pragmatic conditions, such as those proposed by Baker (1995). Emphaticness typically produces a number of effects: (i) contrariety to expectation, (ii) availability of a natural negative gloss of the sort 'and not anyone else' etc., (iii) inducing a particular anaphoric/referential interpretation, (iv) contrastive stress, and (v) giving rise to a particular scope reading (e.g. Edmondson and Plank 1978, and especially Levinson 1991). Take, for example, (9.44).

(9.44)   (Chinese)
  Zhuxi   zongshi yiwei ta/ziji/taziji   dui,
  chairman   always think 3SG/self/3SG-self   right
  bieren   dou   bu   dui.
  other   all   not   right
  'The chairman₁ always thinks that he₁ is right, but others are all wrong.'

The use of the Chinese pronoun *bieren* 'other' is a clear indication that (9.44) conveys an emphatic or contrastive message. This seems to explain why intuitively, the use of *ziji* and *taziji* sound slightly more natural than *ta* on the indexed interpretation. Furthermore, *taziji* is intuitively felt to be more emphatic or contrastive than *ziji*. On my account, the emphaticness or contrastiveness associated with the use of a long-distance reflexive again falls out naturally from the M-principle: it is because the use of a reflexive in these contexts would carry an emphatic or contrastive message that would not be conveyed by the use of either a pronoun or a gap that it is chosen. Furthermore, the fact that the use of *taziji* is more emphatic or contrastive than that of *ziji* can also be explained by the M-principle. Given this principle, it is predicted that the use of a more prolix expression tends to give a more marked message, hence the more emphatic or contrastive reading for *taziji*. Looked at from a slightly different vantage point, an **iconicity principle** is in operation here, namely, the more coding material, the more emphatic or contrastive the message. This analysis can be extended to the use of the morphologically complex emphatics in (9.21)–(9.23) and the 'both reflexives and pronouns' cases of possessive anaphora in (9.20). Furthermore, the repetition of the r-expression in (9.25) may also be given a similar account, for it also seems to carry a contrastive, emphatic message '... but not anyone else'.

Logophoricity

The second dimension of unexpectedness arising from the use of a long-distance reflexive involves logophoricity. **Logophoricity** or **logophora** refers to the phenomenon in which the perspective or point of view of an internal protagonist of a sentence or discourse, as opposed to that of the current, external speaker, is being reported by utilizing some morphological and/or syntactic means. The term 'perspective' or 'point of view' is used here in a technical sense and is intended to encompass words, thoughts, knowledge, emotion, perception, and space-location (Huang 1994, 2000a: 172–204, 2001c, 2002b, 2004, 2007a, 2014). The concept of logophoricity was first introduced in the analysis of African languages like Aghem, Efik, and Tuburi, where a separate paradigm of logophoric pronouns is employed. By way of illustration, consider (9.45).

(9.45)   (Donno Sɔ, Culy 1994)
    a. Oumar   Anta   inyemeñ   waa   be   gi.
       Oumar   Anta   LOG-ACC   seen   AUX   said
       'Oumar₁ said that Anta₂ had seen him₁.'
    b. Oumar   Anta   woñ   waa   be   gi.
       Oumar   Anta   3SG-ACC   seen   AUX   said
       'Oumar₁ said that Anta₂ had seen him₃.'

In (9.45a), what Oumar has said is reported from the perspective of the internal protagonist Oumar, thus the use of the Donno Sɔ logophoric pronoun, which encodes a co-referential reading between it and the matrix subject *Oumar*. By contrast, in (9.45b), Oumar's words are reported from the perspective of the current, external speaker, hence the employment of the regular pronoun, which indicates a locally disjoint reference interpretation.

Cross-linguistically, logophoricity may be morphologically and/or syntactically expressed by one or more of the following mechanisms: (i) logophoric pronouns (e.g. Babungo, Mundani, and Yulu), as in (9.45a); (ii) logophoric addressee pronouns (e.g. Angas, Mapun, and Tikar), as in (9.46); (iii) logophoric verbal affixes (e.g. Ekpeye, Gokana, and Ibibio), as in (9.47); logophoric cross-referencing, as in (9.48); first-person logophoric marking, as in (9.49); and (iv) long-distance reflexives (e.g. Korean, Modern Greek, and Turkish), as in (9.50) (see Huang 2000a: 172–204, 2001c, 2002b, 2004a, 2007a, 2014 for detailed discussion of logophoricity; see also Sells 1987, Zribi-Hertz 1989, Stirling 1993, and Kuno 2004).

(9.46) (Mapun, Frajzyngier 1985)

n-   sat   n-wur   taji   gwar   dim   n   Kaano.
I   say   BEN-3SG   PROHB   ADDR   go   PREP   Kano
'I told him₁ that he₁ may not go to Kano.'

(9.47) (Gokana, Hyman and Comrie 1981).

aè   kɔ   aè   dɔ-ɛ.
he   said   he   fell-LOG
'He₁ said that he₁ fell.'

(9.48) (Akɔɔse, cited in Huang 2014)

a-hɔbe   a   mə-kag
he-said   RP   LOG-should go
'He₁ said that he₁ should go.'

(9.49) (Karimojong, cited in Huang 2014)

abu-papa   tolim   ɛbe   alozi   iŋez   moroto.
AUX-father   say   that   1S-go   3S   Moroto
'The father said that he was going to Moroto'

(9.50) (Marathi, Wali and Subbarao 1991)

Lili₁   samajte   ki   aapan₁   libral   aahot.
Lili   think   that   self   liberal   is
'Lili₁ thinks that self₁ is liberal.'

The use of long-distance reflexives in examples like (9.10), (9.17), (9.43), and (9.50) can be accounted for in terms of the M-principle. Since the grammar allows the unmarked pronoun to be employed to encode co-reference, a speaker will use it if such an interpretation is intended. On the other hand, if the unmarked pronoun is not used, but the marked long-distance reflexive is employed instead, then an M-implicature will be licensed, so that not only co-reference but logophoricity as well is intended.

De se attitude or belief ascription

Thirdly and finally, long-distance reflexives can also be employed to encode a *de se* attitude or belief ascription. What, then, is a *de se* attitude or belief ascription? In the philosophy of language, two types of attitude or belief about oneself are commonly distinguished: (i) attitude or belief held about oneself in a first-person way and (ii) attitude or belief held about oneself in a third-person way. As an example of type (i), consider my belief that I am healthy. This is a belief I hold about myself from a first-person perspective. In other words, it is a belief about myself which I would normally use a first-person personal pronoun *I* to encode, as in (9.51).

(9.51)   I am healthy. (said by Yan Huang)

Next, suppose, unbeknownst to me, I have just been awarded a research prize. I believe that the recipient of the prize is intelligent. While this belief of mine is also about me, it is not a belief which I would normally use the first-person personal pronoun *I* to express. Instead, I would normally use (9.52) to represent this belief of mine.

(9.52)   The recipient of the prize is intelligent.

Attitudes or beliefs of type (i)—self-locating attitudes or beliefs—are considered to be *de se* (Latin 'of oneself'), and attitudes or beliefs of type (ii), to be *de re* (Latin for 'about a/the thing) (see e.g. Castañeda 1966, 1967, 1968, 1989; Lewis 1979; Perry 1979, 2000, 2014; Stalnaker 1981; see also the papers collected in Feit and Capone 2013).

How, then, can the attribution of *de se* attitudes or beliefs from a third-person point of view be represented? Castañeda (1966, 1967) created an artificial pronoun *he*/she*/it** to encode the attribution of *de se* attitudes or beliefs from a third-person perspective. Thus, (9.51) above is represented in (9.53).

(9.53)   Yan Huang said that he* is healthy.

In other words, (9.53) is used to mark the self-conscious self-reference on the part of the reported speaker Yan Huang, who uttered (9.51).

Castañeda called the artificial pronoun he had created a '**quasi-indicator**', and claimed that it is the only device that allows the marking of a *de se* attitude or belief from a third-person viewpoint. Now, do quasi-indicators exist in natural language? The answer is yes. Regarding English, Castañeda suggested *he himself* is a quasi-indicator, as in (9.54). More recently, Chierchia (1989) pointed out that PRO is also a quasi-indicator, as in

(9.55). This proposal is further echoed by Higginbotham (2003) and Schlenker (2003) (but see e.g. Safir 2004 for counterevidence and counterarguments).

(9.54)   John claimed that he himself was an expert on eye photography.
(9.55)   John claimed PRO to be an expert on eye photography.

In Huang (2013), I showed that a long-distance reflexive like *ziji* in (9.10) can function as a quasi-indicator in the sense of Castañeda. In other words, it can be utilized to report on a *de se* attitude or belief to an attributee. The same neo-Gricean pragmatic analysis that has been made of the use of long-distance reflexives to encode logophoricity in the subsection above can also be applied here. Once again, if the unmarked regular pronoun is not employed, but the marked long-distance reflexive is used instead, then an M-implicature will be created to the effect that not only co-reference, but a *de se* attitude or belief ascription, is represented (see also Huang 2000a, 2013c, and Huang 2014 for an alternative Q_{scalar} implicature-based analysis within the same neo-Gricean pragmatic framework).

Regarding both logophoricity and *de se* attitude or belief ascription, also worth noting is that, if relevant, the choice between long-distance reflexives on the one hand and regular pronouns on the other is correlated with that between subjunctive and indicative mood: it is common for the use of a long-distance reflexive to go with subjunctive mood and for the employment of a regular pronoun to go with indicative mood, as (9.43) shows. Once again, the correlation seems to be a reflection of a semantic and pragmatic choice made by an external speaker about the responsibility he or she assumes for the truthfulness of what he or she is reporting. If a regular pronoun like *hann* and indicative mood for the verb like *elskar* are used, it shows that the speaker asserts that the report is true, because the report is *de re*. He or she cannot go on to deny it because doing so will give rise to so-called Moore's paradox (see Chapter 2). If on the other hand, a long-distance reflexive such as *sig* and subjunctive mood for the verb such as *elski* are deployed, it indicates that the speaker does not take the responsibility for the truth of the report, because he or she simply attributes an 'I'-thought to an attributee. He or she can then go on to deny it. Thus, the optionality of long-distance reflexives/regular pronouns and of subjunctives/indicatives provides the speaker with a useful means of expressing his or her attitudes toward the truth of what he or she is reporting, or more broadly, of expressing **evidentiality**, namely, expressing his or her degree of certainty or strength of commitment to a proposition or statement in terms of the reliability of the evidence available (see e.g. Huang 2014 for further discussion).

What I have discussed so far indicates that our revised neo-Gricean pragmatic theory can account for a range of facts relating to intrasentential anaphora that have puzzled and embarrassed Chomsky's syntactic analyses (see Huang 1994: chapters 7 and 8, 2000a: section 5.2, b, and 2007a for an extension of this analysis to discourse anaphora). Another main advantage of my theory is that, conversational implicatures being cancellable, one can always arrive at an interpretation that is best in keeping with our knowledge about the world. One example may suffice to illustrate this point.

(9.56) (Chinese)
    a. bingren   shuo   yisheng   zhidao Ø   mingtian   gei   ta   kaidao.
        patient   say   doctor   know   tomorrow   for   3SG   operate
        'The patient$_1$ says that the surgeon$_2$ knows that (I/you/he$_{2/3}$/we/they ...)
        will operate on him$_1$ tomorrow.'
    b. yisheng   shuo   bingren   zhidao Ø   mingtian   gei   ta   kaidao.
        doctor   say   patient   know   tomorrow   for   3SG   operate
        'The surgeon$_1$ says that the patient$_2$ knows that (I/you/he$_{1/3}$/we/they ...)
        will operate on him$_2$ tomorrow.'

Recollect that, given my pragmatic apparatus in (9.32), the interpretation of an anaphoric expression is subject to the I-principle, unless there is either a Q- or an M-contrast set or both to prevent the applicability of the I-principle. What the I-principle does here is to invite a locally co-referential interpretation for the anaphoric expression. In fact, there appears to be a rigid I-heuristic here: a local subject is in general preferred to a local object; a non-split antecedent is in general favoured over a split one; and a c-commanding antecedent is in general preferred to a non-c-commanding one. If none of these NPs seems to qualify as a possible antecedent, the next, more remote clause will be examined for possibilities in the same order, and so on until the root clause is reached. Failure to find an intrasentential antecedent will lead to the search for a previous discourse antecedent, preferably a topic, or settle for an 'arbitrary' interpretation. However, any anaphoric interpretation generated by my pragmatic apparatus must not run contrary to the RDRP, information saliency, and the general consistency constraints on conversational implicatures. In other words, on my account, all anaphoric interpretations are subject to the requirement of consistency with background assumptions; no interpretation would arise if it is not in keeping with real-world knowledge.

Returning to (9.56), given the I-heuristic, the preferred antecedent for the zero anaphor or gap in (9.56a) is correctly predicted to be the subject of the intermediate clause *yisheng* (the surgeon). However, by the same mechanism, the zero anaphor or gap in (9.56b) would first be interpreted as being preferably co-referential with the subject of the intermediate clause *bingren* (the patient). But this interpretation clearly runs counter to our background assumption that it is stereotypically a surgeon who operates on a patient rather than vice versa. This has the immediate consequence that such an interpretation is ruled out as the preferred interpretation. As a result, the zero anaphor or gap under consideration is I-implicated to be preferably co-referential with the matrix subject *yisheng* in (9.56b)—a correct consequence (see e.g. Huang 1991a, 1994, 2000a for further discussion).

> Have a look at Exercise 6 at the end of this chapter.

9.5. Theoretical implications

In the previous section, I have presented a revised neo-Gricean pragmatic theory of anaphora. In recent years, this theory has generated a new industry of production of pragmatic analyses of anaphora. See, for example, Kim (1993) on Korean, Blackwell (2003) on Spanish, Chiou (2010) and Chiou and Huang (2010) on Modern Greek, Huang (2010b) on switch-reference in Amele and logophoric verbal suffixes in Gokana, and Huang (2010j) on Maori. See also, for example, Demirci (2001) on the acquisition of binding of English reflexives by Turkish L2 learners and Sperlich (2013) on the acquisition of long-distance reflexives in Chinese by Korean and English L2 learners. Furthermore, new progress can confidently be anticipated in the near future.

What, then, are the important implications of our pragmatic theory for current linguistic theorizing? One major implication is that the theory forces a radical rethink of some of the current claims about the nature of grammatical rules and the way in which they interact with pragmatic principles. In the first place, many grammatical rules underlying anaphoric universals such as Chomsky's binding conditions are general, violable tendencies rather than absolute, exceptionless restrictions. Secondly, these rules are not something *sui generis*, but rather have their origins in language use. In other words, they are best seen as, to use Levinson's (1987a) metaphor, **'frozen pragmatics'**—the outcome of a gradual, diachronic process from utterance-token-meaning via utterance-type-meaning to sentence-type-meaning. This, of course, does not mean that these rules as they are today are not part of the grammar. On the contrary, they are and as such they should be dealt with in the grammar. But the point is that if they are the result of a historical grammaticalization process, they can no longer be held as evidence for a biologically pre-programmed human linguistic faculty. Thirdly, as already mentioned, pragmatics and syntax are interconnected in regulating anaphora and binding, though they are distinct levels and modes of linguistic explanation. The interface between pragmatics and syntax may in general be summarized in a Kantian apothegm: pragmatics without syntax is empty; syntax without pragmatics is blind. Furthermore, the extent to which pragmatics and syntax interact varies typologically. There exists a class of languages (such as Chinese, Japanese, and Korean) where pragmatics plays a central role which in familiar European languages (such as English, French, and German) has hitherto been alleged to be played by the grammar. In these pragmatic languages, many of the constraints on anaphora are primarily due to principles of language use rather than rules of grammatical structure. From a diachronic viewpoint, languages seem to change from being more pragmatic to more syntactic; from a synchronic perspective, different languages may simply be at different stages of this evolution.

A second major ramification our pragmatic theory has is concerned with current thinking about important issues such as universals, innateness, and learnability. While a pragmatic approach to anaphora such as mine does not entirely contradict Chomsky's innateness hypothesis, the fact that so many anaphoric processes in such a wide variety of geographically, genetically, and typologically distinct languages can be explained as learnable on the basis of language use does undermine Chomsky's claim to the universality of UG and decreases the plausibility of his innateness hypothesis.[13] This is because anaphora as such can no longer be taken to be mere instantiations of human mental templates. There are aspects of anaphoric universals which clearly are of a grammatical nature; there are also aspects of anaphoric universals which are equally clearly of a pragmatic nature. Put

---

[13] See Huang (2000a), which contains a rich collection of data drawn from a representative range of some 550 of the world's languages.

in a slightly different way, anaphoric universals are the product of both nature and nurture. The challenge before the linguist is to work out what are the grammatical rules and what are the pragmatic principles precisely, what is the relationship between them, and how they interact with each other.

It is encouraging that recent developments in generative grammar seem to be moving towards the view of the pragmatics–syntax interface being advocated in this chapter. In the case of Chomsky's minimalist program, given that the syntax/computational system is neither a phonological nor a semantic component, a large amount of current syntactic explanation has to be shifted to the LF and PF interfaces. As a consequence, syntax has inevitably to interact with semantics and pragmatics in a much more extensive way to link it to the mental world of cognition (e.g. Chomsky 1995: 219–20). This holds, of course, for the study of anaphora.[14] Similarly, the basic notions of **Optimality-theoretic (OT) syntax** are very much in the spirit of the revised neo-Gricean pragmatic theory I have advocated here.[15] In

---

[14] Chomsky has never put forward any systematic pragmatic theory of anaphora. However, in his work on binding, one can find occasional reference to pragmatic principles. One such principle is the 'avoid pronoun' principle (Chomsky 1981: 65). Another is the general discourse principle (Chomsky 1981: 227), which allows binding condition C_1 to be overridden given the appropriate context under certain circumstances, though the relevant circumstances have never been spelled out by Chomsky.

In more recent work on the minimalist program, Chomsky (1995: 138–43, 145–6, 150) argued that both derivation and representation are subject to a kind of 'least effort' guideline: there are no superfluous steps in derivation and there are no superfluous symbols in representation. The economy of derivation and representation is considered to be the functional driving force behind certain innate grammatical rules such as the last resort constraint on movement and the full interpretation principle. Furthermore, on a more global level, this principle is linked to some notion of cost in relation to UG principles and language-specific rules. UG principles are less costly than language-particular rules, therefore, they obtain wherever possible, with language-specific rules employed only if they are not applicable. Chomsky considered the least effort principle of this kind specific to the human language faculty, but more compelling evidence is needed before such a claim can be substantiated (see also Huang 2000a: for a critique of some minimalist analyses of anaphora).

[15] Optimality theory (OT) can best be seen as a revisionist or dissident version of Chomsky's generative grammar. From a cognitive point of view, while Chomsky's principles-and-parameters theory and its minimalist descendent are largely rooted in Fodor's cognitive modularity theory (see Chapter 7), OT is associated at least in part

fact, some of the insights central to an OT syntactic analysis such as competition, hierarchy, and soft constraints (e.g. Legendre, Grimshaw, and Viker 2001; Blutner and Zeevat 2004) have already been independently developed in a pragmatic approach like mine (see also Mattausch 2004 for an attempt to recast a neo-Gricean pragmatic analysis in terms of bidirectional OT). All this, I hope, will open the way for a more interactive approach between the **I[nternalized** and **intensional]**- and **E[xternalized** and **extensional]**-models of language study (Chomsky 1995: 15–17). It seems unlikely that we can provide a satisfactory answer to what Chomsky (1986) has referred to as **Humboldt's problem** and as (a special case of) Plato(-Russell)'s problem without even trying to tackle **Descartes's problem**. In other words, the full understanding of the nature and ontogeny of knowledge of language appears to be partially dependent on a better understanding of the (creative) use of that knowledge.

9.6. Summary

In this chapter, I have discussed the interface between pragmatics and syntax, focusing on anaphora and binding. Section 9.1 outlined Chomsky's views about language and linguistics. Then, Section 9.2 presented Chomsky's binding conditions, and Section 9.3 pointed out some of the problems for these conditions. After that, Section 9.4 provided a revised neo-Gricean

with connectionism (see note 9 of Chapter 7). Next, unlike in the principles-and-parameters theory and the minimalist program, in OT, grammatical regularities are considered to be fundamentally representational and parallel rather than derivational and serial in nature. UG consists of a set of universal but soft (that is, violable) constraints. The grammatical system contains (i) a lexicon, (ii) a set of constraints, (iii) a ranking of constraints, and (iv) two functions: a generator (GEN), which creates a candidate output for the input, and an evaluator (EVAL), which selects the best (or optimal) candidate for the given input among the candidate output produced by the generator. Thus, in OT, universals are expressed in universal but violable constraints. Language variation is accounted for in terms of alternative rankings of the universal constraints. Language acquisition is considered to be a process of constraints ranking and re-ranking within the limits set up by UG (see e.g. Prince and Smolensky 1993, 2004; Archangeli and Langendoen 1997; Blutner and Zeevat 2004. See also Huang 2000a for a discussion of some OT analyses of anaphora).

pragmatic theory of anaphora. Finally, Section 9.5 considered some theoretical implications of the neo-Gricean pragmatic approach to anaphora for
current linguistic theorizing.

Key concepts

pragmatics–syntax interface
anaphora
anaphoric expression
antecedent
NP-anaphora
N-bar-anaphora
logical problem of language acquisition
innateness hypothesis
Universal Grammar (UG)
anaphor
pronominal
r[eferential]-expression
binding conditions A, B, and C
binding
c-command
government category (GC)
long-distance reflexive
binding conditions C_1 and C_2
general pattern of anaphora
revised neo-Gricean pragmatic theory of anaphora
referentiality hierarchy
revised disjoint reference presumption (RDRP)
predicate meaning–reflexivizing strategy correlation
emphaticness or contrastiveness
logophoricity
de se attitude or belief ascription
evidentiality

Exercises and essay questions

1. Of the following grammatical and ungrammatical sentences, which can, and which cannot, be accounted for by Chomsky's binding condition A?
   (i) Susan$_1$ hates herself$_1$.
   (ii) (Norwegian, cited in Huang 2000a)

   *Jon$_1$ foraktet   seg$_1$.

   Jon   despises   self

   'Jon despises himself.'

   (iii) *Chopin$_1$ thought that Liszt$_2$ adored himself$_1$

   (iv) (Marathi, Wali and Subbarao 1991)

   Lili$_1$ samajate   ki   Susi$_2$ aaplyaa-laa$_1$ haste.

   Lili   thinks   that   Susi   self-to   laughs

   'Lili$_1$ thinks that Susi laughs at self$_1$.'

   (v) *Chopin$_1$ believed that himself$_1$ was a poet of the piano.

   (vi) (Icelandic, cited in Huang 2000a)

   Hann$_1$ sagði   að   sig$_1$ vantaði   hæfileika.

   he   said   that   self   lacked-SBJV   ability

   'He said that self lacked ability.'

2. Of the following grammatical and ungrammatical sentences, which are, and which are not, accountable in terms of Chomsky's binding condition A, paying particular attention to c-command?
   (i) Madonna's$_1$ mother$_2$ admired herself$_2$.
   (ii) *Madonna's$_1$ mother$_2$ admired herself$_1$.
   (iii) (Chinese)

   Xiaoming$_1$ de   cuxin   hai   le   ziji$_1$.

   Xiaoming   POSS   carelessness   harm   PFV   self

   'Xiaoming's careless has brought harm to him.'

   (iv) (Zribi-Hertz 1995)

   John's$_1$ face turned red despite himself$_1$.

   (v) *John's$_1$ fortune saved himself$_1$.

   (vi) (Icelandic, cited in Huang 2000a)

   Skoðun   Siggu$_1$ er   að   sig$_1$ vanti   hæfileika.

   Opinion   Sigga's   is   that   self   lacks   talent

   'Sigga's opinion is that self lacks talent.'

3. Of the following grammatical and ungrammatical sentences, which can, and which cannot, be accommodated by Lasnik's binding condition C_1 or C_2?
   (i) Blair$_1$ admired Blair$_2$.
   (ii) *George W. Bush$_1$ thought that Tony Blair admired George W. Bush$_1$.
   (iii) (Vietnamese)

   Ho Chi Minh$_1$ tin   Ho Chi Minh$_1$ sẽ   thăńg.

   Ho Chi Minh   thinks   Ho Chi Minh   will   win

   'Ho Chi Minh$_1$ thinks that Ho Chi Minh$_1$ will win.'

     (iv) Mike's$_1$ father disliked Mike$_1$.

     (v) Victoria and David Beckham$_1$ have one thing in common: she thinks that David$_1$ is a football genius and he$_1$ thinks that David$_1$ is a football genius.

     (vi) *He$_1$ admired Charles Darwin$_1$.

4. Can you explain the contrast between the a and b sentences in terms of the predicate meaning–reflexivizing strategy correlation?

     (i) (Dutch, adapted from Reinhart and Reuland 1993)

        a. Willem   wast   zich.

           Willem   washes   self

           'Willem washes (himself).'

        b. Willem   bewondert   zichzelf.

           Willem   admires   self self

           'Willem admires himself.'

     (ii) (Turkish, König and Siemund 2000, errors corrected)

        a. yaka-mak

           wash

           'wash'

        a'. 'yaka-n-mak

           wash-EMPH

           'wash oneself'

        b. vur-mak

           beat

           'beat'

        b'. (Ø)   kendi   kendi-si-ni   vur-du.

           3SG   self   self-3SG-ACC   beat-PAST-3SG

           'He beat himself.'

5. How can the following cases of possessive anaphora be accounted for in terms of the revised neo-Gricean pragmatic theory?

     (i) (Arabic)

        As'ad$_1$ daxala   maktab-hu$_{1/2}$.

        Asad   enter-PST-3MSG   office-his

        'Asad$_1$ entered his$_{1/2}$ office.'

     (ii) (Telugu, Subbarao and Lalitha Murthy 2000)

        roojaa-ki$_1$ tana$_1$/atani$_2$ amma   anTee   iSTam.

        Roja-DAT   self's/his   mother means liking

        'Roja$_1$ likes self's$_1$/his$_2$ mother.'

     (iii) (Kannada, cited in Huang 2004a)

        raama$_1$ tanna$_1$/avana$_1$ makkaLanna   hoDedanu.

        Rama   self's/his   children-ACC beat

        'Rama$_1$ beat self's$_1$/his$_1$ children.'

6. Can you provide a neo-Gricean pragmatic analysis of the anaphoric patterns in each of the following sentences?

(i) Kylie$_1$ liked herself$_1$.

(ii) Kylie$_1$ liked her$_2$.

(iii) Kylie$_1$ liked Kylie$_2$.

(iv) Kylie$_1$ liked her$_2$ and she$_1$ gave her$_2$ a silk handkerchief.

(v) Kylie$_1$ liked her$_2$ and the woman$_3$ gave her$_2$ a silk handkerchief.

(vi) Barack Obama$_1$ said that he$_1$ would visit France in person.

(vii) Barack Obama$_1$ said that the President$_1$ would visit France in person.

(viii) (Korean)

Lee$_1$-un   caki$_1$/ku$_1$-ka   salang-ey   ppacyessta-ko   malhaysssta.
Lee-TOP   self/he-NOM   love-in   fell-COMP   said
'Lee$_1$ said that self$_1$/he$_1$ was in love.'

7. What is Chomsky's view about language and linguistics?

8. Can the distributional complementarity between anaphors and pronominals dictated by Chomsky's binding conditions A and B be maintained?

9. What are the common ways of reflexive-marking a predicate? Illustrate with your own examples.

10. To what extent can Chomsky's binding conditions be reduced to pragmatics?

11. What is logophoricity? How is logophoricity grammatically marked cross-linguistically?

12. A long-distance reflexive can be used to encode a *de se* attitude or belief ascription. How can this be accounted for in terms of neo-Gricean pragmatics?

13. What are the theoretical implications of the revised neo-Gricean pragmatic analysis of anaphora for current linguistic theorizing?

Further readings

Huang 2000a. Sections 1.2.1, 2.1, 2.3, 3.3, 4.2.

Huang 2004.

Levinson 2000. Chapter 4.

Glossary

For more terms and more detailed definitions, consult *The Oxford Dictionary of Pragmatics*.

accommodation: the pragmatic process in which an explanation is provided for how a missing proposition required by what a speaker has said is supplied by the addressee so that what has been said can be accepted.

***ad hoc* concept**: pragmatic adjustment of a lexical concept in the linguistically decoded logical form of a sentence uttered. The adjustment can be a narrowing or strengthening, a broadening or weakening, or a combination of both.

anaphora: a relation between two or more linguistic elements, in which the interpretation of one (called an anaphoric expression) is in some way determined by the interpretation of the other (called an antecedent).

broad context: any contextual information that is relevant to the working out of what a speaker overtly intends to mean, and to the successful and felicitous performance of a speech act.

communicative principle of relevance: a pragmatic principle which states that every ostensive stimulus (e.g. an utterance) conveys a presumption of its own optimal relevance.

constancy under negation: a property of presupposition, which dictates that a presupposition generated by the use of a lexical item or a syntactic structure remains the same when the sentence containing that lexical item or syntactic structure is negated.

constative: an utterance that is used to make an assertion or a statement.

context: any relevant features of the dynamic setting or environment in which a linguistic unit is systematically used.

conventional implicature: an aspect of non-truth-conditional meaning that arises because of the conventional features attached to a particular lexical item or linguistic construction.

conversational implicature: a meaning or proposition that is expressed implicitly by a speaker in the utterance of a sentence, which is meant without being part of what is said in the strict sense. It is derived from the saying of what is said via Grice's co-operative principle and its component maxims of conversation.

conversational implicature$_F$: a conversational implicature that is generated by a speaker's deliberately flouting one or more of the maxims of conversation.

conversational implicature$_{FO}$: a conversational implicature that is engendered by a speaker's directly observing the maxims of conversation.

(conversational) impliciture: a term coined by Kent Bach, which refers to a third category of speaker-meaning—a category that is implicit in what is said, and that is intermediate between what is said and what is conversationally implicated.

co-operative principle: the overarching principle put forward by Grice in his theory of conversational implicature, which determines the way in which language is used most efficiently and effectively to achieve co-operative, rational interaction in communication.

de se: Latin for 'of oneself'. It refers to the general phenomenon of self-locating attitudes or beliefs, that is, attitudes or beliefs about self.

defeasibility or **cancellability**: the property that a meaning or inference can simply disappear in certain linguistic or non-linguistic contexts.

deictic expression: an expression that has the deictic usage as basic or central. Demonstratives, first- and second-person pronouns, tense markers, adverbs of time and space, and motion verbs are typical deictic expressions. By contrast, a non-deictic expression is an expression that does not have a deictic usage as basic or central. For example, third-person pronouns in English are not taken to be deictic expressions.

deixis: the phenomenon whereby features of context of utterance or speech event are encoded by lexical and/or grammatical means in a language.

direct speech act: a speech act whose illocutionary force and sentence type are directly matched. In addition, an explicit performative, which happens to be in the declarative form, is also taken to be a direct speech act.

discourse, **text** or **textual deixis**: the use of a linguistic expression within some utterance to point to the current, preceding, or following utterances in the same spoken or written discourse.

embedded implicature: a seeming conversational implicature that is engendered locally at the sub-sentential level, typically occurring in a clause that is embedded under a logical operator such as a propositional attitude verb, a conditional, and a comparative.

emotional deixis: the encoding of emotional proximity or distance between a speaker and the entity referred to.

entailment: a semantic relation between propositions or sentences expressing propositions. For *p* to entail *q*, whenever *p* is true, *q* is also true. By contrast, if *p* is false, nothing is said about the truth-value of *q*.

explicature: a term used in relevance theory to refer to an inferential development of one of the incomplete conceptual representations or logical forms encoded by an utterance. It functions to flesh out the linguistically given incomplete logical form of a sentence uttered, yielding fully propositional content.

face: the public self-image that every member of a society claims for him- or herself.

facility condition: a set of conditions that the world must meet for a performative or speech act to be appropriate or felicitous.

free enrichment: a primary pragmatic process whereby the linguistically decoded logical form of a sentence uttered is conceptually enriched.

general pattern of anaphora: reduced, semantically general anaphoric expressions tend to favour locally co-referential interpretations; full, semantically specific anaphoric expressions tend to favour locally non-co-referential interpretations.

generalized conversational implicature (GCI): a conversational implicature that arises without requiring any particular contextual conditions.

Grice's circle: the problem of explaining how what is conversationally implicated can be defined in contrast to and calculated on the basis of what is said, given that what is said seems to both determine and to be determined by what is conversationally implicated.

I-principle: an upper-bounding neo-Gricean pragmatic principle, which may be (and characteristically is) exploited to generate lower-bounding I-implicatures.

illocutionary act: a speech act or action intended to be performed by a speaker in uttering a linguistic expression, by virtue of the conventional force associated with it, either explicitly or implicitly.

impoliteness: any face-aggravating behaviour including verbal behaviour, relative to a particular context, performed by an interlocutor.

indirect speech act: a speech act whose illocutionary force and sentence type are not directly matched.

intrusive construction: a construction in which the truth conditions of the whole depend in part on the conversational implicatures of the parts.

linguistic underdeterminacy thesis: the view that the linguistically encoded meaning of a sentence radically underdetermines the proposition a speaker expresses when he or she utters that sentence.

locutionary act: a speech act of producing a meaningful linguistic expression.

logophoricity: the phenomenon in which the perspective or point of view of an internal protagonist of a sentence or discourse, as opposed to that of the current, external speaker, is being reported by utilizing some morphological and/or syntactic means. The term 'perspective' or 'point of view', used here in a technical sense, is intended to encompass words, thoughts, knowledge, emotion, perception, and space-location.

long-distance reflexive: a reflexive that is bound outside its local syntactic domain, and in some cases even crosses sentence boundaries into discourse.

M-principle: a neo-Gricean pragmatic principle, the basic idea of which is that the use of a marked linguistic expression gives rise to a marked message.

maxims of conversation: a set of nine subprinciples of Grice's co-operative principle classified into four categories: Quality, Quantity, Relation, and Manner.

metalinguistic negation: a device for rejecting a previous utterance on any grounds whatever, including its morphosyntactic form, its phonetic realization, its style or register, or the conversational implicatures it potentially engenders.

narrow context: any contextual information that is relevant to the determination of the content of, or the assignment of, the semantic values to variables such as those concerning who speaks to whom, when, and where.

negative face: an individual's right to freedom of action and his or her need not to be imposed on by others. Negative politeness orients to maintaining the negative face of others. When one employs negative politeness, one tends to opt for the speech strategies that emphasize one's deference for the addressee.

Occam's eraser or **modified Occam's razor**: a particular version of Occam's razor, which dictates that senses or dictionary entries must not proliferate.

Occam's razor: a metatheoretical principle, which dictates that entities are not to be multiplied beyond necessity.

particularized conversational implicature (PCI): a conversational implicature whose generation requires some particular contextual conditions.

performative: an utterance that is used not just to say things, but actively to do things or perform acts as well.

perlocutionary act: a speech act or action that produces consequences or effects on the audience through the utterance of a linguistic expression.

person deixis: the identification of the interlocutors or participant-roles in a speech event.

politeness: any behaviour including verbal behaviour of an interlocutor to maintain his or her face and the face of the individuals he or she is interacting with.

positive face: an individual's desire to be accepted and liked by others. Positive politeness orients to preserving the positive face of others. When one uses positive politeness, one tends to choose the speech strategies that emphasize one's solidarity with the addressee.

pragmatic intrusion: the phenomenon whereby the pragmatically enriched or inferred content enters or intrudes into the conventional, truth-conditional content of what is said.

pragmatics: the systematic study of meaning by virtue of, or dependent on, the use of language. The central topics of inquiry of pragmatics include implicature, presupposition, speech acts, deixis, and reference.

presupposition: a proposition whose truth is taken for granted in the utterance of a sentence. The main function of presupposition is to act as a precondition of some sort for the appropriate use of the sentence. This background assumption will remain in force when the sentence that contains it is negated.

presupposition projection problem: the problem of stating and explaining the presuppositions of complex sentences (as 'wholes') in terms of the presuppositions of their component simple sentences (as 'parts').

presupposition trigger: a lexical item and/or linguistic construction that engenders a presupposition.

proposition: what is expressed by a declarative sentence when that sentence is used to make a statement, that is, to say something, true or false, about some state of affairs in the outside world.

Q- or **Horn scale**: a semantic or lexical scale in which the semantically strong linguistic expression entails the semantically weak one, all linguistic expressions are equally lexicalized, of the same word class, and from the same register, and all are from the same semantic field.

Q-principle: a lower-bounding neo-Gricean pragmatic principle which may be (and characteristically is) exploited to create upper-bounding conversational implicatures.

reference: a relation that involves speakers, linguistic expressions, and the entity, or the set of entities, that these linguistic expressions stand for, or that is picked out by a speaker in using these linguistic expressions.

referring expression: any linguistic expression that can be used in an utterance to refer to a particular entity or set of entities in the external world.

relevance theory: a cognitive-pragmatic theory of utterance interpretation developed by Dan Sperber and Deirdre Wilson. Grounded in a general view of human cognition, the central thesis of the theory is that the human cognitive system works in such a way as to tend to maximize relevance with respect to communication.

saturation: a primary pragmatic process whereby a given slot, position, or variable in the linguistically decoded logical form is contextually filled.

scope principle: a principle which states that a pragmatically determined aspect of meaning is part of what is said (and, therefore, not a conversational implicature) if— and, perhaps, only if—it falls within the scope of logical operators.

semantic transfer: a primary pragmatic process whereby the concept literally expressed by the input proposition is transferred into a different concept, provided that there is a salient functional relation between the old and the new concepts.

sentence: a well-formed string of words put together by the grammatical rules of a language. As a unit of a language system, it is an abstract entity or construct defined within a theory of grammar.

social deixis: the codification of the social status of the speaker, the addressee, or a third person or entity referred to, as well as the social relationships holding between them.

space deixis: the specification of location in space relative to that of the participants at utterance time in a speech event. Other terms include place, spatial, local, and locational deixis.

speech act: the uttering of a linguistic expression whose function is not just to say things but actively to do things or to perform acts as well.

time deixis: the encoding of temporal points and spans relative to the time at which an utterance is produced in a speech event.

truth condition: a condition that the world must meet for a sentence to be true.

truth value: a notion that is associated with proposition. A proposition may be true or false. But the truth or falsity of a proposition may vary from utterance occasion to utterance occasion. However, on a particular occasion, a proposition has a definite truth value, that is, it is either true or false. It is true if and only if it corresponds to some state of affairs that obtains on that occasion, and it is false if and only if it does not.

unarticulated constituent (UC): a propositional or conceptual constituent of a sentence that is not linguistically expressed explicitly in the sentence.

utterance: the use of a particular piece of language—be it a word, a phrase, a sentence, or a sequence of sentences—by a particular speaker on a particular occasion of use.

References

ABBOTT, BARBARA (2006). Where have some of the presuppositions gone? In Birner, B. and Ward, G. (eds.) 1–20.

ABBOTT, BARBARA (2010). *Reference*. Oxford: Oxford University Press.

ABBOTT, BARBARA (forthcoming). Reference. In Huang, Y. (ed.).

ACHIBA, MACHIKO (2003). *Learning to request in a second language: a study of child interlanguage pragmatics*. Clevedon: Multilingual Matters.

AGHA, AZIF (1996). Schema and superposition in spatial deixis. *Anthropological Linguistics* 38: 643–82.

AGYEKUM, KOFI (2004). The socio-cultural concept of face in Akan communication. *Pragmatics and Cognition* 12: 73–95.

ALLAN, KEITH and JASZCZOLT, KASIA (eds.) (2012). *The Cambridge handbook of pragmatics*. Cambridge: Cambridge University Press.

ALLWOOD, JENS (2000). An activity-based approach to pragmatics. In Bunt, H. and Black, W. (eds.) 47–80.

ALPHER, B. (1987). Feminine as the unmarked grammatical gender: buffalo girls are no fools. *Australian Journal of Linguistics* 7: 169–88.

ALSTON, WILLIAM (1994). Illocutionary acts and linguistic meaning. In Tsohatzidis, S. L. (ed.) 29–49.

ALSTON, WILLIAM (2000). *Illocutionary acts and sentence meanings*. Ithaca, NY: Cornell University Press.

ANDERSON, A. R. and BELNAP, NOEL (1975). *Entailments*. 2 vols. Princeton: Princeton University Press.

ANDERSON, A. R. and BELNAP, NOEL (1992). *Entailments*. 2 vols. 2nd edition. Princeton: Princeton University Press.

ANDERSON, STEPHEN R. and KEENAN, EDWARD L. (1985). Deixis. In Shopen, T. (ed.) 259–308.

ANGOURI, JO and LOCHER, MIRIAM A. (eds.) (2012). *Journal of Pragmatics* 44(12). Special issue on theorising disagreement.

ANNAMALAI, E. (2000). Lexical anaphors and pronouns in Tamil. In Lust, B. et al. (eds.) 169–216.

ANSCOMBRE, JEAN-CLAUDE and DUCROT, OSWALD (1977). Deux *mais* en français? *Lingua* 43: 23–40.

ARCHANGELI, DIANA and LANGENDOEN, D. TERENCE (eds.) (1997). *Optimality theory: an overview*. Oxford: Blackwell.

ARIEL, MIRA (1990). *Assessing noun-phrase antecedents*. London: Routledge.

ARIEL, MIRA (2004). Most. *Language* 80: 658–706.

ARIEL, MIRA (2010). *Defining pragmatics*. Cambridge: Cambridge University Press.

ARUNDALE, ROBERT (2010). Constituting face in conversation: face, facework, and interactional achievement. *Journal of Pragmatics* 42: 2078–105.

ASHER, NICHOLAS and LASCARIDES, ALEX (1998). The semantics and pragmatics of presupposition. *Journal of Semantics* 15: 215–38.

ATLAS, JAY D. (1975). Frege's polymorphous concept of presupposition and its role in a theory of meaning. *Semantikos* 1: 29–44.

ATLAS, JAY D. (1977). Negation, ambiguity, and presupposition. *Linguistics and Philosophy* 1: 321–36.

ATLAS, JAY D. (1989). *Philosophy without ambiguity: a logico-linguistic essay*. Oxford: Oxford University Press.

ATLAS, JAY D. (1993). The importance of being 'only': testing the neo-Gricean versus neo-entailment paradigms. *Journal of Semantics* 10: 301–18.

ATLAS, JAY D. (1997). On the modularity of sentence processing: semantic generality and the language of thought. In Nuyts, J. and Pederson, E. (eds.) *Language and conceptualization*. Cambridge: Cambridge University Press. 213–28.

ATLAS, JAY D. (2004). Presupposition. In Horn, L. R. and Ward, G. (eds.) 29–52.

ATLAS, JAY D. (2005). *Logic, meaning, and conversation: semantic underdeterminacy, implicature, and their interface*. Oxford: Oxford University Press.

ATLAS, JAY D. and LEVINSON, STEPHEN C. (1981). It-clefts, informativeness and logical form: radical pragmatics. In Cole, P. (ed.) 1–61.

AUER, PETER (1984). Referential problems in conversation. *Journal of Pragmatics* 8: 627–48.

AUSTIN, J. L. (1962). *How to do things with words*. Oxford: Oxford University Press.

AUSTIN, J. L. (1975). *How to do things with words*. 2nd edition. Oxford: Oxford University Press.

AUSTIN, PADDY (1990). Politeness revisited: the dark side. In Bell, A. and Holmes, J. (eds.) *New Zealand ways of speaking English*. Clevedon: Multilingual Matters. 277–92.

AUSTIN, PETER (1982). The deictic system of Diyari. In Weissenborn, J. and Klein, W. (eds.) 273–84.

BABA, JUNKO (1999). *Interlanguage pragmatics: compliment responses by learners of Japanese and English as a second language*. Munich: Lincom Europa.

BACH, KENT (1994a). Conversational impliciture. *Mind and Language* 9: 124–62.

BACH, KENT (1994b). Semantic slack: what is said and more. In Tsohatzidis, S. (ed.) 267–91.

BACH, KENT (1995). Standardization vs. conventionalization. *Linguistics and Philosophy* 18: 677–86.

BACH, KENT (1997). The semantics–pragmatics distinction: what it is and why it matters. *Linguistische Berichte* 8: 33–50. Repeated in Turner, K. (ed.) (1999), 65–84.

BACH, KENT (1999). The myth of conventional implicature. *Linguistics and Philosophy* 22: 327–66.

BACH, KENT (2000). Quantification, qualification and context: a reply to Stanley and Szabó. *Mind and Language* 15: 262–83.

BACH, KENT (2001). You don't say? *Synthese* 127: 11–31.

BACH, KENT (2004). Pragmatics and the philosophy of language. In Horn, L. R. and Ward, G. (eds.) 463–87.

BACH, KENT (2005). Context *ex machina*. In Szabó, Z. G. (ed.) 15–44.

BACH, KENT (2006a). The top ten misconceptions about implicature. In Birner, B. J. and Ward, G. (eds.) 21–30.

BACH, KENT (2006b). What does it take to refer? In Lepore, E. and Smith, B. (eds.) 516–54.

BACH, KENT (2010). Implicature vs. explicature: what is the difference? In Soria, B. and Romero, E. (eds.) 126–37.

BACH, KENT (2012). Context dependence. In Garcia-Carpintero, M. and Kölbel, M. (eds.) 153–84.

BACH, KENT and HARNISH, ROBERT M. (1979). *Linguistic communication and speech acts*. Cambridge, MA: MIT Press.

BADE, NADINE (2013). Exhaustive interpretation and obligatory presuppositions. Paper presented at the 19th International Congress of Linguists.

BAKER, C. L. (1995). Contrast, discourse prominence, and intensification, with special reference to locally free reflexives in British English. *Language* 71: 63–101.

BALLMER, THOMAS (1975). Einführung und Kontrolle von Diskurswelten. In Wunderlich, D. (ed.) *Linguistische pragmatik*. Berlin: Athenäum-Verlag. 183–206.

BALLMER, THOMAS (1978). *Logical grammar: with special consideration of topics in context change*. Amsterdam: North-Holland.

BAR-HILLEL, YEHOSHUA (1954). Indexical expressions. *Mind* 63: 359–79.

BAR-HILLEL, YEHOSHUA (1971). Out of the pragmatic wastebasket. *Linguistic Inquiry* 2: 401–7.

BARA, BRUNO G. (2010). *Cognitive pragmatics: the mental processes of communication*. Cambridge, MA: MIT Press.

BARGIELA-CHIAPPINI, FRANCESCA and KADAR, DANIEL Z. (eds.) (2011). *Politeness across cultures*. Basingstoke: Palgrave Macmillan.

BARKER, STEPHEN (1991). *Even, still* and counterfactuals. *Linguistics and Philosophy* 14: 1–38.

BARKER, STEPHEN (2000). Is value content a component of conventional implicature? *Analysis* 60: 268–79.

BARKER, STEPHEN (2003). Truth and conventional implicature. *Mind* 112: 1–34.

BARRON, ANNE (2003). *Acquisition in interlanguage pragmatics*. Amsterdam: John Benjamins.

BARRON, ANNE (2005). Offering in Ireland and England. In Barron, A. and Schneider, K. P. (eds.) *The pragmatics of Irish English*. Berlin, New York: Mouton de Gruyter. 141–76.

BARSALOU, LAURENCE (1983). *Ad hoc* categories. *Memory and Cognition* 11: 211–27.

BATORI, ISTVAN (1982). On verb deixis in Hungarian. In Weissenborn, J. and Klein, W. (eds.) 155–65.

BAUERLE, R., REYLE, U., and ZIMMERMAN, T. E. (2003). *Presuppositions and discourse: essays offered to Hans Kamp*. Oxford: Elsevier.

BAX, MARCEL and KADAR, DANIEL (eds.) (2012). *Understanding (im)politeness*. Amsterdam: John Benjamins.

BAYRAKTAROGLU, ARIN (2001). Advice-giving in Turkish: 'superiority' or 'solidarity'? In Bayraktaroglu, A. and Sifianou, M. (eds.) 177–208.

BAYRAKTAROGLU, ARIN and SIFIANOU, MARIA (eds.) (2001). *Linguistic politeness across boundaries: the case of Greek and Turkish*. Amsterdam: John Benjamins.

BEAVER, DAVID I. (1997). Presupposition. In van Benthem, J. and ter Meulen, A. (eds.) *Handbook of logic and language*. Amsterdam: North-Holland. 939–1008.

BEAVER, DAVID I. (2001). *Presupposition and assertion in dynamic semantics*. Stanford: CSLI Publications.

BEAVER, DAVID I. (2008). As brief as possible (but not briefer). *Theoretical Linguistics* 34: 213–28.

BEAVER, DAVID I. and GEURTS, BART (2011). Presupposition. In Zalta, E. N. (ed.) *Stanford Encyclopedia of Philosophy*. The main part of this article is reprinted in Maienborn, C., von Heusinger, K., and Portner, P. (eds.) 2432–60.

BEAVER, DAVID I. and GEURTS, BART (2012). Presupposition. In Maienborn, C., von Heusinger, K., and Portner, P. (eds.) 2432–60.

BECHTEL, WILLIAM and ABRAHAMSEN, ADELE (1991). *Connectionism and the mind: an introduction to parallel processing in networks*. Oxford: Blackwell.

BECKER, ANGELIKA and MARY, CARROL (1997). *The acquisition of spatial relations in a second language*. Amsterdam: John Benjamins.

BECKWITH, SEONAID and DEWAELE, JEAN-MARC (2012). The effect of two years abroad on the development of apologies in the Japanese L2 of adult English native speakers. In Ruiz de Zarobe, L. and Ruiz de Zarobe, Y. (eds.) 275–306.

BELNAP, NOEL (1969). Questions: their presuppositions, and how they can fail to arise. In Lambert, K (ed.) *The logical way of doing things*. New Haven: Yale University Press.

BENZ, ANTON, JÄGER, GERHARD, and VAN ROOIJ, ROBERT (eds.) (2006). *Game theory and pragmatics*. London: Palgrave Macmillan.

BERG, JONATHAN (2002). Is semantics still possible? *Journal of Pragmatics* 34: 349–59.

BERGMAN, MARC L. and KASPER, GABRIELE (1993). Perception and performance in native and non-native apology. In Kasper, G. and Blum-Kulka, S. (eds.) 82–107.

BERTLOTET, ROD (1994). Are there indirect speech acts? In Tsohatzidis, S. (ed.) 335–49.

BEZUIDENHOUT, ANNE (2002). Generalized conversational implicatures and default pragmatic inferences. In Campbell, J. K. et al. (eds.) *Meaning and truth: investigations in philosophical semantics*. New York: Seven Bridges Press. 257–83.

BEZUIDENHOUT, ANNE (2010). The coherence of contextualism. *Mind and Language* 21: 1–10.

BEZUIDENHOUT, ANNE (forthcoming). Contextualism and semantic minimalism. In Huang, Y. (ed.).

BEZUIDENHOUT, ANNE and CUTTING, C. (2002). Literal meaning, minimal propositions and pragmatic processing. *Journal of Pragmatics* 34: 433–56.

BEZUIDENHOUT, ANNE and MORRIS, ROBIN K. (2004). Implicature, relevance and default pragmatic inference. In Novek, I. and Sperber, D. (eds.) 257–82.

BHAT, DARBHE (2004). *Pronouns*. Oxford: Oxford University Press.

BIANCHI, CLAUDIA (2004a). Semantics and pragmatics: the distinction reloaded. In Bianchi, C. (ed.) 1–11.

BIANCHI, CLAUDIA (ed.) (2004b). *The semantics/pragmatics distinction*. Stanford: CSLI Publications.

BIANCHI, CLAUDIA (2011). Contextualism. In Sbisà, M., Östman, J.-O., and Verschueren, J. (eds.) *Philosophical perspectives for pragmatics*. Amsterdam: John Benjamins. 53–70.

BIRNER, BETTY and WARD, GREGORY (eds.) (2006). *Drawing the boundaries of meaning*. Amsterdam: John Benjamins.

BISHOP, D. (1997). *Uncommon understanding*. Hove: Psychology Press.

BLACKWELL, SARAH E. (2003). *Implicatures in discourse: the case of Spanish NP anaphora*. Amsterdam: John Benjamins.

BLAKEMORE, DIANE (1987). *Semantic constraints on relevance*. Oxford: Blackwell.

BLAKEMORE, DIANE (2002). *Relevance and linguistic meaning: the semantics and pragmatics of discourse markers*. Cambridge: Cambridge University Press.

BLAKEMORE, DIANE (2004). Discourse markers. In Horn, L. R. and Ward, G. (eds.) 221–40.

BLASS, REGINA (1990). *Relevance relations in discourse: a study with special reference to Sissala*. Cambridge: Cambridge University Press.

BLOOM, PAUL (2000). *How children learn the meanings of the words*. Cambridge, MA: MIT Press.

BLOOM, PAUL (2002). Mindreading, communication and the learning of names for things. *Mind and Language* 17: 37–54.

BLOOMFIELD, LEONARD (1962). *The Menomini language*. New Haven: Yale University Press.

BLUM-KULKA, SHOSHANA, HOUSE, JULIANE, and KASPER, GABRIELE (eds.) (1989). *Cross-cultural pragmatics: requests and apologies*. Norwood: Ablex.

BLUM-KULKA, SHOSHANA and OLSHTAIN, E. (1984). Requests and apologies: a cross-cultural study of speech act realization patterns (CCSARP). *Applied Linguistics* 5: 196–213.

BLUTNER, REINHARD (1998). Lexical pragmatics. *Journal of Semantics* 15: 115–62.

BLUTNER, REINHARD (2004). Pragmatics and the lexicon. In Horn, L. R. and Ward, G. (eds.) 488–514.

BLUTNER, REINHARD (forthcoming). Formal pragmatics. In Huang, Y. (ed.).

BLUTNER, REINHARD and ZEEVAT, HENK (eds.) (2004). *Optimality theory and pragmatics*. New York: Palgrave Macmillan.

BÖER, STEVEN E. and LYCAN, WILLIAM G. (1976). *The myth of semantic presupposition*. Bloomington: Indiana University Linguistic Club.

BORG, EMMA (2004). *Minimal semantics*. Oxford: Clarendon Press.

BORG, EMMA (2007). Minimalism versus contextualism in semantics. In Preyer, G. and Peter, G. (eds.) 546–71.

BORG, EMMA (2009). On three theories of implicature: default theory, relevance theory and minimalism. *International Review of Pragmatics* 1: 63–83.

BORG, EMMA (2010). Semantic minimalism. In Cummings, L. (ed.) 423–5.

BOTHA, RUDOLF P. (1989). *Challenging Chomsky: the generative garden game*. Oxford: Blackwell.

BOTNE, ROBERT (2005). Cognitive schemas and motion verbs: COMING and GOING in Chindali (Eastern Bantu). *Cognitive Linguistics* 16: 43–80.

BOUSFIELD, DEREK (2008). *Impoliteness in interaction*. Amsterdam: John Benjamins.

BRAUN, DAVID (1995). What is character? *Journal of Philosophical Logic* 24: 227–40.

BRAUN, DAVID (1996). Demonstratives and their linguistic meanings. *Noûs* 30: 145–73.

BREHENY, RICHARD, KATSOS, NAPOLEON, and WILLIAMS, JOHN (2006). Are scalar implicatures generated by default? *Cognition* 100: 434–63.

BROWN, J. K. (1975). Iroquois women: an ethnohistoric note. In Reiter, R. (ed.) *Toward an anthropology of women*. New York: Monthly Review Press. 235–51.

BROWN, PENELOPE (forthcoming). Politeness and impoliteness. In Huang, Y. (ed.).

BROWN, PENELOPE and LEVINSON, STEPHEN C. (1978). Politeness: some universals in language usage. In Goody, E. N. (ed.) *Questions and politeness*. Cambridge: Cambridge University Press. 56–310.

BROWN, PENELOPE and LEVINSON, STEPHEN C. (1987). *Politeness: some universals in language usage*. Cambridge: Cambridge University Press.

BROWN, PENELOPE and LEVINSON, STEPHEN C. (1993). 'Uphill' and 'downhill' in Tzeltal. *Journal of Linguistic Anthropology* 3: 46–74.

BROWN, ROGER W. and GILMAN, ALBERT (1960). The pronouns of power and solidarity. In Sebeok, T. A. (ed.) *Style in language*. Cambridge, MA: MIT Press. 253–76.

BUBLITZ, WOLFRAM and NORRICK, NEAL (eds.) (2011). *Foundations of pragmatics*. Berlin: De Gruyter Mouton.

BÜHLER, KARL (1934). The deictic field of language and deictic words. In Jarvella, R. J. and Klein, W. (eds.) 9–30.

BULTINCK, BERT (2005). *Numerous meaning: the meaning of English cardinals and the legacy of Paul Grice*. Oxford: Elsevier.

BUNT, HARRY and BLACK, WILLIAM (eds.) (2000). *Abduction, belief and context in dialogue: studies in computational pragmatics*. Amsterdam: John Benjamins.

BURGESS, ALEXIS G. and BURGESS, JOHN P. (2011). *Truth*. Princeton, NJ: Princeton University Press.

BURQUEST, DONALD A. (1986). The pronoun system of some Chadic languages. In Wiesemann, U. (ed.) 70–102.

BURTON-ROBERTS, NOEL (1989). *The limits to debate*. Cambridge: Cambridge University Press.

BURTON-ROBERTS, NOEL (1999). Presupposition-cancellation and metalinguistic negation: a reply to Carston. *Journal of Linguistics* 35: 347–64.

BURTON-ROBERTS, NOEL (2007a). Varieties of semantics and encoding: negation, narrowing/loosening and numericals. In Burton-Roberts, Noel (ed.) 90–114.

BURTON-ROBERTS, NOEL (ed.) (2007b). *Pragmatics*. London: Palgrave Macmillan.

BURTON-ROBERTS, NOEL (2010). Cancellation and intention. In Soria, B. and Romero, E. (eds.) 138–55.

BURZIO, LUIGI (1991). The morphological basis of anaphora. *Journal of Linguistics* 27: 81–105.

BURZIO, LUIGI (1996). The role of the antecedent in anaphoric relations. In Fredin, R. (ed.) *Current issues in comparative grammar*. Dordrecht: Kluwer. 1–45.

BYON, ANDREW (2006). The role of linguistic indirectness and honorifics in achieving linguistic politeness in Korean requests. *Journal of Politeness Research* 2: 247–76.

CAP, PIOTR (2011). Micropragmatics and macropragmatics. In Bublitz, W. and Norrick, N. (eds.) 51–75.

CAPONE, ALESSANDRO (2009). Are explicatures cancellable? Toward a theory of the speaker's intentionality. *Intercultural Pragmatics* 6: 55–83.

CAPONE, ALESSANDRO, LO PIPARO, FRANCO, and CARAPEZZA, MARCO (eds.) (2014). *Perspectives on linguistic pragmatics*. New York: Springer.

CAPPELEN, HERMAN and HAWTHORNE, JOHN (2007). Locations and binding. *Analysis* 67: 95–105.

CAPPELEN, HERMAN and LEPORE, ERNIE (2005). *Insensitive semantics*. Oxford: Blackwell.

CARLSON, GREGORY (1977). A unified analysis of the English bare plural. *Linguistics and Philosophy* 1: 413–56.

CARLSON, GREGORY (2004). Reference. In Horn, L. and Ward. G. (eds.) 74–96.

CARNAP, RUDOLF (1942). *Introduction to semantics*. Cambridge, MA: Harvard University Press.

CARRUTHERS, PETER and SMITH, PETER (eds.) (1996). *Theories of theories of mind*. Cambridge: Cambridge University Press.

CARSTON, ROBYN (2002). *Thoughts and utterances: the pragmatics of explicit communication*. Oxford: Blackwell.

CARSTON, ROBYN (2004). Relevance theory and the saying/implicating distinction. In Horn, L. R. and Ward, G. (eds.) 633–56.

CARSTON, ROBYN (2010a). Modularity. In Barber, A. and Stainton, R. J. (eds.) *Concise encyclopedia of philosophy of language and linguistics*. Oxford: Elsevier. 480–1.

CARSTON, ROBYN (2010b). Explicit communication and 'free' pragmatic enrichment. In Soria, B. and Romero, E. (eds.) 217–85.

CASTAÑEDA, H.-N. (1966). 'He': a study in the logic of self-consciousness. *Ratio* 8: 130–57.

CASTAÑEDA, H.-N. (1967). Indicators and quasi-indicators. *American Philosophical Quarterly* 4: 85–100.

CASTAÑEDA, H.-N. (1968). On the logic of attributions of self-knowledge to others. *The Journal of Philosophy* 65: 439–56.

CASTAÑEDA, H.-N. (1989). *Thinking, language, and experience*. Minneapolis: University of Minnesota Press.

CERIA, VERÓNICA G. and SANDALO, FILOMENA (1995). A preliminary reconstruction of Proto-Waikurúan with special reference to pronominals and demonstratives. *Anthropological Linguistics* 37: 169–91.

CHALMERS, D. (1993). Connectionism and compositionality: why Fodor and Pylyshyn were wrong. *Philosophical Psychology* 6: 305–19.

CHANG, Y. (2008). How to say no: an analysis of cross-cultural difference and pragmatic transfer. *Language Sciences* 10: 1–17.

CHAPMAN, SIOBHAN (2005). *Paul Grice: philosopher and linguist*. London: Palgrave Macmillan.

CHASTAIN, CHARLES (1975). Reference and context. *Minnesota Studies in the Philosophy of Science* 7: 194–269.

CHEMLA, EMMANUEL (2008). An epistemic step for antipresuppositions. *Journal of Semantics* 25: 141–73.

CHEMLA, EMMANUEL and SCHLENKER, PHILIPPE (2012). Incremental vs. symmetric accounts of presupposition projection: an experimental approach. *Natural Language Semantics* 20: 177–226.

CHEMLA, EMMANUEL and SPECTOR, BENJAMIN (2011). Experimental evidence for embedded scalar implicatures. *Journal of Semantics* 28: 359–400.

CHEN, RONG (2010a). Pragmatics between East and West: Similar or different? In Trosborg, A. (ed.) 167–88.

CHEN, RONG (2010b). Compliment and compliment response research: A cross-cultural survey. In Trosborg, A. (ed.) 79–101.

CHEN, RONG and YANG, DAFU (2010). Responding to compliments in Chinese: has it changed? *Journal of Pragmatics* 42: 1951–63.

CHEN, YUAN-SHAN, CHEN, CHUN-YIN, and CHANG, MIAO-HSIA (2011). American and Chinese complaints: strategy use from a cross-cultural perspective. *Intercultural Pragmatics* 8: 253–75.

CHENG, DONGMEI (2011). New insights on compliment responses: a comparison between native English speakers and Chinese L2 speakers. *Journal of Pragmatics* 43: 2204–14.

CHIERCHIA, GENARO (1989). Anaphora and attitudes *de se*. In Bartsch, R., van Bentham, J., and van Emde Boas, P. (eds.) *Language in context*. Dordrecht: Foris. 1–31.

CHIERCHIA, GENNARO (2004). Scalar implicatures, polarity phenomena, and the syntax/pragmatics interface. In Belletti, A. (ed.) *Structures and beyond*. Oxford: Oxford University Press. 39–103.

CHIERCHIA, GENNARO (2006). Broaden your views: implicatures of domain widening and the 'logicality' of language. *Linguistic Inquiry* 37: 535–90.

CHIERCHIA, GENNARO (2013). *Logic in grammar: polarity, free choice, and intervention*. Oxford: Oxford University Press.

CHIERCHIA, GENNARO, FOX, DANNY, and SPECTOR, BENJAMIN (2012). Scalar implicature as a grammatical phenomenon. In Maienborn, C., von Heusinger, K., and Portner, P. (eds.) 2297–331.

CHIERCHIA, GENNARO and McCONNELL-GINET, SALLY (2000). *Meaning and grammar*. 2nd edition. Cambridge, MA: MIT Press.

CHIOU, MICHAEL (2010). *NP-anaphora in Modern Greek: a partial neo-Gricean pragmatic approach*. Newcastle upon Tyne: Cambridge Scholars Publishing.

CHIOU, MICHAEL and HUANG, YAN (2010). NP-anaphora in Modern Greek: a partial neo-Gricean pragmatic approach. *Journal of Pragmatics* 42: 2036–57.

CHOMSKY, NOAM (1981). *Lectures on government and binding*. Dordrecht: Foris.

CHOMSKY, NOAM (1982). *On the generative enterprise*. Dordrecht: Foris.

CHOMSKY, NOAM (1986). *Knowledge of language: its nature, origin and use*. New York: Praeger.

CHOMSKY, NOAM (1995). *The minimalist program*. Cambridge, MA: MIT Press.

CHOMSKY, NOAM (2012). *The science of language: interviews with James Gilvray*. Cambridge: Cambridge University Press.

CLARK, BILLY (2013). *Relevance theory*. Cambridge: Cambridge University Press.

CLARK, EVE V. (2004). Pragmatics and language acquisition. In Horn, L. R. and Ward, G. (eds.) 562–77.

CLARK, HERBERT H. (1996). *Using language*. Cambridge: Cambridge University Press.

CLIFTON JR., C. and DUBE, C. (2010). Embedded implicatures observed. *Semantics and Pragmatics* 3: 1–13.

COHEN, L. JONATHAN (1971). Some remarks on Grice's views about the logical particles of natural language. In Bar-Hillel, Y. (ed.) *Pragmatics of natural languages*. Dordrecht: Reidel. 50–68.

COHEN, L. JONATHAN (1977). Can the conversationalist hypothesis be defended? *Philosophical Studies* 31: 81–90.

COLARUSSO, JOHN (1989). East Circassian (Kabardian dialect) In Hewitt, B. G. (ed.) *The indigenous languages of the Caucasus*, vol. 2. New York: Caravan Books. 261–355.

COLE, PETER (ed.) (1978). *Syntax and semantics 9: pragmatics*. London: Academic Press.

COLE, PETER (ed.) (1981). *Radical pragmatics*. London: Academic Press.

COLE, PETER and MORGAN, JERRY (eds.) (1975). *Syntax and semantics 3: speech acts*. London: Academic Press.

COMRIE, BERNARD (1976). Linguistic politeness axes: speaker-addressee, speaker-reference, speaker-bystander. Pragmatic microfiche 1.7: A3–B1.

COMRIE, BERNARD (1985). *Tense*. Cambridge: Cambridge University Press.

COMRIE, BERNARD (1989). Some general properties of reference-tracking system. In Arnold, D. et al. (eds.) *Essays on grammatical theory and universal grammar*. Oxford: Oxford University Press. 37–51.

CORAZZA, EROS (2007). Contextualism, minimalism, and situationalism. *Pragmatics and Cognition* 15: 115–37.

CORBETT, GREVILLE G. (1991). *Gender*. Cambridge: Cambridge University Press.

CORBETT, GREVILLE G. (2000). *Number*. Cambridge: Cambridge University Press.

CORDELLA, MARISA (1990). Apologising in Chilean Spanish and Australian English. *Australian Review of Applied Linguistics* 7: 66–92.

COULMAS, FLORIAN (1981). Poison to your soul: thanks and apologies contrastively viewed. In Coulmas, F. (ed.) *Conversational routine: explorations in standardized communication situations and prepatterned speech*. The Hague: Mouton. 131–48.

COULMAS, FLORIAN (1982). Some remarks on Japanese deictics. In Weissenborn, J. and Klein, W. (eds.) 209–21.

COULSON, S. (2001). *Semantic leaps*. Cambridge: Cambridge University Press.

COWELL, ANDREW (2007). Arapaho imperatives: indirectness, politeness and communal 'face'. *Journal of Linguistic Anthropology* 17: 44–60.

CROFT, WILLIAM (1994). Speech act classification, language typology and cognition. In Tsohatzidis, S. (ed.) 460–77.

CULPEPER, JONATHAN (2011). *Impoliteness: using language to cause offence*. Cambridge: Cambridge University Press.

CULY, CHRISTOPHER (1994). Aspects of logophoric marking. *Linguistics* 32: 1055–94.

CUMMINGS, LOUISE (2005). *Pragmatics: a multidisciplinary perspective*. Edinburgh: Edinburgh University Press.

CUMMINGS, LOUISE (ed.) (2010). *The pragmatics encyclopaedia*. London: Routledge.

CUMMINGS, LOUISE (2013). Clinical pragmatics and theory of mind. In Capone, A., Lo Piparo, F., and Carapezza, M. (eds.) 25–56.

CUMMINGS, LOUISE (forthcoming). Clinical pragmatics. In Huang, Y. (ed.).

CYSOUW, MICHAEL (2002). 'We' rules: the impact of an inclusive/exclusive opposition on the paradigmatic structure of person marking. In Simon, H. and Wiese, H. (eds.) 41–62.

CYSOUW, MICHAEL (2003). *The paradigmatic structure of person marking*. Oxford: Oxford University Press.

DAHL, ÖSTEN (1985). *Tense and aspect systems*. Oxford: Blackwell.

DANZIGER, E. (1994). Out of sight, out of mind: person, perception and function in Mopan Maya spatial deixis. *Linguistics* 32: 885–907.

DASCAL, MARCELO (1981). Contextualism. In Parret, H. et al. (eds.) *Possibilities and limitations of pragmatics*. Amsterdam: John Benjamins. 153–77.

DASCAL, MARCELO (1994). Speech act theory and Gricean pragmatics: some differences of detail that make a difference. In Tsohatzidis, S. (ed.) 323–34.

DAVIES, MARTIN and STONE, TONY (eds.) (1995). *Mental simulation: philosophical and psychological essays*. Oxford: Blackwell.

DAVIS, WAYNE A. (1998). *Implicature: intention, convention, and principle in the failure of Gricean theory*. Cambridge: Cambridge University Press.

DAVITT, MICHAEL (2004). The case for referential descriptions. In Reimer, M. and Bezuidenhout, A. (eds.) 280–305.

DE JONGE, C. C. (2001). Natura artis magistra: ancient rhetoricians, grammarians, and philosophers on natural word order. In van der Wouden, T. and Broekhuis, H. (eds.) *Linguistics in the Netherlands 2001*. Amsterdam: John Benjamins. 159–66.

DE SOUSA MELO, CANDIDA (2002). Possible directions of fit between mind, language and the world. In Vanderveken, D. and Kubo, S. (eds.) 109–17.

DEMIRCI, MAHIDE (2001). Acquisition of binding of English reflexives by Turkish L2 learners: a neo-Gricean pragmatic account. *Journal of Pragmatics* 33: 753–75.

DENNY, J. P. (1982). Semantics of the Inuktitut (Eskimo) spatial deictics. *International Journal of American Linguistics* 48: 359–84.

DIESSEL, HOLGER (1999). *Demonstratives: form, function and grammaticalization*. Amsterdam: John Benjamins.

DILLER, ANTHONY (1993). Diglossic grammaticality in Thai. In Foley, W. A. (ed.) 393–420.

DIXON, R. M. W. (1972). *The Dyirbal language of North Queensland*. Cambridge: Cambridge University Press.

DIXON, R. M. W. (1977). *A grammar of Yidiɲ*. Cambridge: Cambridge University Press.

DIXON, R. M. W. (1980). *The languages of Australia*. Cambridge: Cambridge University Press.

DIXON, R. M. W. (2003). Demonstratives: a cross-linguistic typology. *Studies in Language* 27: 61–112.

DONNELLAN, KEITH (1966). Reference and definite descriptions. *Philosophical Review* 75: 281–304.

DONNELLAN, KEITH (1970). Proper names and identifying descriptions. *Synthese* 21: 335–58.

DONNELLAN, KEITH (1978). Speaker reference, descriptions and anaphora. In Cole, P. (ed.) 47–68.

DORAN, RYAN, BAKER, RACHEL E., MCNABB, YARON, LARSON, MEREDITH, and WARD, GREGORY (2009). On the non-unified nature of scalar implicature: an empirical investigation. *International Review of Pragmatics* 1: 211–48.

DORAN, RYAN, WARD, GREGORY, LARSON, MEREDITH, MCNABB, YARON, and BAKER, RACHEL E. (2012). A novel experimental paradigm for distinguishing between what is said and what is implicated. *Language* 88: 124–54.

DUCROT, OSWALD (1972). *Dire et ne pas dire*. Paris: Hermann.

DUCROT, OSWALD (1973). *La prevue et le dire*. Paris: Mame.

DUFON, MARGARET A., KASPER, GABRIELE, TAKAHASHI, SATOMI, and YOSHINAGA, NAOKO (1994). Bibliography on linguistic politeness. *Journal of Pragmatics* 21: 527–78.

DUMITRESCU, D. (2006). *Noroc!, Merci!, Qué Linso!, Sorry*: some polite speech acts across cultures. *Southwest Journal of Linguistics* 25: 1–37.

DUMMETT, MICHAEL (1973). *Frege: philosophy of language*. London: Duckworth.

DUMMETT, MICHAEL (1981). *Frege: philosophy of language*. 2nd edition. London: Duckworth.

DURANTI, ALESSANDRO (1992). Language in context and language as context: the Samoan respect vocabulary. In Duranti, A. and Goodwin, C. (eds.) 77–100.

DURANTI, ALESSANDRO (1997). *Linguistic anthropology*. Cambridge: Cambridge University Press.

DURANTI, ALESSANDRO and GOODWIN, CHARLES (eds.) (1992). *Rethinking context: language as an interactive phenomenon*. Cambridge: Cambridge University Press.

EBSWORTH, MIRIAM E. and BODMAN, JEAN (1993). Expressing gratitude in American English. In Kasper, G. and Blum-Kulka, S. (eds.) 64–81.

EBSWORTH, MIRIAM E., BODMAN, JEAN W., and CARPENTER, MARY (1996). Cross-cultural realization of greeting in American English. In Gass, S. M. and Neu, J. (eds.) 89–107.

EDMONDSON, JEROLD A. and PLANK, FRANS (1978). Great expectations: an intensive *self* analysis. *Linguistics and Philosophy* 2: 373–413.

EDMONDSON, WILLIS and HOUSE, JULIA (1991). Do learners talk too much? The waffle phenomenon in interlanguage pragmatics. In Philippson, R. et al. (eds.) *Foreign language pedagogy research*. Clevedon: Multilinugal Matters.

ELBOURNE, PAUL D. (2005). *Situations and individuals*. Cambridge, MA: MIT Press.

ELBOURNE, PAUL D. (2013). *Definite descriptions*. Oxford: Oxford University Press.

ELLEN, GINO (2001). *A critique of politeness theories*. Manchester: St. Jerome Publishing.

ELLIS, ROD (1994). *The study of second language acquisition*. Oxford: Oxford University Press.

ENFIELD, NICOLAS (2003). Demonstratives in space and interaction: data from Lao speakers and implications for semantic analysis. *Language* 79: 82–117.

EVANS, GARETH (1973). The causal theory of names. *Proceedings of the Aristotelian Society*: Supplementary Volume 47: 187–208.

EVANS, GARETH (1977). Pronouns, quantifiers, and relative clauses (I). *Canadian Journal of Philosophy* 7: 467–536.

EVANS, GARETH (1980). Pronouns. *Linguistic Inquiry* 11: 337–62.

EVANS, GARETH (1982). *The varieties of reference*. Oxford: Clarendon Press.

EVANS, NICHOLAS (1993). Code, inference, placedness and ellipsis. In Foley, W. A. (ed.) 241–80.

FARGHAL, MOHAMMED and HAGGAN, MADELINE (2006). Compliment behaviour in bilingual Kuwaiti college students. *International Journal of Bilingual Education and Bilingualism* 9: 94–118.

FARMER, ANN K. and HARNISH, ROBERT M. (1987). Communicative reference with pronouns. In Verschueren, J. and Bertuccelli-Papi, M. (eds.) 547–65.

FARNCESCOTTI, R. M. (1995). *Even*: the conventional implicature approach reconsidered. *Linguistics and Philosophy* 18: 153–73.

FAUCONNIER, GILLES (1975). Pragmatic scales and logical structure. *Linguistic Inquiry* 6: 353–75.

FAUCONNIER, GILLES (1985). *Mental spaces*. Cambridge, MA: MIT Press.

FEIT, NEIL and CAPONE, ALESSANDRO (eds.) (2013). *Attitudes* de se*: linguistics, epistemology and metaphysics*. Stanford: CSLI Publications.

FELIX-BRASDEFER, CESAR (2008). *Politeness in Mexico and the United States: a contrastive study of the realization and perception of refusals*. Philadelphia: Benjamin.

FELIX-BRASDEFER, CESAR and HASLER-BARKER, MARIA (2012). Complimenting and responding to a compliment in the Spanish FL classroom. In Ruiz de Zarobe, L. and Ruiz de Zarobe, Y. (eds.) 241–73.

FENG, GUANGWU (2010). *A theory of conventional implicature and pragmatic markers in Chinese*. Bingley: Emerald.

FETZER, ANITA (forthcoming). Context. In Huang, Y. (ed.).

FILLMORE, CHARLES J. (1971). *The Santa Cruz lectures on deixis*. Bloomington, IN: Indiana University Linguistic Club.

FILLMORE, CHARLES J. (1982). Towards a descriptive framework for spatial deixis. In Jarvella, R. J. and Klein, W. (eds.) 31–59.

FILLMORE, CHARLES J. (1997). *Lectures on deixis*. Stanford: CSLI Publications.

FINKBEINER, RITA, MEIBAUER, JORG, and SCHUMACHER, PETRA B. (eds.) (2012). *What is a context? Linguistic approaches and challenges*. Amsterdam: John Benjamins.

FODOR, JERRY (1983). *The modularity of mind*. Cambridge, MA: MIT Press.

FODOR, JERRY (2001). Language, thought and compositionality. *Mind and Language* 16: 1–15.

FODOR, JERRY and PYLYSHYN, Z. (1988). Connectionism and cognitive architecture: a critical analysis. *Cognition* 28: 3–71.

FOLEY, WILLIAM A. (ed.) (1993). *The role of theory in language description*. Berlin: Mouton de Gruyter.

FORTESCUE, MICHAEL (1984). *West Greenlandic Eskimo*. London: Croom Helm.

FOX, DANNY (2007). Free choice and the theory of scalar implicature. In Sauerland, U. and Stateva, P. (eds.) *Presupposition and implicature in compositional semantics*. Basingstoke: Palgrave Macmillan. 71–120.

FRAJZYNGIER, ZYGMUNT (1985). Logophoric systems in Chadic. *Journal of African Languages and Linguistics* 7: 23–37.

FRAJZYNGIER, ZYGMUNT and CURL, TRACI S. (eds.) (2000). *Reflexives: forms and functions*. Amsterdam: John Benjamins.

FRASER, BRUCE (1988). Motor oil is motor oil: an account of English nominal tautologies. *Journal of Pragmatics* 12: 215–20.

FRASER, BRUCE (1990). Perspectives on politeness. *Journal of Pragmatics* 14: 219–36.

FRASER, BRUCE (2010). Discourse markers. In Cummings, L. (ed.) 125–30.

FREGE, GOTTLOB (1892). Über Sinn and Bedeutung. Zeitschrift für Philosophie und Philosophisch Kritik 100: 25–50. Trans. as On sense and reference. In Geach, P. and Black, M. (eds.) (1952). *Translations from the philosophical writings of Gottlob Frege*. Oxford: Blackwell. 56–78.

FREGE, GOTTLOB (1918–1919). *The thought: a logical inquiry*. Translation in *Mind* 55: 289–311.

FREI, HENRI (1944). Systèmes de déictiques. *Acta Linguistica* 4: 111–29.

FRISSON, S. and PICKERING, M. J. (2007). The processing of familiar and novel senses of a word: why reading Dickens is easy but reading Needham can be hard. *Language and Cognitive Processes* 22: 595–613.

FRITZ, THOMAS A. (2003). 'Look here, what I am saying!': speaker deixis and implicature as the basis of modality and future tense. In Lenz, F. (ed.) 135–51.

FUKUSHIMA, SAEKO (2002). *Requests and culture: politeness in British English and Japanese*. Bern: Peter Lang.

GAJEWSKI, JON and SHARVIT, YAEL (2012). In defense of the grammatical approach to local implicature. *Natural Language Semantics* 20: 31–57.

GANDOUR, JACKSON T. (1978). On the deictic use of verbs of motion *come* and *go* in Thai. *Anthropological Linguistics* 20: 381–94.

GAO, H. J., ZHOU, Q. Q., and CHOW, D. (2012). A variationist study of compliment responses in Chinese. *International Journal of Applied Linguistics* 22: 347–73.

GARCÉS-CONEJOS BLITVICH, PILAR (2010). Introduction: the *status-quo* and *quo vadis* of impoliteness research. *Intercultural Pragmatics* 7: 535–59.

GARCIA-CARPINTERO, MANUEL (2000). A presuppositional account of reference-fixing. *Journal of Philosophy* 97: 109–47.

GARCIA-CARPINTERO, MANUEL and KÖLBEL, MAX (2008). *Relative truth*. Oxford: Oxford University Press.

GARCIA-CARPINTERO, MANUEL and KÖLBEL, MAX (eds.) (2012). *The Continuum companion to the philosophy of language*. London: Continuum.

GARRETT, MERRILL and HARNISH, ROBERT M. (2007). Experimental pragmatics: testing for implicature. *Pragmatics and Cognition* 15: 65–90.

GASS, SUSAN M. and HOUCK, NOËL (2000). *Interlanguage refusals: a cross-cultural study of Japanese-English*. Berlin: Mouton de Gruyter.

GASS, SUSAN M. and NEU, JOYCE (eds.) (1996). *Speech acts across cultures: challenges to communication in a second language*. Berlin: Mouton de Gruyter.

GATHERCOLE, VIRGINIA C. (1977). A study of the comings and goings of the speakers of four languages: Spanish, Japanese, English and Turkish. *Kansas Working Papers in Linguistics* 2: 61–94.

GAUKER, CHRISTOPHER (2003). *Words without meaning*. Cambridge, MA: MIT Press.

GAZDAR, GERALD (1979). *Pragmatics: implicature, presupposition and logical form*. London: Academic Press.

GEACH, PETER THOMAS (1962). *Reference and generality*. Ithaca, NY: Cornell University Press.

GEURTS, BART (1998). Presuppositions and anaphors in attitude contexts. *Linguistics and Philosophy* 21: 545–601.

GEURTS, BART (1999). *Presuppositions and pronouns*. Oxford: Elsevier Science.

GEURTS, BART (2009). Scalar implicature and local pragmatics. *Mind and Language* 24: 51–79.

GEURTS, BART (2010). *Quantity implicature*. Cambridge: Cambridge University Press.

GEURTS, BART and POUSCOULOUS, NAUSICAA (2009). Embedded implicatures?!? *Semantics and Pragmatics* 2: 1–34.

GEURTS, BART and VAN TIEL, BOB (2013). Embedded scalars. *Semantics and Pragmatics* 6, article 9: 1–37.

GHOMESHI, JILIA, JACKENDOFF, RAY, ROSEN, NICOLE, and RUSSELL, KEVIN (2004). Contrastive focus reduplication in English. *Natural Language and Linguistic Theory* 22: 307–57.

GIBBS, RAYMOND (1999). Speakers' intentions and pragmatic theory. *Cognition* 69: 355–9.

GIBBS, RAYMOND (2002). A new look at literal meaning in understanding what is said and what is implicated. *Journal of Pragmatics* 34: 457–86.

GIBBS, RAYMOND and MOISE, JESSICA (1997). Pragmatics in understanding what is said. *Cognition* 62: 51–74.

GODDARD, CLIFF (2011). *Semantic analysis: a practical introduction*. 2nd edition. Oxford: Oxford University Press.

GOFFMAN, ERVING (1967). *Interaction ritual: essays on face-to-face behavior*. New York: Anchor Books.

GOFFMAN, ERVING (1979). Footing. *Semiotica* 25: 1–29.

GORDON, DAVID and LAKOFF, GEORGE (1975). Conversational postulates. In Cole, P. and Morgan, J. (eds.) 83–106.

GREEN, GEORGIA, M. (1975). How to get people to do things with words: the whimperative question. In Cole, P. and Morgan, J. (eds.) 107–42.

GREEN, GEORGIA, M. (1996). *Pragmatics and natural language understanding*. 2nd edition. Mahwah, NJ: Lawrence Erlbaum.

GREEN, MITCHELL (1995). Quantity, volubility and some varieties of discourse. *Linguistics and Philosophy* 18: 83–112.

GREEN, MITCHELL (1998). Direct reference and implicature. *Philosophical Studies* 91: 61–90.

GREENBERG, J. H. (ed.) (1963). *Universals of language*. Cambridge, MA: MIT Press.

GREENBERG, J. H., FERGUSON, C. A., and MORAVCSIK, E. A. (eds.) (1978). *Universals of human language*, 4 vols. Stanford: Stanford University Press.

GRENOBLE, L. (1994). Discourse deixis and information tracking. *Proceedings of the Annual Meeting of the Berkeley Linguistics Society* 20: 208–19.

GRICE, H. P. (1957). Meaning. *Philosophical Review* 66: 377–88.

GRICE, H. P. (1961). The causal theory of perception. *Proceedings of the Aristotelian Society*. Supplementary volume 35: 121–68.

GRICE, H. P. (1969). Utterer's meaning and intentions. *Philosophical Review* 78: 147–77.

GRICE, H. P. (1975). Logic and conversation. In Cole, P. and Morgan, J. (eds.) 41–58.

GRICE, H. P. (1978). Further notes on logic and conversation. In Cole, P. (ed.) 113–28.

GRICE, H. P. (1981). Presupposition and conversational implicature. In Cole, P. (ed.) 183–98.

GRICE, H. P. (1989). *Studies in the way of words*. Cambridge, MA: Harvard University Press.

GRODNER, D., KLEIN, N., CARBARY, K., and TANENHAUS, M. (2007). Experimental evidence for rapid interpretation of pragmatic *some*. Paper presented at XPRAG, Berlin.

GU, YUEGUO (1990). Politeness phenomena in Modern Chinese. *Journal of Pragmatics* 14: 237–57.

HAIMAN, JOHN (1985a). *Natural syntax*. Cambridge: Cambridge University Press.

HAIMAN, JOHN (ed.) (1985b). *Iconicity in syntax*. Amsterdam: John Benjamins.

HALL, ALISON (2008). Free enrichment or hidden indexicals? *Mind and Language* 23: 426–56.

HAMILTON, SIR WILLIAM (1860). *Lectures on logic*. Vol. 1. Edinburgh: Blackwood.

HANKS, WILLIAM F. (1992). The indexical ground of deictic reference. In Duranti, A. and Goodwin, C. (eds.) 43–76.

HANKS, WILLIAM F. (2011). Deixis and indexicality. In Bublitz, W. and Norrick, N. (eds.) 315–46.

HARLEY, HEIDI and RITTER, ELIZABETH (2002). Person and number in pronouns: a feature-geometric analysis. *Language* 78: 482–526.

HARNISH, ROBERT M. (1976). Logical form and implicature. In Beaver, T., Katz, J., and Langendoen, D. T. (eds.) *An integrated theory of linguistic ability*. New York: Crowell. 313–92.

HARRIS, RANDY ALLEN (1993). *The linguistic wars*. Oxford: Oxford University Press.

HARRIS, STEPHEN G. (1984). *Culture and learning: tradition and education in northeast Arnhem land*. Canberra: Australian Institute of Aboriginal Studies.

HARRISON, S. P. (1976). *Makilese reference grammar*. Honolulu: University of Hawaii Press.

HASSALL, TIM (2001). Do learners thank too much in Indonesian? *Australian Review of Applied Linguistics* 24: 97–112.

HASSALL, TIM (2003). Requests by Australian learners of Indonesian. *Journal of Pragmatics* 35: 1903–28.

HATFIELD, HUNTER and HAHN, JEE-WON (2011). What Korean apologies require of politeness theory? *Journal of Pragmatics* 43: 1303–17.

HAUGH, MICHAEL (2007). The discursive challenge to politeness research: an interactional alternative. *Journal of Politeness Research* 3: 295–317.

HAUGH, MICHAEL and SCHNEIDER, KLAUS P. (eds.) (2012). *Journal of Pragmatics* 44 (9). Special issue on (im)politeness across Englishes.

HAUSER, MARC (1996). *The evolution of communication*. Cambridge, MA: MIT Press.

HAVILAND, JOHN B (1979). Guugu Yimidhirr brother-in-law language. *Language in Society* 8: 365–93.

HAVILAND, JOHN B. (1997). Shouts, shrieks, and shots: untruly political conversations in indigenous Chiapas. *Pragmatics* 7: 547–74.

HAWKINS, JOHN A. (1991). On (in)definite articles: implicatures and (un)grammaticality prediction. *Journal of Linguistics* 27: 405–42.

HEADLAND, PAUL (1986). Social rank and Tunebo requests. In Huttar, G. and Gregerson, K. (eds.) 1–34.

HEATH, J. (1980). Nunggubuyu deixis, anaphora, and culture. In Kreiman, J. and Ojeda, A. E. (eds.) *Pronouns and anaphora*. Chicago, IL: Chicago Linguistic Society. 151–65.

HEESCHEN, VOLKER (1982). Some systems of spatial deixis in Papuan languages. In Weissenborn, J. and Klein, W. (eds.) 81–109.

HEIM, IRENE (1982). The semantics of definite and indefinite noun phrases. PhD dissertation. University of Massachusetts at Amherst.

HEIM, IRENE (1983). On the projection problem for presuppositions. *Proceedings of the West Coast Conference on Formal Linguistics* 2: 114–25.

HEIM, IRENE (1991). Artikel und Definitheit. In von Stechow, D. A. and Wunderlich, D. (eds.) *Semantics: an international handbook of contemporary research*. Berlin: De Gruyter Mouton.

HEIM, IRENE (1992). Presupposition projection and the semantics of attitude verbs. *Journal of Semantics* 9: 183–221.

HELMBRECHT, JOHANNES (2003). Politeness distinctions in second person pronouns. In Lenz, F. (ed.) 185–202.

HERBERT, ROBERT (1991). The sociology of compliment work: an ethnocontrastive study of Polish and English compliments. *Multilingua* 10: 381–402.

HERRING, S. C. (1994). Discourse functions of demonstrative deixis in Tamil. *Proceedings of the Annual Meeting of the Berkeley Linguistics Society* 20: 246–59.

HIGGINBOTHAM, JAMES (2003). Remembering, imaging, and the first person. In BARBER, A. (ed.) *Epistemology of Language*. Oxford: Oxford University Press. 496–535.

HILL, CLIFORD (1982). Up/down, front/back, left/right: a contrastive study of Hausa and English. In Weissenborn, J. and Klein, W. (eds.) 11–42.

HIMMELMANN, NIKOLAUS (1997). *Deiktikon, artikel, nominalphrase*. Tübingen: Niemeyer.

HIRSCHBERG, JULIA (1991). *A theory of scalar implicature*. New York: Garland.

HO, D. (1976). On the concept of face. *The American Journal of Sociology* 81: 867–84.

HOBBS, JERRY R. (2004). Abduction in natural language understanding. In Horn, L. R. and Ward, G. (eds.) 724–41.

HOLDCROFT, DAVID (1994). Indirect speech acts and propositional content. In Tso-hatzidis, S. (ed.) 350–64.

HOLMES, JANET (1986). Compliments and compliment responses in New Zealand English. *Anthropological Linguistics* 28: 485–508.

HONG, WEI (1998). *Request patterns in Chinese and German: a cross-cultural study*. Munich: Lincom Europa.

HOPPER, ROBIN (2002). Deixis and aspect: the Tokelanan directional particles *mai* and *atu*. *Studies in Language* 26: 283–313.

HORGAN, TERENCE and TIENSON, JOHN (1996). *Connectionism and the philosophy of psychology*. Cambridge, MA: MIT Press.

HORN, LAURENCE R. (1972). On the semantic properties of logical operators in English. PhD dissertation. University of California at Los Angeles.

HORN, LAURENCE R. (1984). Toward a new taxonomy for pragmatic inference: Q-based and R-based implicature. In Schiffrin, D. (ed.) *Meaning, form, and use in context: linguistic applications*. Washington DC: Georgetown University Press. 11–42.

HORN, LAURENCE R. (1985). Metalinguistic negation and pragmatic ambiguity. *Language* 61: 121–74.

HORN, LAURENCE R. (1988). Pragmatic theory. In Newmeyer, F.J. (ed.) *Linguistics: the Cambridge survey*, vol. 1: 113–45.

HORN, LAURENCE R. (1989). *A natural history of negation*. Chicago: University of Chicago Press.

HORN, LAURENCE R. (1992). The said and the unsaid. *SALT II: Proceedings of the 2nd Conference on Semantics and Linguistic Theory*. 163–202.

HORN, LAURENCE R. (1996). Presupposition and implicature. In Lappin, S. (ed.) 299–320.

HORN, LAURENCE R. (2004). Implicature. In Horn, L. R. and Ward, G. (eds.) 3–28.

HORN, LAURENCE R. (2006). The border wars: a neo-Gricean perspective. In von Heusinger, K. and Turner, K. (eds.) 21–48.

HORN, LAURENCE R. (2007a). Neo-Gricean pragmatics: a Manichaean manifesto. In Burton-Roberts, N. (ed.) *Pragmatics*. London: Palgrave Macmillan. 158–83.

HORN, LAURENCE R. (2007b). Toward a Fregean pragmatics: *Voraussetzung, Nebengedanke, Andeutung*. In Kecskes, I. and Horn, L. R. (eds.) *Explorations in pragmatics: linguistic, cognitive and intercultural aspects*. Berlin: Mouton de Gruyter. 39–69.

HORN, LAURENCE R. (2009). WJ-40: implicature, truth, and meaning. *International Review of Pragmatics* 1: 3–34.

HORN, LAURENCE R. (2012). Implying and inferring. In Allan, K. and Jaszczolt, K. (eds.) 69–86.

HORN, LAURENCE R. and BAYER, SAMUEL (1984). Short-circuited implicature: a negative contribution. *Linguistics and Philosophy* 7: 397–411.

HORN, LAURENCE R. and WARD, GREGORY (eds.) (2004). *The handbook of pragmatics*. Oxford: Blackwell.

HOTTENROTH, PRISKA-MONIKA (1982). The system of local deixis in Spanish. In Weissenborn, J. and Klein, W. (eds.) 133–53.

HOUCK, NOEL and GASS, SUSAN M. (1996). Non-native refusals: a methodological perspective. In Gass, S. M. and Neu, J. (eds.) *Speech acts across cultures*. Berlin: Mouton de Gruyter. 45–64.

HOUSE, JULIA (1988). 'Oh excuse me please': apologizing in a foreign language. In Kettemann B. et al. (eds.) *Englisch als zweitsprache*. Tübingen: Narr. 303–27.

HOUSE, JULIA (2005). Politeness in Germany. In Hickey, L. and Stewart, M. (eds.) *Politeness in Europe*. Clevedon: Multilingual Matters.

HOZA, JACK (2007). *It's not what you sign, it's how you sign it: politeness in American Sign Language*. Washington, DC: Gallaudet University Press.

HU, HSIEN CHIN (1944). The Chinese concept of 'face'. *American Anthropologists* 46: 45–64.

HUANG, YAN (1987). The preference organisation of adjacency pairs in English conversation (written in Chinese). *Xiandai Waiyu* 3: 10–18.

HUANG, YAN (1991a). A neo-Gricean pragmatic theory of anaphora. *Journal of Linguistics* 27: 301–35.

HUANG, YAN (1991b). A pragmatic analysis of control in Chinese. In Verschueren, J. and Bertuccelli-Papi, M. (eds.) 113–45.

HUANG, YAN (1992a). Against Chomsky's typology of empty categories. *Journal of Pragmatics* 17: 1–29.

HUANG, YAN (1992b). Empty categories in Chinese (written in Chinese). *Zhongguo Yuwen* 1992 (5): 383–93.

HUANG, YAN (1994). *The syntax and pragmatics of anaphora: a study with special reference to Chinese*. Cambridge: Cambridge University Press.

HUANG, YAN (1995). On null subjects and null objects in generative grammar. *Linguistics* 33: 1081–123.

HUANG, YAN (1996). A note on the head-movement analysis of long-distance reflexives. *Linguistics* 34: 833–40.

HUANG, YAN (2000a). *Anaphora: a cross-linguistic study*. Oxford: Oxford University Press.

HUANG, YAN (2000b). Discourse anaphora: four theoretical models. *Journal of Pragmatics* 32: 151–76.

HUANG, YAN (2001a). Reflections on theoretical pragmatics. *Waiguoyu* 131: 2–14.

HUANG, YAN (2001b). Anaphora. In Smelser, N. J. and Baltes, P. B. (eds.) *International encyclopedia of the social and behavioural sciences*, 26 vols. New York: Elsevier Science. Vol. 1: 486–90.

HUANG, YAN (2001c). Marking of logophoricity in West African, East and South Asian languages. In *Proceedings of the 6th International Conference on the Languages of East, Southeast Asia and West Africa*. St Petersburg: University of St Petersburg Oriental Press. 224–38.

HUANG, YAN (2001d). Anaphora and word order. In Palek, B. and Fujimura, O. (eds.) *Item order*. Prague: Charles University Press. 329–46.

HUANG, YAN (2002a). Typology of coreferential anaphora and neo-Gricean pragmatics: implications for a newly defined artificial language. *Journal of Universal Language* 3: 31–56.

HUANG, YAN (2002b). Logophoric marking in East Asian languages. In Güldemann T. and von Roncador, M. (eds.) *Reported discourse*. Amsterdam: John Benjamins. 213–24.

HUANG, YAN (2003). On neo-Gricean pragmatics. *International Journal of Pragmatics* 13: 87–110.

HUANG, YAN (2004a). Anaphora and the pragmatics-syntax interface. In Horn, L. R. and Ward, G. (eds.) 288–314.

HUANG, YAN (2004b). Neo-Gricean pragmatic theory: looking back on the past; looking ahead to the future. *Waiguoyu* 149: 2–25.

HUANG, YAN (2005). Pragmatic intrusion into what is said: explicature, pragmatically enriched said, implicIture or implicAture? Paper presented at the 27th Meeting of the German Linguistic Society.

HUANG, YAN (2006a). Speech acts. In Brown, K. (ed.) *The encyclopedia of languages and linguistics*. 2nd edition. 14 vols. New York: Elsevier Science. Vol. 11: 656–66.

HUANG, YAN (2006b). Neo-Gricean pragmatics. In Brown, K. (ed.) *The encyclopedia of languages and linguistics*. 2nd edition. 14 vols. New York: Elsevier Science. Vol. 8: 586–90.

HUANG, YAN (2006c). Anaphora, cataphora, exophora, logophoricity. In Brown, K. (ed.) *The encyclopedia of languages and linguistics*. 2nd edition. 14 vols. New York: Elsevier Science. Vol. 1: 231–8.

HUANG, YAN (2006d). Coreference: identity and similarity. In Brown, K. (ed.) *The encyclopedia of languages and linguistics*. 2nd edition. 14 vols. New York: Elsevier Science. Vol. 3: 203–5.

HUANG YAN (2007a). *The syntax and pragmatics of anaphora: a study with special reference to Chinese.* Reprint. Cambridge: Cambridge University Press.

HUANG, YAN (2007b). The grammaticalization and lexicalization of space deixis: a cross-linguistic analysis. *Waiguoyu* 167: 2–18.

HUANG, YAN (2009). Neo-Gricean pragmatics and the lexicon. *International Review of Pragmatics* 1: 118–53.

HUANG, YAN (2010a). Neo-Gricean pragmatic theory of conversational implicature. In Heine, B. and Narrog, H. (eds.) *The Oxford handbook of linguistic analysis.* Oxford: Oxford University Press. 607–31.

HUANG, YAN (2010b). Switch-reference in Amele and logophoric verbal suffix in Gokana: a generalized neo-Gricean pragmatic analysis. In Shu, D. F. and Turner, K. (eds.) *Contrasting meaning in languages of the East and West.* Berlin: Peter Lang. 75–101.

HUANG, YAN (2010c). Anaphora, pragmatics of. In Cummings, L. (ed.) 33–7.

HUANG, YAN (2010d). Anglo-American and European Continental traditions. In Cummings, L. (ed.) 37–40.

HUANG, YAN (2010e). Implicature. In Cummings, L. (ed.) 234–8.

HUANG, YAN (2010f). Impliciture. In Cummings, L. (ed.) 238–40.

HUANG, YAN (2010g). Neo-Gricean pragmatics. In Cummings, L. (ed.) 370–5.

HUANG, YAN (2010h). Scalar implicature. In Cummings, L. (ed.) 441–4.

HUANG, YAN (2010i). What is said. In Cummings, L. (ed.) 520–2.

HUANG, YAN (2010j). Binding and anaphora in Maori: a neo-Gricean pragmatic account. Paper presented at the 8th International Conference on Oceanic Linguistics.

HUANG, YAN (2011). Types of inference: entailment, presupposition, and implicature. In Bublitz, W. and Norrick, N. (eds.) 397–421.

HUANG, YAN (2012a). *The Oxford dictionary of pragmatics.* Oxford: Oxford University Press.

HUANG, YAN (2012b). Relevance and neo-Gricean pragmatic principles. In Schmid, H.-J. (ed.) *Cognitive pragmatics.* Berlin: Mouton de Gruyter. 25–46.

HUANG, YAN (2013a). Micro- and macro-pragmatics: remapping their terrains. *International Review of Pragmatics* 5: 129–62.

HUANG, YAN (2013b). Bayesian probabilistic model of discourse anaphoric comprehension, linguistic typology, and neo-Gricean pragmatics. *Theoretical Linguistics* 39: 95–108.

HUANG, YAN (2013c). *De se* attitude/belief attribution and neo-Gricean truth-conditional pragmatics: logophoric expressions in West African languages and long-distance reflexives in East, South, and Southeast Asian languages. In Feit, N. and Capone, A. (eds.) 185–209.

HUANG, YAN (2013d). Semantics and pragmatics. In Kaldis, B. (ed.) *Encyclopedia of philosophy and social sciences.* London: Sage Publications. Vol. 2: 858–60.

Huang, Yan (2013e). *Unarticulated constituents in neo-Gricean pragmatics*. Paper presented at the 1st International Pragmatic Conference of the Americas.

Huang, Yan (2014). Logophoricity and neo-Gricean truth-conditional pragmatics. In Capone et al. (eds.) 217–42.

Huang, Yan (ed.) (forthcoming). *The Oxford handbook of pragmatics*. Oxford: Oxford University Press.

Huang, Yi Ting, Spelke, Elizabeth, and Snedeker, Jesse (2010). When is four far more than three? Children's generalization of newly acquired number words. *Psychological Science* 21(4): 600–6.

Hudson, Joyce (1986). An analysis of illocutionary verbs in Walmutjari. In Hutter, G. and Gregerson, K. (eds.) 63–83.

Hurewitz, Felicia, Papafragou, Anna, Gleitman, Lila, and Gelman, Roger (2006). Asymmetries in the acquisition of numbers and quantifiers. *Language Learning and Development* 2: 77–96.

Hurford, James R. and Heasley, Brendan (1983). *Semantics: a coursebook*. Cambridge: Cambridge University Press.

Huttar, George and Gregerson, Kenneth (eds.) (1986). *Pragmatics in non-western perspective*. Arlington: The Summer Institute of Linguistics and the University of Texas at Arlington.

Hwang, J. (1990). 'Deference' versus 'politeness' in Korean speech. *International Journal of the Sociology of Language* 82: 41–55.

Hyman, Larry and Comrie, Bernard (1981). Logophoric reference in Gokana. *Journal of African Languages and Linguistics* 3: 19–37.

Hyslop, Catriona (1993). Towards a typology of spatial deixis. Honours thesis. The Australian National University.

Ide, Sachiko (1989). Formal forms and discernment: two neglected aspects of universals of linguistic politeness. *Multilingua* 8: 223–48.

Imai, Shingo (2003). Spatial deixis. PhD dissertation. State University of New York at Buffalo.

Ingram, D. (1978). Typology and universals of personal pronouns. In Greenberg, et al. (eds.) 213–47.

Ippolito, M. (2010). Embedded implicatures? Remarks on the debate between globalist and localist theories. *Semantics and Pragmatics* 3(5): 1–15.

Israel, Michael (2004). The pragmatics of polarity. In Horn, L. and Ward, G. (eds.) 701–23.

Jackendoff, Ray (1983). *Semantics and cognition*. Cambridge, MA: MIT Press.

Jackendoff, Ray (1990). *Semantic structure*. Cambridge, MA: MIT Press.

Jackendoff, Ray (1992). *Languages of the mind*. Cambridge, MA: MIT Press.

Jackendoff, Ray (1997). *The architecture of the language faculty*. Cambridge, MA: MIT Press.

Jaggar, Philip J. and Buba, Malami (1994). The space and time adverbials NAN/CAN in Hausa: cracking the deictic code. *Language Sciences* 16: 387–421.

JANSSEN, THEO (1997). Compositionality. In van Benthem, J. and ter Meulen, A. (eds.) *Handbook of logic and language.* Amsterdam: North-Holland. 417–73.

JARVELLA, ROBERT and KLEIN, WOLFGANG (eds.) (1982). *Speech, place and action: studies in deixis and related topics.* Chichester: John Wiley and Sons.

JIANG, XIANGYING (2012). Politeness and facework in Chinese language and culture. In Ruiz de Zarobe, L. and Ruiz de Zarobe, Y. (eds.) 129–52.

JOBERT, MANUEL and JAMET, DENIS (eds.) (2013). *Aspects of linguistic impoliteness.* Newcastle upon Tyne: Cambridge Scholars Publishing.

JUCKER, ANDREAS and TAAVITSAINEN, IRMA (2013). English historical pragmatics. Edinburgh: Edinburgh University Press.

JUNGBLUTH, KONSTANZE (2003). Deictics in the conversational dyad: findings in Spanish and some cross-linguistic outlines. In Lenz, F. (ed.) 13–40.

JURAFSKY, DANIEL (2004). Pragmatics and computational linguistics. In Horn, L. and Ward, G. (eds.) 578–604.

KADAR, DANIEL and MILLS, SARA (eds.) (2011). *Politeness in East Asia.* Cambridge: Cambridge University Press.

KADMON, NIRIT. (2001). *Formal pragmatics: semantics, pragmatics, presupposition, and focus.* Oxford: Blackwell.

KAMP, HANS and REYLE, UWE (1993). *From discourse to logic: introduction to model theoretic semantics of natural languages, formal logic and discourse representation theory.* Dordrecht: Kluwer.

KAPLAN, DAVID (1978). Dthat. In Cole, P. (ed.) 221–43.

KAPLAN, DAVID (1989). Demonstratives: an essay on the semantics, logic, metaphysics, and epistemology of demonstratives and other indexicals. In Almog, J. et al. (eds.) *Themes from Kaplan.* Oxford: Oxford University Press. 481–563.

KARTTUNEN, LAURI (1969). Problems of reference in syntax. PhD dissertation. Indiana University.

KARTTUNEN, LAURI (1971). Some observations on factivity. *Papers in Linguistics* 5: 55–69.

KARTTUNEN, LAURI (1973). Presuppositions of compound sentences. *Linguistic Inquiry* 4: 169–93.

KARTTUNEN, LAURI (1974). Presupposition and linguistic context. *Theoretical Linguistics* 1: 182–94.

KARTTUNEN, LAURI and PETERS, STANLEY (1979). Conventional implicature. In Oh, C-K. and Dineen, A. D. (eds.) *Syntax and semantics 11: presupposition.* London: Academic Press. 1–56.

KASANGA, LUANGA and LWANGA-LUMU, JOY-CHRISTINE (2007). Cross-cultural linguistic realisation of politeness: a study of apologies in English and Setswana. *Journal of Politeness Research* 3: 65–92.

KASHER, ASA (1976). Conversational maxims and rationality. In Kasher, A. (ed.) *Language in focus: foundations, methods and systems.* Dordrecht: Reidel. 197–216.

KASHER, ASA (ed.) (1998). *Pragmatics: critical concepts.* 6 vols. London: Routledge.

KASPER, GABRIELE and BLUM-KULKA, SHOSHANA (eds.) (1993). *Interlanguage pragmatics*. Oxford: Oxford University Press.

KATZ, JERROLD J. (1977). *Propositional structure and illocutionary force*. New York: Crowell.

KAY, PAUL (1990). Even. *Linguistics and Philosophy* 13: 59–111.

KEATING, ELIZABETH (1998). Honor and stratification in Pohnpei, Micronesia. *American Ethnologist* 25: 399–411.

KEENAN, ELINOR OCHS (1976). The universality of conversational implicature. *Language in Society* 5: 67–80.

KEMPSON, RUTH (1975). *Presupposition and the delimitation of semantics*. Cambridge: Cambridge University Press.

KIM, SUN-HEE (1993). Division of labor between grammar and pragmatics: the distribution and interpretation of anaphora. PhD dissertation. Yale University.

KING, JEFFREY and STANLEY, JASON (2005). Semantics, pragmatics, and the role of semantic content. In Szabó, Z. G. (ed.) *Semantics vs. pragmatics*. Oxford: Clarendon Press. 111–64.

KITA, S. (ed.) (2003). *Pointing: where language, culture and cognition meet*. Mahwah, NJ: Erlbaum.

KÖNIG, EKKEHARD and SIEMUND, PETER (2000). Intensifiers and reflexives: a typological perspective. In Frajzyngier, Z. and Curl, T. S. (eds.) 41–74.

KORTA, KEPA and PERRY, JOHN (2008). The pragmatic circle. *Synthese* 165: 347–57.

KORTA, KEPA and PERRY, JOHN (2011). *Critical pragmatics*. Cambridge: Cambridge University Press.

KOUTLAKI, SOPHIA A. (2002). Offers and expressions of thanks as face enhancing acts: tæ'arof in Persian. *Journal of Pragmatics* 34: 1733–56.

KRAHMER, EMIEL (1998). *Presupposition and anaphora*. Stanford: CSLI.

KRIPKE, SAUL (1972). Naming and necessity. In Davidson, D. and Harman, G. (eds.) *Semantics of natural language*. Dordrecht: Reidel.

KRIPKE, SAUL (1977). Speaker's reference and semantic reference. *Midwest Studies in Philosophy* 2: 255–76.

KRIPKE, SAUL (1980). *Naming and necessity*. Cambridge, MA: Harvard University Press.

KRIPKE, SAUL (2009). Presupposition and anaphora: remarks on the formulation of the projection problem. *Linguistic Inquiry* 40: 367–86.

KROON, FREDERICK (1987). Causal descriptivism. *Australian Journal of Philosophy* 65: 1–17.

KUNO, SUSUMU (2004). Empathy and direct discourse perspectives. In Horn, L. R. and Ward, G. (eds.) 315–43.

LAKOFF, GEORGE (1972). Hedges: a study in meaning criteria and the logic of fuzzy concepts. *Chicago Linguistic Society* 8: 183–228.

LAKOFF, GEORGE (1987). *Women, fire, and dangerous things: what categories reveal about the mind*. Chicago: University of Chicago Press.

LAKOFF, ROBIN (1971). If's, and's and but's about conjunction. In Fillmore, Charles J. and Langendoen, D. Terence (eds.). *Studies in linguistic semantics*. New York: Holt, Rinehart and Winston. 114–49.

LAKOFF, ROBIN (1973). The logic of politeness or minding your p's and q's. *Chicago Linguistic Society* 9: 292–305.

LALITHA MURTHY, B. and SUBBARAO, K. V. (2000). Lexical anaphors and pronominals in Mizo. In Lust B. et al. (eds.) 777–840.

LAM, BARRY (2010). Are Cantonese speakers really descriptivists?: revisiting cross-cultural semantics. *Cognition* 115: 320–9.

LANDMAN, FRED (1986). Conflicting presuppositions and modal subordination. *Papers from the Regional Meeting of the Chicago Linguistics Society* 22: 105–207.

LANGACKER, RONALD (1987). *Foundations of cognitive grammar*. Vol 1. Stanford: Stanford University Press.

LANGENDOEN, D. TERENCE and SAVIN, HARRIS (1971). The projection problem for presuppositions. In Fillmore, C. and Langendoen, D. T. (eds.) *Studies in linguistic semantics*. New York: Holt, Rinehart and Winston. 373–88.

LAPPIN, SHALOM (ed.) (1997). *The handbook of contemporary semantic theory*. Oxford: Blackwell.

LASNIK, HOWARD (1989). *Essays on anaphora*. Dordrecht: Kluwer.

LE PAIR, R. (1996). Spanish request strategies: a cross-cultural analysis from an intercultural perspective. In Jaszczolt, K. M. and Turner, K. (eds.) *Contrastive semantics and pragmatics*. Oxford: Elsevier. 651–70.

LEE, CHEN LENG (2009). Compliments and responses during Chinese New Year celebrations in Singapore. *Pragmatics* 19: 519–41.

LEECH, GEOFFREY N. (1983). *Principles of pragmatics*. London: Longman.

LEECH, GEOFFREY N. (2007). Politeness: is there an East-West divide? *Journal of Politeness Research* 3: 167–206.

LEE-WONG, SONG MEI (2000). *Politeness and face in Chinese culture*. Frankfurt am Main: Peter Lang.

LEGENDRE, GÉRALDINE, GRIMSHAW, JANE, and VIKNER, STEN (2001). *Optimality-theoretic syntax*. Cambridge, MA: MIT Press.

LENZ, FRIEDRICH (ed.) (2003). *Deictic conceptualisation of space, time and person*. Amsterdam: John Benjamins.

LEONARD, R. A. (1985). Swahili demonstratives: evaluating the validity of competing semantic hypotheses. *Studies in African Linguistics* 16: 281–95.

LEPORE, ERNIE and SMITH, BARRY (eds.) (2006). *The Oxford handbook of philosophy of language*. Oxford: Oxford University Press.

LEVINSON, STEPHEN C. (1983). *Pragmatics*. Cambridge: Cambridge University Press.

LEVINSON, STEPHEN C. (1987a). Minimization and conversational inference. In Verschueren, J. and Bertuccelli-Papi, M. (eds.) 61–129.

LEVINSON, STEPHEN C. (1987b). Pragmatics and the grammar of anaphora. *Journal of Linguistics* 23: 379–434.

LEVINSON, STEPHEN C. (1988). Putting linguistics on a proper footing: explorations in Goffman's concepts of participation. In Drew, P. and Wootton, A. (eds.) *Erving Goffman: exploring the interactional order*. Cambridge: Polity. 161–293.

LEVINSON, STEPHEN C. (1989). A review of Relevance. *Journal of Linguistics* 25: 455–72.

LEVINSON, STEPHEN C. (1991). Pragmatic reduction of the binding conditions revisited. *Journal of Linguistics* 27: 107–61.

LEVINSON, STEPHEN C. (1995). Three levels of meaning. In Palmer, F. (ed.) 90–115.

LEVINSON, STEPHEN C. (1996). Frames of reference and Molyneux's question: cross-linguistic evidence. In Bloom, P. et al. (eds.) *Language and space*. Cambridge, MA: MIT Press. 109–69.

LEVINSON, STEPHEN C. (2000). *Presumptive meanings: the theory of generalized conversational implicature*. Cambridge, MA: MIT Press.

LEVINSON, STEPHEN C. (2003). *Space in language and cognition: explorations in cognitive diversity*. Cambridge: Cambridge University Press.

LEVINSON, STEPHEN C. (2004). Deixis and pragmatics. In Horn, L. R. and Ward, G. (eds.) 97–121.

LEWIS, DAVID (1979a). Attitudes *de dicto* and *de se*. *The Philosophical Review* 88: 513–43.

LEWIS, DAVID (1979b). Scorekeeping in a language game. *Journal of Philosophical Logic* 8: 339–59.

LI, CHARLES N. and THOMPSON, SANDRA A. (1976). Subject and topic: a new typology of language. In Li, C. N. (ed.) *Subject and topic: a new typology of language*. London: Academic Press. 457–98.

LIN, Y. L., WOODFIELD, H., and REN, W. (2012). Compliments in Taiwan and Mainland Chinese: the influence of region and compliment topic. *Journal of Pragmatics* 44: 1486–1502.

LÖBNER, SEBASTIAN (1985). Definites. *Journal of Semantics* 4: 279–326.

LÖBNER, SEBASTIAN (2000). Polarity in natural language: predication, quantification and negation in particular and characterizing sentences. *Linguistics and Philosophy* 23: 213–308.

LOCHER, MIRIAM A. (2004). *Power and politeness in action: disagreements in oral communication*. Berlin: Mouton de Gruyter.

LOCHER, MIRIAM A. and BOUSFIELD, DEREK (eds.) (2008). *Impoliteness in language*. Berlin: Mouton de Gruyter.

LOCHER, MIRIAM A. and GRAHAM, SAGE I. (eds.) (2010). *Interpersonal pragmatics*. Berlin: De Gruyter Mouton.

LOCHER, MIRIAM A. and WATTS, RICHARD J. (2005). Politeness theory and relational work. *Journal of Politeness Research* 1: 9–33.

LOCHER, MIRIAM A. and WATTS, RICHARD J. (2008). Relational work and impoliteness: negotiating norms of linguistic behaviour. In Locher, M. and Bousfield, D. (eds.) 77–100.

Lorenzo-Dus, N. (2001). Compliment responses among British and Spanish university students: a contrastive study. *Journal of Pragmatics* 33: 107–27.

Lust, Barbara, Wali, K., Gair, James, and Subbarao, K. V. (eds.) (2000). *Lexical anaphors and pronouns in selected South Asian languages*. Berlin: Mouton de Gruyter.

Lycan, William G. (1991). *Even* and *even if. Linguistics and Philosophy* 14: 115–50.

Lyons, John (1977). *Semantics*. 2 vols. Cambridge: Cambridge University Press.

Lyons, John (1987). Semantics. In Lyons et al. (eds.) *New horizons in linguistics* 2. London: Penguin. 152–78.

Lyons, John (1995). *Linguistic semantics*. Cambridge: Cambridge University Press.

MacDonald, L. (1990). *A grammar of Tauya*. Berlin: Mouton de Gruyter.

MacFarlane, John (2007). Semantic minimalism and nonindexical contextualism. In Preyer, G. and Peter, G. (eds.) 240–50.

MacFarlane, John (2009). Nonindexical contextualism. *Synthese* 166: 231–50.

McGinn, Colin (1981). The mechanism of reference. *Synthese* 49: 157–86.

Machery, Edouard, Mallon, Ron, Nichols, Shaun, and Stich, Stephen (2004). Semantics: cross-cultural style. *Cognition* 92 (3): B1–B12.

Machery, Edouard, Olivola, Christopher, and De Blanc, Molly (2009). Linguistic and metalinguistic intuitions in the philosophy of language. *Analysis* 69: 689–94.

Maienborn, Claudia, von Heusinger, Klaus, and Portner, Paul (eds.) (2012). *Semantics: an international handbook of natural language meaning*. Vol. 3. Berlin: De Gruyter Mouton.

Majid, A., Bowerman, M., Kita, S., Haun, D., and Levinson, Stephen C. (2004). Can language restructure cognition? The case for space. *Trends in Cognitive Sciences* 8: 108–14.

Malotki, Eckehart (1982). Hopi person deixis. In Weissenborn, J. and Klein, W. (eds.) 223–52.

Manning, H. Paul (2001). On social deixis. *Anthropological Linguistics* 43: 54–100.

Mao, Luming Robert (1994). Beyond politeness theory: 'face' revisited and renewed. *Journal of Pragmatics* 21: 451–86.

Margri, Giorgio (2009). A theory of individual-level predicates based on blind mandatory scalar implicatures. *Natural Language Semantics* 17: 245–97.

Marmaridou, Sophia S. A. (2000). *Pragmatic meaning and cognition*. Amsterdam: John Benjamins.

Marquez-Reiter, Rosina (2000). *Linguistic politeness in Britain and Uruguay: a contrastive study of requests and apologies*. Amsterdam: John Benjamins.

Marti, Genoveva (2012). Reference. In Garcia-Carpintero, M. and Kölbel, M. (eds.) 109–24.

Marti, Luisa (2006). Unarticulated constituents revisited. *Linguistics and Philosophy* 29: 135–66.

Martinet, A. (1962). *A functional view of language*. Oxford: Clarendon Press.

MATE, D. and TIRASSA, M. (2010). Knowledge. In Cummings, L. (ed.) 239–42.

MATSUMOTO, YO (1995). The conversational condition on Horn scales. *Linguistics and Philosophy* 18: 21–60.

MATSUMOTO, YOSHIKO (1988). Reexamination of the universality of face: politeness phenomena in Japanese. *Journal of Pragmatics* 12: 403–26.

MATSUMOTO, YOSHIKO (1989). Politeness and conversational universals: observations from Japanese. *Multilingua* 8: 207–21.

MATTAUSCH, JASON (2004). Optimality theory pragmatics and binding phenomena. In Blutner, R. and Zeevat, H. (eds.) 63–90.

MATTHEWS, PETER H. (1995). Syntax, semantics, and pragmatics. In Palmer, F. (ed.) 48–60.

MEIBAUER, JÖRG (2008). Tautology as presumptive meaning. *Pragmatics and Cognition* 16: 439–70.

MEIBAUER, JÖRG and STEINBACH, MARKUS (eds.) (2011). *Experimental pragmatics/ semantics*. Amsterdam: John Benjamins.

MEINI, CRISTINA (2010). Modularity of mind thesis. In Cummings, L. (ed.) 275–8.

MEIRA, SÉRGIO (2003). 'Addressee effects' in demonstrative systems: the cases of Tiriyó and Brazilian Portuguese. In Lenz, F. (ed.) 3–11.

MERIN, ARTHUR (1994). Algebra of elementary social acts. In Tsohatzidis, S. (ed.) 234–66.

MERIN, ARTHUR (1999). Information, relevance, and social decision making: some principles and results of decision-theoretic semantics. In Moss, L. S., Ginzburg, J., and de Rijke, M. (eds.) *Logic, language, and computation*. Vol 2. Stanford: CSLI Publications. 179–221.

MERIN, ARTHUR (2003). Probabilistic and deterministic presuppositions. In Bauerle, R. et al. (eds.)

MEY, JACOB L. (2001). *Pragmatics: an introduction*. 2ⁿᵈ edition. Oxford: Blackwell.

MILL, JOHN STUART (1843). *A system of logic, ratiocinative and inductive, being a connected view of the principles of evidence, and the methods of scientific investigation*. London: John W. Parker.

MILLER, ROY A. (1967). *The Japanese language*. Chicago: University of Chicago Press.

MILLS, SARA (2003). *Gender and politeness*. Cambridge: Cambridge University Press.

MITHUN, MARIANNE (1999). *The languages of native North America*. Cambridge: Cambridge University Press.

MIZUTANI, OSAMU and MIZUTANI, NOBUKO (1987). *How to be polite in Japanese*. Tokyo: Japan Times.

MONTALBETTI, MARIO (2003). Reference transfers and the Giorgione problem. In Barss, A. (ed.) *Anaphora: a reference guide*. Oxford: Blackwell. 127–39.

MORGAN, JERRY L. (1978). Two types of convention in indirect speech acts. In Cole, P. (ed.) 261–80.

MORRIS, CHARLES (1938). *Foundations of the theory of signs.* Chicago: University of Chicago Press.

MÜHLHÄUSLER, PETER and HARRÉ, ROM (1990). *Pronouns and people.* Oxford: Blackwell.

MURSY, AHMAD and WILSON, JOHN (2001). Towards a definition of Egyptian complimenting. *Multilingua* 20: 133–54.

NADEN, ANTHONY (1986). Social context and Mampruli greetings. In Huttar, G. and Gregerson, K. (eds.) *Pragmatics in non-western perspective.* Arlington: The Summer Institute of Linguistics and the University of Texas at Arlington. 161–99.

NEALE, STEPHEN (1992). Paul Grice and the philosophy of language. *Linguistics and Philosophy* 15: 509–59.

NELSON, GAYLE L., CARSON, J., AL BATAL, MAHMOUD, and EL BAKARY, WAGUIDA (2002). Cross-cultural pragmatics: strategy use in Egyptian Arabic and American English refusals. *Applied Linguistics*: 23: 163–89.

NELSON, GAYLE L., EL BAKARY, WAGUIDA, and AL BATAL, MAHMOUD (1996). Egyptian and American compliments: focus on second language learners. In Gass, S. M. and Neu, J. (eds.) 109–28.

NEMO, FRANÇOIS (1999). The pragmatics of signs, the semantics of relevance, and the semantics-pragmatics interface. In Turner, K. (ed.) *The semantics/pragmatics interface from different points of view.* Oxford: Elsevier. 343–417.

NEMO, FRANÇOIS and CADIOT, P. (1997). Un problème insoluble? *Revue de sémantique et pragmatique* 1: 15–22, 2: 9–40.

NGUYEN, THI THUY MINH and HO, GIA ANLLE (2013). Requests and politeness in Vietnamese as a native language. *Pragmatics* 23: 685–714.

NICOLLE, STEVE and CLARK, BILLY (1999). Experimental pragmatics and what is said: a reply to Gibbs and Moise. *Cognition* 69 (3): 337–54.

NOVECK, IRA A. (2001). When children are more logical than adults: experimental investigations of scalar implicature. *Cognition* 78: 165–88.

NOVECK, IRA A. and REBOUL, ANNE (2008). Experimental pragmatics: a Gricean turn in the study of language. *Trends in Cognitive Sciences* 12: 425–31.

NOVECK, IRA A. and SPERBER, DAN (eds.) (2004). *Experimental pragmatics.* New York: Palgrave Macmillan.

NOVECK, IRA A. and SPERBER, DAN (2007). The why and how of experimental pragmatics: the case of 'scalar inference'. In N. Burton-Roberts (ed.) 184–212.

NUNBERG, GEOFFREY (1979). The non-uniqueness of semantic solutions: polysemy. *Linguistics and Philosophy* 3: 143–84.

NUNBERG, GEOFFREY (1993). Indexicality and deixis. *Linguistics and Philosophy* 16: 1–44.

NUNBERG, GEOFFREY (1995). Transfers of meaning. *Journal of Semantics* 12: 109–32.

NUNBERG, GEOFFREY (2004). The pragmatics of deferred interpretation. In Horn, L. R. and Ward, G. (eds.) 344–64.

NWOYE, ONUIGBO (1989). Linguistic politeness in Igbo. *Multilingua* 8: 259–75.

Nwoye, Onuigbo (1992). Linguistic politeness and socio-cultural variations of the notion of face. *Journal of Pragmatics* 18: 309–28.

O'Driscoll, Jim (1996). About face: a defence and elaboration of universal dualism. *Journal of Pragmatics* 25: 1–32.

Ogiermann, Eva (2009a). *On apologising in negative and positive politeness cultures.* Amsterdam: John Benjamins.

Ogiermann, Eva (2009b). Politeness and indirectness across cultures: a comparison of English, German, Polish and Russian requests. *Journal of Politeness Research* 5: 189–216.

Ogiermann, Eva (2012). About Polish politeness. In de Zarobe, L. R. and de Zarobe, Y. R. (eds.) *Speech acts and politeness across languages and cultures.* Bern: Peter Lang. 27–52.

Ogiermann, Eva and Suszczyńska, Malgorzata (2011). On (im)politeness behind the iron curtain. In Bargiela-Chiappini, F. and Kadar, D. (eds.) 194–215.

Ohasi, Jun (2008). Linguistic rituals for thanking in Japanese. *Journal of Pragmatics* 40: 2150–74.

Olshtain, Elite and Weinbach, Liora (1993). Interlanguage features of the speech act of complaining. In Kasper, G. and Blum-Kulka, S. (eds.) 108–22.

Othman, Normala (2011). Pragmatic and cultural considerations of compliment responses among Malaysian-Malay speakers. *Asiatic* 5: 86–103.

Palmer, Frank (ed.) (1995). *Grammar and meaning: essays in honour of Sir John Lyons.* Cambridge: Cambridge University Press.

Pan, Yuling and Kadar, Daniel Z. (2011). *Politeness in historical and contemporary Chinese.* London: Continuum.

Panizza, D. and Chierchia, Gennaro (2008). Two experiments on the interpretation of numerals. Paper presented at Workshop on Experimental Pragmatics/ Semantics, the 30th Annual Convention of the German Society of Linguistics.

Papafragou, Anna and Musolino, Julien (2003). Scalar implicatures: experiments at the semantics-pragmatics interface. *Cognition* 86: 253–82.

Parker, E. (1986). Mundani pronouns. In Wiesemann, U. (ed.) 131–66.

Peccei, Jean Stilwell (1999). *Pragmatics.* London: Routledge.

Pedersen, Jan (2010). The different Swedish *tack*: an ethnopragmatic investigation of Swedish thanking and related concepts. *Journal of Pragmatics* 42: 1258–65.

Perrault, C. Raymond (1990). An application of default logic to speech act theory. In Cohen, P. (ed.) *Intentions in communication.* Cambridge, MA: MIT Press. 161–86.

Perry, John (1979). The problem of the essential indexical. *Nous* 13: 3–21.

Perry, John (1986). Thought without representation. *Proceedings of the Aristotelian Society* Supplementary Volume 60: 137–51.

Perry, John (1993). *The problem of the essential indexical and other essays.* Oxford: Oxford University Press.

PERRY, JOHN (1998). Indexicals, contexts and unarticulated constituents. In Aliseda-Llera, A., van Glabbeek, R., and Westerstahl, D. (eds.) *Computing natural language*. Stanford: CSLI Publications. 1–11.

PERRY, JOHN (2000). Castañeda on *he* and *I*. In Perry, J. (ed.) *The problem of the essential indexical and other essays*. Expanded edition. Stanford: CSLI publications. 77–100.

PERRY, JOHN (2013). Self-locating belief. In Neit, F. and Capone, A. (eds.) 385–408.

PETERSON, ELIZABETH (2010). Perspective and politeness in Finnish requests. *Pragmatics* 20: 401–23.

PLAT, J., WEBER, H., and HO, MIAN LIAN (1983). *Varieties of English around the world: Singapore and Malaysia*. Amsterdam: John Benjamins.

POPPER, KARL (1973). *Objective knowledge*. Oxford: Oxford University Press.

PORTNER, PAUL (2005). *What is meaning? Fundamentals of formal semantics*. Oxford: Blackwell.

POSNER, R. (1980). Semantics and pragmatics of sentence connectives in natural language. In Searle, J. R., Kiefer, F., and Bierwisch, M. (eds.) *Speech act theory and pragmatics*. Dordrecht: Reidel. 169–203.

POTTS, CHRISTOPHER (2005). *The logic of conventional implicatures*. Oxford: Oxford University Press.

PREDELLI, STEFANO (2005). *Contexts, meaning, truth, and the use of language*. Oxford: Oxford University Press.

PREYER, GERHARD and PETER, GEORG (eds.) (2005). *Contextualism in philosophy*. Oxford: Oxford University Press.

PREYER, GERHARD and PETER, GEORG (eds.) (2007). *Context-sensitivity and semantic minimalism: new essays on semantics and pragmatics*. Oxford: Oxford University Press.

PRINCE, ALAN and SMOLENSKY, PAUL (2004). *Optimality theory: constraint interaction in generative grammar*. Oxford: Blackwell.

PRUCHA, J. (1983). *Pragmalinguistics: East European tradition*. Amsterdam: John Benjamins.

PUSTEJOVSKY, JAMES (1995). *The generative lexicon*. Cambridge, MA: MIT Press.

PUTNAM, HILARY (1965). How not to talk about meaning. Reprinted in Putnam, H. *Philosophical papers*, vol. 2. Cambridge: Cambridge University Press. 117–31.

PUTNAM, HILARY (1975). The meaning of 'meaning'. Reprinted in Putnam, H. *Philosophical papers*, vol. 2. Cambridge: Cambridge University Press. 215–71.

PUTNAM, HILARY (1981). *Reason, truth and history*. Cambridge: Cambridge University Press.

QUINE, W. V. O. (1953). *From a logical point of view*. Cambridge, MA: Harvard University Press.

RAY, TAPAS S. (2000). Lexical anaphors and pronouns in Oriy. In Lust, B. et al. (eds.) 575–636.

REBOUL, ANNE (2004). Conversational implicatures: nonce or generalized? In Novek, I. and Sperber, D. (eds.) 322–32.

RECANATI, FRANÇOIS (1989). The pragmatics of what is said. *Mind and Language* 4: 295–329.

RECANATI, FRANÇOIS (1993). *Direct reference: from language to thought*. Oxford: Blackwell.

RECANATI, FRANÇOIS (1994). Contextualism and anti-contextualism in the philosophy of language. In Tsohatzidis, S. (ed.) 156–66.

RECANATI, FRANÇOIS (2001). What is said. *Synthese* 125: 75–91.

RECANATI, FRANÇOIS (2004a). *Literal meaning*. Cambridge: Cambridge University Press.

RECANATI, FRANÇOIS (2004b). Pragmatics and semantics. In Horn, L. R. and Ward, G. (eds.) 442–62.

RECANATI, FRANÇOIS (2005a). 'What is said' and the semantics/pragmatics distinction. In Bianchi, C. (ed.) 45–64.

RECANATI, FRANÇOIS (2005b). Literalism and contextualism: some varieties. In Preyer, G. and Peter, G. (eds.) 171–96.

RECANATI, FRANÇOIS (2008). Moderate relativism. In Garcia-Carpintero, M. and Kölbel, M. (eds.) 41–62.

RECANATI, FRANÇOIS (2010). *Truth-conditional pragmatics*. Oxford: Oxford University Press.

REESINK, G. P. (1987). *Structures and their function in Usan: a Papuan language of Papua New Guinea*. Amsterdam: John Benjamins.

REIMER, MARGA and BEZUIDENHOUT, ANN (eds.) (2004). *Descriptions and beyond*. Oxford: Oxford University Press.

REINHART, TANYA and REULAND, ERIC (1993). Reflexivity. *Linguistic Inquiry* 24: 657–720.

REULAND, ERIC (2011). *Anaphora and language design*. Cambridge MA: MIT Press.

RICHARD, M. (1990). *Propositional attitudes: an essay on thoughts and how we ascribe them*. Cambridge: Cambridge University Press.

RIEBER, STEPHEN (1997). Conventional implicatures as tacit performatives. *Linguistics and Philosophy* 20: 51–72.

ROBERTS, CRAIGE (1996). Anaphora in intensional contexts. In Lappin, S. (ed.) 215–46.

ROBERTS, CRAIGE (2004). Context in dynamic interpretation. In Horn, L. and Ward, G. (eds.) 197–220.

ROSALDO, MICHELLE Z. (1982). The things we do with words: Ilongot speech acts and speech act theory in philosophy. *Language in Society* 11: 203–37.

ROSS, JOHN ROBERT (1970). On declarative sentences. In Jacobs, R. and Rosenbaum, P. S. (eds.) *Readings in English transformational grammar*. Waltham: Ginn. 222–72.

ROTHSCHILD, DANIEL (2007). Presuppositions and scope. *Journal of Philosophy* 104: 71–106.

RUE, YONG-JU and ZHANG, GRACE QIAO (2008). *Request strategies: a comparative study in Mandarin Chinese and Korean.* Amsterdam: John Benjamins.

RUHI, SÜKRIYE (2006). Politeness in compliment responses: a perspective from naturally occurring exchanges in Turkish. *Pragmatics* 16 (6): 43–101.

RUIZ DE ZAROBE, LEYRE and RUIZ DE ZAROBE, YOLANDA (eds.) (2012). *Speech acts and politeness across languages and cultures.* Bern: Peter Lang.

RUSSELL, BENJAMIN (2006). Against grammatical computation of scalar implicatures. *Journal of Semantics* 23: 361–82.

RUSSELL, BERTRAND (1905). On denoting. *Mind* 14: 479–93.

RUSSELL, BERTRAND (1957). Mr. Strawson on referring. *Mind* 66: 385–9.

RYLE, GILBERT (1954). *Dilemmas.* Cambridge: Cambridge University Press.

SACKS, HARVEY and SCHEGLOFF, EMANUEL (1979). Two preferences in the organization of reference to persons in conversation and their interaction. In Psathas, G. (ed.) *Everyday language: studies in ethnomethodology.* New York: Irvington. 15–21.

SADOCK, JERROLD M. (1974). *Toward a linguistic theory of speech acts.* New York: Academic Press.

SADOCK, JERROLD M. (1978). On testing for conversational implicature. In Cole, P. (ed.) 281–98.

SADOCK, JERROLD M. (1994). Toward a grammatically realistic typology of speech acts. In Tsohatzidis, S. (ed.) 394–406.

SADOCK, JERROLD M. (2004). Speech acts. In Horn, L. R. and Ward, G. (eds.) 53–73.

SADOCK, JERROLD M. and ZWICKY, ARNOLD M. (1985). Speech act distinctions in syntax. In Shopen, T. (ed.) vol. 1: 155–96.

SAEED, JOHN I. (2003). *Semantics.* 2nd edition. Oxford: Blackwell.

SAFIR, KENNETH (2004). Person, context and perspective. *Rivista di Linguistica* 16: 107–53.

SALGADO, ELIZABETH FLORES (2011). *The pragmatics of requests and apologies: developmental patterns of Mexican students.* Amsterdam: John Benjamins.

SALMON, NATHAN (1991). The pragmatic fallacy. *Philosophical Studies* 63: 83–97.

SALMON, NATHAN (2004). The good, the bad and the ugly. In Reimer, M. and Bezuidenhout, A. (eds.) 230–60.

SAUERLAND, ULI (2004). Scalar implicatures in complex sentences. *Linguistics and Philosophy* 27: 367–91.

SAUL, JENNIFER (2002). What is said and psychological reality: Grice's project and relevance theorists' criticisms. *Linguistics and Philosophy* 25: 347–72.

SAVIC, MILICA (2014). *Politeness through the prism of requests, apologies and refusals.* Newcastle upon Tyne: Cambridge Scholars Publishing.

SBISÀ, MARINA (2009). Speech act theory. In Verschueren, J. and Östman, Jan-Ola (eds.) *Key notions for pragmatics.* Amsterdam: John Benjamins. 229–44.

SCHEGLOFF, EMANUEL (1996). Some practices for referring to persons in talk-in-interaction: a partial sketch of a systematics. In Fox, B. (ed.) *Studies in anaphora*. Amsterdam: John Benjamins. 437–85.

SCHLADT, M. (2000). The typology and grammaticalization of reflexives. In Frajzyngier, Z. and Curl, T. S. (eds.) 103–24.

SCHLENKER, PHILIPPE (2003). A plea for monster. *Linguistics and Philosophy* 26: 29–120.

SCHLENKER, PHILIPPE (2007). Anti-dynamics: presupposition projection without dynamic semantics. *Journal of Logic, Language and Information*. 16: 325–56.

SCHLENKER, PHILIPPE (2008). Be articulate: a pragmatic theory of presupposition. *Theoretical Linguistics*: 157–212.

SCHLENKER, PHILIPPE (2012). Maximize Presupposition and Gricean reasoning. *Natural Language Semantics* 20: 391–429.

SCHÖLL, THOMAS (2011). *The acquisition of politeness in the language of children*. Munich: GRIN Verlag.

SCHUTZ, ALFRED (1970). *Reflections on the problems of relevance*. New Haven: Yale University Press.

SCOLLON, RONALD and SCOLLON, SUZANNE WONG (1995). *Intercultural communication: a discourse approach*. Oxford: Blackwell.

SEARLE, JOHN R. (1958). Proper names. *Mind* 67: 166–73.

SEARLE, JOHN R. (1969). *Speech acts: an essay in the philosophy of language*. Cambridge: Cambridge University Press.

SEARLE, JOHN R. (1975a). A taxonomy of speech acts. In Gunderson, K. (ed.) *Minnesota studies in the philosophy of science 9: language, mind and knowledge*. 344–69.

SEARLE, JOHN R. (1975b). Indirect speech acts. In Cole, P. and Morgan, J. L. (eds.) 59–82.

SEARLE, JOHN R. (1979). *Expression and meaning: studies in the theory of speech acts*. Cambridge: Cambridge University Press.

SEARLE, JOHN R. (1983). *Intentionality: an essay in the philosophy of mind*. Cambridge: Cambridge University Press.

SEARLE, JOHN R. (1992). *The rediscovery of the mind*. Cambridge, MA: MIT Press.

SEARLE, JOHN R. (1996). *The construction of social reality*. Oxford: Blackwell.

SEARLE, JOHN R. (2002). *Consciousness and language*. Cambridge: Cambridge University Press.

SEARLE, JOHN R. and VANDERVEKEN, DANIEL (1985). *Foundations of illocutionary logic*. Cambridge: Cambridge University Press.

SELLS, PETER (1987). Aspects of logophoricity. *Linguistic Inquiry* 18: 445–79.

SEUREN, PETER (2000). Presupposition, negation and trivalence. *Journal of Linguistics* 36: 1–37.

SEUREN, PETER (2004). *Chomsky's minimalism*. Oxford: Oxford University Press.

SHARIATI, MOHAMMAD and CHAMANI, FARIBA (2010). Apology strategies in Persian. *Journal of Pragmatics* 42: 1689–99.

SHARIFIAN, FARZAD (2005). The Persian cultural schema of *shekasteh-nafsi*: a study of compliment reponses in Persian and Anglo-Australian speakers. *Pragmatics and Cognition* 13: 337–61.

SHIBATANI, MASAYOSHI (1990). *The languages of Japan*. Cambridge: Cambridge University Press.

SHIBATANI, MASAYOSHI (1999). Honorifics. In Brown, K. and Miller, J. (eds.) *Concise encyclopedia of grammatical categories*. New York: Elsevier Science. 192–201.

SHOPEN, TIM (ed.) (1985). *Language typology and syntactic description*. 3 vols. Cambridge: Cambridge University Press.

SIDNELL, JACK (2009). Deixis. In Verschueren, J. and Ostman, J.-O. (eds.) *Key notions for pragmatics*. Amsterdam: John Benjamins. 114–38.

SIDNELL, JACK and ENFIELD, N. (forthcoming). In Huang, Y. (ed.).

SIEBOLD, KATHRIN (2012). Implicit and explicit thanking in Spanish and German. In Ruiz de Zarobe, L. and Ruiz de Zarobe, Y. (eds.) 155–71.

SIEWIERSKA, ANNA (2004). *Person*. Cambridge: Cambridge University Press.

SIFIANOU, MARIA (1992). *Politeness phenomena in England and Greece: a cross-cultural perspective*. Oxford: Clarendon Press.

SIFIANOU, MARIA (2001). 'Oh, how appropriate!' Compliments and politeness. In Bayraktaroglu, A. and Sifianou, M. (eds.) 391–430.

SIGURÐSSON, HALLDÓR Á. (1990). Long-distance reflexives and moods in Icelandic. In Maling, J. and Zaenen, A. (eds.) *Syntax and semantics 24: Modern Icelandic syntax*. London: Academic Press. 309–46.

SIMON, HORST J. and WIESE, HEIKE (eds.) (2002). *Pronouns: grammar and representation*. Amsterdam: John Benjamins.

SIMONS, MANDY (2003). Presupposition and accommodation: understanding the Stalnakerian picture. *Philosophical Studies* 112: 251–78.

SIMONS, MANDY (2014). On the conversational basis of some presuppositions. In Capone, A. et al. (eds.) 329–48.

SINHA, ANJANI KUMAR (1972). On the deictic uses of 'coming' and 'going' in Hindi. *Papers from the Regional Meeting of the Chicago Linguistic Society* 8: 351–8.

SLOBIN, DAN I. (1996). From 'thought and language' to 'thinking for speaking'. In Gumperz, J. J. and Levinson, S. C. (eds.) *Rethinking linguistic relativity*. Cambridge: Cambridge University Press. 70–96.

SMITH, BERRY (1990). Towards a history of speech act theory. In Burkhardt, A. (ed.) *Speech acts, meaning and interactions: critical approaches to the philosophy of John R. Searle*. Berlin: W. de Gruyter. 29–61.

SMITH, NEIL (2004). *Chomsky: ideas and ideals*. 2nd edition. Cambridge: Cambridge University Press.

SOAMES, SCOTT (1979). A projection problem for speaker presuppositions. *Linguistic Inquiry* 10: 623–66.

SOAMES, SCOTT (1982). How presuppositions are inherited: a solution to the projection problem. *Linguistic Inquiry* 13: 483–545.

SOAMES, SCOTT (1989). Presupposition. In Gabbay, D. and Guenthner, F. (eds.) *Handbook of philosophical logic*. Vol 4. Dordrecht: Reidel. 553–616.

SOAMES, SCOTT (2002). *Beyond rigidity: the unfinished semantic agenda of Naming and Necessity*. Oxford: Oxford University Press.

SORIA, BELEN and ROMERO, ESTHER (eds.) (2010). *Explicit communication*. Basingstoke: Palgrave Macmillan.

SPECTOR, BENJAMIN (2006). Aspects de la pragmatique des opérateurs logiques. PhD dissertation. Université de Paris 7.

SPERBER, DAN and WILSON, DEIRDRE (1986). *Relevance: communication and cognition*. Oxford: Blackwell.

SPERBER, DAN and WILSON, DEIRDRE (1987). Précis of Relevance. *Behavioral and Brain Sciences*. 10: 697–710.

SPERBER, DAN and WILSON, DEIRDRE (1995). *Relevance: communication and cognition*. 2nd edition. Oxford: Blackwell.

SPERBER, DAN and WILSON, DEIRDRE (2002). Pragmatics, modularity and mindreading. *Mind and Language* 17: 3–23.

SPERLICH, DARCY (2013). The acquisition of long-distance reflexives in Chinese as an interlanguage: an experimental study. PhD dissertation. University of Auckland.

STALNAKER, ROBERT C. (1972). Pragmatics. In Davidson, D. and Harman, G. (eds.) *Semantics of natural language*. Dordrecht: Reidel. 380–97.

STALNAKER, ROBERT C. (1973). Presuppositions. *The Journal of Philosophical Logic* 2: 447–57.

STALNAKER, ROBERT C. (1974). Pragmatic presupposition. In Munitz, M. and Unger, P. (eds.) *Semantics and philosophy*. New York: New York University Press. 197–214.

STALNAKER, ROBERT C. (1978). Assertation. In Cole, P. (ed.) 315–22.

STALNAKER, ROBERT C. (1981). Indexical belief. *Synthese* 49: 129–51.

STALNAKER, ROBERT C. (1998). On the representation of context. *Journal of Logic, Language and Information* 7: 3–19.

STALNAKER, ROBERT C. (1999). *Context and content*. Oxford: Oxford University Press.

STANLEY, JASON (2000). Context and logical form. *Linguistics and Philosophy* 23: 391–434.

STANLEY, JASON (2002). Making it articulated. *Mind and Language* 17: 149–68.

STANLEY, JASON (2005). Semantics in context. In Preyer, G. and Peter, G. (eds.) 221–54.

STANLEY, JASON and SZABÓ, ZOLTÁN G. (2000a). On quantifier domain restriction. *Mind and Language* 15: 219–61.

STANLEY, JASON and SZABÓ, ZOLTÁN G. (2000b). Reply to Bach and Neale. *Mind and Language* 15: 295–8.

STIRLING, LESLEY (1993). *Switch-reference and discourse representation*. Cambridge: Cambridge University Press.

STRAWSON, PETER F. (1950). On referring. *Mind* 59: 320–44.

STRAWSON, PETER F. (1952). *Introduction to logical theory*. London: Methuen.

STRAWSON, PETER F. (1964). Intention and convention in speech acts. *Philosophical Review* 73: 290–302.

STRECKER, IVO (1993). Cultural variations in the notion of 'face'. *Multilingua* 12: 119–41.

SUBBARAO, K. V. and LALITHA MURTHY, B. (2000). Lexical anaphors and pronouns in Telugu. In Lust, B. et al. (eds.) 217–76.

SUSZCZYŃSKA, MALGORZATA (1999). Apologizing in English, Polish and Hungarian: different languages, different strategies. *Journal of pragmatics* 31: 1053–65.

SZABÓ, ZOLTÁN G. (2005a). Introduction. In Szabó, Z. G. (ed.) 1–14.

SZABÓ, ZOLTÁN G. (ed.) (2005b). *Semantics versus pragmatics*. Oxford: Clarendon Press.

TAAVITSAINEN, IRMA and JUCKER, ANDREAS H. (2003). *Diachronic perspectives on address term systems*. Amsterdam: John Benjamins.

TAKAHASHI, TOMOKO and BEEBE, LESLIE M. (1987). The development of pragmatic competence in Japanese learners of English. *JALT Journal* 8: 131–55.

TAKAHASHI, TOMOKO and BEEBE, LESLIE M. (1993). Cross-linguistic influence in the speech act of correction. In Kasper, G. and Blum-Kulka, S. (eds.) 138–57.

TANG, CHEN-HSIN and ZHANG, GRACE QIAO (2009). A contrastive study of compliment responses among Australian English and Mandarin Chinese speakers. *Journal of Pragmatics* 42: 1951–63.

TAYLOR, KENNETH (2001). Sex, breakfast, and descriptus interruptus. *Synthèse* 128: 45–61.

TERKOURAFI, MARINA (2008). Toward a unified theory of politeness, impoliteness, and rudeness. In Locher, M. and Bousfield, D. 45–74.

TERKOURAFI, MARINA (2012). Politeness and pragmatics. In Allan, K. and Jaszczolt, K. M. (eds.) 617–37.

THOMAS, JENNY (1995). *Meaning in interaction: an introduction to pragmatics*. London: Longman.

THOMASON, RICHMOND H. (1990). Accommodation, meaning, and implicature: interdisciplinary foundations for pragmatics. In Cohen, P. R., Morgan, J., and Pollack, M. E. (eds.) *Intentions in communication*. Cambridge, MA: MIT Press. 325–64.

TOMASELLO, MICHAEL (2004). *Constructing a language: a usage-based theory of language acquisition*. Cambridge, MA: Harvard University Press.

TRAUGOTT, ELIZABETH CLOSS (2004). Historical pragmatics. In Horn, L. R. and Ward, G. (eds.) 538–61.

TRAUGOTT, ELIZABETH CLOSS and DASHER, RICHARD D. (2001). *Regularity in semantic change*. Cambridge: Cambridge University Press.

TRAVIS, CHARLES (1981). *The true and the false: the domain of the pragmatic*. Amsterdam: John Benjamins.

TRAVIS, CHARLES (1985). On what is strictly speaking true. *Canadian Journal of Philosophy* 15: 187–229.

TRAVIS, CHARLES (1997). Pragmatics. In Hale, B. and Wright, C. (eds.) *A companion to the philosophy of language*. Oxford: Blackwell. 87–107.

TROSBORG, ANNA (1995). *Interlanguage pragmatics: requests, complaints, and apologies*. Berlin: Mouton de Gruyter.

TROSBORG, ANNA (ed.) (2010). *Pragmatics across languages and cultures*. Berlin: De Gruyter Mouton.

TRUDGILL, PETER (2000). *Sociolinguistics: an introduction to language and society*. 4th edition. London: Penguin.

TSOHATZIDIS, SAVAS L. (ed.) (1994). *Foundations of speech act theory: philosophical and linguistic perspectives*. London: Routledge.

TURNER, KEN (1997). Semantics vs. pragmatics. In Verschueren et al. (eds.) *Handbook of pragmatics*. Amsterdam: John Benjamins. 1–23.

TURNER, KEN (ed.) (1999). *The semantics-pragmatics interface from different points of view*. New York: Elsevier Science.

UEDA, K. (1974). Sixteen ways to avoid saying 'no' in Japanese. In Condon, J. C. and Saito, M. (eds.) *Intercultural encounters with Japan: communication, contact and conflict*. Tokyo: Simul Press.

URMSON, J. O. (1956). *Philosophical analysis: its development between the two wars*. Oxford: Clarendon Press.

VAN DER SANDT, ROB (1988). *Context and presupposition*. London: Croom Helm.

VAN DER SANDT, ROB (1992). Presupposition projection as anaphora resolution. *Journal of Semantics* 9: 333–77.

VAN EIJK, JAN (1997). *The Lillooet language: phonology, morphology, syntax*. Vancouver: University of British Columbia Press.

VAN KUPPEVELT, J. (1996). Inferring from topics: scalar implicatures as topic-dependent inferences. *Linguistics and Philosophy* 19: 393–443.

VAN MULKEN, D. (1996). Politeness markers in French and Dutch requests. In Jaszczolt, K. M. and Turner, K. (eds.) *Contrastive semantics and pragmatics*. New York: Elsevier Science. 689–702.

VAN ROOIJ, ROBERT (2004). Relevance in bidirectional Optimality Theory. In Blutner R. and Zeevat, H. (eds.) 173–210.

VAN ROOIJ, ROBERT and SCHULZ, K. (2004). Exhaustive interpretation of complex sentences. *Journal of Logic, Language and Information* 13: 491–519.

VANDERVEKEN, DANIEL (1990). *Meaning and speech acts vol 1: principles of language use*. Cambridge: Cambridge University Press.

VANDERVEKEN, DANIEL (1991). *Meaning and speech acts vol 2: formal semantics of success and satisfaction*. Cambridge: Cambridge University Press.

VANDERVEKEN, DANIEL (1994). A complete formulation of a simple logic of elementary illocutionary acts. In Tsohatzidis, S. (ed.) 99–131.

VANDERVEKEN, DANIEL (2002). Universal grammar and speech act theory. In Vanderveken, D. and Kubo, S. (eds.) 25–62.

VANDERVEKEN, DANIEL and KUBO, SUSUMU (eds.) (2002). *Essays in speech act theory*. Amsterdam: John Benjamins.

VERSCHUEREN, JEF (ed.) (1991). *Levels of linguistic adaptation*. Amsterdam: John Benjamins.

VERSCHUEREN, JEF (1995). The pragmatics perspective. In Verschueren et al. (eds.).

VERSCHUEREN, JEF (1999). *Understanding pragmatics*. London: Arnold.

VERSCHUEREN, JEF and BERTUCCELLI-PAPI, MARIA (eds.) (1987). *The pragmatics perspective*. Amsterdam: John Benjamins.

VERSCHUEREN, JEF, ÖSTMAN, O. H., BLOMMAERT, J., and BULCAEN, C. (eds.) (1995). *Handbook of pragmatics*. Amsterdam: John Benjamins.

VINCENTE, BEGOÑA (2002). What pragmatics can tell us about (literal) meaning: a critical note on Bach's theory of impliciture. *Journal of Pragmatics* 32: 403–21.

VON HEUSINGER, KLAUS and TURNER, KEN (2006a). (By way of an) introduction: a first dialogue on the semantics-pragmatics interface. In von Heusinger, K. and Turner, K. (eds.) 1–18.

VON HEUSINGER, KLAUS and TURNER, KEN (eds.) (2006b). *Where semantics meets pragmatics*. Oxford: Elsevier.

VOORHOEVE. C. L. (1975). Central and western trans New Guinea Phylum languages. In Wurm, S. A. (ed.) *New Guinea area languages and language study 1*. Canberra: Pacific Linguistics C-38. 345–459.

WALI, KASHI and SUBBARAO, K. V. (1991). On pronominal classification: evidence from Marathi and Telugu. *Linguistics* 29: 1093–110.

WALKER, R. (1975). Conversational implicatures. In Blackburn, S. (ed.) *Meaning, reference and necessity*. Cambridge: Cambridge University Press. 133–81.

WALKINSHAW, IAN (2009). *Learning politeness: disagreement in a second language*. New York: Peter Lang.

WARD, GREGORY L. (2004). Equatives and deferred reference. *Language* 80: 262–89.

WARD, GREGORY L. and HIRSCHBERG, JULIA (1991). A pragmatic analysis of tautological utterances. *Journal of Pragmatics* 15: 507–20.

WATKINS, L. J. (1984). *A grammar of Kiowa*. Lincoln: University of Nebraska Press.

WATTS, RICHARD J. (2003). *Politeness*. Cambridge: Cambridge University Press.

WATTS, RICHARD J. (2008). Rudeness, conceptual blending theory and relational work. *Journal of Politeness Research* 4: 289–317.

WATTS, RICHARD J., IDE, SACHIKO, and EHLICH, KONRAD (eds.) (2005). *Politeness in language: studies in its history, theory and practice*. 2nd edition. Berlin: Mouton de Gruyter.

WEBBER, BONNIE LYNN (1991). Structure and ostension in the interpretation of discourse deixis. *Language and Cognitive Processes* 6: 107–35.

WEINER, M. (2006). Are all conversational implicatures cancellable? *Analysis* 66: 127–30.

WEISSENBORN, JÜRGEN and KLEIN, WOLFGANG (eds.) (1982). *Here and there: cross-linguistic studies on deixis and demonstration*. Amsterdam: John Benjamins.

WEIZMAN, ELDA (1993). Interlanguage requestive hints. In Kasper, G. and Blum-Kulka, S. (eds.) 123–37.

WELKER, KATHERINE (1994). Plans in the common ground: toward a generative account of conversational implicature. PhD dissertation. Ohio State University.

WIERZBICKA, ANNA (1987). Boys will be boys. *Language* 63: 95–114.

WIERZBICKA, ANNA (1991). *Cross-cultural pragmatics: the semantics of human interaction*. Berlin: Mouton de Gruyter.

WIESEMANN, URSULA (ed.) (1986). *Pronominal systems*. Tübingen: Narr.

WILKINS, DAVID and HILL, DEBORAH (1995) When 'GO' means 'COME': questioning the basicness of basic motion verbs. *Cognitive Linguistics* 6: 209–59.

WILSON, DEIRDRE (1975). *Presupposition and non-truth-conditional semantics*. New York: Academic Press.

WILSON, DEIRDRE (2010). Relevance theory. In Cumming, L. (ed.) 393–9.

WILSON, DEIRDRE and CARSTON, ROBIN (2007). A unitary approach to lexical pragmatics: relevance, inference and ad hoc concepts. In Burton-Roberts, N. (ed.) 230–59.

WILSON, DEIRDRE and SPERBER, DAN (1993). Linguistic form and relevance. *Lingua* 90: 1–25.

WILSON, DEIRDRE and SPERBER, DAN (2004). Relevance theory. In Horn, L. R. and Ward, G. (eds.) 607–32.

WILSON, GEORGE (1991). Reference and pronominal description. *Journal of Philosophy* 88: 359–87.

WITTGENSTEIN, LUDWIG (1953). *Philosophical investigations*. Oxford: Blackwell.

WONG, MAY L. Y. (2010). Expressions of gratitude by Hong Kong speakers of English: research from the International Corpus of English in Hong Kong (ICE-HK). *Journal of Pragmatics* 42: 1243–57.

YU, MING-CHUNG (2003). On the universality of face: evidence from Chinese compliment response behaviour. *Journal of Pragmatics* 35(10): 1679–710.

YUEN, LI (2002). Compliments and compliments responses in Kunming Chinese. *Pragmatics* 12: 183–226.

YULE, GEORGE (1996). *Pragmatics*. Oxford: Oxford University Press.

ZEEVAT, HENK (2012). Objection marking and additivity. *Lingua* 122: 1886–98.

ZEITOUN, ELIZABETH (1997). The pronominal system of Mantauran (Rukai). *Oceanic Linguistics* 36: 114–48.

ZEYREK, DENIZ (2001). Politeness in Turkish and its linguistic manifestations: a socio-cultural perspective. In Bayraktaroglu, A. and Sifianou, M. (eds.) 43–74.

ZEYREK, DENIZ (2012). Thanking in Turkish: a corpus-based study. In Ruiz de Zarobe, L. and Ruiz de Zarobe, Y. (eds.) 53–88.

ZHU, HUA, LI, WEI, and QIAN, YUAN (2000). The sequential organisation of gift offering and acceptance in Chinese. *Journal of Pragmatics* 32: 81–103.

ZIFF, P. (1960). *Semantic analysis*. Ithaca: Cornell University Press.

ZIPF, GEORGE K. (1949). *Human behavior and the principle of least effort: an introduction to human ecology*. Cambridge, MA: Addison-Wesley.

ZRIBI-HERTZ, ANNE (1989). Anaphor binding and narrative point of view: English reflexive pronouns in sentence and discourse. *Language* 65: 695–727.

ZWICKY, ARNOLD M. (1974). Hey, whatsyaname! *Papers from the Regional Meeting of the Chicago Linguistic Society* 10: 787–801.

Suggested solutions
to exercises

Chapter 1

1. The propositional content of (i)–(viii) is THE SHOPKEEPER HAD REDUCED THE PRICES.
2. Entailment
      (i) Yes
      (ii) No
      (iii) No
      (iv) Yes
      (v) Yes
      (vi) No
      (vii) Yes
      (viii) No

Chapter 2

1. The violated maxim is the maxim of Relation.
2. Opted-out maxims
      (i) Quality
      (ii) Quantity
      (iii) Relation
      (iv) Quality
      (v) Manner
      (vi) Quality
      (vii) Manner
      (viii) Relation
      (ix) Quantity
      (x) Quality
3. The conversational implicature Joe failed to work out is that there might be some honey in the beehive in the oak tree. It is a conversational implicature$_O$.
4. The conversational implicature of Mary's reply is that what John said is absurdly incorrect. This is a conversational implicature$_F$. The maxims of Quality and Relation are flouted. The conversational implicature of the clergyman's response is that he did not think that the person who spoke to him (that is, Lord

Rutherford) was Lord Rutherford. This is also a conversational implicature$_F$. The maxims of Quality and Relation are also flouted.

5. The conversational implicature in question is that President Kennedy and the United States of America would stand by the people of West Berlin. The maxim of Quality is flouted.

6. Generalized versus particularized conversational implicature
    (a) is the generalized conversational implicature (GCI)
    (b) is the particularized conversational implicature (PCI)

7. It is because of the Navajo taboo of not speaking the name of the dead, as pointed out by the author of the novel. The example is not a real counterexample to Grice's first sub-maxim of Quantity: what it shows is that this sub-maxim can be overridden by a sociolinguistic rule.

8. Q-implicatures and their types
    (i) The man Mary is chatting with is not her husband; Q$_{scalar}$ implicature
    (ii) The speaker may or may not love his wife—he doesn't know which; Q$_{clausal}$ implicature
    (iii) Please don't roast, boil, steam, or bake the bean sprouts; Q$_{unordered\ alternate}$ implicature
    (iv) Xiaoming does not hate/loathe cheese; Q$_{scalar}$ implicature
    (v) Her uncle is not the president; Q$_{ordered\ alternate}$ implicature
    (vi) The Smiths have not married yet; Q$_{ordered\ alternate}$ implicature
    (vii) John will send it perhaps as an e-mail or perhaps not as an e-mail; perhaps as an attachment or perhaps not as an attachment; Q$_{clausal}$ implicature
    (viii) The speaker's brother has not got Barack Obama's autograph; Q$_{ordered\ alternate}$ implicature
    (ix) The two impressionist paintings are not identical; Q$_{scalar}$ implicature
    (x) Peter is either a chief or a gardener; Q$_{scalar}$ implicature

9. Q-implicatures
    (i) The sprinter can't run 100m in less than 9.8 seconds
    (ii) The sprinter can run 100m in more than 9.8 seconds

10. It is because the seven lexical expressions under discussion have two opposite orientations. Although the word *lukewarm* is defined as 'moderately warm, tepid; not zealous, indifferent' in *The Concise Oxford Dictionary of Current English*, it functions as a weaker version of *cool/cold/freezing* rather than *warm/hot/boiling*. As pointed out in Horn (1989 and personal communication), this can be shown by the contrastive behaviours of *lukewarm* using the following diagnostic tests.
    (i) a. The tea is not just lukewarm, but downright cool!
        b. Her greeting was lukewarm, if not downright chilly!
        c. The prime minister's reception was lukewarm, verging on cool.
    (ii) a. ?The tea is not just lukewarm, but downright warm!
        b. ?Her greeting was lukewarm, if not downright friendly!
        c. ?The prime minister's reception was lukewarm, verging on warm.

11. Metalinguistic versus descriptive negation
    (i) Descriptive negation
    (ii) Metalinguistic negation
    (iii) Descriptive negation
    (iv) Metalinguistic negation
    (v) Metalinguistic negation
    (vi) Descriptive negation
    (vii) Descriptive negation
    (viii) Metalinguistic negation
    (ix) Metalinguistic negation
    (x) Metalinguistic negation

12. I-implicatures
    (i) John is reading two modern European languages other than modern English at Oxford University
    (ii) If and only if you let me see the manuscript will I make a donation to the library
    (iii) The children ate the whole cake and all the apples after dinner
    (iv) His female secretary talked learnedly about the internet
    (v) The police first moved in and then the suspects were arrested, or
        The police moved in and thereby caused the suspects to be arrested, or
        The police moved in in order to arrest the suspects
    (vi) John and Mary scrubbed the carpet afresh together
    (vii) The speaker has no idea if John is in a sexual/romantic relationship
    (viii) a. The apple is red on its peel
           b. The watermelon is red inside its flesh
           c. The pencil is painted red or has red lead
           d. The book is red on its cover
           e. The house is red on its outside
    (ix) I usually have a hen egg for breakfast in the morning
    (x) Something smells bad/stinks here

13. M-implicatures
    (i) John went to a particular university or a particular university campus without doing the things (such as studying for a degree) that are socially stereotypically associated with the institution, as conventionally I-implicated by its corresponding a utterance. The same is true of *John went to church/the church, jail/the jail,* and *school/the school.*
    (ii) John didn't stop the alarm in the normal way
    (iii) Mary has a dress whose colour can't be described exactly as pink
    (iv) John had the ability to swim the English Channel, but he didn't
         Cf. the I-implicature of the a utterance, namely, John could swim the English Channel, and he did
    (v) John drank considerably more Pinot Noir for dinner yesterday evening than the uttering of the a sentence would suggest
    (vi) That may not be his father; he could be his stepfather

(vii) Peter is an extremely rich businessman

(viii) Their new boss is less friendly than the uttering of the a sentence would suggest

14. Conventional implicatures

(i) John is going to finish his thesis

(ii) Although it is hard to believe, the two families live opposite each other

(iii) Others, besides his sister, belly-danced in a Lebanese restaurant two nights a week; and of those under consideration, his sister was among the least likely to do so, or

His sister is the least likely (in a contextually invoked set) to belly-dance in a Lebanese restaurant two nights a week

(iv) Someone other than Mike forgot to ring the client

(v) The VIPs' arrival is expected

(vi) Mary was born in London. By contrast, her husband was an immigrant from Pakistan

(vii) It was difficult for John to complete his thesis on virtual reality technology

(viii) The addressee is socially superior to or distant from the speaker

Chapter 3

1. Presuppositions

(i) The burglar had been filmed on closed circuit television

(ii) John ought to have done, or intended to do, the washing up

(iii) John had an/the accident

(iv) Professor Matthews had solved one of evolution's great mysteries

(v) John was off cigarettes before

(vi) Someone moved to Spain

(vii) Miriam's husband was having an affair

(viii) Mary wasn't emptying the shopping bag before. Note that other aspectual/change-of-state predicates include *continue*, *quit*, *resume*, and *start*.

(ix) John doesn't know how to use an iPad

(x) There are cats

(xi) John missed the interview

(xii) John's brother used all the printer paper

(xiii) William Shakespeare existed

(xvi) Someone gave her a rose

(xv) Helen has a mother-in-law

(xvi) Looked at economically, something else is easy to solve

2. Presuppositions

(i) John wasn't a professional footballer

(ii) John read mathematics at Harvard University

(iii) Bill cheated in the final exam

(iv) John hadn't had a bath for three weeks

(v) Peter is rich. But compare and contrast

John isn't as tall as Peter, which may not carry the presupposition that Peter is tall.

(vi) Susan was wearing a fur coat

(vii) Jamie walked into the study

(viii) Mary is a lawyer and Susan is a lawyer

3. The use of *as a part of good parental correction* seems to presuppose that smacking is a part of good parental correction. If it is a part of good parental correction, it should of course not be a criminal offence in New Zealand. In other words, the referendum question was made inherently biased towards a no vote by the presupposition.

4. Presuppositions or not

(i) No. It is a conversational implicature.

(ii) Yes

(iii) Yes

(iv) No. It is a conventional implicature.

(v) No

(vi) No. It is an entailment.

(vii) No. It is a conventional implicature.

(viii) No. It is a conventional implicature.

5. Putative presuppositions and their cancellations

(i) Manchester United lost the game, cancelled by overt denial

(ii) Dr Smith was promoted to an associate professor, cancelled by real-world knowledge, namely, universities normally do not promote a person after he or she has left them. (Needless to say, what we are talking about here is a promotion within the same university where Dr Smith had been working for some time.)

(iii) Someone fancies Henry, cancelled by reduction arguments

(iv) Charles finished running the 400 metres, cancelled by real-world knowledge

(v) Neil Armstrong was the first man to travel in space, cancelled by real-world knowledge, namely Yuri Gagarin was the first man to travel in space

(vi) The news was announced, cancelled by explicit suspension

(vii) He is the Tsar of Russia, cancelled by overt denial

(viii) Cambridge wins the boat race, cancelled by the $Q_{clausal}$ conversational implicature, namely, Cambridge may not win the boat race

(ix) The vase fell to the ground and broke, cancelled by real-world knowledge or by the immediate linguistic context

(x) There would be a buoyant demand for homes soon, cancelled by the use of a propositional attitude verb

(xi) She had had some tea, cancelled by overt denial

(xii) His father was an infamous Red Guard during Mao's Cultural Revolution in China, cancelled by the use of 'I don't know'

6. Entailments versus presuppositions under negation and in modal contexts
   If (i) is negated, as in (ii), or put in modal contexts, as in (iii) and (iv), its
   entailment will not survive. (I use '~ ‖-' to stand for 'does not entail'.)

   (i) The nursery teacher sold nine Christmas raffle tickets.

      ~ ‖- The nursery teacher sold eight Christmas raffle tickets

   (ii) The nursery teacher didn't sell nine Christmas raffle tickets.

      ~ ‖- The nursery teacher sold eight Christmas raffle tickets

   (iii) It's possible/there's a chance that the nursery teacher sold nine Christmas
   raffle tickets.

      ~ ‖- The nursery teacher sold eight Christmas raffle tickets

   (iv) The nursery teacher could/should/ought to sell nine Christmas raffle tickets.

      ~ ‖- The nursery teacher sold eight Christmas raffle tickets

   On the other hand, the presupposition will get through under the same
   circumstances. This is shown by (v) and (3.36) and (3.37) in the text.

   (v) The nursery teacher didn't sell nine Christmas raffle tickets.

      >> There is a nursery teacher

   On the basis of the above comparison, the conclusion we can draw is that there
   are at least some linguistic contexts in which entailments cannot survive but
   presuppositions can.

Chapter 4

1. Performatives versus constatives
   - (i) Constative
   - (ii) Performative
   - (iii) Constative
   - (iv) Performative
   - (v) Performative
   - (vi) Constative
   - (vii) Performative
   - (viii) Constative

2. Explicit versus implicit performatives
   - (i) Implicit
   - (ii) Implicit
   - (iii) Explicit
   - (iv) Implicit
   - (v) Implicit
   - (vi) Explicit

3. Performative verbs
   - (i) Yes
   - (ii) Yes
   - (iii) Yes

(iv) No

(v) No

(vi) Yes

4. Performatively versus non-performatively

(i) Non-performatively

(ii) Performatively

(iii) Performatively

(iv) Non-performatively

(v) Performatively

(vi) Non-performatively

5. Felicity condition violated

The Austinian felicity condition Diana violated is B (i). It is a misfire.

6. Locutionary, illocutionary, and perlocutionary acts

(i) Locution: The mother uttered the words 'Give me that *Playboy* magazine' to her son meaning 'Hand that *Playboy* magazine over to me', with *me* referring to the mother.

Illocution: The mother requested (or ordered) her son to give her the *Playboy* magazine. Or the mother performed the speech act of requesting (or ordering) her son to give her the *Playboy* magazine.

Perlocution: The mother persuaded her son to give her the *Playboy* magazine. Or the son refused to give his mother the *Playboy* magazine.

(ii) Locution: The dean's secretary uttered the word 'Coffee?' to the professor, meaning 'Would you like a coffee?'

Illocution: The dean's secretary offered a coffee to the professor. Or the dean's secretary performed the speech act of offering a coffee to the professor.

Perlocution: The professor accepted the coffee from the dean's secretary with thanks. Or the professor declined the coffee from the dean's secretary with thanks.

7. Searlean felicity conditions

(i) Questioning

(i) Propositional content: any proposition or propositional function

(ii) Preparatory: (a) S does not know the answer, i.e. for a yes/no question, he does not know whether p is true or false; for a WH-question, he does not know the missing information. (b) It is not obvious to both S and H that H will provide the information at that time without being asked

(iii) Sincerity: S wants this information

(iv) Essential: the utterance of e counts as an attempt to elicit this information from H where p stands for the proposition expressed in the speech act

(ii) Thanking

(i) Propositional content: past act A done by H

(ii) Preparatory: *S* believes that *A* benefits *S*

(iii) Sincerity: *S* feels grateful or appreciative for *A*

(iv) Essential: the utterance of *e* counts as an expression of gratitude or appreciation

(iii) Warning

(i) Propositional content: future event or state, etc. *E*

(ii) Preparatory: *S* has reason to believe that *E* will occur and that it is not in *H*'s interest

(iii) Sincerity: *S* believes that *E* is not in *H*'s best interest

(iv) Essential: the utterance of *e* counts as an undertaking that *E* is not in *H*'s best interest where *E* stands for event

8. Classification of speech acts

(i) Directive

(ii) Expressive

(iii) Directive

(iv) Commissive

(v) Declaration

(vi) Declaration

(vii) Representative

(viii) Expressive

9. Direct versus indirect speech acts

(i) Indirect

(ii) Direct

(iii) Indirect (No one cares!)

(iv) Indirect

(v) Indirect

(vi) Direct

10. FTA-avoiding strategies

(i) Don't perform the FTA

(ii) On record, with negative politeness redress

(iii) Off record

(iv) On record, without redress

(v) On record, with positive politeness redress

Order of politeness, starting with the strongest: (i), (iii), (ii), (v), (iv)

11. Interlanguage compliment response

The main pragmatic error here is that the Chinese L2 learner of English uses self-denigrating as the response to the foreign visitor's compliment. The typical response by a native speaker of English here would be acceptance/thanking. The error is largely the result of the influence of the typical compliment response formula in Chinese, as pointed out in the text.

Chapter 5

1. Used deictically, and if so, gesturally or symbolically?
   (i) Yes, symbolically
   (ii) Yes, gesturally
   (iii) Normally, no. *You* is used as impersonal here.
   (iv) Yes, gesturally
   (v) No. *He* is used anaphorically here.
   (vi) *There* is used both anaphorically and deictically in a symbolic way. *His* is used anaphorically.
2. Yiddish joke
   The Hebrew teacher should have used 'my slippers' rather than 'your slippers'. He forgot the fact that in deixis, my 'I' is your 'you', my 'here' is your 'there', and my 'this' is your 'that'. This is also true of 'my', that is, his 'my slippers' is his wife's 'your slippers'.
3. Deictic projection
   (i) No
   (ii) Yes, the deictic centre has been projected onto the next station.
   (iii) No
   (iv) Yes, the deictic centre has been shifted to New Zealand. So *next summer* is not next British summer but next New Zealand summer.
   (v) No
   (vi) Yes, the deictic centre has been projected onto the addressee.
   (vii) Yes, the deictic centre has been shifted to the northern hemisphere.
   (viii) No
4. Why is (ii) anomalous?
   The *us* in *let's* has to be understood inclusively. This explains why (i) is OK but (ii) is anomalous. In (i), the speaker and the addressee can both go to the airport to collect a third person, whereas in (ii), the speaker and the addressee cannot both go to the airport where one of them already is.
5. Why is *we* used?
   (i) *We* is used here to show that the doctor has taken the perspective of the patient or identified him or her with the patient.
   (ii) This is known as the 'business' *we*. *We* is used here to indicate 'I + powerful', expressing both the *we* as office and the *we* of the group.
6. Use of *here*
   (i) The region referred to is restricted to the speaker's place and excludes that of the addressee.
   (ii) The region referred to is of broad extent and includes both the speaker and the addressee(s).
   (iii) The place referred to is a small segment of the body of the speaker.
   (iv) The region referred to is a deferred place using a map in the common perceptual field of the interlocutors.

7. Deictically versus non-deictically
   (i) (a) Deictically
   (i) (b) Non-deictically
   (ii) (a) Non-deictically
   (ii) (b) Deictically
8. *Go* versus *come*
   (i) Since *go* designates movement away from the speaker's location at the time of speaking, and the use of *there* indicates that the location it encodes will be away from the speaker, both readings of *we* are possible.
   (ii) Given that one of the conditions for the use of *come* is movement towards the addressee's location at arrival time, and *there* establishes that one of the interlocutors—namely, the addressee—will be away from the speaker at arrival time, the addressee is excluded from *we*.
9. Deictic expressions and their types
   (i) I (person), here (space), there (space)
   (ii) Good morning (time), ladies and gentlemen (person, social), this (space)
   (iii) We (person), this year (time), that (discourse), I (person)
   (iv) I (person), came (space), you (person), last week (time), there (space)
   (v) Good afternoon (time), Sir (person, social), I (person), you (person)
   (vi) I (person), that person (emotional)

Chapter 6

1.   (i) Yes
   (ii) Yes
   (iii) No
   (iv) Yes
   (v) Yes
   (vi) Yes
   (vii) Yes
   (viii) Yes
   (ix) Yes
   (x) Yes
2. Type of referring expression and category of reference
   (i) Proper name, definite reference
   (ii) Demonstrative pronoun, demonstrative reference
   (iii) Proper name, definite reference
   (iv) Indefinite description, generic reference
   (v) Indefinite description, indefinite reference
   (vi) Possessive NP, definite reference
   (vii) Partially descriptive proper name, definite reference
   (viii) Indefinite partially descriptive proper name, indefinite reference

(ix) Incomplete definite description, definite reference

(x) The natural kind term *silver* does not belong to any of the categories of reference discussed in this book. The most common view in the philosophy of language is that it stands for a substance, understood as a universal of some kind (Fred Kroon, personal communication).

(xi) Definite description, arguably generic reference of some kind

(xii) Definite description, definite reference

3. Type of anaphoric use

   (i) Bridging-cross reference.
   (ii) E-type
   (iii) Referential
   (iv) Bound-variable
   (v) 'Laziness'
   (vi) 'Laziness'
   (vii) Bound-variable
   (viii) Referential

4. Semantic referent and speaker's referent

   In this case, there is a mistake in the definite description. Although the man used the definite description *the woman reading a newspaper*, what he has clearly talked about is the woman who was browsing a magazine. Therefore, the semantic referent of the definite description *the woman reading a newspaper* is the woman who was indeed reading a newspaper but who was obscured partly by the fountain and the speaker's referent was the fake-newspaper reader, namely, the woman who was browsing a magazine.

5. Semantic referent and speaker's referent

   In this case of misattribution, the semantic referent of the demonstrative description *that man* is George W. Bush and the speaker's referent is Barack Obama.

6. Transferred referents

   (i) The hotel guest who is staying in Room 336
   (ii) The Obama administration
   (iii) The person with a pretty face
   (iv) The exterior of John's car
   (v) e.g. the New Zealand Rugby Team, the French Rugby Team
   (vi) The speaker's address and telephone number
   (vii) e.g. the customer who is eating the roast beef he has ordered
   (viii) The passenger who is sitting in seat 16A
   (ix) The voters in the Botley ward
   (x) The people in Pearl Harbor, the Japanese attack on Pearl Harbor on the morning of December 7 1941
   (xi) John's email address etc.
   (xii) The mobile phone in her handbag

Chapter 7

1. Explicatures
    (i) The speaker has visited the Great Wall in China at some point in his life
    (ii) The thieves have stolen everything that is valuable
    (iii) Much of the Walled Garden at the Botanic Garden is made up of approximately rectangular botanical family borders
    (iv) e.g. The oven is hot enough for cooking the lamb moussaka
    (v) e.g. Jane has found a small burrowing insectivore
    (vi) e.g. Nobody in our class understood the professor's talk on genetic engineering
    (vii) The building collapsed a relatively long time after the bomb went off
    (viii) The explicature of this sentence uttered is that the lexical concept encoded by *heart* underwent an *ad hoc* adjustment involving both broadening (i.e. to include 'heart' that is made of chocolate) and narrowing (i.e. to exclude 'heart' that is a human or animal organ).
    (ix) e.g. John told Steve that John had won the prize
    (x) The speaker hasn't shaved this morning
    (xi) There was an Italian waiter in the pizza restaurant they went to
    (xii) e.g. The children are coming from a small town in Russia
2. Higher-order explicatures
    (i) The speaker tells (the addressee) frankly that she doesn't fancy him (who is not the addressee)
    (ii) a. The father is telling his son to pick up the books scattered on the floor
        b. It is moderately desirable to the father (and achievable) that his son pick up the books scattered on the floor
        c. The father is requesting his son to pick up the books scattered on the floor
    (iii) a. The speaker believes that their European patent has been granted
        b. The speaker is glad that their European patent has been granted
    (iv) a. John is telling his wife that he will not drink heavily any more
        b. John's wife prefers his not drinking heavily any more
        c. John is promising his wife that he will not drink heavily any more
3. Implicated premises and conclusions
    (i) Implicated premise
       The Last Emperor directed by Bernardo Bertolucci is a period epic
       Implicated conclusion
       Mary does not want to go and watch *The Last Emperor*
    (ii) Implicated premise
       If the kitchen is closed, dinner will not be served
       Implicated conclusion
       The guest is too late for dinner

(iii) Implicated premise

If one's paper is one of the best submitted to a conference, it will be accepted for presentation at that conference

Implicated conclusion

Steve's paper has been accepted for presentation at the conference

(iv) Implicated premise

If Lucy has been paying a lot of visits to London lately, she may have a boyfriend there

Implicated conclusion

Lucy may have a boyfriend in London these days

(v) Implicated premise

If it's snowing heavily outside, it's not possible to play football

Implicated conclusion

John (and the speaker) can't play football outside

(vi) Implicated premise

Chinese supermarkets normally sell soy sauce, and if they are open, one can buy soy sauce there

Implicated conclusion

John can buy soy sauce in the small Chinese supermarket—which is open—just around the corner

4. Strong and weak implicatures

Strong implicatures:

Implicated premise

A vegetarian does not eat any beef or pork

Implicated conclusion

Mary will not have any beef or pork

Weak implicatures: e.g.

Implicated premise

A vegetarian does not eat any lamb

Implicated conclusion

Mary will not have any lamb

Implicated premise

People who are vegetarians are also environmentalists

Implicated conclusion

Mary is an environmentalist

Chapter 8

1. Saturation/completion, free enrichment/expansion, semantic transfer/deferred/transferred reference, and loosening

   (i) I haven't been to Australia before (free enrichment/expansion)
   (ii) Christmas is a considerable time away (free enrichment)

(iii) Mary isn't slim enough for being a fashion model (saturation/completion)
(iv) Roughly speaking, the tram is full (loosening/expansion)
(v) In all probability John is going to marry the woman who has a pretty face (semantic transfer/deferred/transferred reference)
(vi) The Tibetan Buddhist temple is a considerable distance away (free enrichment)
(vii) Peter and Susan drove to LA together (expansion)
Their car broke down roughly half way (expansion)
(viii) This laptop is cheaper than that one (saturation/completion)
(ix) A book written by Confucius is on the top shelf. It is bound in leather (semantic transfer/deferred/transferred reference)
(x) She's a real beauty with high-functioning brains (free enrichment)
(xi) The children stood in an approximate circle around the Christmas tree (loosening/expansion)
(xii) The semantics/pragmatics conference starts at nine or a few minutes later (expansion)
(xiii) Susan lost everything that is valuable (free enrichment/expansion)
(xiv) People say that he owns a painting by van Gogh (semantic transfer/deferred/transferred reference)

2. Pragmatic intrusion and types
(i) Yes. M-implicature.
(ii) Yes. $Q_{-scalar}$ implicature
(iii) Yes. I-implicature
(iv) Yes. M-implicature
(v) Yes. I-implicature
(vi) Yes. M-implicature
(vii) Yes, $Q_{-scalar}$ implicature
(viii) Yes. $Q_{-scalar}$ implicature

Chapter 9

1. Binding condition A pattern
(i) Yes
(ii) No. *Seg* in Norwegian is an anaphor in the Chomskyan sense. As such, it should be able to be bound within its local domain, given binding condition A. But this is not the case.
(iii) Yes
(iv) No. *Aaplyaa-laa* in Marathi is bound in a long-distance way outside its local domain, which is the embedded clause.
(v) Yes
(vi) No. *Sig* in Icelandic is bound in a long-distance way outside its local domain, which is the embedded clause.

2. Binding condition A pattern (c-command)
   (i) Yes
   (ii) Yes
   (iii) No. Here *Xiaoming* does not c-command *ziji* (self).
   (iv) No. The same is true of *John* and *himself.*
   (v) Yes
   (vi) No. In this Icelandic example, *Siggu* does not c-command *sig* (self).

3. Binding condition C_1 or C_2 pattern
   (i) Yes
   (ii) Yes
   (iii) Yes, if binding condition C_1 is allowed to be subject to parametric variation with regard to Vietnamese; otherwise, no.
   (iv) Yes
   (v) No. Given Lasnik's binding condition C_2, *he* and *David* must be free. But they are bound or co-indexed.
   (vi) Yes

4. Predicate meaning–reflexivizing strategy correlation
   (i) In the (a) sentence, since 'wash' is used here as a reflexive- or self-directed predicate, the use of the morphologically simplex *zich* (self) is enough. By contrast, in the (b) sentence, 'admire' is an other-directed predicate. Consequently, the more marked, morphologically complex *ziczelf* (self self) has to be used.
   (ii) 'Wash' is a reflexive- or self-directed predicate in Turkish. When it is reflexive-marked, a simple emphatic marker is used, as in (a'). By comparison, 'beat' is an other-directed predicate. When it is reflexive-marked, the more complex 'self self' has to be employed, as in (b').

5. Possessive anaphora
   (i) This is a case of 'pronoun only' possessive anaphora. The preferred co-referential interpretation between 'Asad' and 'his' is due to the I-principle.
   (ii) This is a case of 'reflexive only' possessive anaphora. The co-referential interpretation between 'Roja' and 'self's' is due to the I-principle. The disjoint in reference reading is due to the Q-principle (<self's, his>).
   (iii) This is a case of 'both reflexive and pronoun' possessive anaphora. The co-referential interpretation between 'Rama' and 'self's' and the preferred co-referential interpretation between 'Rama' and 'his' are due to the I-principle. The emphatic reading arising from the use of 'self's' is due to the M-principle ({his, self's}).

6. Neo-Gricean pragmatic analyses of anaphoric patterns
   (i) The co-referential interpretation is due to the I-principle. A less radical alternative is to say that this interpretation is due to binding condition A.
   (ii) The disjoint in reference interpretation is due to the Q-principle (<himself, him>) and the RDRP.
   (iii) The same as in (ii). (<herself, Kylie>)

(iv) The disjoint in reference interpretation between *Kylie* and *her* is due to the Q-principle (<herself, her>), as is the disjoint in reference reading between *she* and *her* (<herself, her>). The preferred co-referential interpretation between *Kylie* and *she* is due to the I-principle.

(v) The same as in (iv), except that the disjoint in reference interpretation between *Kylie* and *the woman* is due to the M-principle ({she, the woman}).

(vi) The co-referential interpretation is due to the I-principle.

(vii) The same as in (vi). In addition, the use of *the President* is subject to the M-principle ({he, the President}), which engenders the M-implicated difference between a man and his office.

(viii) The co-referential interpretation between *Lee* and *caki* (self) is due to the I-principle, as is the preferred co-referential interpretation between *Lee* and *ku*. The use of the marked *caki* is subject to the M-principle ({ku, caki}), which gives rise to the emphatic, *de se*, or logophoric reading, depending on context.

Index of languages, language families, and language areas

This index includes all the individual languages, larger genetic groupings of languages, and larger non–genetic, geographic groupings of languages referred to in this book.

Index of names

Index of subjects

absolute ranking (R) 145
abuse 125, 132, 166
accommodation 108–12, 375
  global/*de facto* 110
  intermediate 111
  local/*de jure* 110
accommodation module 109
ad hoc concept construction 278–9, 375
adjacency pair 158–9
adjective interpretation 60–1
ambiguity 8, 61, 275, 305
  lexical 8, 275, 305
  syntactic/structural 8, 275
  syntactic/structural–lexical 275
  systematic 61
anaphor 10–13, 341–51
anaphora 9–13, 59, 235–8,
    338–70, 375
  bound-variable 235
  bridging-cross reference 59, 237–8
  E-type 236–7
  general pattern of 353
  identity of reference 235
  identity of sense 235
  possessive 347–8, 360–2
  pronoun of 'laziness' 237
  referential 235
  revised neo-Gricean pragmatic
    apparatus for 354–7
  revised neo-Gricean pragmatic theory
    of 10–13, 351–70
Andeutungen 73; *see also* conventional
  implicature
antipresupposition 113
Atlas principle 112
audibility 200

Austinian typology of speech act 132
  behabitive 132
  commissive 132
  exercitive 132
  expositive 132
  verdictive 132
availability principle 324–5, 328
'avoidance' language 209–10, 215

bidirectional Optimality theory 68,
    369–70
binding 10–13, 341–51, 358–9, 367–70
binding condition 11–12, 342–51, 358–9
  A 11–12, 342–9, 358–9
  B 11–12, 342–3, 345–9, 358–9
  C 11–12, 349–50, 358–9
  elimination of 12, 350–1
bridging-cross reference 59, 237–8
'brother-in-law' language 209–10

charity 303
circumstance of evaluation 310
classical Gricean pragmatic
    theory 25–43, 288–93
cognitive/contextual effect 269
cognitive modularity 285–6
cognitive pragmatics theory 268
common ground 16–17, 106
completion 315
conceptual meaning 284
conditional perfection 59
conjunction buttressing 58–9
connectionism 285, 369–70
connotation 239
constative 119–23, 375
constitutive rule 131

Printed and bound by CPI Group (UK) Ltd, Croydon, CR0 4YY